"Why should not the New Englander be in search of new adventures?"
THOREAU: *Walden*

NORTH AMERICA
Country Inns and Back Roads

22nd Year—Revised Annually

New England, West Coast,
Canada, Middle Atlantic, South, Midwest,
Rocky Mountains

**By Norman T. Simpson
The Berkshire Traveller**

PERENNIAL LIBRARY

HARPER & ROW, PUBLISHERS, New York
Cambridge, Philadelphia, San Francisco, Washington
London, Mexico City, São Paulo, Singapore, Sydney

TRAVEL BOOKS BY NORMAN T. SIMPSON

Country Inns and Back Roads, North America
Country Inns and Back Roads, Britain and Ireland
Country Inns and Back Roads, Continental Europe
Bed and Breakfast, American Style

COVER PAINTING: Charlotte Inn, Edgartown, Martha's Vineyard Island,
Massachusetts, by John Loeper
DRAWINGS: Janice Lindstrom

COUNTRY INNS AND BACK ROADS, North America, 22nd Edition, 1987.
Copyright © 1987 by Harper & Row, Publishers, Inc. All rights reserved. Printed
in the United States of America. No part of this book may be used or reproduced
in any manner whatsoever without written permission except in the case of brief
quotations embodied in critical articles and reviews. For information address
Harper & Row, Publishers, Inc., 10 East 53rd Street, New York, N.Y. 10022.
Published simultaneously in Canada by Fitzhenry & Whiteside Limited, Toronto.

First PERENNIAL LIBRARY edition published 1986. Second PERENNIAL
LIBRARY edition published in 1987.

ISSN: 70-615664
ISBN: 0-06-096167-8

87 88 89 90 91 10 9 8 7 6 5 4 3 2 1

Contents

WEST INDIES

PREFACE

What have we come to?

Just as this book was going to press I received some mail that was both interesting and distressing.

It was an announcement by a national lodging chain of a plan to construct as many as 200 "country inns" almost instantly. Among the items that caught my eye was the statement that each inn would have a front porch that, according to their plan, would become "a hallmark and statement of excellence." Furthermore, the inns would have clapboard exteriors and window shutters that would also contribute, so this corporation claims, substantially to a "sense of arrival, curb appeal, and exciting new personality."

Taking only twenty weeks from ground-breaking to grand opening, all of these inns would be clean, crisp, and brand new (they refuse to franchise older properties), and each would have a registered country inn sign.

When my early editions of *CIBR*, over twenty years ago, aroused the first stirrings of interest in country inns, little did I realize that there would some day be a chain of "instant country inns" stamped out by some corporation.

I am happy to say by an interesting contrast, all of the inns included in this book have been well established for many years and have been carefully selected after one or more visits by me.

Each of the inns in this book reflects the unique personality of the innkeepers and their families—innkeepers who, in many instances have gladly abandoned the ways of corporate living and alluring incomes in the cities and suburbs to start a second career.

The innkeepers will undoubtedly meet you at the door, cosset to your wishes, provide information about the arts and recreation in the area, make suggestions that will add to the enjoyment of your stay, and perhaps join you in one of the public rooms for conversation and an exchange of ideas. These are the things that only dedicated owner-innkeepers can provide.

In the American tradition they have, with the aid of helpful neighbors, shifted, hauled, pulled, and bulldozed to make their inn as comfortable and inviting as possible. Frequently, new rooms have been added, still preserving the ambience of the original, venerable building. Additional bathrooms, parlor areas, and other conveniences have been designed, always faithful to the original architectural integrity.

The hallmarks and statements of excellence are found not on front porches or in window shutters, but in the dedication given to personal innkeeping, which is reflected in the care expressed in the individual furnishings, decorations, and attention to guests' needs.

No, these are decidedly not part of a national lodging chain. There are no "registered signs," and ninety percent of these inns are situated in older buildings, reflecting the stages of our country's architectural heritage. In fact, many are on the National Register of Historic Places. Restoration, with the advice of state and national organizations, far from being instant, has taken hundreds of painstaking hours. Previously hidden facades, fireplaces, and original wallpapers have been discovered and in some cases lovingly restored.

Furnishings have often been brought from the previous homes of the present innkeepers and their families or might even be family heirlooms. Members of the community have sometimes contributed such interesting decorations as clocks and teapots and other personal items. Antiques abound.

The inns in this book, almost without exception, are kept and operated by highly involved owner-innkeepers and their families. They have ideals and purpose, and they see in the inn the opportunity to carry on with a tradition of personal innkeeping, which actually predates the Christian era. Because they are owner-innkeepers, the happiness and well-being of every guest is important to them.

No...clapboard exterior siding, window shutters, and specially designed front porches do not an inn make. Not even registered signs!

Now to other matters....

From the beginning, I found that innkeepers had no forum where they might exchange ideas and views and simply talk shop, so a small informal innkeepers' association was formed, and meetings were held every year to provide such a forum. From one meeting a year, this idea grew into the Independent Innkeepers' Association, Inc., where upwards of twenty meetings a year are held throughout North America. One large meeting is held every year, to which hoteliers from Britain and the Continent are also invited.

Many of these inns have "twin inns" located in Britain and Europe, which are included in my *CIBR* books dealing with those areas. You'll see displays in the inns with photographs and brochures from their "twin inns" across the water.

I learned about innkeeping from innkeepers, and it never stops. The inn picture has changed radically in the past twelve years. Whereas in the early days the book was really a guide to almost every existing country inn, now with the marked proliferation of inns, the book has become highly selective—based, of course, on my personal choices. With the limitation on the number of inns to be included, there is a waiting list each year. Because inns are omitted when they change owners, and occasionally for other reasons, the principle behind this book is each year to find a few good replacement inns in various parts of North America, to keep in touch and visit all of them as frequently as possible, and to concentrate on quality rather than quantity.

Many of these inns are in other guides similar to this. However, the uniqueness of this book lies in the selection of inns. It's not merely a collection of inns, it is a combination of inns from all parts of North America with many important common denominators. In some cases, a decision was put in abeyance for a year or two to allow more "seasoning."

Inns are far from static. They are constantly changing and evolving. That's why we painstakingly revise and rewrite much of the book every year, as a result of continuing contact.

So that the reader may see just how long each inn has been a part of *Country Inns and Back Roads*, after the heading of each write-up, we have inserted the date the inn was first included in the book. As you will see, quite a few inns go back to the early years.

In this edition I have added an entirely new group of inns on the islands of Nevis and Saint Kitts in the West Indies. I visited them in the winter of 1986 and enjoyed it so much that I returned again in March, 1987, this time in the company of several innkeepers from North America, also in search of a holiday in the sun.

To our readers in Great Britain and other countries in Europe:

Welcome to North America! Many of you are making your first visit and we're delighted that you'll be experiencing some of the *real* United States and Canada by visiting these country inns. Incidentally, all of them will be very happy to help you make arrangements and reservations at other inns in the book.

Further Notes:

Here are some basic guidelines for reservations and cancellations in most of the inns listed in this book:

A deposit is required for a confirmed reservation. Guests are requested to please note arrival and departure dates carefully. The deposit will be forfeited if the guest arrives after date specified or departs before the final date of reservation. Refund will be made only if cancelled from 7 to 14 days (depending on the policy of the individual inn) in advance of arrival date and a service charge will be deducted from the deposit.

A number of inns have nearby airports where private planes may land, and further information may be obtained directly from each inn. We have indicated those inns near such airports by putting the following symbol at the end of each inn's directions.

Southern New England

Eastern Time Zone

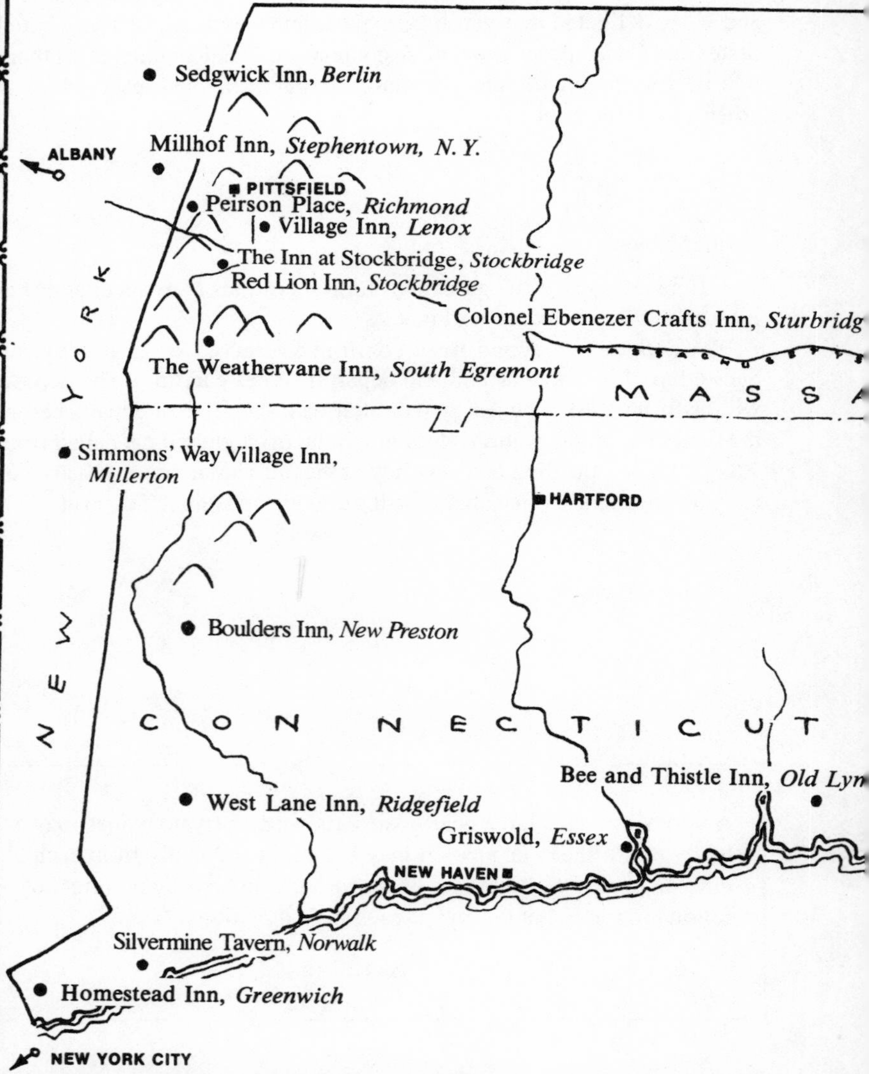

Sedgwick Inn, *Berlin*

ALBANY

Millhof Inn, *Stephentown, N.Y.*

PITTSFIELD
Peirson Place, *Richmond*
Village Inn, *Lenox*

The Inn at Stockbridge, *Stockbridge*
Red Lion Inn, *Stockbridge*

Colonel Ebenezer Crafts Inn, *Sturbridge*

NEW YORK

The Weathervane Inn, *South Egremont*

MASSACHUSETTS

MASSA

Simmons' Way Village Inn, *Millerton*

HARTFORD

Boulders Inn, *New Preston*

CONNECTICUT

Bee and Thistle Inn, *Old Lyme*

West Lane Inn, *Ridgefield*

Griswold, *Essex*

NEW HAVEN

Silvermine Tavern, *Norwalk*

Homestead Inn, *Greenwich*

NEW YORK CITY

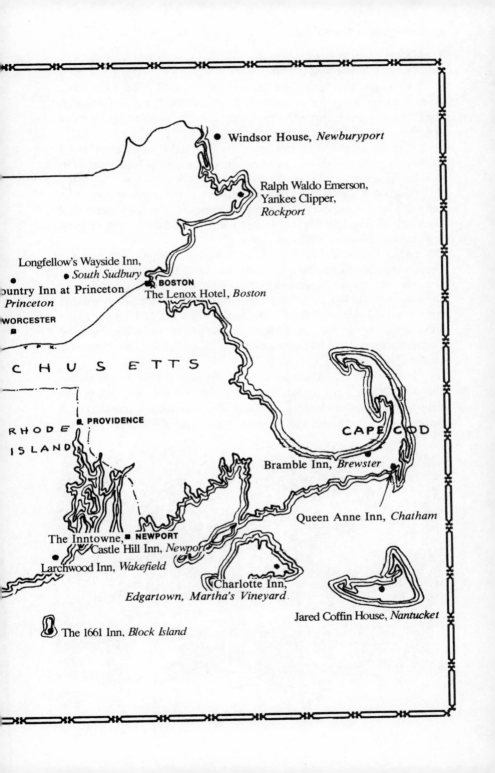

Windsor House, *Newburyport*

Ralph Waldo Emerson,
Yankee Clipper,
Rockport

Longfellow's Wayside Inn,
South Sudbury

Country Inn at Princeton
Princeton

WORCESTER

BOSTON
The Lenox Hotel, *Boston*

CHUSETTS

RHODE
ISLAND

PROVIDENCE

CAPE COD

Bramble Inn, *Brewster*

Queen Anne Inn, *Chatham*

The Inntowne, NEWPORT
Castle Hill Inn, *Newport*

Larchwood Inn, *Wakefield*

Charlotte Inn,
Edgartown, Martha's Vineyard

Jared Coffin House, *Nantucket*

The 1661 Inn, *Block Island*

BEE AND THISTLE INN
Old Lyme, Connecticut (1984)

Although I first visited the Bee and Thistle Inn in 1982, it has taken a succession of visits to bring the inn, the village itself, and, in particular, the lovely ambience created by the Lieutenant River into complete focus for me.

It really happened on my last visit. Bob and Penny Nelson and I strolled out across the broad lawns and fields behind this handsome 1756 building down to the river banks.

"Someday I'm going to have a gazebo here," quoth Penny. "Our neighbor across the river is Roger Tory Peterson, the world-renowned authority on bird life. He has written many guide books, and we have some of his paintings hanging in the inn."

When I remarked on the similarity of this riverside idyll to many French impressionist paintings, Penny was quick to point out that American painters who had gone to France to paint their pastoral settings and then come to Old Lyme, stayed right on this river and decided they didn't have to go to France any more. "The natural beauty of Old Lyme was the ideal subject matter for American artists who painted in the Barbizon and Impressionist styles. Old Lyme was one of the earliest art colonies in this country."

Bob continued, "There are at least fifty houses here, ranging from the late 17th century to the present, which are not only artistically captivating, but also worthy of study for their architectural and historical importance. Lyme Street was designated as a historic district in 1970."

This love of beauty and fine things was reflected throughout the inn. Many of the architectural features enhance an atmosphere of friendly open-heartedness. The many fireplaces, antiques, sunlit porches, the lovely carved staircase, the three canopied beds and the four-posters, and the old quilts and afghans plainly show the Nelsons' love for the quality of things in both the past and present.

"I hope you'll return sometime after the first of November," said Penny. "We are serving English tea, November through April, on Monday, Wednesay, and Thursday from 3:30 until 5:00. We have an ever-growing collection of individual china teapots, and the menu includes hot fresh scones with fresh whipped cream and raspberry jam, assorted tea sandwiches, tea breads, and a dessert of the day. Guests have their choice of Darjeeling tea or herbal teas. It's the greatest fun."

As we reluctantly returned to the main inn, passing through the English garden, which is one of Penny's delights, I commented on all the flowers. "There are giant phlox, asters, lupines, iris, peonies, and bleeding heart," she said. "Everyone enjoys the peace and quiet and the lovely colors."

I asked Bob and Penny as we walked through the front door what it was that moved guests to return several times to the Bee and Thistle. "Many of them say that we are what they thought an inn would be like—a gracious home, giving them a chance to sit and talk, have a lovely dining experience with caring people in attendance.

"We give all of our new guests a map of all the places to see when they arrive and we guide them on spending their day. It's important for us to inform people on the many things to do in the area."

In previous editions of this book I have described more of the inn itself, including the menus and the common rooms. This time I thought that our readers might like to know more about Bob and Penny Nelson, and the wonderful atmosphere of Old Lyme, which helps to make the Bee and Thistle an enjoyable experience.

BEE AND THISTLE INN, 100 Lyme St. (Rte. 1), Old Lyme, CT 06371; 203-434-1667. An 11-guestroom (2 rooms with shared bath) inn located in an as-yet-unspoiled Connecticut village, near the border of Rhode Island. Breakfast, lunch, and dinner served daily, except Tues. Sun. brunch. Open year-round. Conveniently located to visit Gillette Castle, Goodspeed Opera House, and Essex steam train and train rides. Mystic Seaport, Essex Village, Ivoryton Summer Theater nearby. No pets. Bob and Penny Nelson, Innkeepers.

Directions: Coming north on I-95, take a left at the bottom of Exit 70. At the first light take a right. At the second light, take a left and then follow Rte. 1 (Lyme Street) to inn.

BOULDERS INN
Lake Waramaug, New Preston, Connecticut (1970)

I'm not much of a sailor but I could easily see that Jim Woollen is. We were skimming along on Lake Waramaug, enjoying a midsummer's day. When we came about, I looked back toward the beach in front of the Boulders Inn and followed the gentle curve of the lawn upward among the trees to the inn itself, with its formidable first floor of great glacier boulders and its traditional New England gambrel roof.

It was an early August midafternoon and I remarked to Jim on what a pretty lake this was, completely surrounded by hills and the many old cottages on the shore. "Yes, we've had very little construction here, and I think it's much the same as it was eighty years ago. At the turn of the century there were eight inns along the shoreline, but the tempo has dropped now, with only four. It's nice and quiet.

"Next year, come back on the Fourth of July," he continued. "It's just about an hour or so from Stockbridge, isn't it? The homeowners set off flares in unison all around the shore, and would you believe that their signal is a man parachuting out of a plane over the lake with a flare in his boot!"

Jim and his wife, Carolyn, are coming up to their tenth year at the Boulders. I can remember an earlier conversation with them, when they explained that their objective was to provide a small intimate retreat where care, attention, and a homelike atmosphere would blend with the physical setting and all the facilities. I asked Jim whether he felt they had achieved those objectives. "Yes," he replied, "we try to create a rather serene environment that has no pressures." They've made many tangible improvements during their ten years, including extending the outdoor dining room area with two terrace decks overlooking the lake. They've also installed fireplaces in the little cottages, along with patios or balconies.

"Besides all of the amenities—boats, tennis courts, bicycles, and wonderful trails for walks and hikes," Jim added, "we think that one of the ways to increase our guests' enjoyment is to provide a dining experience that is always interesting. Food is very important, and so we've put a big emphasis on that department.

"For instance, at breakfast, you come into the dining room and are first confronted with our 'cold table,' where there are freshly squeezed juices, fresh fruit, and dry cereal, and bowls of dried fruit to put on the cereal, if you wish. Boulders' coffee cake, a wonderful, heavenly sour cream and cinnamon cake, is waiting for all. The waitress will tell you about the eggs or omelets, all with a variety of fillings, as well as pancakes with real maple syrup, sausage, ham, or bacon, and don't forget the whole-wheat toast.

"Dinner is by candlelight, and we have entrées such as boned duck breast, Kashmir lamb, and very often an oriental dish as a special offering. Our chef likes to prepare dishes with curry, as well."

The Boulders and the lake are reminiscent of the English Lake Country, and it's hard to realize that New York City is just eighty miles to the south. When this lovely lake freezes over, guests can go skating on it, toboggan on the ski hill behind the inn, and cross-country ski on the mountain trails starting from the back door.

Jim's hand tightened on the tiller as his practiced eye saw something that I had missed. "Here comes a good gust," he said. "Let's take it as far as we can."

BOULDERS INN, Lake Waramaug, New Preston, CT 06777; 203-868-7918. A 14-guestroom year-round resort-inn, 20 mi. north of Danbury, 40 mi. west of Hartford. Modified American plan Memorial Day to Labor Day. Breakfast, lunch, and dinner served to travelers, except Mon. dinner. Sept. thru May, breakfast served daily; dinner Tues. thru Sat. Open Thanksgiving; closed Christmas Eve and Christmas Day. Tennis, swimming, boating, sailing, fishing, antiquing, hiking, riding, and downhill skiing nearby; 40 min. from chamber music concert series, July thru Aug. Suitable for children over 6. No pets. The Woollen Family, Innkeepers.

Directions: From I-84, take exit 7 and follow Rte. 7 north to Rte. 202 (formerly 25) thru New Milford. Proceed 8 mi. to New Preston, then 1½ mi. to inn on Rte. 45.

GRISWOLD INN
Essex, Connecticut (1974)

If you've never been to New England, I could give you a list of towns that are absolute "musts." Right near the top of the list is Essex, Connecticut.

In the first place, each summer, sailors from all over the world make Essex a port of call. A common sight are these "boaters," who have moored at the end of the street and come up to do some shopping in their faded jeans and boat shoes, stopping in at the Griswold Inn for lunch.

In fact, that's what *I* was doing at the very moment. Innkeeper Bill Winterer and I had been strolling for a while on the main street, doing a little window shopping in some of the fine stores of the village, which is another reason for a visit. We had seated ourselves underneath the upstairs gallery on one of the wooden benches that line both sides of the entrance. It was a warm summer afternoon in August, and people-watching was at its best

I like to get Bill started on some of the historical events that took place in Essex. He is a graduate of the nearby New London Coast Guard Academy and truly a man of the sea himself.

"Only five families have owned the inn since 1776. The Tap Room was built in 1738 and was the first schoolhouse in Essex. It was rolled on logs drawn by a team of oxen down the main street to where we are now.

"Most of Essex was burned during the War of 1812 except the Griswold, which billeted some of the officers from the British fleet."

The Gris has a very high historic profile. The Steamboat Dining Room was recently restored to conform to the period of the remainder of the building. Lovely paned windows have been added, and some of the marine collection is now displayed there. It is notable for the mural on the end wall that actually rocks back and forth, creating the impression of being on an old Connecticut River steamship of the 19th century.

Within its many dining rooms and parlors, the inn has a remarkable collection of marine paintings, including some by Antonio Jacobsen. The collection includes prints, ship models, firearms, binnacles, ship's clocks, a potbellied stove, humorous posters and prints, and a genuine popcorn machine. Vicky, Bill's wife, has been working over the past several years organizing everything. "Our plan is to publish a book that can be made available to our guests. This will list each piece in the collection, along with the history of the artist. Oliver Jensen, the original founder and publisher of *American Heritage*, has agreed to write the foreword."

Our talk turned quite naturally to the cuisine. "Over the past six months or so we have been doing a considerable amount of research on our New England cuisine and we've added several items to the menu," he

remarked. "The deeper we dig into the subject the more we realize how authentically New England our cuisine really is. Menus and recipes have been handed down from year to year, from innkeeper to innkeeper, and from chef to chef. In addition to the New England specialties, we've also added some Creole cooking, following recipes of Sala Griswold's wife, who hailed from New Orleans."

So our chatting eddied back and forth with our shared enthusiasm for history, good books, and good inns. It was a wonderfully pleasant summer's day for two old friends.

GRISWOLD INN, Main St., Essex, CT 06426; 203-767-0991. A 22-guestroom inn in a waterside town, steps away from the Connecticut River. European plan. Complimentary continental breakfast served daily to inn guests. Lunch and dinner served daily to travelers. Hunt breakfast served Sun. Closed Christmas Eve and Christmas Day. Near the Eugene O'Neill Theatre, Goodspeed Opera House, Ivoryton Playhouse, Gillette Castle, Mystic Village, Valley Railroad, and Hammonasset State Beach. Day sailing on inn's 44-foot ketch by appointment. Bicycles, tennis, and boating nearby. Victoria and William G. Winterer, Innkeepers.

Directions: From I-95 take Exit 69 and travel north on Rte. 9 to Exit 3, Essex. Turn right at stoplight and follow West Ave. to center of town. Turn right onto Main St. and proceed down to water and inn.

THE HOMESTEAD INN
Greenwich, Connecticut (1969)

As frequently as I have visited the Homestead over the years, I'm always delightfully re-surprised at the truly residential nature of its location. There's been an inn here for a very long time with a long procession of different innkeepers and many different types of accommodations; now, however, I believe the Homestead has reached the pinnacle of its success.

Today, the inn reflects the sensitivities and tastes of Lessie Davison and Nancy Smith, two attractive and talented women who saw the possibilities in restoring this 185-year-old farmhouse that is just a few moments from I-95.

The inn began its life as a farmhouse, built in 1799. In 1859 it was sold to innkeepers who completely remodeled it in the distinctive "Carpenter Gothic" architecture of the Victorian era.

The inn is set back from the road in a lovely old orchard and gardens, and the sloping lawn is highlighted by handsome hydrangea bushes. There are now twenty-four guest rooms, all with different decorative

themes. They are handsomely furnished, including many antiques and such comforts as clock radios, electric blankets, two pillows for every head, lots of books and magazines, and very modern bathrooms. In many ways, the guest rooms resemble those at Rothay Manor in the Lake Country of England.

Although many of the guest rooms are in the main house, some very careful attention has been given recently to the remodeling of other buildings on the property, and guests may now enjoy a variety of rooms, some with queen-sized beds and balconies or porches, as well as a queen-bedded suite, with a lovely, large, cathedral-ceilinged bedroom and a front porch overlooking the neighbor's apple orchard.

The Homestead is the perfect alternative to the busy, noisy New York hotels, and provides a very pleasant country-type atmosphere for city dwellers who want to leave the canyons of steel for the peaceful lanes of Greenwich.

One of the main reasons for the continuing success of the Homestead is La Grange Restaurant. The chef is Jacques Thiebeult from Paris, who trained in France, Switzerland, England, and at Le Cirque and Le Cygne restaurants in New York.

The *New York Times* restaurant reviewer awarded three stars to La Grange, pointing out that the restaurant "pays attention to every detail: salads, warm, crusty rolls, even a choice of loose tea, all are part of the seamlessly smooth dining performance."

The menu offerings include French country paté, cream of asparagus soup, scallops of veal with chestnuts, striped bass, and shad roe with bacon. Desserts include créme brulée, chocolate mousse cake, almond tart, and almond cake with chestnut filling.

Incidentally, I learned recently that William Inge wrote *Picnic* here during the 1950s. This, of course, was long before Lessie and Nancy arrived on the scene, bringing with them impeccable taste and a gratifying attention for detail. I'm sure, were he to revisit now, Mr. Inge would find the atmosphere and cuisine even more inspiring.

THE HOMESTEAD INN, 420 Field Point Rd., Greenwich, CT 06830; 203-869-7500. A 24-guestroom inn located in the residential area of a suburb, 45 min. north of New York City. Lunch served Mon. thru Fri.; dinner served daily except Labor Day, Christmas, New Year's. Located a short distance from Conn. countryside and shore scenes. Accessible by train from New York City. No amusements for children under 12. No pets. Lessie Davison, Nancy Smith, Innkeepers.

Directions: The inn is 3 min. from Rte. I-95. Take Exit 3 in Greenwich; from NYC, turn left; from New Haven, turn right off ramp. Turn left onto Horseneck Ln. at light, just before railroad overpass. Go to next traffic light; turn left onto Field Point Rd., and continue approx. 1/4 mi. to inn on the right.

The date in parenthesis in the heading represents the first year the inn appeared in the pages of Country Inns and Back Roads.

SILVERMINE TAVERN
Norwalk, Connecticut (1975)

"Meet Miss Abigail," said Frank Whitman. "She's the only woman permitted by Connecticut law to stand within three feet of a bar."

I spoke courteously, but Miss Abigail just stood there in her crinoline and lace, looking inscrutable. The walls behind her, and in fact in all of the dining rooms, were covered with old farm implements and tools, as well as American primitive paintings.

Frank and I continued our tour of the Silvermine Tavern. "The Tavern was named for the town," he said. "That name, in turn, came from an old as-yet-unfounded rumor about a silver mine discovered by an early settler. The old post office was here at the four corners."

We passed through two low-ceilinged sitting rooms brimming with antiques. There were fireplaces in each, and one had an old clock with wooden works. Frank pointed out the beams of the original inn as well as the old-fashioned Colonial hinges on the doorway. Some of the oil paintings of the Colonial ladies and gentlemen looked rather forbidding.

"You can imagine that we're quite popular with honeymooners," he said. "They like to wander the country roads and to feed the ducks and swans on the Mill Pond." There is a Country Store just across the street from the Tavern where the old counters and display tables have some very interesting adaptations of Colonial skills and crafts. In the back room of the store, a museum has antique tools and gadgets and a fine collection of Currier and Ives prints.

The Tavern at various times has served as a country inn, a gentleman's country seat, and a town meeting place. It has a very large outdoor dining area overlooking the Silvermine River and the Mill Pond with ducks and swans. Summer terrace dining among the oaks, maples, pines, and poplar trees is very popular with playgoers to the Westport Playhouse and the Stratford Shakespeare Theatre nearby. I like the Silvermine in the winter also, when the many fireplaces are crackling and the candles create a romantic feeling.

Some of the New England dishes on the menu include indian pudding, bread pudding, honeybuns, native scrod, lobster, scallops, and oysters. On Thursday night there is a buffet that includes roast beef, corned beef, and fried chicken. On Wednesday and Friday night during the summer there is a barbecue, and there is a Sunday brunch buffet, with as many as twenty-five different offerings on the big tables.

When my tour of the Tavern and all the buildings at the crossroads was over, I went back to ask Miss Abigail if she'd care to join me for dinner. I suggested the chicken pie. No reply. I pointed out that all the breads and desserts were homemade—even the ice cream. Still she remained inscrutable.

But I didn't feel too badly when Frank assured me that she hasn't spoken to anyone in years.

SILVERMINE TAVERN, Perry Ave., Norwalk, CT 06850; 203-847-4558. A 10-guestroom country inn in the residential section of Norwalk. European plan includes continental breakfast. Lunch and dinner served to travelers daily. Open year-round. Closed Christmas Day and Tuesdays during winter. Long Island Sound and beaches 6 mi. away. Golf, tennis, and fishing nearby. Francis C. Whitman, Innkeeper.

Directions: From New York or New Haven via I-95, take Exit 15. Pick up the new Rte. 7 going north. At the end of Rte. 7 (approx. 1 mi.) turn right, go to first stoplight, turn right. At next stoplight by firehouse turn right onto Silvermine Ave. Proceed down Silvermine Ave. about 2 mi. to Tavern. From I-84 and Danbury take old Rte. 7 south to Norwalk. Watch for Kelly Greens, ½ mi. south of Merritt Pkwy. on the left; turn right on Perry Ave., opposite Kelly Greens. Follow Perry Ave. 2 mi. to Tavern. From Merritt Pkwy. take Exit 39 south on old Rte. 7 and follow above directions.

I do not include lodging rates in the descriptions, for the very nature of an inn means that there are lodgings of various sizes, with and without baths, in and out of season, and with plain and fancy decoration. Travelers should call ahead and inquire about the availability and rates of the many different types of rooms.

WEST LANE INN
Ridgefield, Connecticut (1980)

"Basically, I think that we have three different types of guests that find their way to our little inn." Maureen Mayer and I were seated on the broad front porch of the West Lane Inn enjoying a generous continental breakfast. "By the way," she added, "if you'd like a bigger breakfast, we have an à la carte breakfast menu that offers, among other things, grapefruit, sliced bananas, berries, yogurt, corn flakes, and poached eggs."

I might add that this breakfast was served at a table with real linen tablecloths and napkins.

One of the things that sets West Lane Inn apart is the many additional amenities this attractive innkeeper provides for her guests. For example, there is a clock in every guest room, as well as a computerized phone system, a radio-TV, individual heating and air conditioning controls, and one-day laundry and dry-cleaning service, and a basket of fruit, cheese, and crackers is presented to newly arrived guests.

"Among our guests are families being relocated to the Ridgefield-Fairfield-Danbury area who need a comfortable, roomy place in which to stay while they look for a new home. Many come and stay for a week or two. I decided that they would be much more comfortable if we had accommodations that reflected the feeling of the area, so we have rooms with decks overlooking our lawn and the forest in the rear. Some of these have fireplaces and kitchen facilities. You see, guests can literally establish a little home for a short time. One of our bathrooms is designed for the handicapped, similar to the one at the West Mountain Inn in Vermont."

I observed that Ridgefield itself would be an ideal suburban place in which to live. Within commuting distance of New York and driving distance of the many corporations which are relocating in Fairfield County, Ridgefield is a most pleasant town with large graceful trees and excellent small shops. "There's also a very active community here," Maureen remarked. "We have a historical society, a library, the Ridgefield Symphony, the League of Women Voters, and various men's service clubs, sports groups, and business groups."

West Lane Inn is set back from the village street with a broad lawn enhanced by azaleas, tulips, roses, and maple and oak trees. It was originally built as a mansion in the early 1800s and the guest rooms are unusually commodious.

The other types of guests are commercial travelers, both men and women, and vacationers who enjoy country-inn hospitality. "I think we understand commercial travelers very well and we've done everything possible to have them feel that this is really a 'home away from home.'

"As far as the country-inn travelers are concerned, we're at sort of a

crossroads for north-south, east-west travel, and many couples on their way to or from New England come back and stay every year."

The West Lane could well be a model for other bed-and-breakfast inns everywhere. Every lodging room is spotless and the furnishings and decorating are all part of a harmonious color scheme. Overnight guests are coddled even further with heated towel racks and wonderful, new, large, fluffy bath sheets.

One of the things that also appeals to me is the 100%-cotton sheets on every bed in the inn. When was the last time you slept in a bed that had 100%-cotton sheets? Outstanding!

WEST LANE INN, 22 West Lane, Ridgefield, CT 06877; 203-438-7323. A 20-guestroom (several suites with kitchens) inn approx. 1 hr. from N.Y.C., in a quiet residential village in southwest Connecticut. Open every day in the year. Breakfast and light snacks available until 10:30 p.m. Convenient to many museums and antique shops. Golf, tennis, swimming, and xc skiing and other outdoor recreation available nearby. No pets. Maureen Mayer, Innkeeper.

Directions: From New York: follow I-684 to Exit 6, turn right on Rte. 35, 12 mi. to Ridgefield. Inn is on left. From Hartford: Exit I-84 on Rte. 7 south and follow Rte. 35 to Ridgefield.

A number of inns have nearby airports where private airplanes may land. An airplane symbol at the end of the inn directions indicates that there is an airport nearby. Consult inn for further information.

THE BRAMBLE INN
Brewster, Cape Cod, Massachusetts (1977)

Every time I travel on Route 124, the road that leads from Exit 10 on the Mid-Cape Highway toward Brewster, I am most pleased with its wonderful "country" feeling. The bike trails leading off the road provide another diversion for travelers and natives alike. Among other things, it passes the Pleasant Lake General Store, another interesting step back into life as it was lived on the Cape a few years ago—just the battered red building in itself would indicate that.

Route 124 joins Route 6A, the north shore road of the Cape, also with many lovely villages and pleasant views. Upon turning right, one can almost see the Bramble Inn sign in the distance on the left-hand side.

There have been some very interesting changes at the Bramble Inn. It has been owned and operated for well over a year by Ruth and Cliff Manchester, who have had many years of experience in the accommodations field. Ruth is a very experienced gourmet cook, as we shall learn in just a few moments.

Other changes can be found, for example, in the handsome oriental rugs on the wide floorboards, and the dining room, which has changed almost completely with new decorations. The Manchesters have also worked hard redoing all of the bedrooms, and have put another bathroom in the 1849 House, adjacent to the present inn building. It now has five rooms, all with private baths.

The inn is now open from mid-March to mid-January. This means it's possible to travel to the Cape in the off-season and have a very pleasant country inn experience and perhaps enjoy the Cape at a more leisurely pace.

The continental breakfast, served on the porch every morning and included in the cost of the room, consists of homemade muffins, which are invariably different every day, juice, coffee, and other items of that nature.

The dinner menu is quite different. Now, it's a four-course price-fixed dinner that changes almost nightly. As Ruth Manchester points out, "There's a choice of five items from each course and it's really given me the opportunity to offer some dinners that present me with a real challenge. Among our more popular main dishes are tenderloin of beef with Roquefort and a white wine sauce, and rack of lamb with a cracked peppercorn and mustard backing. However, our most sought-after recipes—also requested by both *Bon Appetit* and *Gourmet*—are the lettuce and scallion bisque and our chocolate terrine with coffee cream sauce.

"Dinner is served Tuesday through Sunday in season, and Thursday through Sunday off season," Ruth explained.

Guest rooms at the top of the stairs in the main inn have flowered

wallpaper, antiques, country furniture, and will have private baths. There's a definite tilt to the doors and the floors, adding to the fun. The same is true of the five additional guest rooms, all with their own baths, in the 1849 House.

For those readers who have already made the acquaintance of the previous owners, Karen Etsell and Elaine Brennan, the authors of *How To Open A Country Inn*, I'm happy to report that they have moved almost directly across from the inn on Route 6A, and when last I had a chance to chat with them, they were redoing an old Cape house and were going to make a portion of it into a gift shop.

THE BRAMBLE INN, Route 6A, Main St., Brewster, Cape Cod, MA 02631; 617-896-7644. An 8-guestroom (private baths) village inn in the heart of one of Cape Cod's north-shore villages. Lodgings include continental breakfast. Dinner served Tues. thru Sun. in season; Thurs. thru Sun. in fall and winter. Open mid-March to mid-Jan. Swimming, sailing, water sports, golf, recreational and natural attractions within a short drive. Adjacent to tennis club. This is a small, intimate inn and does not meet the needs of most children. No pets. Cliff and Ruth Manchester, Innkeepers.

Directions: Take Exit 10 from Rte. 6. Turn left (north) and follow Rte. 124 to the intersection of Rte. 6A (4 mi.). Turn right, $1/10$ mi. to inn.

I do not include lodging rates in the descriptions, for the very nature of an inn means that there are lodgings of various sizes, with and without baths, in and out of season, and with plain and fancy decoration. Travelers should call ahead and inquire about the availability and rates of the many different types of rooms.

CHARLOTTE INN
Edgartown, Martha's Vineyard, Massachusetts (1979)

It's true. Yes, in last year's edition I said that there was always something new happening at the Charlotte Inn, and my most recent visit confirmed this.

Gery and Paula Conover were taking me on an extensive tour of the fifth dwelling that makes up the ever-growing complex called the Charlotte Inn. This was the Summer House, about which I had written while it was still being redesigned and redecorated.

First, perhaps I will provide a little background about the inn itself. It is located on south Summer Street in Edgartown on Martha's Vineyard Island, off the southern coast of Cape Cod. The main house, like many other Edgartown houses, is a classic three-story white clapboard with a widow's walk on the top. It is the former home of a Martha's Vineyard sea captain. Guest rooms are individually furnished with their own private baths and are very quiet and impeccably clean. Several rooms have working fireplaces and there are many four-poster beds. There are lots of fresh flowers, books, magazines, good reading lamps, and perhaps, most important of all, a very romantic atmosphere.

Besides this main house, there is a carriage house with a cathedral ceiling and unusual adornments, about which I wrote several years ago, as well as a "garden house" across the street from the main inn. This has been decorated with a French country look, and, as is the case with the other guest rooms throughout the inn and annex, the furnishings and decorations have been done with great care and taste. This house also provides houseguests with a private lounge of their own, where they may enjoy the fireplace, play games, watch TV, and get acquainted.

Now, back to the Summer House. Entering through a downstairs hallway, I immediately felt as if I were in a British inn. There are English

prints, particularly of old London inns and coffeehouses, throughout the hallways and guest rooms, along with some ancient tennis rackets, an old straw hat, and even a hard hat for horseback riding.

The guest rooms in the Summer House are highly individual. There are pineapple bedposts, brass beds, carved antique headboards, beautiful chests, handsome silver, and positively scrumptious bathrooms. One has a tub from 1912 that weighs about a thousand pounds and had to be lifted through the window by a crane.

Mike Brisson and his wife, Joan, are now running l'etoile, the inn restaurant. I had a chance to talk with Mike about their philosophy. "We try to achieve food that is very simple but is elegant on the plate," he said. "I think our menu is sophisticated but we both feel that it is very palatable. We try to build on the natural ingredients, using flavors and seasonings with subtlety. We like our guests to think of their dinner as a whole rather than picking out one item on a plate."

Among the entrées on this *prix-fixe* dinner are roast supremes of baby pheasant, sauté of lobster and mussels in a puff pastry box, rack of lamb, and grilled swordfish steak with champagne and shrimp sauce. Incidentally, *Bon Appetit* will be featuring the restaurant in an article sometime in 1987, as will *Travel and Leisure*.

October is an ideal time to be at Martha's Vineyard. The weather is usually pleasantly chilly in the morning and warms up as the hours go by. The island and the ferries are not crowded, and it's possible to enjoy the Vineyard as a place with its own personality.

CHARLOTTE INN, So. Summer St., Edgartown, Martha's Vineyard Island, MA 02539; 617-627-4751. A 24-guestroom combination inn—art gallery and restaurant on a side street, a few steps from the harbor. European plan. Continental breakfast served to inn guests. Open year-round. L'etoile restaurant open for dinner from mid-March through New Year's Day, also winter weekends. Boating, swimming, beaches, fishing, tennis, riding, golf, sailing, and biking nearby. No pets. Not suitable for children under 15. Gery and Paula Conover, Innkeepers.

Directions: The Woods Hole/Vineyard Haven Ferry runs year-round and automobiles may be left in the parking lot at Woods Hole. Taxis may be obtained from Vineyard Haven to Edgartown (8 mi.). Check with inn for ferry schedules for all seasons of the year. Accessible by air from Boston and New York. ◢

The date in parenthesis in the heading represents the first year the inn appeared in the pages of Country Inns and Back Roads.

JARED COFFIN HOUSE
Nantucket Island, Massachusetts (1969)

Because I am a great saver of letters and mementos, I ran across this letter from one of my readers, written in 1975, who visited the Jared Coffin House in that year. Let me share some of it with you:

"Having written for our first *Country Inns*. . . while in Frankfurt, Germany (U.S. Army), to ease the homesickness, our enjoyment was limited to paging through to see where we already had visited. Until this Easter week, having five days off together (a rarity on our work schedules), we picked a route to Nantucket by way of Wakefield, Rhode Island, where we enjoyed a delicious meal at the Larchwood Inn. It was certainly a good start.

"But we were totally unprepared for our first visit to Nantucket. Our first surprise was the beauty of the island in early April—crocuses in bloom, sun, and fresh breezes. Mr. Read gave us his front Crewel Embroidery Room in the main house. He was there as we left the next day, and he made us feel so much at home. He is as warm as the inn.

"Being from a family who lived in Oahu, my husband was intrigued by the Hawaiian influences, and as we both love the sea and anything to do with boats we were really incredibly surprised at such a lovely spot in the ocean and yet so close.

"Your book is the best $3.95 we've ever spent. [Well, it certainly was 1975!] We hope you'll be expanding it to some of the European countries." [Our first European edition was published in 1975, and it has been going on ever since.]

Thank you very much, and I'm glad to have the opportunity to share some of your thoughts. If you recognize this letter in this edition do drop me a line; I'd like to know how things are going.

Things are certainly going well at the Jared Coffin House. Phil Read's most recent note points out the fact that he and Peggy have been managing the inn for twenty years and have owned it for ten. "It's been great," he declares. "We still love it and look forward to coming to it each day."

There have been some changes in those years. In addition to the main house of the inn, built in 1845, Phil and Peggy Read have acquired over the years the Harrison Gray House (1841), the Henry Coffin House (1821), the Swain House (1700s), the Eben Allen Wing (1857), and the Daniel Webster House. Three of these are physically connected; the others are only thirty feet away. Each is unique in its own way. All of the rooms have private baths and telephones, and some even have television.

The inn is furnished with period antiques reflecting the worldwide voyages of the Nantucket whalers and a way of life that has now passed forever from the American scene.

To the best of my knowledge, the island of Nantucket, which is thirty miles at sea and can be reached either by ferry or plane, has only one house that has a Victorian design. All other houses pre-date the Victorian era and are either of Colonial or Georgian design.

"Shortly after the Great Fire of 1846 burned out most of the center of the town, the English brick walls and Welsh slate roof of the J.C. House resisted the fire and helped stop its spread. During the following year the Nantucket Steamboat Company bought the house for use as a hotel, naming it "The Ocean House."

Nantucket is a very lively place during the height of the summer season, and it is necessary to have reservations at the Jared Coffin well in advance. I suggest a trip in middle-to-late fall or early spring. The cobblestone streets and the shops will not be crowded, and you can enjoy the beauty and intriguing history of both the inn and the island.

JARED COFFIN HOUSE, Nantucket Island, MA 02554; 617-228-2400; reservations: 617-228-2405 (M-F 10-6). A 58-guestroom village inn, 30 mi. at sea. European plan. Breakfast, lunch, and dinner served daily (food service in Tap Room only in Jan., Feb., Mar.). Please verify accommodations before planning a trip to Nantucket in any season. Swimming, fishing, boating, golf, tennis, riding, and bicycles nearby. Philip and Margaret Read, Innkeepers.

Directions: Accessible by air from Boston, New York, and Hyannis, or by ferry from Woods Hole and Hyannis, Mass. Automobile reservations are usually needed in advance: 617-540-2022. Cars are not recommended for short stays. Ferry service from Hyannis available May thru Dec.: 617-426-1855; Woods Hole, Jan.-Mar. Inn is located 300 yards from ferry dock.

THE QUEEN ANNE INN
Chatham, Cape Cod, Massachusetts (1981)

One of my readers suggested that a good subtitle for this book might be "Conversations with Innkeepers." Actually, I think that's true because in going back over the book now and then, I find that a great deal of what I have written has actually been a result of conversations. That's what I was doing right now, having a conversation with innkeeper Guenther Weinkopf.

This conversation was quite different from the one we had while we were cruising the Chatham Harbor, and he had pointed out the many landmarks and points of natural beauty. On this occasion we were on the deck of my bedroom, overlooking the lovely spacious lawn of the inn and we could just glimpse the players on the tennis courts. Each of the second- and third-floor rooms has its own private deck, and there is a great profusion of flowers of all kinds, providing just the right touch to the wonderful greenness of the scene.

"We've worked very hard to achieve this," Guenther said, "and now after rearranging and planning and re-planning, I think we've finally got it right." My bedroom, typical of most of the bedrooms at the inn, was furnished in beautiful antiques with matching quilts and draperies. The beds have carved headboards and there are private baths in every room. Some even have working fireplaces.

"One of the things that pleases me most," he went on, "is the fact that our guests are enjoying our beautiful and exciting new boats. They can water-ski or enjoy the coastal sightseeing excursions to Monomoy and Nantucket Islands. As you know I have a U.S. Coast Guard Captain's license now and I'm running these trips myself."

On an earlier excursion, Guenther explained that Monomoy Island is almost legendary. It extends fifteen miles into the Atlantic, pointing towards Nantucket, and is now a wildlife sanctuary providing a habitat for many different animals and birds, including snow egrets, blue herons, terns, wild swans, Canada geese, ducks, seals, and deer.

It's hard for me to realize that Sonja, my first guide at the Queen Anne, whom I met in 1981, has now finished her first year at Tufts. However, Guenther and Nicole's second daughter Lisa is now working at the reception desk. Bert, their son, is a ball boy, pro shop operator at the tennis courts, and also doubles as crew on boat excursions.

I had dinner in the summer with my old friends, Pete and Jane Johnston, and we were all tremendously impressed by not only the unusual number of offerings but also the delicious food. I particularly enjoyed a special dish called "Atlantic Delicacies," consisting of lobster, scallops, mussels, and shrimp glazed with a white wine sauce. Lobsters are on the menu whenever they are available. The Queen Anne is open every day of the year, and there is a program of fall and winter culinary events, including fowl and game dinners prepared with herbs from the garden.

As Guenther and I left the deck, heading for the tennis courts, he said, "You know, our new fitness center with the inside lap-pool and sauna is particularly enjoyed by our guests in the winter months. We also have an outdoor fitness trail for running and jogging. It's a wonderful place for an off-season weekend."

THE QUEEN ANNE INN, 70 Queen Anne Rd., Chatham, MA 02633; 617-945-0394. A 30-guestroom village inn on Cape Cod on the picturesque south shore. Full American, modified American, or European plans. Open year-round. Breakfast, dinner, Sunday brunch, and Tuesday clambake served to travelers. Restaurant hours limited in fall and winter. Call for reservations. Near all of the Cape's scenic, cultural, and historical attractions. Tennis, swimming, sauna on grounds. Water skiing, deep-sea fishing, sailing, bicycles, backroading, beach walking nearby. No recreational facilities for children on grounds. Nicole and Guenther Weinkopf, Innkeepers.

Directions: From Boston, take Rte. 3 south to Sagamore Bridge, crossing Cape Cod Canal. Continue on Rte. 6 to Exit 11; take Rte. 137 south to Rte. 28 and turn left. This is Chatham's Main St. Turn right into Queen Anne Rd. From New York, take I-95 north to Providence, RI, I-95 to Wareham, and Rte. 6 to Sagamore Bridge (see directions above).

THE LENOX HOTEL
Boston, Massachusetts (1985)

I like Boston. It is really a civilized city. To me the Lenox Hotel and Boston go hand-in-glove.

The time was 7:00 a.m. and the streaks of a mid-October dawn over the city were giving way to a full-fledged day. I was seated in the window of my corner room on the eighth floor of the Lenox, looking east. One by one, the street lamps were flickering out and the tail lights of the early morning traffic were becoming more obscure. There, indeed, was a potpourri of Boston architecture in front of me, with restrained 19th-century business buildings cheek-by-jowl with the single bell tower and spire of a church. The trees on Boylston Street still had a generous tinge of the fall colors. A seagull swooped by my window and perched on the very top of a modern Boston building on the opposite corner. Through the other window I could look down the street towards the Charles River and Cambridge on the other side. The runners and joggers were already out. By the way, the Lenox provides a jogger's guide to Boston.

Now the sun poked its way up over the harbor and I glanced around this most "unhotel" of all hotel rooms. A good substantial Hitchcock-style side chair was augmented by two excellent regular chairs and, of course, a Boston rocker. The furniture, draperies, and wallpaper were all in a most pleasing New England style. There wasn't a single piece of furniture that wouldn't have been in place at one of the *CIBR* country inns found throughout New England.

Perhaps most surprising and gratifying of all was a working fireplace. "This took a lot of doing and designing," Gary Saunders told me. "But we comply with all of the Boston codes and many of our guests can enjoy the fun of actually having a wood fire in their fireplace at a hotel in the city. They should indicate their preference when making reservations; not all of the rooms have working fireplaces."

The Lenox Hotel, a small, turn-of-the-century establishment, conveniently located in the Back Bay area of Boston (next door to Copley Square) is something of a rarity in these days of corporate ownership—a family-run hotel, whose owners are very visible. Gary Saunders and his father, Roger, along with other members of the family, have owned the hotel for the past twenty-five years.

Delmonico's, the main dining room, with a Victorian decor, has an impressive and sophisticated menu. Hearty New England fare is served in the Olde London Pub and Grille, for which the main paneling, posts, and tables were shipped over from England.

Another feature is Diamond Jim's piano bar, which offers young vocalists the opportunity to get a little "on stage" experience. I was pleased to be one of the judges during the fall of 1986 for the finals of the great "Piano Bar Sing-off."

There is one particular convenience that guests at the Lenox enjoy, which pleases me very much, and that's the airport and limousine service, available at a reasonable charge for guests arriving and departing. This is particularly handy for those of us who have to fly out of the Logan Airport in Boston. Incidentally, I must admit that I also enjoyed the valet parking service that eliminates the hassle of finding a garage that isn't full.

I must soon be on my way for a quick trip back to the Berkshires on the Massachusetts Turnpike, but before long I would return again to the Lenox Hotel and my civilized city.

THE LENOX HOTEL, 710 Boylston St., Boston, MA 02116; 1-800-225-7676 (Mass.: 617-536-5300). A 220-guestroom conservative hotel in Boston's Back Bay area. Breakfast, lunch, and dinner served every day. Open all year. All contemporary hotel conveniences provided. Drive-in garage with valet parking service. Convenient to business, theaters, sightseeing, and shopping. The Saunders Family, Innkeepers; Jacques Gasnier, General Manager.

Directions: If arriving by automobile, take Exit 22 from the Mass. Tpke., the Copley Square ramp, and turn left on Dartmouth St. for 2 blocks to Newbury St. Take a left on Newbury St. for 1 block to Exeter St., take a left on Exeter for 1 block and the hotel is ahead at the corner of Exeter and Boylston Sts. An airport limo service between Logan Airport and the Lenox is available for a nominal fee.

RALPH WALDO EMERSON
Rockport, Massachusetts (1973)

"When it comes to rocks, ocean, and sky, I think we have more than our share," said Gary Wemyss. Gary pointed out to the breakwater about three miles in front of the "Emerson," as it is known to most of its guests. "In 1946, it was about three times the length it is now, but storms and heavy seas have beaten it down until now in places it is barely visible. The far left end originally formed a harbor of refuge for sailing ships, but the builders ran out of money and gave up the construction.

"There is a reef out there beyond the breakwater known as 'Dry Salvages,' which was an inspiration for the T.S. Eliot poem. The town is trying to get the federal government to rebuild the breakwater because it protects us in winter's heavier storms."

Preoccupation with reefs, the ocean, and the swooping gulls is one of the big attractions at this country inn in Pigeon Cove. It is run by Gary Wemyss, the son of the innkeepers at the Yankee Clipper, about a mile away. The two inns make an interesting contrast, because the Emerson is built along somewhat conventional lines and has many rooms overlooking the water, whereas the Clipper is tucked away among the rocks overlooking the water and is much smaller.

Gary pointed to two lighthouses on Thatcher's Island. "They are the only twin lighthouses on the Eastern Seaboard. However, only one of them has a working light. People like to sit out here in the evening and watch the stars over the ocean and the circling beam from the lighthouse.

"In recent years there's been an increased interest in whale watching, and from May through November there are cruises with naturalists on board. We see some fin-backed whales, but there are humpbacked whales primarily. They come here to feed and they are so tame you can almost reach out and touch them. The naturalists can determine a great many things by looking at the flukes, and they can give you all kinds of information about the whales. The cruises leave primarily from Gloucester, although some leave from Rockport. Plane spotters are often used to determine where the whales are located. You can virtually always see whales. I think it's one of the most thrilling and touching experiences anyone can have to be so close to these wonderful creatures."

Gary explained that the guests include people of all interests and ages. "I think they mix well here," he said. "Everyone seems to enjoy the things that are here—the village, the shore, and of course the proximity to the sea. There is a real feeling of being relaxed and away from urban pressures, and I think that draws a lot of people together. It is such a relief just to have a few days' holiday."

Well, any kind of a holiday usually includes an emphasis on food, and at the Emerson the emphasis is on food from the nearby ocean waters, especially lobster. "People come to this part of New England for lobster, so we try to serve it as frequently as possible," Gary remarked. "Sometimes our guests go up to the Clipper for dinner, or people staying there come down here. It is part of the advantage of having two inns run by the same family."

Ocean, rocks, sky, reefs, lighthouses, bobbing lobster pots, plenty of home-cooked food—all close to Rockport, Massachusetts, one of the most picturesque towns on the New England coast—that's what the Ralph Waldo Emerson is all about. It has provided vacationers with diversion and relaxation for many years.

RALPH WALDO EMERSON, 1 Cathedral Ave., Pigeon Cove, Rockport, MA 01966; 617-546-6321. A 36-guestroom oceanside inn, 40 mi. from Boston. Modified American and European plans. Breakfast and dinner served daily from July 1 to Labor Day; bed and breakfast only during remainder of the year. Pool, sauna, and whirlpool bath on grounds. Tennis, golf nearby. Courtesy car. No pets. Gary and June Wemyss, Innkeepers.

Directions: Take I-95 to Rte. 128 to Rte. 127 (Gloucester). Proceed 6 mi. on Rte. 127 to Rockport and continue to Pigeon Cove.

YANKEE CLIPPER INN
Rockport, Massachusetts (1973)

Nineteen eighty-six was a banner year at the Yankee Clipper Inn. It was the fortieth anniversary of the beginnings of the Clipper by Fred and Lydia Wemyss in 1946. It was also their fiftieth wedding anniversary year and the twenty-fifth wedding anniversary year for their daughter, Barbara, and her husband, Bob.

The Clipper is actually three different buildings. One is The Inn, a gracious ocean-front mansion with antique furnishings, some canopy beds, glass-enclosed porches, and a dining room right on the ocean. All the meals are served in this building. The Quarterdeck, just a few paces away, features unsurpassed views of the ocean through large picture windows and lots of sitting space to enjoy the view. The Bulfinch House

was designed by the early-American architect Bulfinch, who also designed the Massachusetts State House. It is a classic early-19th-century New England house of clipper ship days with period furnishings.

The rooms in the Inn and Quarterdeck are offered with breakfast and dinner from mid-May to the end of October under the modified American plan.

The inn is open in winter on a bed-and-breakfast basis in the two ocean-front buildings. Dinner is served on Fridays and Saturdays in winter, and there is a Sunday brunch. Sitting in front of the fireplace in the afternoon, sipping hot mulled cider and munching homemade goodies with the other guests is really a lot of fun. The innkeepers have a better chance to get to know the guests, and many guests come back two or three times during the winter and again during the summer.

Spring in Rockport, one of the most photographable and paintable villages on the New England coast, has become an annual musical treat. Starting in late March through June there are events such as the Rockport Community Chorus, the Cape Ann Symphony, and the annual Rockport Chamber Music Festival.

One of the more exciting things for guests to do is to take a whale-watch boat trip out to the feeding grounds off Stellwagen Banks, the main fishing grounds for the local fleet. These boats have naturalists on board who give a commentary on each individual whale sighted, their habits, how often they've been seen, and much other information. These trips last from four to five hours, and at least a two-day stay at the Clipper would be necessary.

There is also much to occupy the time of both the active and more contemplative guests at the Yankee Clipper. A heated salt-water pool is sheltered by lovely garden walls d beautiful shade trees. Many guests spend the greater part of the day in the comfortable deck chairs, looking out over the sunlit waters of the bay.

Whether active or contemplative, guests' appetites seem to increase, and the menu has always been one of the special features over the past forty years. Incidentally, lobster dinners are one of the most continually popular reasons that guests return to the Yankee Clipper.

YANKEE CLIPPER INN, P.O. Box 2399, Rockport, MA 01966; 617-546-3407. A 28-guestroom intimate inn on the sea, 40 mi. from Boston. Modified American plan from mid-May to end of Oct. Dining room open to the public. The Quarterdeck and main inn open Nov. 1 to mid-May for bed-and-breakfast. (Closed Dec. 24 to 26.) Heated outdoor pool, ocean view, shoreline walks. Many antique shops and other stores within walking distance. No facilities for infants and children under 3. No pets. Fred and Lydia Wemyss, Owners; Bob and Barbara Wemyss Ellis, Innkeepers.

Directions: Take I-95 to Rte. 128 to 127 (Gloucester). Proceed 6 mi. on Rte. 127 to Rockport and continue to Pigeon Cove.

A number of inns have nearby airports where private airplanes may land. An airplane symbol at the end of the inn directions indicates that there is an airport nearby. Consult inn for further information.

I do not include lodging rates in the descriptions, for the very nature of an inn means that there are lodgings of various sizes, with and without baths, in and out of season, and with plain and fancy decoration. Travelers should call ahead and inquire about the availability and rates of the many different types of rooms.

WINDSOR HOUSE
Newburyport, Massachusetts (1980)

Judith Crumb was telling me how much Newburyport has to offer. "Bird watchers, nature lovers, hikers, and beachcombers love the Parker River Wildlife Refuge with its beautiful beaches, and there are day and evening whale-watch cruises with a marine specialist aboard, as well as harbor tours on a lovely river boat. We can make arrangements for bicycle touring, too, which is more and more popular. Of course," she said as she warmed to her subject, "if you want something really romantic, there's the historic Newburyport tour in a horse-drawn carriage.

"We have a wide variety of comedy, drama, and musicals in our year-round theater in Newburyport, and in the summer we have the Castle Hill Music Festival in Ipswich, the North Shore Music Theatre in Beverly, and the Hampton Playhouse in Hampton, New Hampshire. And there are regular outdoor concerts in our new waterfront park."

I thought she'd told me everything and we'd start our tour of the house, but she put a restraining hand on my arm. "And we mustn't forget that Newburyport is an increasingly important center for fine art, with 18th- and 19th-century painting and antiques, as well as contemporary art, in several excellent galleries. We've definitely moved away from the 'Sunday painter school,' and some very fine work is being exhibited."

Now we headed for the kitchen, as she continued her conversation. "The Windsor House was started in 1785 and completed in 1787 as a private residence. By 1796 it was being used as both a residence and a ship's chandlery. The kitchen here was the original shipping and receiving room, as you can see from those big outside doors.

"The brick wall with the fireplace is part of a firewall that also goes to the top story and separates the warehouse section from the living section. The posts and beams throughout the entire house were built by ships' carpenters, the same men who built the clipper ships."

The kitchen is really the pulse of the Windsor House. Not only do all the guests gather around in the morning to enjoy Judith's prandial skill, but, as she says, "It's the place where we all gather at any time during the day and tell tall tales and get acquainted."

There were interesting contrasts between the rooms on the warehouse side of the firewall and the residential section. The Merchant's Suite on the first floor was the original chandlery. It has its own street entrance and is filled with antiques from 19th-century provisioners' shops, including scales, display boxes, and a bootjack. It's ideal for folks who have difficulty with stairs, or a family with small children.

Rooms on the residential side of the house tend to have wood paneling and other graceful features that would befit a residence.

Judith and her colleague, Jim Lawbaugh, share the breakfast duties,

and he has developed his own sausage recipe. Incidentally, his two sons, Richard and Paul, are frequently in residence at the inn. A rather informal supper with the innkeepers may be enjoyed with special advance arrangement.

The door opened and two guests, who had been doing the walking tour of Newburyport with the Clipper Trail folder, returned for a warming cup of coffee and a little conversation. "We decided to stay for two more days, there's just too much to see."

We all readily agreed.

WINDSOR HOUSE, 38 Federal St., Newburyport, MA 01950; 617-462-3778. A 6-guestroom inn (private and shared baths) in the restored section of Newburyport. Open year-round. Breakfast served to all guests. Supper with the innkeepers by special arrangement. Located in the Merrimack River Valley, 3 mi. from Plum Island and the Parker River National Wildlife Refuge. A short walk from the restored 19th-century retail area, restaurants, and museums. Also nearby: deep sea fishing, swimming, art galleries, antique shops, family ski area, horseback riding, and year-round theater. Some trundle beds available for children. Babysitters provided. Small dogs welcome. Judith Crumb and Jim Lawbaugh, Innkeepers.

Directions: From Boston and Maine: From I-95 use exit to Rte. 113, turn right onto High St. (Rte. 1A) and proceed 3 mi. to Federal St., turn left. Inn on left across from Old South Church (Rte. 1A is scenic drive from Boston or New Hampshire).

LONGFELLOW'S WAYSIDE INN
South Sudbury, Massachusetts (1967)

Off Route 20 there's a wonderful country road marked "Wayside Inn" that leads past the Wayside Inn Gristmill, the Martha and Mary Chapel, and right to the inn itself on the left. Set in a beautiful grove of trees, high hedges, and wooden fences, the inn looks out over a pond. Never mind that it's the site of one of America's oldest country inns, or that history has been made within its walls, the point is that the setting and the building make it a wonderful country inn experience at any time.

Built around 1702, the inn originally was called Howe's Tavern. In 1775, led by innkeeper Ezekiel Howe, the Sudbury farmers were among the men at nearby Concord, and Revolutionary War soldiers found sustenance at the inn's tables. Today, all musters of the Sudbury Minutemen

take place at the inn as preparations are made for their annual reenactment of the march from Sudbury to Concord on April 19. The 200th anniversary of the Battle of Lexington and Concord was celebrated in 1975.

Henry Wadsworth Longfellow immortalized the inn in 1863 with his *Tales of a Wayside Inn,* and thereafter it was known by its new name. Thanks to a grant from the Ford Foundation, the buildings and priceless antiques have been preserved as a historical and literary shrine. The inn is filled with preserved and restored antiques. It combines being a museum with the more practical function of providing lodging and food.

The dining room specializes in such good New England fare as Massachusetts duckling in orange sauce, baked Cape Cod scallops, roast beef, stuffed fillet of sole, muffins made from meal stone-ground at the Gristmill, and indian pudding served with ice cream.

I must echo the advice of innkeeper Frank Koppeis that anyone who is expecting to visit Longfellow's Wayside Inn, either for a meal or lodgings, should be sure to make a reservation in advance.

The gift shop is well worth noting. It is filled with mementos, including prints of the inn and of the Gristmill, and also Longfellow's Wayside Inn history and recipes—a combination history and cookbook in one. It has some absolutely splendid color photographs showing some of the typical dishes they serve here, including their special recipe for meatloaf. By the way, baked beans should always contain molasses and curry powder. As I looked through this book before dinner I became even hungrier.

There were also some recordings of tunes reminiscent of the Wayside Inn, performed by the Sudbury Ancient Fife and Drum Company, which created such a stir a few years ago when we had a *Country Inns and Back Roads* meeting here.

Two of the guest rooms, which escaped damage by a fire in 1955, are over the original inn and are most Colonial in flavor, with wood paneling, exposed beams, and wide floorboards, and are reached by narrow, twisty stairs. The other, later, guest rooms are comfortably and attractively furnished in more of a country Victorian style. All have fresh red roses in them.

I believe that the Longfellow's Wayside experience is particularly enhanced by the fact that the building and grounds and the atmosphere have been so well taken care of. Even though this is one of the most popular places in North America for lunches and dinners, and there are literally thousands of people coming here every year, it has a wonderful set-apart feeling about it, as if it's been waiting for you to arrive.

LONGFELLOW'S WAYSIDE INN, Wayside Inn Rd., Off Rte. 20, South Sudbury, MA 01776; 617-443-8846. A 10-guestroom historic landmark inn, midway between Boston and Worcester. European plan. Lunch and dinner served daily except Christmas. Breakfast served to overnight guests. Within a short distance of Concord, Lexington, and other famous Revolutionary War landmarks. Francis Koppeis, Innkeeper.

Directions: From the west, take Exit 11A from Mass. Tpke., and proceed north on Rte. 495 to Rte. 20. Follow Rte. 20, 7 mi. east to inn. From the east, take Exit 49 from Rte. 128. Follow Rte. 20 west 11 mi. to inn.

The date in parenthesis in the heading represents the first year the inn appeared in the pages of Country Inns and Back Roads.

COUNTRY INN AT PRINCETON
Princeton, Massachusetts (1983)

It was an absolutely magnificent day at the height of the fall foliage season. After parking my car, I walked around the north end of the Country Inn at Princeton out onto the lawn, which I shared with some pigeons and blue jays, and just stood on the terrace for a moment looking over the rolling northern Massachusetts countryside. The autumn colors of rust, yellow, and orange blended with the high hills in the far distance and were complemented by the perfect blue of the sky. I walked across the terrace, with its handsome white outdoor furniture and glass-topped tables, and onto the porch, lush with hanging flowers.

Later, enjoying iced tea on the sunny porch, I asked Don Plumridge about the obvious coordination between the furnishings and decorations of the inn and the menu offerings.

"We offer country products of New England, and the game and wild fowl are not only very popular on our menu, but we are using them as artifacts and decorative pieces around the inn. You see, we have bird collections and wood carvings everywhere. This feeling of natural freshness is carried into both of our dining rooms."

"Flowers and floral motifs are essential to us," Maxine declared. "I spend a great deal of time gathering and arranging the flowers, and we have expanded our own garden tremendously."

Interestingly enough, this decorative theme is continued in the Washburn dining room with arrangements of pheasants and with wall mountings of boar heads, deer heads, and others. Mr. Washburn, the original builder, was apparently a good friend of Theodore Roosevelt's and they hunted wild game together.

There are six guest rooms—some are spacious parlor-size suites—each uniquely decorated with authentic antiques and attractive bedroom furniture, and with views of the countryside or forest. Two of them are the largest bedrooms I have ever seen in a real country inn. Since breakfast is served in the privacy of the guest rooms, all have small tables for dining.

Maxine and Don are very proud to have a new French chef, Larbi Dahrouch, who comes to them from a successful, twelve-year association as executive sous chef to internationally known chef Jean-Louis Palladin. His American–French nouvelle cuisine will feature such dishes as roasted loin of Vermont lamb with shallot and onion flan; a tajine of mallard duck, done by a Moroccan method and served with dates, honey, and cumin; and fresh medallions of venison loin with mushrooms, parsley, and garlic, and served with cauliflower purée.

"Our most exciting innovation is the Private Gourmet Dinner Party evenings," Don declared. "Approximately every six weeks or so we close

the inn to all general public dining on a Thursday night. Invitations have been extended to all guests who visit and dine here, and they arrive about seven o'clock for social greetings and introductions. Remember, they all have demonstrated one thing in common: the willingness to explore the *un*common since the entire evening's bill-of-fare has not been disclosed in advance. This dinner is a seven-course meal with wines, and the entire purpose is to provide a social culinary evening for those of our guests whose dining experience and love of adventure make them want to explore an even higher elevation of refined dining, and it gives Frank a further opportunity to show his skills."

Put all these factors together in such a romantic setting and one might have what one guest describes in the guest book as "a perfect country inn."

COUNTRY INN AT PRINCETON, 30 Mountain Rd., Princeton, MA 01541; 617-464-2030. A 6-guestroom late-Victorian mansion, 50 mi. from Boston and 14 mi. north of Worcester. Open all year except Christmas. Dinner reservations Wed. thru Sun. evenings. Sun. brunch. Closed Mon. and Tues. Near Wachusett Ski Resort, Audubon and Wildlife Society, Mt. Wachusett State Reservation. Tennis, swimming, fishing, hiking, nature trails nearby. Downhill and xc skiing, 3 mi. Lodging for couples only, no accommodations for children. Sorry, no pets. Don and Maxine Plumridge, Innkeepers.

Directions: From Boston, follow Rte. 2 west to Rte. 31 south. From Conn. and Mass. Tpke. (90), follow Rte. 290 north to Rte. 190; then take Exit 5 and continue on Rte. 140. At Rte. 62 turn left 4 mi., and turn right at post office and flashing light. With the town common on your left, the inn is 200 yards up Mountain Rd. on right.

COLONEL EBENEZER CRAFTS INN
Sturbridge, Massachusetts (1981)

If you're traveling on the Massachusetts Turnpike there are two reasons to stop off in Sturbridge. One is to take advantage of the really exceptional lodgings at the Colonel Ebenezer Crafts Inn and to enjoy dinner or lunch at the Publick House.

The other is to pay a serious visit to Sturbridge Village, a restored 19th-century environment. Such a visit would take at least two and a half hours to skim it and longer to really recognize its significance and appreciate all the work that has gone into it.

The village covers over 200 acres with farms, shops, a tavern, a blacksmith shop, and a working gristmill. All of the nearly forty buildings were moved here from throughout New England and then restored and authentically furnished. Year-round, costumed men and women demonstrate skills that have almost disappeared today.

To get to the Publick House, where one must check in for the Colonel Ebenezer Crafts Inn, if you're coming to Sturbridge from the Massachusetts Turnpike be sure to take the first exit to the right, marked "Route 20 West." Follow that to Route 131, turn left, and you're on your way not to old Sturbridge Village, but to today's contemporary Sturbridge Village. On the way you'll pass the Sturbridge Town Hall, the Federated Church, the library, the village green, and the Publick House on your right.

On the June day I arrived at Colonel Ebenezer Crafts Inn, the apple trees on the ridge had shed their blossoms and the small green apples gave promise of good things to come in future months. The lawn was neatly mowed to the edge of the woods and the birds almost seemed to signal my arrival with a pleasant welcome. I walked up the stone steps to the porch with its long deacon's bench and rang the bell. I was greeted by the hostess, Pat Bibeau.

Each of the guest rooms has its own bath and shower, and there's almost always a bowl of apples in each room for guests to enjoy. Pat commented that she frequently turns down the beds in the evening and also leaves cookies. Both of these are nice country inn touches. There is a comfortable terrycloth robe provided for the use of each guest at the poolside or after a shower.

The rooms are very light and airy and are furnished either in antiques or good reproductions. There were a number of chenille bedspreads, including one called "The Pride of Sturbridge."

The living room really invites guests to get acquainted, and I was delighted to find a generously supplied bookcase and also stacks of the *National Geographic,* which makes wonderful bedtime reading.

The exterior landscaping for the inn includes a beautiful brick patio where guests may have morning breakfast or afternoon tea, surrounded by plants and an herb garden. A stone stairway leads from the patio to the pool area, and shrubbery has been planted to form a live sundial around the flagpole.

Because guests at the Colonel Ebenezer Crafts Inn take a great many of their meals at the nearby Publick House, it is of interest to know that luncheons and dinners there include excellent New England clam chowder, as well as New England dishes such as lobster pie, broiled native scallops, double-thick lamb chops, deep dish apple pie—à la mode or with cheddar cheese—and indian pudding served with vanilla ice cream.

COLONEL EBENEZER CRAFTS INN, c/o Publick House, Box 187, Sturbridge, MA 01566; 617-347-3313. A 10-guestroom bed-and-breakfast inn in a historic village, 18 mi. from Worcester. Old Sturbridge Village nearby. Lodging rates include continental breakfast and afternoon tea. (Lunch and dinner available at nearby Publick House.) Open year-round. Swimming pool on grounds. Tennis nearby. Buddy Adler, Innkeeper.

Directions: From Mass. Tpke. take Exit 9; follow signs to Sturbridge on Rte. 131. From Hartford follow I-84, which becomes I-86. Take Exit 3.

"European plan" means that rates for rooms and meals are separate. "American plan" means that meals are included in the cost of the room. "Modified American plan" means that breakfast and dinner are included in the cost of the room. The rates at some inns include a continental breakfast with the lodging.

PEIRSON PLACE
Richmond, Massachusetts (1979)

If you are like I am, then I know you enjoy the idea that there are certain places in the world where the past and the present become a continuum. I find it in certain Scandinavian farmhouse inns that have been lived in by the same family literally for centuries, and also in special places in Germany and Austria, where there is this sense of a continuation with the past. At Peirson Place I have the same feeling that the house and the furniture and the grounds and the view and the atmosphere have remained for the most part unchanged.

This point came home to me when I was once again strolling through the grounds of Peirson Place, and Margaret Kingman told me that the Cogswell House was built in 1762 by Joseph Cogswell. A few years later, a tannery was built on the land by Nathan Peirson, starting a connection through a later marriage between the Cogswells and the Peirsons. "Even our groundskeeper, Russell Chapman, who has maintained all of the trails and landscaping for eighteen years, belongs on the place as well. Nathan Peirson was a tanner, Russell's ancestor a harness maker. Each generation has worked on the property since 1790."

Peirson Place is really very unusual, and Margaret and her son, Lou, have created an intimate country inn that is markedly different from other accommodations in the Berkshires, and, in fact, from most other places. She has many guests who have been returning each year because they enjoy the shaded quiet of the Victorian gazebo, the tranquility of the woods, and the quietude of the pond.

Bird watchers have myriad feathered friends to observe, and guests also enjoy riding bicycles and swimming and the use of the sauna.

Peirson Place is open year around, and during the winter it provides very warm and cozy quarters to accommodate cross-country skiers, who actually do not have to leave the grounds to enjoy that favorite outdoor sport. A good point for me to mention is that lunches and dinners are available on weekends at all times; however, special arrangements can be made for midweek repasts with advance notice.

Speaking of those lunches and dinners, I discovered that many people prefer the dinners at Peirson Place, particularly during the summer, and most particularly on the Friday evenings of Tanglewood. For example, the fare might include a chilled fruit soup, chicken, pasta, a fresh vegetable salad, and melon for dessert. Another menu might be minestrone, fetuccini Alfredo, and strawberry shortcake. Still a third might be cream of broccoli soup, a scallop casserole, and dutch apple pie. Each menu has three courses: soup, an entrée, and dessert. By the way, this combination lunch/dinner is served all afternoon; as Margaret says, "People seem to want to eat all day long."

Breakfasts are also rather special, and include whole-grain cereals with honey, maple syrup, milk or cream, raisin bran, various cheeses, toast, muffins, and pastries.

As we continued walking around the grounds, stopping at the grape arbor—a favorite place for weddings—she told me that many guests are fascinated by the fact that her great-grandfather, her mother, and she were all born in the same room in the Peirson house, which has very sumptuous rooms. It has been in the family since the 18th century.

Although Peirson Place is sometimes referred to as an "obscure inn," Margaret insists that she and the guests enjoy the obscurity.

PEIRSON PLACE, Richmond, MA 01254; 413-698-2750. A 10-guest-room (private and shared baths) country house 6 mi. from Pittsfield on Rte. 41. Open year-round. Minimum stay of 2 nights during Tanglewood season and holiday weekends. Complimentary breakfast. Near all the scenic attractions of the Berkshire Hills, including Tanglewood, Hancock Shaker Village, and marvelous backroading in 3 states. Pond, sauna, badminton, darts, boating on grounds. Tennis, golf, horseback riding, etc., nearby. No facilities to amuse children under 12. No pets. The Kingman Family, Innkeepers.

Directions: From Boston: Take Mass. Tpke. to Exit 1. Follow Rte. 41 north through Richmond. Peirson Place is on left-hand side. From New York: Leave Taconic State Pkwy. at Rte. 295 and continue east to Rte. 41. Turn left. From Albany: New York Thruway (Berkshire Spur) to State Line Exit; left on Rte. 22 to Rte. 295; right on Rte. 295 to Rte. 41. Turn left.

THE VILLAGE INN
Lenox, Massachusetts (1977)

"We're actually beginning our sixth year as innkeepers; it hardly seems possible that that much time has passed." I was having dinner in the Harvest Restaurant at the Village Inn with innkeepers Cliff Rudisill and Ray Wilson. We were reminiscing about their early days here, when they took over the inn in January of 1982, weathered the winter, and worked on learning the ropes and becoming acclimated.

"After Easter that year," Ray said, "we spent two weeks in England and visited seven country house hotels, sampling marvelous cuisine and learning our way around English teas. As a matter of fact, because of meeting Bronwen Nixon at Rothay Manor, we came back and established an English Afternoon Tea, which we've been serving ever since. Rothay Manor is our 'Twin Inn' in England."

These two men, both from Texas, have established their own unique style at the Village Inn, a two-and-a-half-story yellow clapboard building with a basic Federal design. Built in 1771, and ultimately adapted to meet various needs over many years, it became an inn in 1775, and has been one ever since. Two rear wings were once well-constructed barns, forming an L- shaped sheltered terrace with a lawn on which there are a number of beautiful maples. Plantings of iris, daffodils, petunias, roses, and tulips brighten the picture during the warmer weather, and the interior of the inn is enhanced by flowers throughout all months of the year.

On the floors above, authentic New England rooms and suites are available for overnight guests or for those with longer stays in mind. All of them have their own bathrooms, many have four-poster beds, and some have working fireplaces. All of the rooms have new Colonial wallpaper and new curtains and carpets. They are air conditioned in the summer. There is a separate TV on the first floor as well.

The Tavern in the old cellar is now completely remodeled and features professional entertainment on the weekends.

Parking at the inn is in the rear, and it's now possible to enter through a back entrance just off the parking lot, making ingress to the inn more convenient.

On that particular evening I was truly enjoying roast quail with a mousse-like dressing of mushrooms, pecans, and pinenuts served in a wine sauce. It was positively ambrosial. Other menu offerings from the regional American cuisine included a Shaker entrée, which on that evening happened to be Shaker chicken in a cider sauce made from locally pressed cider, and a Shaker dessert—chocolate bread pudding with a custard sauce.

But let's return to the style that Cliff and Ray have brought to the inn in the past few years. Besides the English tea, served every afternoon with the inn's own scones and Devonshire-style clotted cream, High Tea is offered one Sunday a month from January through May, preceded by an hour of live chamber music. One of the artists is Pamela Smith, who recently made her debut at the Metropolitan Opera.

On this subject, Cliff said, "You know, Tanglewood is just a mile down the road, and we continue the tradition of good music all year long. We always have good classical music playing in the background, and our grand piano in the large common room is frequently played by guests who share their talent with us." The inn has also been acquiring some very handsome paintings, including those of William and James Hart and other Hudson River School painters.

The Village Inn in Lenox—an inn of graceful style.

THE VILLAGE INN, Church St., Lenox, MA 01240; 413-637-0020. A 28-guestroom inn (private baths) in a historic Berkshire town, 4 mi. from Stockbridge, 8 mi. from Pittsfield, and 1 mi. from Tanglewood. Breakfast and afternoon tea served daily to travelers. Dinner served Wed. thru Sun. Open every day of the year. Lenox is located in the heart of the Berkshires with many historical, cultural, and recreational features. Swimming in pleasant nearby lakes. All seasonal sports, including xc and downhill skiing available nearby. No entertainment for children under 10. No pets. Personal checks accepted. Cliff Rudisill and Ray Wilson, Innkeepers.

Directions: After approaching Lenox on Rte. 7, one of the principal north-south routes in New England, exit onto Rte. 7A to reach the village center and Church St. When approaching from the Mass. Tpke. (Exit 2) use Rte. 20W about 4 mi. and turn left onto Rte. 183 to center of town.

THE WEATHERVANE INN
South Egremont, Massachusetts (1984)

"Good evening, folks, how are you? I'm the innkeeper, Vince Murphy." While I was having a welcome cup of tea in front of the very cozy fireplace at the Weathervane Inn on a midwinter afternoon, Vincent Murphy excused himself at least four times to welcome new guests. Vince is a man who has the knack for making people feel welcome immediately.

Among the things that I look for in an inn are qualities of memorability. Besides innkeeper Murphy, who is, as he says, "a private investigator from the streets of New York," there are many other memorable features.

For example, there's Anne Murphy with the laughing eyes and a most pleasant manner with all of the guests. Then there's Patricia (or Trish), Anne and Vince's daughter, who had just returned from a Florida vacation at the time of my visit and must have knocked them dead on the beaches, because she had a super suntan to go with her Irish good looks.

The Weathervane Inn, listed in the National Register of Historic Places, is a small cluster of buildings set off the highway, with sections dating back to 1785. It is located in the lovely little village of South Egremont in the Berkshires, where there are many pre-1800 houses and a graceful church. Replete with wide-board floors, beautiful moldings, and an original fireplace that served as a heating and cooking unit with a beehive oven, the inn has a comfortable, warm atmosphere.

There are eleven very attractively furnished country inn guest rooms, with private baths, enhanced by Anne's eye for design and her needlework. Antique maple high double beds and some king-sized beds, all with coordinated linens, along with Anne's handmade pierced lampshades, all combine to make each room distinctive. There are many dried flower arrangements, ball fringe curtains, books and magazines, and good reading lamps.

I talked to Anne about the menu at the Weathervane. "Well," she said, "the kitchen is my domain and I'm very proud of the response that our guests have had to our entrées. Our specialties have been Cornish hens with kiwi sauce, veal Dijonnaise, pork tenderloin Normandy, duckling with black cherries, seafood Mornay, and soups like split pea, New England chowders, and a hearty borscht. We've had to print our recipe for celery seed dressing because so many of our diners requested it."

Vince came cruising by and decided to make his contribution: "Let me tell you about our desserts—Trish is the pastry chef par excellence! The best homemade pies with the best crust. All kinds of fresh fruit combinations—blueberry-peach, strawberry-blueberry, peach-nectarine, and pear-blueberry. And her cheesecake and chocolate chip walnut pie get nothing but raves!"

There are two dining areas, including a new dining room overlooking the garden and the swimming pool, with a glimpse of the antique shop in a barn that has a feeling somewhat akin to the Sturbridge Village buildings. The shop specializes in early quilts and folk furniture, and inn guests often wander back there to browse.

Eventually, we all sat down in front of the fireplace, next to a sort of little pub corner, and for an hour and a half I was beguiled by the various members of the Murphy family. Vince really *is* a private investigator, but he takes all of the "Mike Hammer" jokes with exceptionally good grace and even adds a few of his own. "I did that for many years in the city," he said, "and I still go in about one day a week, but all of us have taken up this new life here in the country. As a matter of fact, I'm even a member of the South Egremont Volunteer Fire Department!"

THE WEATHERVANE INN, Rte. 23, South Egremont, MA 01258; 413-528-9580. An 11-guestroom village inn in the Berkshire foothills. Modified American plan in summer; in winter, modified American plan, Thurs. through Sun. Breakfast served to houseguests. Dinner served to travelers Fri. and Sat. Open year-round. Swimming pool on grounds. Golf, tennis, bicycling, backroading, hiking, horseback riding, fishing, downhill and xc skiing nearby. Tanglewood, Jacob's Pillow, Berkshire Playhouse, Norman Rockwell Museum, and great antique shops all nearby. No pets. Vincent, Anne, and Patricia Murphy, Innkeepers.

Directions; From New York City follow Sawmill River Pkwy. to Taconic Pkwy. to Rte. 23 east. South Egremont and the inn are about 2 mi. past the Catamount Ski area.

THE RED LION INN
Stockbridge, Massachusetts (1967)

"What is your favorite country inn?"

That's a question I hear literally hundreds of times a year. Quite truthfully I have no favorite. I love them all. If I didn't, I'm sure that I couldn't include them in this book. However, there is one country inn to which I feel very close. That's the Red Lion Inn in Stockbridge.

I feel very close to it for many reasons, not the least of which is that I can see it through my office window, just a half-square away. (A little play on words there.)

I'm close to it for many other reasons as well, because, like all of the residents of my village, I have a proprietary interest in the Red Lion. We who live in Stockbridge were dismayed to learn in 1967 that the old inn, originally erected in 1793, enlarged and improved over many years, then almost completely destroyed by fire in 1896, was possibly going to be

torn down and replaced by a gasoline station. We were very much relieved when Jack and Jane Fitzpatrick, owners of Country Curtains, acquired the property, reopened it in 1967, and turned it into a thriving concern.

Like the visitors in Stockbridge, I have spent many a pleasant time rocking on the broad front porch and enjoying lunch at the Widow Bingham's Tavern with my friends. I have attended at least four conferences of *CIBR* innkeepers at the Red Lion over the past twenty-three years. Like many other village inns, it is the center of a great deal of our social activity, including wedding receptions, political gatherings, anniversary parties—in general, a meeting place for villagers.

From the start, the Fitzpatricks have made the Red Lion a family affair, with Jack and Jane being joined by their two daughters, Nancy and Ann. They are all very much involved.

The Fitzpatricks are also the owners of Blantyre, an imposing stone mansion of a former estate, just a few miles from the center of

Stockbridge. Blantyre has sumptuously proportioned bedrooms and two proper courts for playing croquet, as well as a swimming pool and tennis courts. Arrangements may be made through the Red Lion for accommodations there, except in the winter when it is closed.

One of the most enjoyable times at the Red Lion is Christmas, when the inn is decorated "to the nines" with Christmas greens and trim and 2,000 feet of laurel roping. The ceiling-high tree in the lobby shimmers with hundreds of handmade ornaments.

Ann Fitzpatrick's candy sculptures are restored to their familiar spots throughout the public rooms. During the holiday season, there is afternoon harp music, a visit from Santa, and a concert by bell ringers. Children can hang decorations they have made on the children's tree in the hallway by the gift shop. The Christmas spirit continues with a group of carolers, who gather on the front porch at Epiphany. Incidentally, the Red Lion Christmas trees adorning the top of the porch are kept lighted until long after Christmas.

Betsy Herrick, the innkeeper, easily recognizable by her shining blond hair, pointed out to me recently that Stockbridge is a five-season town: winter, spring, summer, autumn, and fall foliage. "It is the first country-inn experience for many people," she commented, "and we want to make it a memorable one. The Berkshire Theatre Festival, the Boston Symphony at Tanglewood, and Jacob's Pillow Dance Festival are open in the summer. In the winter we've got lots of downhill and cross-country skiing. Fortunately, the Norman Rockwell Museum, which contains many of his original paintings, is open every day except Tuesday year-round."

THE RED LION INN, Stockbridge, MA 01262; 413-298-5545. A 95-guestroom historic village inn, dating back to 1773, in the Berkshire hills. European plan. Breakfast, lunch, and dinner. Open year-round. Adjacent to Tanglewood, Norman Rockwell's Old Corner House Museum, the Berkshire Playhouse, Jacob's Pillow, Chesterwood Gallery, Mission House, and major ski areas. Outdoor pool. Tennis, golf, boating, fishing, hiking, mountain climbing, and xc skiing nearby. Jack and Jane Fitzpatrick, Owners; Betsy Herrick, Innkeeper.

Directions: From the Taconic State Pkwy., take Exit 23 (N.Y. Rte. 23) to Mass. Rte. 7. Proceed north to Stockbridge. From the Mass. Tpke., Exit 2 at Lee, and follow Rte. 102 to Stockbridge.

The date in parenthesis in the heading represents the first year the inn appeared in the pages of Country Inns and Back Roads.

THE INN AT STOCKBRIDGE
Stockbridge, Massachusetts (1986)

What a wonderful, gorgeous Berkshire afternoon! The last forty-five minutes of an October sun was streaming across the meadows, lighting up the swaying trees and the two-story columns of the Inn at Stockbridge with a wondrous golden light. I pulled around the circular driveway and stood for a moment on the steps drinking in the entire scene, almost reluctant to join Lee Weitz and other guests for the usual afternoon wine and cheese.

Anticipating my mood, Lee opened the front door of the inn and said, "Oh, I know how you feel, it's so wonderful that you almost hate to come inside. But come on in, because we're all having such a good time in here!" Lee introduced me to some of the guests, all of whom had enjoyed a wonderful afternoon walking or driving in the Berkshires.

I trailed off into the library, another very large room furnished in a most comfortable way, quite reminiscent of an English country house with deep chintz-covered sofas and another big fireplace. Then I crossed over to the other side of the house to see the fourteen-place Chippendale dining room table, where I have had breakfast quite a few times myself. You see, I live about a mile away from the Inn at Stockbridge.

I returned and sank down on a sofa, immediately becoming engrossed in conversation with a couple from California who were traveling with CIBR. "We love it here," they said. "It's our third time and it's like coming home again. What we particularly remember is the good time around the breakfast table, when people are so stimulating and fascinating."

Lee came and spirited me upstairs to look at some of the beautiful guest rooms. These are all most attractively furnished and decorated, and all have interesting names. "I like to furnish every room entirely differently," Lee commented, as we moved from room to room. "Fortunately, this was a lovely, spacious private house for many years and so most of the bedrooms are unusually large. All of them have views of the countryside."

Each of them has some little hidden things, such as candy or little flower arrangements or something special to make the room more distinctive.

Some rooms have a view of a spacious patio where, during the warm weather, the tables are set with pink tablecloths and napkins and fresh flowers. It's all very festive. Beyond the patio is a graceful, secluded swimming pool.

As we rejoined the group in the living room I asked Lee about dinners. "We serve a lighter main course instead of roast prime ribs of beef or heavy cuts of steak," she remarked. "There are light things like fish, chicken, salads, soup, good wholesome homemade bread, and desserts that are appealing but lower in calories. We serve the evening meal in the dining room or out on the patio. There's one menu for dinner; we post it in the morning and the guests can make a reservation that day. When they call off-season we will ask them if they want dinner, which is always served at a set time.

"I have to tell you," she went on, "that people in the summertime love the breakfast out on the patio. Many of them take pictures because the setting is so pretty. Breakfast might include a soufflé or eggs Benedict or a thick slice of french toast with whipped Grand Marnier butter. This makes it taste like crêpes Suzette, but even better. There's also fresh fruit, blueberry pancakes, herbed eggs with cheese and mushrooms, and many other things. We make our own coffee with a French roast blend."

Yes indeed, there was much more to say about the Inn at Stockbridge. It is a most pleasant, intimate inn experience.

THE INN AT STOCKBRIDGE, Rte. 7, Box 618, Stockbridge, MA 01262; 413-298-3337. A 7-guestroom (5 with private bath) country house about 1 mi. north of the center of Stockbridge. Closed during winter months. Lodgings include a full breakfast. Dinner available by request and advance reservation. Convenient to all of the Berkshire cultural and recreational attractions. A summer swimming pool on grounds. No facilities for children under 10. No pets. Lee and Don Weitz, Innkeepers.

Directions: From N.Y.C.: take any of the main highways north to Stockbridge, and continue north on Rte. 7 for 1.2 mi. Look for small sign on the right after passing under the Mass. Tpke. Inn cannot be seen from the road. From Mass. Tpke: exit at Lee, take Rte. 102 to Stockbridge and turn right on Rte. 7 going north for 1.2 mi. as above.

INN AT CASTLE HILL
Newport, Rhode Island (1976)

I was enjoying a few moments of quiet on the porch of one of the Harbor Houses at the Inn at Castle Hill watching the water traffic on Narragansett Bay. In the foreground, a young fisherman wearing very high orange boots was taking in his nets, and in the middle distance I counted at least seventeen sailboats, including one of the famous twelve-meter yachts that are used in the America's Cup Races. In the far distance there was the presence of the famous Newport Bridge, which soars over the bay to Jamestown.

Each one of the Harbor Houses is beautifully furnished with its own bathroom and is roomy enough to accommodate three people comfortably. All of them are newly decorated and the bright white walls and gay curtains and bedspreads are just perfect for the waterside atmosphere.

In addition to these lodgings, there are several rooms in the main mansion of the Inn at Castle Hill. This was once the property of the eminent naturalist Alexander Agassiz, who built Castle Hill one hundred

years ago as a summer residence. It has remained unchanged in character and many of the original furnishings, including oriental rugs and the handcrafted oak and mahogany paneling, are still intact. "This was done before Newport really became a chic society hideout," said Paul McEnroe, the innkeeper at Castle Hill. "Agassiz built this mansion for himself and was really one of the forerunners of Newport's later resplendence."

Paul and I strolled along the grassy bank to the deck of the main house where luncheon was served in full view of the everchanging panorama of sea, sky, and ships. The menu featured several enticing offerings, including a variety of omelets, crêpes, quiches, and salads.

Our conversation naturally led to the dinners at the inn, and Paul explained that the inn takes a limited number of diners each night. "They must be spaced just right. Dinner takes two to two-and-a-half hours, so we naturally cater to people who are not in a hurry. Our dinners are now 98 per cent by reservation, and we only hold a table ten minutes. We always request that they not be late in order to avoid any misunderstandings.

"The evening meal is oriented to French cuisine and includes hot and cold hors d'oeuvres, soups, salads, fish, fowl, lamb, veal, and beef, all cooked and served in the continental manner. We also have a nonsmoking dining room."

The European flavor of the Inn at Castle Hill is considerably reinforced by the road that leads from Ocean Drive through a small section of woods. It reminds me of the Barbizon Forest, about two hours south of Paris, which inspired a school of French painters, including Millet. When I remarked to Paul on this resemblance to inns that I have visited in Europe, he responded enthusiastically, "That's exactly what we've tried to achieve. After all, this inn was built as a mansion and we're trying to recreate the elegance of Newport's past by having a menu, service, and furnishings that best suit our ideals. Jackets are required at dinner and no jeans, not even designer style, are allowed in the dining rooms. I'm sure that's the way it was eighty years ago."

INN AT CASTLE HILL, Ocean Dr., Newport, RI 02840; 401-849-3800. A 20-guestroom mansion-inn on the edge of Narragansett Bay. European plan. Continental breakfast served to houseguests only. Lunch and dinner served daily to travelers. Dining room closed from Dec. 1 to week before Easter. Guestrooms open all year. Lounge open winter weekends. Near the Newport mansions, Touro Synagogue, the Newport Casino, and National Lawn Tennis Hall of Fame, the Old Stone Mill, the Newport Historical Society House. Swimming, sailing, scuba diving, walking on grounds. Bicycles and guided tours of Newport nearby. No pets. Jens Thillemann, Manager; Paul McEnroe, Innkeeper.

Directions: After leaving Newport Bridge, follow Bellevue Ave., which becomes Ocean Dr. Look for inn sign on left, about 2 mi. out of town.

"European plan" means that rates for rooms and meals are separate. "American plan" means that meals are included in the cost of the room. "Modified American plan" means that breakfast and dinner are included in the cost of the room. The rates at some inns include a continental breakfast with the lodging.

THE INNTOWNE
Newport, Rhode Island (1982)

No matter how many times I've done it, it still gives me a tremendous lift to cross over the bridge from Jamestown to Newport, Rhode Island. Not only is this approach one of the most convenient ways to reach Newport, it affords a wonderful view of Newport Harbor.

It was a lovely day in mid-May, and as soon as I parked the car I spied Paul McEnroe, well tanned and as young-looking as the day I met him in 1966. He immediately took me into the Mary Street House, a new addition to the main inn since my last visit. Each of the rooms has been decorated with care and subtlety by Ione Williams, who with her husband, Rod, is also the owner of the Inn at Sawmill Farm in West Dover, Vermont.

The Mary Street House proved to be a fitting complement to the Inntowne, and all of the decorations and furnishings were a continuation of the earlier themes that had been established a few years ago when Paul and his wife, Betty, relocated in Newport after living for many years in New York State. Paul is also the innkeeper of the Inn at Castle Hill. After spying the architectural integrity of the original, old, dilapidated brick building on the corner of Mary and Thames, he decided to convert it into an elegant bed-and-breakfast inn and call it the Inntowne Inn.

The lobby-living room area has some handsome antiques, including an old grandfather's clock in a beautiful inlaid antique case, and one wall is a bookcase decorated with ivy plantings and a beautiful model ship. It's like being in a living room of a very elegant house of two hundred years ago, because the atmosphere is decidedly Colonial, rather than Victorian.

Betty joined us, and while we were having a cup of afternoon tea, a regular event at the Inntowne, I heard the receptionist responding to a phone call, explaining that there were no TV's, no telephones, and no elevators. Upon checking in, guests are advised that arrangements can be made for parking in a special lot just up the street.

Breakfast at the Inntowne includes very tasty croissants and muffins, and something I am always delighted to find: freshly squeezed orange juice.

I asked Paul about the best time to come to Newport. "If someone is looking for a nice quiet time and a nice quiet country inn within the city, I think the fall or even the winter is lovely. The crowds are gone and you can get into all of the restaurants and there is still much to see and do.

"We're taking more and more reservations for people in the wintertime," he continued. "There are three mansions open on weekends in the winter. The indoor tennis facilities are open, the shopping and wharf areas, and the fine restaurants are all at their best. The drive along the ocean is magnificent."

Betty added, "Christmas in Newport is a wonderful time to come. The city is very active with many events scheduled, including parades, Christmas tree decorations, and there are candles in all the windows. The town is most tastefully decorated. There is a special calendar published for December, and there is something happening every day. Although we are closed Christmas Eve and Christmas Day, we are open throughout the rest of the Christmas season."

As I departed after a really pleasant visit with Paul and Betty, it occurred to me that there was a distinct resemblance between the Inntowne and the Residence du Bois in Paris. Each has a soothing air of quietude, somewhat away from the hustle and bustle of the city.

THE INNTOWNE, 6 Mary St., Newport, RI 02840; 401-846-9200. An elegant 20-guestroom bed-and-breakfast inn in the center of the city of Newport overlooking the harbor, serving continental breakfast and afternoon tea. Open every day. Reservations by telephone only between 9 a.m. and 11 p.m. Convenient for all of the Newport historical and cultural attractions, which are extremely numerous. No recreational facilities available; however, tennis and ocean swimming are nearby. Not adaptable for children of any age. No pets. Betty and Paul McEnroe, Innkeepers.

Directions: After crossing Newport bridge, turn right at first exit sign, and right again at bottom of ramp. Drive straight to Thames Street; Inntowne is on corner of Thames St. and Mary St., across from Brick Marketplace.

LARCHWOOD INN
Wakefield, Rhode Island (1969)

Frank Browning and I were talking about lobsters, a subject that is near and dear to the hearts of those of us who are fortunate enough to live near New England's coastal waters. The Larchwood Inn certainly qualifies in this respect, since it's just a few minutes from the great beaches of southern Rhode Island.

"We buy from one source, and we know we're getting the best," he told me. "On Monday, we have special dinners of either twin lobsters or prime rib, and it is one of our most popular nights in the week. We always have a full-sized lobster every night and twin lobsters on Monday. I hope your readers will reserve ahead for lobsters because there's always a great demand. By the way, on Mondays in the summertime we have Al Conte, who is a cabaret performer and a piano player. It really livens things up."

I wandered into one of the dining rooms, where there is a mural depicting the southern Rhode Island beaches. The tables were very attractively set for the next meal with green tablecloths. I noticed the living room had been redecorated since my last visit. It was very pleasant, with comfortable chairs and a fireplace with a very impressive ship's model on the mantel. There was also an exotic bird in a cage.

At this point, Frank returned, and I asked him about the ship's model. "That is a three-masted schooner, called *L'Astrolabe*, and everything was built to scale by a friend of mine. See the little boys on the deck—he thought of everything."

The Larchwood is a large mansion, dating back to 1831, in the village of Wakefield, set in the middle of a large parklike atmosphere with

copper, beech, ginkgo, pin oak, spruce, mountain ash, maple, Japanese cherry trees, evergreens, dogwoods, and a very old mulberry tree. In all, there are three acres of trees and lawn.

The interior has many Scottish touches, including quotations from Robert Burns and Sir Walter Scott, and photographs and prints of Scottish historical and literary figures.

The conversation naturally turned once again to menu items, since Frank was the chef here for many years and is now carefully supervising the kitchen and dining room.

"We're in the process right now of working with the South County Hospital. They are coming out with low-cholesterol items, and they came to us to ask if we could cooperate with them. We're working on seven or eight items in our restaurant for their program. There will be lighter things, including different ways to serve chicken and fish."

I asked him about breakfasts, and I'm very glad I did. "We make the french toast with our own bread and offer it with either sour cream or whipped cream and warm strawberries. The strawberries make it absolutely fantastic. It's something that our guests really appreciate, along with our selection of different omelets."

Besides guest rooms in the main inn, there are additional attractively furnished guest rooms in the Holly House, a 150-year-old building across the street from the inn. Guests at the Holly House can enjoy breakfast, lunch, and dinner at the Larchwood Inn dining room.

My eye caught a card on the table that had a Catholic, Jewish, and Protestant grace, and also one from Robert Burns, which I am going to share with everyone.

> *Some ha' e meat and canna eat*
> *And some ha' e nane that want it,*
> *But we ha' e meat and we can eat,*
> *So let the Lord be thankit.*

LARCHWOOD INN, 176 Main St., Wakefield, RI 02879; 401-783-5454. A 19-guestroom (some shared baths) village inn just 3 mi. from the famous southern R.I. beaches. European plan. Breakfast, lunch, dinner served every day of the year. Swimming, boating, surfing, fishing, xc skiing, and bicycles nearby. Francis Browning, Innkeeper.

Directions: From Rte. 1, take Pond St. exit and proceed ½ mi. directly to inn.

THE 1661 INN
Block Island, Rhode Island (1976)

A few years before my first visit to Block Island, Joan, Justin, Rita, Mark, and Rick Abrams had discovered the 1661 Inn during one of their many sailing adventures from Providence. At that time it was a small hotel named the Florida House. Later, it was renamed the 1661 Inn by the Abramses, in honor of the year that Block Island was settled by colonists from New England.

"At that time, we gave each of the bedrooms the name of one of the original brave settlers," Joan explained. "Our family spent many hours consulting books for authentic New England decor and redoing all the rooms. We decorated with many of our own antiques and Early American paintings."

A few years later, after Rita Abrams and Steve Draper were married, the house next door to the 1661 Inn was acquired. Steve, who is a natural-born planner and builder, set about completely remodeling what was to become the 1661 Guest House. All of the bedrooms were done over and private decks were added. The guest house is completely heated and is open all year.

Perhaps Steve did not know the Abrams family's penchant for remodeling and rebuilding, but he soon found out about it! Joan and Justin decided to restore one of the island's historic summer hotels, the Manisses Hotel, also owned by the Abrams family.

The two accommodations offer interesting contrasts: the 1661 House has a distinctly Colonial and early-19th-century atmosphere, while the Manisses has a mid-19th-century-resort opulence.

In recent years, three of the bedrooms overlooking the dining deck at the 1661 Inn were enlarged and now enjoy glorious views of the ocean

from their own deck. Directly above them, three second-floor bedrooms have their own decks, so that there are seven rooms with sea views and decks. Each room has been decorated in Colonial-period furniture, wallpaper, and draperies. There are Winslow Homer prints and quite a few original watercolors and drawings of Block Island houses.

Breakfast is an extravaganza with fresh fruit, corned beef hash, scrambled eggs, quiche, choices of breakfast meat, small, red potatoes, roasted first, then baked in the oven with spices, and at least one or two special dishes, such as chicken tetrazzini and vegetable casseroles. All the muffins, jams, and breads are homemade.

The evening menu features such regional dishes as Block Island clam chowder, flounder, lobster, swordfish, johnnycake, indian pudding, and blackberry flummery. I must say that the baked stuffed flounder with mussels and clams is a joy. Guests may take lunch at the Manisses.

May I take a moment to point out that Block Island is a very singular experience during what is usually known as the "off season." This is any time after the middle of October. There are wonderful beaches to walk, bikes to ride, and the island, with a population of only 600 during the winter, becomes a very private experience. Rita and Steve and their two boys are always on hand in the Guest House to help island winter visitors make it a really beautiful experience.

THE 1661 INN, Box 367, Block Island, RI 02807; 401-466-2421 or 2063. A 25-guestroom island inn off the coast of R.I. and Conn. in Block Island Sound; 11 private baths. Open from Memorial Day thru Columbus Day weekend. Breakfast served to travelers daily. (Guest House open year-round; continental breakfast included in off-season rates; dinner upon request.) Lawn games on grounds. Tennis, bicycling, ocean swimming, sailing, snorkeling, diving, salt and fresh water fishing nearby. Block Island is known as one of the best bird observation areas on the Atlantic flyway. The Abrams Family, Innkeepers.

Directions: By ferry from Providence, Pt. Judith, and Newport, R.I.,and New London, Ct. Car reservations must be made in advance for ferry. Cars are a convenience, but not needed on the island. By air from Newport, Westerly, and Providence, R.I., New London and Waterford, Ct., or by chartered plane. Contact inn for schedules.

A number of inns have nearby airports where private airplanes may land. An airplane symbol at the end of the inn directions indicates that there is an airport nearby. Consult inn for further information.

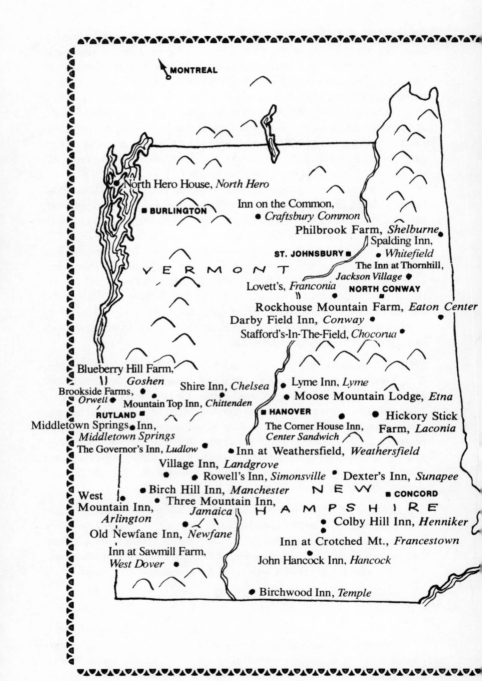

MONTREAL

North Hero House, *North Hero*

Inn on the Common,
● *Craftsbury Common*

Philbrook Farm, *Shelburne* ●
)) Spalding Inn,
● *Whitefield*

BURLINGTON

ST. JOHNSBURY ■

V E R M O N T

The Inn at Thornhill,
Jackson Village ●

Lovett's, *Franconia*   NORTH CONWAY
■

Rockhouse Mountain Farm, *Eaton Center*

Darby Field Inn, *Conway* ●

Stafford's-In-The-Field, *Chocorua* ●

Blueberry Hill Farm,
\) *Goshen*   Shire Inn, *Chelsea*   ● Lyme Inn, *Lyme*
Brookside Farms, ● ●   ● Moose Mountain Lodge, *Etna*
Orwell ● Mountain Top Inn, *Chittenden*
RUTLAND ■   ■ HANOVER   ● Hickory Stick
Middletown Springs ● Inn,   The Corner House Inn,   Farm, *Laconia*
Middletown Springs   *Center Sandwich*
The Governor's Inn, *Ludlow* ●   ● Inn at Weathersfield, *Weathersfield*

Village Inn, *Landgrove*
●   ● Rowell's Inn, *Simonsville* ● Dexter's Inn, *Sunapee*
● Birch Hill Inn, *Manchester*   N E W   ■ CONCORD
West ●   ● Three Mountain Inn,
Mountain Inn,   *Jamaica*)) H A M P S H I R E
Arlington   ● ∠ \   ● Colby Hill Inn, *Henniker*
Old Newfane Inn, *Newfane*))
Inn at Sawmill Farm,   Inn at Crotched Mt., *Francestown*
West Dover ●   ●
John Hancock Inn, *Hancock*

● Birchwood Inn, *Temple*

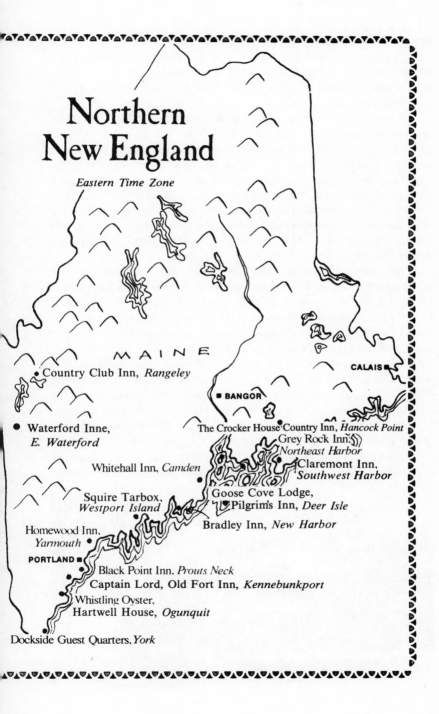

Northern New England

Eastern Time Zone

MAINE

Country Club Inn, *Rangeley*

CALAIS

BANGOR

Waterford Inne, *E. Waterford*

The Crocker House Country Inn, *Hancock Point*
Grey Rock Inn, *Northeast Harbor*

Whitehall Inn, *Camden*

Claremont Inn, *Southwest Harbor*

Squire Tarbox, *Westport Island*

Goose Cove Lodge, Pilgrim's Inn, *Deer Isle*

Bradley Inn, *New Harbor*

Homewood Inn, *Yarmouth*

PORTLAND

Black Point Inn, *Prouts Neck*
Captain Lord, Old Fort Inn, *Kennebunkport*

Whistling Oyster, Hartwell House, *Ogunquit*

Dockside Guest Quarters, *York*

BLACK POINT INN
Prouts Neck, Maine (1969)

I drove up the circular driveway to the canopied entrance of the Black Point Inn, and there sat a sedate black London taxicab. I couldn't help but reflect that it was, like the inn itself, a throwback to the days of New England's past.

Normand Dugas, the innkeeper, had seen me through his office window and came out to tell me about "Wally, the cab." "In 1981, an English company sent over a couple of their famous London taxicabs as samples, hoping to corner the market left open by the demise of the Checker Cab Company. However, it all came to naught, and after a number of adventures I acquired one of the cabs. The staff named it 'Wally.' With a four-cylinder diesel engine, Wally has a top speed of fifty miles an hour and gets about fifty miles to the gallon. He seats five people comfortably, and we use him for transporting people back and forth to the airport and for sedate afternoon rides."

We walked upstairs into the lobby, where the grandfather's clock tolled exactly twelve noon, which meant it was thirty minutes before lunch. A few of the guests were on the porch overlooking the bay side of Prouts Neck, and a few others were in the enclosed sunporch, playing cards or knitting. Ordinarily, lunch would be served poolside, but today being a bit too foggy, it was served in the regular inn dining room.

Last summer, twelve-year-old Peter Dugas, who wants to be a writer/historian, put together a one-and-half-hour walking trip on the Cliff Walk, where he gives the history of Prouts Neck, going back to the days of the Indian massacres. He'll repeat his guided tour this year, too.

Another interesting addition to the Black Point is the "Atlantic House Library." The Atlantic House Hotel, also on Prouts Neck, is now closed after 146 years of continuous operation, and the BPI acquired most of their library books and some other memorabilia. A lovely outside

deck just off the library has been constructed for nice sunny-day reading.

Norm and I walked into the indoor swimming pool room, which he tells me has been extremely well received by all of the inn guests. Those staying slightly off season have particularly appreciated this pool, since the ocean is too cold before mid-June and after mid-September. The walls of the room are lined in beautiful California red cedar, and the pool overlooks the rose garden and the putting green. This also includes a group jacuzzi, sauna, and exercise area.

The Black Point Inn is one of the few remaining American plan hotels that were so numerous on the New England coast sixty and seventy years ago. It has quiet dignity, personal service, and attention to details.

For the active, sports-minded guest, there's just about everything: an 18-hole golf course, tennis courts, sailing, fishing, swimming, beach walking, and clambering over rocks.

In many respects, the Black Point is a throwback to the F. Scott Fitzgerald era. Gentlemen wear coats and ladies don colorful dresses for dinner. The small orchestra plays for dancing in the evening and at poolside during lunches.

Rooms are more readily available during the months of June and July. During recent years, the weather in early June has been exceptional, and it is sometimes possible to call and make a reservation a day ahead; however, August is always a full month.

One hundred years ago, the American painter Winslow Homer found in this section of the rocky Maine coastline the inspiration and atmosphere that enabled him to create some of his greatest works. In fact, he walked these sandy shores and climbed these same rocks. His studio is located just a few minutes' walk from the front door of the inn.

Prouts Neck became popular as a summer resort at the end of the 19th century, and time has brought few changes to this lovely neck of land stretching out into the Atlantic. The sea, birds, water, sky, and trees, all of which go to make such desirable tranquility, are still here today.

BLACK POINT INN, Prouts Neck, ME 04070; 207-883-4126. An 80-guestroom luxury resort-inn on Rte. 207, 10 mi. south of Portland. Open May to late Oct. American plan during July and Aug. Optional MAP May, June, Sept., Oct. During high season, 3-night minimum stay. Indoor pool, jacuzzi, and sauna, fresh-water whirlpool, heated salt-water pool, bicycles, sailing, dancing, golf, tennis, and ocean bathing all within a few steps. No children under 8 during July and Aug. No pets. Normand H. Dugas, Innkeeper.

Directions: From Maine Tpke., take Exit 7. Turn right at sign marked Scarborough and Old Orchard Beach. At second set of lights turn left on Rte. 207. Follow 4.3 mi. to Prouts Neck.

THE BRADLEY INN
Pemaquid Point, New Harbor, Maine (1981)

I reached out and put my hands on the firm stone base of the Pemaquid Point Lighthouse. It radiated a wonderful warmth borrowed from the brilliant September sun, so I sat down and rested against it, attempting to draw into myself some of its strength and nobility. It was my lighthouse.

Immediately in front of me, this selfsame sun created momentary jewels where the Atlantic gently lapped against the striated rocks that stretched out toward Spain. Overhead, sea birds wheeled and turned and talked to each other incessantly. I closed my eyes and my thoughts drifted back to my arrival at the Bradley Inn, just a short, pleasant walk from my lighthouse.

This time I had taken Route 32 off Route 1 at Waldoboro, south of Rockland. This is a delightful experience through back-country Maine. Travelers who are trying to get pell-mell from one inn to another may never leave I-95 for Route 1, and that's unfortunate, for here is a good alternate back road that's hard to beat. It comes out just a few moments from the Bradley Inn. If you're traveling north from the Bradley Inn, ask any member of the Ek family and they will put you on Route 32.

Well, I found the Ek family, Ed, Louine, and Grandma, in excellent spirits because many new features had been added to the inn; in fact, the front of it was quite different from the last time I visited. The dining room has also been enlarged to encompass the former old-fashioned screened-in porch, with an addition that forms a lounge with a piano, all done in knotty pine and bentwood chairs. Both the dining room and lounge have a pleasant view across the fields.

A visit to this country inn on the rocky coast of Maine is in many respects a step backward in time. Most of the guest rooms share bathrooms and conveniences "down the hall," and the furniture came from Ed and Louine's former home. Besides decorator sheets and pillowcases in bright colors, these moderately sized rooms have firm mattresses. Smoking, incidentally, is not permitted in the guest rooms.

The menu includes such hearty offerings as prime ribs of beef, several chicken and veal dishes, and much seafood from the local waters, when available, including scallops, sole, swordfish, haddock, and lobster. Sunday brunch is always a happy occasion.

With new areas in the inn and much new decorating, the Bradley Inn has taken on wonderful new dimensions; however, there is a simplicity and purposefulness, in some ways personified by a small plaque in each room, which reads in part: "Let the guest sojourning here know that in this home our life is simple. What we cannot afford we do not offer, but what good cheer we can give, we give gladly. We make no strife for appearance's sake. We will not swerve from our path for you. . . .

"For, while you are with us, we would have you enjoy the blessings of a home, health, love and freedom, and we pray that you may find the final blessing of life—peace."

Janice Lindstrom, our artist, has sketched the Pemaquid Point Lighthouse, which I, along with, I'm sure, most of the guests at the Bradley Inn, find delightful.

THE BRADLEY INN, Rte. 130, 361 Pemaquid Point, New Harbor, ME 04554; 207-677-2105. A 13-guestroom (shared baths) country inn near Pemaquid Lighthouse on Maine's rocky coast, 15 mi. from Damariscotta. Open mid-May to Jan. Continental breakfast included in room rate. Open daily to the public for dinner from mid-June to mid-Oct.; on weekends only Oct. to Jan., March to June. Restaurant is closed Christmas Eve, Christmas Day, Jan., Feb. Tennis, swimming, golf, canoeing, backroading, woodland walks, xc skiing all available nearby. Many cultural, historical, and recreational facilities nearby. No pets. No smoking in rooms. Edwin and Louine Ek and Grandma, Innkeepers.

Directions: From south: Maine I-95 to Brunswick/Bath Coastal Rte. 1 Exit. Follow Rte. 1 through Brunswick, Bath, and Wiscasset. Exit Business Rte. 1 at Damariscotta. Turn right at top of hill (white church), follow Rte. 130, 14 mi. to Pemaquid Pt. From north: Rte. 1; exit at Business Rte. 1, Damariscotta. Turn left at white church onto Rte. 130. Follow 130, 14 mi. to Pemaquid Pt.

The date in parenthesis in the heading represents the first year the inn appeared in the pages of Country Inns and Back Roads.

THE CAPTAIN LORD MANSION
Kennebunkport, Maine (1975)

I remember it very well; in fact, it was only last summer. It was a Wednesday morning in mid-July and I joined the Captain Lord breakfast group at nine-thirty. (There had been an earlier breakfast group at eight-thirty.) Many of the guests were seated in a large but somewhat formal dining room enjoying coffee and planning the day's activities. A large jigsaw puzzle was on the dining room table and a couple of guests were playing chinese checkers in one corner. The Chippendale chairs, beautiful cabinets, and crystal chandelier were indications that this was indeed an important room during the many years of the mansion's existence.

Meanwhile, the morning breakfast chimes were rung, and almost as one, the waiting guests rose, crossed the hallway, and walked into the ample Captain Lord kitchen, where breakfast is served.

I took advantage of the moment to walk around and admire the handsome woodwork and lovely period wallpapers of this mansion, built during the War of 1812. Captain Nathaniel Lord answered the needs of idle carpenters and sailors by engaging them to build this stately home, using timbers intended for ships.

I walked to the front of the house where a beautiful curving banister led up a rather formal staircase to the third floor. Throughout the mansion, Rick and Bev have collected antiques, oriental rugs, and other tasteful objets d'art. One parlor has been set aside as a gift shop offering attractive mementos of the area, as well as smaller items such as cups, saucers, plates and the like.

Ample use has been made of the generously sized hallways, both on the second and third floors, with handsome cabinets, antique children's sleighs, duck decoys, quilts, prints of sailing ships, a spinning wheel,

and even a basket of washed wool. Many of the rooms have been named after ships that probably sailed from Kennebunkport.

I peeked into a few of the spotless guest rooms whose doors were open, and once again fluffy comforters, handmade quilts or 100% wool blankets, and Posturepedic mattresses reigned supreme. There are eight rooms with queen-sized beds and two rooms with king-sized beds.

Well, we were quite a group at breakfast. There were several couples from New Jersey, and a couple who had been married in Francestown, New Hampshire, just the day before. We all had great fun guessing what our various occupations were and also how long we had been married. There was lots of laughter and also many comments about the fact that breakfast, consisting of orange juice, homemade breads, muffins, or toast and coffee and, if desired, a soft-boiled egg, was not only plentiful, but extremely tasty as well.

We were all seated around the lovely harvest table, which provides just the right amount of intimacy to make this whole experience even more fun. Our conversation turned to what we looked for at an inn, and we decided that congeniality among the guests was a very important quality. It was definitely agreed by all present that the Captain Lord should get very high marks for having congenial guests!

Before I departed, I had a chance to talk to Rick about their newly acquired wonderful copper eagle weathervane. "It was actually originally here at the Captain Lord Mansion," he said. "I was the most persistent bidder for it at an auction in Lebanon, Maine, and as the auctioneer gaveled my winning bid, he told the crowd, 'the eagle is going back home to the Captain Lord Mansion in Kennebunkport.' "

THE CAPTAIN LORD MANSION, Box 800, Kennebunkport, ME 04046; 207-967-3141. A 16-guestroom mansion-inn in a seacoast village. Lodgings include breakfast. No other meals served. Open year-round. Near the Rachel Carson Wildlife Refuge, the Seashore Trolley Museum, the Brick Store Museum, and lobster boat tours. Bicycles, hiking, xc skiing, deep sea fishing, golf, indoor swimming, and tennis nearby. No children under 12. No pets. No credit cards. Bev Davis and Rick Litchfield, Innkeepers.

Directions: Take Exit 3 (Kennebunk) from the Maine Tpke. Take left on Rte. 35 and follow signs through Kennebunk to Kennebunkport. Take left at traffic light at Sunoco station. Go over drawbridge and take first right onto Ocean Ave., then take fifth left off Ocean Ave. ($^3/_{10}$ mi.). The mansion is in the second block on left. Park behind building and take brick walk to office.

THE CLAREMONT HOTEL AND COTTAGES
Southwest Harbor, Maine (1974)

The year was 1884. Grover Cleveland (Democrat) defeated James G. Blaine (Republican) for president. London opened the first underground railroad. Auguste Rodin created his famous sculpture *Burghers of Calais*. Harry Truman was born. The Ringling Brothers circus was organized in Baraboo, Wisconsin. The Statue of Liberty was completed and presented to the United States. Women first competed in Wimbledon tennis, and the Washington Monument was completed.

It was also the year that the Claremont Hotel was opened. Its creator was Captain Jesse Pease, a native of Rockland and a well-known sea captain. During that first year, 146 names were entered on the register. Many of these came from New York and Boston and enjoyed a simple, modest vacation at the Claremont. There were oil lamps and pitchers and basins in each room. Hot baths were ordered in advance for twenty-five cents.

Considerable contribution to the progress of this now-century-old establishment came during the long tenure of the Philips family, who owned it for sixty years. During that time, more bedrooms and a new dining room were added, and such improvements as an elevator and a sprinkling system were installed.

In 1968, the Claremont was sold to Mr. and Mrs. Allen McCue of Yarmouth, Maine, who have continued in all of the traditions, as well as adding new cottages and making many improvements, including a wing with a spectacular view of Somes Sound.

During 1984, the Claremont celebrated its centennial in a most auspicious way with a series of very interesting events, some of which I suspect will be continued during many summers to come. The official birthday was celebrated on August 18, and I told Jay Madeira, who has been the innkeeper for most of the ten years I have been visiting the Claremont, how sorry I was to miss such an important affair.

On the waters of Somes Sound, the Claremont is situated in a most interesting community with an identity of its very own. It always intrigues me that there are two different aspects to Southwest Harbor. On one side of the small peninsula is a working harbor with lots of fishing boats and the hustle and bustle of people who make their living with the cooperation of the sea. On the other side is a more tranquil scene, with sailboats and launches. This view over the water to Northeast Harbor is the one which is enjoyed by Claremont guests as they sit in the boathouse or on the front porch of the inn itself.

On each visit I have been struck by the wide variety of entertainment and recreation available for people vacationing on Mount Desert Island. All of the natural attractions of the area are within a very convenient distance; however, in recent years the Claremont has become well known for an important tournament of 9-wicket croquet—a game which has been played on the lawn of the inn since its earliest days. Players and spectators alike enjoy the Claremont Croquet Classic, a unique event for Claremont visitors. Many guests and staff return year after year to enjoy the serene atmosphere and the beautiful views.

Now the Claremont, on the National Register of Historic Places, is well into its second hundred years!

THE CLAREMONT HOTEL AND COTTAGES, Southwest Harbor, ME 04679; 207-244-5036. A 22-guestroom (mostly private baths) rambling summer hotel with rooms also in two adjacent guest houses; on Somes Sound, Mt. Desert Island, 24 mi. south of Ellsworth. Hotel and dining room open mid-June thru mid-Sept. Breakfast and dinner served to guests and the public. Lunch served in the boathouse during July and Aug. Guest-house rooms and housekeeping cottages available May thru Oct. Hotel and Phillips House rooms available only on mod. American plan during the season. Off-season, all rooms available either EP or MAP while hotel is open. Tennis, rowboats, croquet, badminton, golf, bicycles, riding, boating, and sailing rental nearby. No credit cards. Personal checks accepted. The McCue Family, Owners; John Madeira, Jr., Manager.

Directions: From Maine Tpke., exit at Augusta and proceed east on Rte. 3 to U.S. 1. At Ellsworth, pick up Rte. 3 again and follow Rte. 102 on Mt. Desert Island to Southwest Harbor. Follow inn signs approaching and in Southwest Harbor.

THE COUNTRY CLUB INN
Rangeley, Maine (1981)

We were all gathered at one of the focal points at the Country Club Inn—the deck, with its sweeping panorama of sky, lake, and mountains. There were innkeepers Bob and Sue Crory, their daughter, Marge, and her husband, Steve Jameson, and the Crorys' son, Bob, Jr. There was also an extra guest, Ann Leger, from Philbrook Farm Inn in Shelburne, New Hampshire, who had driven up with me for the day. Sue was telling me how pleasant it was to have Marge, Steve, and Bob Jr. with them at the inn.

"I think a lot of it is with the returning guests," she said. "They look for them as soon as they arrive. It's always a case of 'Oh, where's Margie?' Or, 'Is Bob here this year?' Our staff is small enough anyway so that they all become like a family. Of course, we all change our hats around here and move from one job to another, but having members of the family makes everything a lot more personal."

There's no doubt that there are two emphases at the Country Club Inn; the first is the familylike atmosphere and the second is the really incredible scenery. Rangeley, Maine, is one of those places in the world

that has a special kind of charisma. There are few locations that offer such beauty and grandeur in all seasons. It's a combination of wide skies, vast stretches of mountain woodland, and the placid aspect of the Rangeley Lake that has been drawing people to this part of western Maine since long before the roads were as passable and numerous as they are today.

Bob Crory joined in: "I spent my boyhood summers working in Maine resorts and then went on to major in hotel administration at the University of New Hampshire. Sue and I had many different jobs, but all the time we knew that what we wanted was to have our own resort inn, small, cozy and comfortable. We found it in the Country Club Inn because we're small, but this coziness plus all the things there are to do here, like the swimming pool, the golf course, and the backroading make it a really good experience."

All of the guest rooms at the Country Club Inn have a picture window with a view of the lake and each one has a double bed and a twin bed, which, as Bob says, "makes everybody happy." The dining room also has this same view of the lake that reminds me of a similar stretch of lake and mountains in certain sections of Scotland, Loch Ness being one.

Sweeping an arm towards the view, Bob said, "September is a golden month. This whole panorama becomes a pageant of changing colors. You can see the colors coming down from the top of the mountains into the valley enveloping the countryside in brilliance. We also frequently can see the northern lights at that time. Of course, our big fireplace is going all the time."

The Country Club Inn has been open in both summer and winter in the past few years as there are lots of wintertime activities in the woods of western Maine, including tobogganing, snowmobiling, cross-country skiing, and downhill skiing at Saddleback and Sugarloaf. It's at times like these that guests appreciate the sauna most.

As Ann and I were leaving, Ann remarked, "I didn't realize how close the front door of the lodge is to the first tee on the public golf course. Next time let's come earlier and play at least nine holes!"

THE COUNTRY CLUB INN, P.O. Box 680C, Rangeley, ME 04970; 207-864-3831. A 25-guestroom (private baths) resort-inn on Rangeley Lake in western Maine, 45 mi. from Farmington. Modified American plan. Open mid-May to mid-Oct. and late Dec. to late Mar. Breakfast and dinner served to travelers by reservation. Near many cultural, historic, and recreational attractions. Swimming pool and lake swimming, horseshoes, volley ball, croquet, and bocci on grounds; 18-hole golf course adjacent. Fishing, canoeing, hiking, tennis nearby. Winter sports—snowmobiling and xc skiing at doorstep. Downhill skiing at Saddleback and Sugarloaf Mts. Bob and Sue Crory, Innkeepers.

Directions: From Maine Tpke., take Auburn Exit 12 and follow Rte. 4 to Rangeley. From Vt. and N.H., take I-91 to St. Johnsbury; east on Rte. 2 to Gorham, and Rte. 16 north to Rangeley. From Bar Harbor, Rte. 1A to Rte. 2 to Rte. 4. From Montreal, Rte. 10 to Rte. 112 to Rte. 147, to Rte. 114; then Rte. 26 to Rte. 16 to Rte. 4.

THE CROCKER HOUSE COUNTRY INN
Hancock Point, Maine (1987)

Finding a beguiling, secluded place for an overnight stay on a trip to Canada via U.S. 1 would delight many a weary traveler. And it could be the perfect solution for those who enjoy the activity and excitement of Bar Harbor, Acadia National Park, and Blue Hill, but also want a quiet hideaway nearby. On Hancock Point, three minutes from the ocean, the Crocker House Country Inn is all of the above.

The entrance leads into a living room that is eclectic, to say the least, with good comfortable old wicker furniture, a big window seat, some rather striking modern primitive paintings, a very handsome rug of Indian design, a backgammon set, and lots of growing plants. At the very moment I walked in I was greeted with a flute concerto by Jean Pierre Rampal wafting from the stereo. It all seemed quite casual and quite natural.

The guest rooms are bright and cheerful. Almost all of them have been redecorated and some have stenciling on the upper walls. They are large enough to accommodate two people very comfortably.

Innkeeper Richard Malaby told me a little bit about the past history of this part of Maine. "A lot of people think that the most northern part of Maine is Ellsworth and Bar Harbor," he remarked. "Hancock was once a thriving shipbuilding community and also the terminus of the Washington, D.C., to Bar Harbor express train. It was the port from which the famed Sullivan Quarry shipped its cobblestones to pave the streets of Boston, New York, and Philadelphia. I'm afraid that the Crocker House is a lone survivor of those days of the past."

He continued, his eyes alight with enthusiasm, "Up here we're rather out of the way, but we have quite a few of our own activities. For instance, the Monteux Symphony Orchestra performs biweekly in Hancock during June and July and the Somesville Acadia Repertory Theater provides professional theater during the summer. Hancock is the site of one of the two reversing tidal falls in North America.

"We have clay tennis courts available for our guests a short stroll away, and the ocean is just a three-minute walk from our front door. Many guests come to enjoy Acadia National Park and then stay on here an extra day to recover from all of that activity."

One might expect the dinner menu to consist of good hearty up-country Maine food; therefore, I was quite surprised to find some international dishes such as poached salmon Florentine, coquilles St. Jacques, and veal Monterey, which I ordered. It is very thinly sliced veal, sautéed in madeira with avocado and tomato and topped with Monterey jack cheese. The menu also has baked stuffed lobster, soft-shell crabs, broiled swordfish, broiled halibut Dijon, and other treasures from the sea.

If you happen to be there on Sunday, the brunch is very spiffy indeed, with brandied french toast, eggs Benedict, steak and eggs, and something interesting called "create your own omelet."

In the morning, after a very pleasant continental breakfast, I walked around this little neck of land, enjoying the birch trees and the grass beside the water. It's great for bicycling and running, and I came upon a little harbor with lots of sailboats and mountains in the distance and lobster traps bobbing in the tide. Would you believe that not a single motorcar passed in either direction during my morning walk?

Taken all-in-all, I found the experience at the Crocker House Country Inn most refreshing. I particularly enjoyed my conversation with innkeeper Malaby, who, because of the relatively small size of the inn, can take the time to meet his guests and to share some of his enthusiasm about this quiet, sequestered corner of the Maine coast.

We are delighted to welcome Crocker House to the pages of *Country Inns and Back Roads* for the first time.

THE CROCKER HOUSE COUNTRY INN, Hancock Point, ME 04640; 207-422-6806. A 10-guestroom (private baths) secluded country inn about 8 mi. north of Ellsworth, Me. Breakfast and dinner served daily. Open from May 1 to Thanksgiving. (Check for possible opening during winter months.) Bicycles and dock moorings available for guests. Tennis, swimming, and walking nearby. Just 30 min. from Mount Desert Island, Acadia National Park, and Bar Harbor. Blue Hill and the east Penobscot peninsula easily accessible. Richard Malaby, Innkeeper.

Directions: Follow Rte. 1 approx. 8 mi. north from Ellsworth. Turn right at sign for Hancock Point and continue approx. 5 mi.

DOCKSIDE GUEST QUARTERS
York, Maine (1975)

"There must be something special that happens here on the Fourth of July; don't I remember that you have a special little celebration?"

Harriette Lusty and I were having a light luncheon on the porch of the dining room at Dockside Guest Quarters. It was a day such as I have experienced here many times in the past, watching the wonderful harbor traffic as all kinds of craft make their way through the harbor to the ocean. Even though it had been a very hot day out on I-95, here on this lovely porch there was a wonderful breeze that made even sitting in the sun a joy.

"Oh, we do some very wonderful things here on the Fourth of July," Harriette exclaimed. "We have a very large flag that is brought out, unfolded, and placed on the lawn, because it is much too large for any flagpole. At noontime we set off our cannon, and the waitresses and all of our chambermaids come over and stand by. It's really quite a ceremony and we leave one of our postcards at each door, inviting all the guests to come up to the shoot. It takes place right over there by the flagpole. We use that little brass one-pounder cannon originally kept in the hallway near the front door. Everybody gets into a wonderful Independence Day mood."

The Dockside Guest Quarters is composed of the original New England homestead of the 1880s, called the Maine House, and other multi-unit cottage buildings of a contemporary design, each with its own porch and water view. Some have a casual studio feeling and some have kitchenettes.

The innkeepers are David and Harriette Lusty. David is a real "State of Maine" man, complete with a wonderful Down East accent. They have raised four sons at Dockside, two of whom may be returning to the family inn after gaining experience in the hospitality field.

Harriette continued, "The days in early June can be spent in many different ways. We have a number of sandy beaches, and swimming is at its best when the sun is highest at midday and in early afternoon. It's also great fun to wander around the stretches of beach and have them almost entirely to one's self. Golf and tennis are available at the golf club, and the marina has rental sailboats and outboards. We're doing something very interesting during the month of June; we have arranged a special bargain package that includes a sightseeing cruise with a luncheon stop at Portsmouth Harbor. We are arranging several other similar expeditions for our guests. It also includes a lobster dinner and very attractive pre-season rates."

There's always a great deal of history to share in the York area, and this time I learned about the famous statue that is the figure of a Confederate soldier, instead of a "Boy in Blue." David tells me that they have now

located the town somewhere in South Carolina where the statue of the Union soldier has been resting for almost a hundred years. Everybody has decided that they're going to leave the statues the way they are. "After all," said David, "that war has long been over."

So the combination of Dockside life, generous dollops of history, the pleasant vista from Dockside of the harbor craft, and the opportunity to enjoy a good dinner at the Dockside dining room, managed by Steve and Sue Roeder, makes staying at this little seaside inn an enjoyable experience in any season of the year—perhaps just a tad more satisfying in June.

DOCKSIDE GUEST QUARTERS, P.O. Box 205, Harris Island Rd., York, ME 03909; 207-363-2868. An 18-guestroom (some studio suites with kitchenettes) waterside country inn 10 mi. from Portsmouth, N.H. American plan available. Continental breakfast served to houseguests only. Dockside Dining Room serves lunch and dinner to travelers daily except Mon. Open from Memorial Day weekend in May thru Columbus Day (in Oct.). York Village is a National Historic District. Lawn games, shuffleboard, badminton, fishing, sailing, and boating from premises. Golf, tennis, and ocean swimming nearby; safe and picturesque paths and roadways for walks, bicycling, and jogging. Credit cards are not welcome for amounts over fifty dollars. Personal checks accepted for payment of food and lodgings incurred by registered guests. David and Harriette Lusty, Innkeepers.

Directions: From I-95, take the last exit before the northbound toll gate at York to U.S. 1, then to Rte. 1A. Follow 1A thru center of Old York Village, take Rte. 103 (a side street off Rte. 1A leading to the harbor), and watch for signs to the inn immediately after crossing bridge.

GOOSE COVE LODGE
Deer Isle, Maine (1981)

Innkeeper Elli Pavloff's letter, dated August 31, read in part: "Last Friday night we were sitting up in our apartment above the main lodge listening to a group of guests, one of them with a guitar, singing songs. (The Beatles and Simon and Garfunkel seemed to have displaced 'Now is the Hour' and 'It's a Long Way to Tipperary.') It was after the lobster cookout on the beach.

"I thought: 'There is no other place and no other moment I'd rather be living in!' This is the reward for innkeeping, seeing people happy, relaxed, at peace, at one with the world.

"The Goose Cove environment does it really. We just work along with it—the ocean, the nature trails, the fresh air, the social hour, the family-style meals, the camaraderie and friendships that spring up among the guests—peace flows in and we can actually see people, renewed, recreated in the space of a week. It's wonderful to be a part of the process."

Goose Cove Lodge is a resort-inn on Deer Isle. It is on the modified American plan, and all guests take breakfast and dinner in the dining room, which has an expansive view of Goose Cove. There is a one-week-minimum-stay policy during July and August. Typically, guests arrive about 5:30 on Saturday, which is the beginning of the Goose Cove week. They are shown to their cottage or room and told that hors d'oeuvres have just been set out in the Lodge and that the dinner bell will ring at 6:30. A little later, George and Elli Pavloff greet them and introduce them to other guests. Then it's time for the Saturday evening buffet, and already first-timers are beginning to realize that many of the other guests have been coming to Goose Cove for quite a few years.

At breakfast the first morning, everybody is given an orientation to Deer Isle and apprised of the many choices available for various activities. By that evening they're all eager to share the day's experiences. Perhaps they've gone on a boat ride to the outer islands, taken a drive to Bar Harbor, spent the day walking the nature trails, visited the crafts and antique stores, or had a deep muscle massage or a sailing lesson or expedition.

On Friday night, the lobster cookout on the beach is like the last night of summer camp. Physical and mental tensions are erased, faces are relaxed, and fellowship is high. Guests are exchanging addresses at breakfast the next morning, and George and Elli and their staff are all saying goodbye. The result is obvious and in marked contrast to those guests who are trying to 'do' New England in a week by touching down briefly in a different place each night.

Lest I forget, most of the accommodations are in cottages with native stone fireplaces. Aromatic wood has been used for walls, beams, shelves, bookcases, and the like. Most have a peaked roofs and exposed overhead beams, and all of the cottages sit on the great granite rocks adjacent to Goose Bay, and all have wonderful views. Each of the rustic lodges has its own bathroom facilities and in some there is an extra bedroom.

George had a P.S. on Elli's letter: "Another delight of this season is the willingness of our guests to share their talent with one another, these include slide shows, music making, and informal lectures."

GOOSE COVE LODGE, Sunset, Deer Isle, ME 04683; 207-348-2508. A 22-guestroom (60 people) resort-inn on beautiful Penobscot Bay approx. 1 hr. from Rte. 1 at Bucksport. Open mid-May to mid-Oct. Modified American plan mid-June to mid-Sept.; 7-day minimum stay (Sat.-Sat.) in July and Aug.; 2-day minimum stay other times. Meals served to houseguests only. Swimming, boating, canoeing, hiking, and bird watching all available at the inn. Other outdoor sports, including backroading, golf, tennis, etc., nearby. Especially adaptable for children of all ages. Elli and George Pavloff, Innkeepers.

Directions: From Bucksport, drive 4 mi. north on Rte. 1 and turn right on Rte. 15 down the Blue Hill Peninsula to Deer Isle Village. Turn right in village at sign to Sunset, Maine. Proceed 3 mi., turn right at Goose Cove Lodge sign. Follow dirt road 1½ mi. to inn.

GREY ROCK INN
Northeast Harbor, Maine (1976)

Janet Millet and I were seated in a new, trim sitting room that had been created on the second floor of the Grey Rock Inn since my last visit. Bathed in the afternoon sunshine, it's a perfect place for a quiet cup of tea, and that's exactly what we were having.

"I call it a little upstairs sitting room," she said. "I put on the last of the wallpaper in June, and as you see I've decorated it with other things of which I am very fond. I put some wicker furniture in here, including a Victorian bird cage with some colorful peacocks, and there is some geranium ivy. It's supposed to have pink blossoms, but they haven't come out just yet. That Japanese screen is one of my favorites and it's decorated with jade and mother-of-pearl."

Janet is British and she has an innate admiration for things British. For example, she loves, as do most Britons, "a lovely fireplace." Fortunately, Grey Rock is on the coast of upper Maine and there is plenty of firewood right from her own little forest to supply the two living-room/parlor fireplaces with ample wood.

I usually tease her about being British and this time I asked, "What are some British touches that you use here at Grey Rock?"

"Well, we serve a very good strong cup of tea. English breakfast tea," she replied rather firmly. "Another English touch is the unusual reception and drawing room, also used as our breakfast room. We have a very large selection of books and British magazines."

"Is there anything that you particularly liked and remembered from growing up in England that you have introduced in the bedrooms?" I asked.

"Yes, my lovely down-feather pillows. We used to have down-feather mattresses when I was a girl, but I've got the very best down-feather pillows here for Grey Rock. We have all kinds of other English touches too, with lots of flowers and bright and gay fabrics in all of the guest rooms."

I must admit that Grey Rock has a very authentic English country house feeling—the same feeling I enjoy so much when visiting in England. Some of the guest rooms on the second floor have very good views of the corner of the harbor.

One of the focal points is a porch off the reception area that gives one the sensation of sitting in the treetops. There are evergreen trees all around it and big hanging tuberous begonias. It's a very pleasant place for breakfast in the morning.

"Elegant" is an excellent word to describe Grey Rock, and almost immediately new arrivals are struck by Janet's unusual collection of wicker pieces, which are rare art forms. For example, there is a tea table on wheels, a chaise lounge, three or four wicker table lamps, a wicker floor lamp, wicker love seats, a wicker desk, a wicker plant stand for two plants, and wing chairs in wicker. These are all in the main sitting room and another smaller adjacent parlor.

These wicker pieces blend beautifully with the unusual collection of oriental memorabilia that Janet has gathered over the years, making the inn somewhat reminiscent of a New England house of a century ago, when sea captains brought back the wonderful treasure of the Orient on

their clipper ships. Particularly impressive are the collection of fans and the exquisite framed oriental paintings on silk. As part of the harmonious whole, fresh flowers complete the picture.

Grey Rock literally sits on a rocky ledge above the town of Northeast Harbor, well within its own forested area, where trails lead into the woods. There is no amusement or recreation on the grounds for smaller children. The entire kaleidoscope of the wonderful natural attractions of Mount Desert Island is literally at the front door.

GREY ROCK INN, Harborside Rd., Northeast Harbor, ME 04662; 207-276-9360. A 12-guestroom village inn adjacent to Acadia National Park and all of the attractions of this unusual region. European plan. Continental breakfast served to houseguests only. No other meals served. Small cottage available for minimum 4-night stay. Season from early spring to Nov. 1. Children 14 yrs. and older preferred. No pets. No credit cards. No smoking in guest rooms. Janet Millet, Innkeeper.

Directions: Located on the right side of Rte. 198 approaching the town of Northeast Harbor. Note sign for inn. Do not try to make a right turn at this point, but proceed about one block, turn around and approach the inn on the left, up the steep hill.

HOMEWOOD INN
Yarmouth, Maine (1973)

"Tell me about the kind of guests who come to Homewood," I said to Fred Webster as we were strolling about the grounds.

"Well, I think that we appeal to a great many people of all ages and preferences," he said. "For instance, we have one guest who comes for three weeks in late June each year and tells us to put through no phone calls and not to bother him and his wife for clambake reservations or anything else. It happens that he's about to leave now and we haven't seen him once! Of course, there are others who like to chat with the staff and the family and who mix well around the pool and the tennis courts with the other guests. One of the things that attracts almost every guest is the L. L. Bean store."

The L. L. Bean store in nearby Freeport is just one of the many reasons to remain several nights at the Homewood Inn. The inn has been operated for a number of years by the Webster family and has a view of some of the 365 Calendar Islands. Many of the single and double cottages that make up most of the inn complex have fireplaces and kitchen facilities and are set among the juniper, cedar, maple, and Norway pine trees. There is a multitude of flowers, including roses, phlox, snapdragons, marigolds, petunias, and dozens of other flowering plants and shrubs.

Guests are frequently delighted to discover that they are sharing their waterside environment with many varieties of land and shore birds. Colleen Webster told me that a few years ago she looked out of her window and saw a moose walking on the property. "It seemed to me to be as big as a house," she declared. "Eventually it strolled down the road, passed some of our cottages, and entered the water and swam off into the distance. We do have seals on our offshore rocks, but this is the first time I've ever seen a moose. As a matter of fact, I hope it's the last time!"

Homewood Inn has been on this particular spot on Casco Bay for many, many years. It was originally started by Fred Webster's mother and father and is being continued by Fred and his wife, Colleen.

The Inn Shop has been operated by Fred's mother, Doris Gillette, and her husband, Ted. They scout around the crafts shops in Maine seeking out unusual gifts. Incidentally, they are still very active people at 86 and 87 years of age.

In the summer, I've always enjoyed being at Homewood on a Wednesday night so that I can have fun at the regular Wednesday night clambake—a real Down East feast, with lobster, steak, clams, and chicken served outdoors at rustic tables. No other evening meals are offered.

Meanwhile, Fred and I walked over the path he had cut in the field by the woods, through the new pine-tree farm, and we were accompanied by Bonnie, a full-bred collie. She flushed out a pileated woodpecker and a cedar waxwing as we strolled along.

The Homewood is certainly well named; it's very homelike and looks happily settled among the woods, fields, and harbor. Its informal atmosphere invites vacationers, especially those with children, to enjoy a real country resort-inn experience. Sooner or later everyone meets at the lodge, around the pool, or at the tennis courts.

HOMEWOOD INN, Drinkwater Point, P.O. Box 196B, Yarmouth, ME 04096; 207-846-3351. A 42-guestroom (including suites and cottages with fully equipped kitchens) waterside inn on Casco Bay, 20 min. north of Portland. Breakfast served to houseguests and travelers. A steak and lobster cookout is held each Wed. night during summer (advance reservation). Open June 12 through Oct. 14. Bicycles (including tandems), pool, tennis, croquet court, hiking, salt-water swimming on grounds. Golf, riding, fishing, boating, state parks, theater nearby. Fred and Colleen Webster and Ted and Doris Gillette, Innkeepers.

Directions: From the south, take Exit 9 from Maine Tpke. (I-95) to Rte. 1-N, or Yarmouth exit from I-295 to Rte. 1-N and follow signs to inn. From north (Brunswick area) take I-95 to Yarmouth exit. Then take Rte. 88 and follow signs to inn.

A number of inns have nearby airports where private airplanes may land. An airplane symbol at the end of the inn directions indicates that there is an airport nearby. Consult inn for further information.

OLD FORT INN
Kennebunkport, Maine (1976)

"Beaches are fun and I enjoy salt water, but to me there's something very special about having the privacy and quietness of a swimming pool."

A group of us were seated around the pool at the Old Fort Inn when this particular observation was made by a Canadian guest. Someone else had said, "I like to play tennis and I like to know that not only is there a good tennis court here, but there are frequently people who play a good game."

The Old Fort Inn is a very special kind of country inn that provides a complete change of pace from the hustle and bustle of Kennebunkport. A few years ago, the main building of the hotel that originally had been on the property was torn down, and the handsome stone carriage house was converted into twelve large bedrooms with electric heat, fully equipped kitchen facilities, Laura Ashley wallpapers, and daily maid service. The rooms are large enough so that guests can stay for longer periods without feeling cramped.

Guests gather at the main lodge in a converted barn, built around 1880. It has a big fireplace that serves as a focal point on spring and fall evenings, and its open deck next to the swimming pool makes it a very comfortable place where guests may gather in the warmer weather.

The innkeepers are David and Sheila Aldrich, two very attractive people from California, who came here a few years ago and have made the Old Fort Inn and Kennebunkport their new home. They are considerably assisted by their perky daughter, Shana, who must be at least ten years old by this time.

I think it might be fun if I shared a description of my bedroom at the Old Fort Inn. For one thing, it's large enough to be comfortable for two people, with plenty of room for a third person on the little sofa bed. There is a big double cannonball bed with blue sheets and a harmonizing blue comforter, blue carpeting, and a blue cover on the daybed. There are good reading lights on both sides of the bed. A fully equipped kitchenette, including a stove with an oven and separated from the rest of the room by a divider, gives guests the option of preparing their own meals. A wood table and chairs for two, a Victorian table with an attractive lamp, a wicker armchair, and a beautifully refinished chest of drawers complete the picture. A painting of a duck is part of the great collection of duck decoys and paintings found throughout the inn.

A large over-sized closet contains extra pillows (something I commend at all times). By the way, David and Sheila have provided such thoughtful things as a laundry with a dryer in the same building.

I think I can safely say that Kennebunkport, Maine, is one of the few fast-disappearing places in the world that lives up to its advance billing.

The village still retains much of the ambience it had when clipper ships sailed from its shores. The lovely old sea captains' houses remain, and the beautiful streets and winding river make it a very pleasant vacation experience.

During my most recent visit I found that guests spend quite a bit of time in the antique shop that's mainly Sheila's project. "David and I feel that it has added considerably to the attractiveness of the inn," she said.

Spring is an excellent time to visit this part of the Maine coast, and between mid-April and mid-June, and November and mid-December, David and Sheila have arranged for a very special midweek "Escape Plan" that I'm sure many of our readers would find most attractive.

OLD FORT INN, Old Fort Ave., P.O. Box M, Kennebunkport, ME 04046; 207-967-5353. A 14-guestroom resort-inn within walking distance of the ocean in a historic Maine town. Includes an ample continental breakfast, and a full kitchen is provided with each apartment. Daily maid service. Fireplace lodge. Open from mid-Apr. to mid-Dec. Heated pool, tennis court, shuffleboard and bicycles on grounds. Golf, saltwater swimming, and boating nearby. Not comfortable for children under 12. No pets. Sheila and David Aldrich, Innkeepers.

Directions: Take Exit 3 (Kennebunk) from the Maine Turnpike. Take left on Rte. 35 and follow signs through Kennebunk to Kennebunkport. Take left at traffic light at Sunoco station. Go over drawbridge and take first right on Ocean Ave. Take Ocean Ave. to the Colony Hotel; turn left in front of the Colony, go to the Y in the road, go right ¼ mi. Inn is on left.

THE PILGRIM'S INN
Deer Isle, Maine (1980)

Travelers really have to be looking for Deer Isle and the Pilgrim's Inn. It's a good hour's drive from U.S. 1, east of Bucksport, to the Blue Hill Peninsula. Deer Isle sits just off the southern flank of the mainland and no matter how you arrive it's necessary to cross over the suspension bridge at Eggemoggin Reach.

This is really "down home" Maine and even the 1939 bridge has failed to disturb the naturalness of both the islanders and the area.

A four-story, gambrel-roofed gray house, this building has overlooked the long harbor on the front and the millpond in the rear since 1793. Jean and Dud Hendrick moved here a few years ago after acquiring the Pilgrim's Inn. Much of the original building has remained almost

completely unchanged, with the original Colonial feature of two large rooms and a kitchen on the ground floor still intact. One of these rooms is the Common Room of the present-day inn.

Most of the guest rooms are quite large with richly hued pine floorboards, wood stoves, country furniture, and a selection of books and magazines. They are enhanced by coordinated Laura Ashley fabrics, used for curtains, lampshades, quilts, and cushions.

Although I visited there last summer as part of a hilarious dinner party with some friends from nearby Blue Hill, where everybody vowed that it was "the best time ever," I'd like to share a portion of a yearly letter that Dud and Jean write me.

"We have now purchased and redecorated an enchanting house in the village, which we call 'Number 15.' 'Enchanting' understates it. Number 15 sits over the harbor, affording the occupants unparalleled sunset views from its back deck. It is completely furnished and equipped so that guests may choose to prepare their own meals if they are so foolish as to pass up Jean's fabulous cuisine. It is the quintessential honeymoon cottage or retreat for four friends (it has a hide-a-bed in front of the fireplace in the living room in addition to the upstairs bedroom)."

The letter went on to say that one of the first-floor parlors of the main inn has now been made into a warm reading room and library. "We discovered that guests really don't have a room in which they can quietly read, free of socializing fellow travelers. Now they do."

The Pilgrim's Inn provides far more than can really be done in a single or two-night stay. Guests can bike, hike, sail, canoe, and even learn to kayak in whitewater or the sea with a certified instructor. Guests also play tennis and golf, and do many of the less-energetic things. The mail boat run to Isle au Haute is a most romantic day trip, and the sailing here is terrific. There are many, many art galleries and crafts shops a short distance away, and Acadia National Park is just close enough for a day trip.

Pilgrim's Inn, as I said before, is a special place, so tell only your very special friends about it.

THE PILGRIM'S INN (originally The Ark), Deer Isle, ME 04627; 207-348-6615. A 13-guestroom (some shared baths) inn in a remote island village on the Blue Hill Peninsula on the Maine coast. Modified American plan, May 15 to Nov. 1, includes a hearty breakfast and a creative dinner. In season, outside dinner reservations are accepted. A 4-day minimum reservation is requested in Aug. Bicycles, badminton, ping-pong, regulation horseshoes, croquet, and a rowboat for the millpond on the grounds. All types of cultural and recreational advantages, including golf, fishing, sailing, hiking, and browsing nearby. No pets. Dud and Jean Hendrick, Innkeepers.

Directions: From Boston, take I-95 to Brunswick exit. Take coastal Rte. 1 north past Bucksport. Turn right on Rte. 15, which travels to Deer Isle down the Blue Hill Peninsula. At the village, turn right on Main St. (Sunset Rd.) and proceed one block to the inn on the left side of the street, opposite the harbor.

"European Plan" means that rates for rooms and meals are separate. "American Plan" means that meals are included in the cost of the room. "Modified American Plan" means that breakfast and dinner are included in the cost of the room. The rates at some inns include a continental breakfast with the lodging.

THE SQUIRE TARBOX INN
Westport Island, Maine (1974)

Karen Mitman and I were walking through the woods behind the Squire Tarbox Inn toward Squam Creek. We were two people being escorted by seven lively, handsome Nubian goats in various shades of brown and beige. It being June, we passed through patches of buttercups and lupine, and our group occasionally paused while one of the goats decided to nibble.

"Come on, Garbo," Karen called. "We call her Garbo because she thinks she's kind of dramatic. Another one is Garbanzo Bean because she has a humorous side to her. Opal is our Southern belle from Luray, Virginia." We arrived at the serene saltwater marsh that has a little dock and a screened-in shed for just sitting and looking through the binoculars provided.

"Most of our guests are from the big city, and it's just nice for them to come here and sit. It is quiet, and the combination of the water and the sky and the clouds and the little marshy island and the trees is so pleasing to them."

The Squire Tarbox is a very quiet inn in a section of Maine that is sufficiently off the beaten track to be unspoiled and natural. The main house has both the wainscoting of the early 1800s and the rustic wide-board construction of the 1700s. It is quite small—nine guest rooms have a cozy "up country" feeling with Colonial prints and colors and some working fireplaces. A large hearth with the original bake oven, pumpkin pine floors, and hand-hewn beams set the tone for this rambling Colonial farmhouse with its hip roof and pale yellow narrow clapboards and apple green shutters.

There are several choices for sitting around in front of fireplaces to enjoy reading or conversation, especially in a captivating barn with large doors that open out on a screened-in sundeck. There is a player piano, an antique music box, Colonial wooden toys, and English wooden puzzles for further amusement.

Karen and her husband, Bill, are very friendly, conversational people, who make innkeeping seem almost deceptively simple. Their background at the Copley Plaza in Boston must have much to do with this.

Karen and I sat in the little shed and continued our conversation while the goats cavorted on the pine needles. "I know you remember when we brought in our first goats," she said. "We were a little hesitant, but they have been a most rewarding experience for our guests. Now we have a new cheese-processing room and have packaged some goat cheese for sale to our guests. The cheese is served every night before dinner as well."

Our conversation turned naturally to food and she mentioned that the Squire Tarbox is on the modified American plan, which includes breakfast and dinner. "Dinner is served at seven o'clock and usually begins with a soup that could be made with fruit or vegetables. The second course is a salad, and the main course is fish or chicken and is always served with three vegetables that reflect some creative thinking, such as minted glazed carrots, cranberries with red cabbage, or broccoli with lemon butter. One of the most popular desserts is a chocolate concoction known as the Squire's 'Sin Pie.' "

Karen had to return to the inn and suggested that I might find it interesting just to sit here and enjoy the sounds of silence. So she took all of the goats and set back up the hill. I mused that this simple little path through the woods down to the saltwater marsh provides guests with the unique opportunity to have the feeling of really being in the country. I had known the Squire Tarbox through three sets of owners during the past eighteen years, but felt that Karen and Bill have put enthusiasm and know-how together in generous portions to bring Squire Tarbox to the height of its career.

THE SQUIRE TARBOX INN, Westport Island, R.D. 2, Box 620, Wiscasset, ME 04578; 207-882-7693. A 9-guestroom (5 private baths) restored Colonial home midway between Boston and Bar Harbor on Rte. 144 in Westport, 10 mi. from Wiscasset. Modified American plan—includes continental breakfast and full leisurely dinner. Also serving dinner to travelers. Open late May to late Oct. Within a 30-min. drive of beaches, harbor shops, and museums of midcoast Maine. No amusements for children under 14. Bill and Karen Mitman, Innkeepers.

Directions: From Maine Tpke., take Exit 9 and follow Rte. 95 to Exit 22. Take Rte. 1 to Rte. 144, 7 mi. north of Bath. Follow Rte. 144 to Wiscasset–Westport Bridge. The inn is located 6 mi. south of bridge on Westport Island.

THE WATERFORD INNE
East Waterford, Maine (1980)

Three of us were seated on the screened-in porch, which has a lovely view of the meadows and had actually only been completed the day before, so both Rosalie and Barbara Vanderzanden, innkeepers at the Waterford Inne, were feeling very proud and happy.

"This is something that we've been wanting to do for years," said Barbara. "It seems that we have about one major project every year; one year it was the new kitchen and, of course, this year it's the porch. It also provides us with additional dining space on warm evenings."

My eye happened to travel to what was one of the most sumptuous-looking vegetable gardens I have ever seen, and it prompted a question: "What are some of the things that you grow in your own garden for your kitchen?"

"Well, we grow practically all our own herbs," explained Rosalie, who is Barbara's mother and the cook. "We like fresh herbs in the salad dressing. We also have tomatoes, brussels sprouts, broccoli, peppers, squash, and pumpkins. I'm surprised at how fussy pumpkins are to grow."

"What about some of your other main dishes?" I asked. "You have one main dish every night, don't you?"

"Well, we like baked ham with peach glaze, breast of chicken with heavy cream, various kinds of roasts, and beef Stroganoff. We serve a fixed-price dinner every evening for both houseguests and visitors. We do all our own baking, and our guests seem to enjoy it very much."

At the Waterford Inne, located in the little-known Oxford Hills area of western Maine, "small and tidy" is beautiful. It can be truthfully said that the Waterford Inne is an intimate inn. The inn is small enough to provide a really cozy country inn experience. The original house was built in 1825 and has five upstairs bedrooms that step out of the 19th century. These are augmented by four additional rooms created in a wing leading to a very large barn.

All of the bedrooms have been carefully decorated, usually with some theme in mind. For example, the Chesapeake Room has a fireplace stove and a private porch. The decorations are in the Eastern Shore theme, with duck decoys and water fowl. Even the sheets and towels have colorful water fowls on them. All of the rooms have either antiques or attractive country furniture. My bed was a four-poster with a lace canopy.

Guests gather in the main living room, where there are many different books and magazines, including several from England, because Barbara and Rosalie are Anglophiles and in fact followed *Country Inns and Back Roads, Britain and Ireland* in a trip they made to England.

Well, our chat was over, and as Rosalie went to the kitchen, Barbara

and I strolled around to take a closer look at the big barn. "The Oxford Hills section of Maine abounds in much beautiful scenery," she remarked. "It's hard to drive more than four or five miles without coming to a lake. It's quite a popular area for summer camps, so we are rather well booked in advance for the camp visitation weekends. Many camp parents stay at the inn and then stay on extra days, because it's such a lovely, tranquil experience."

THE WATERFORD INNE, Box 49, East Waterford, ME 04233; 207-583-4037. A 9-guestroom farmhouse-inn in the Oxford Hills section of southwest Maine, 8 mi. from Norway and South Paris. Closed March and April. Breakfast and dinner served to travelers by reservation. European plan. Within a short distance of many recreational, scenic, and cultural attractions in Maine and the White Mountains of New Hampshire. Cross-country skiing and badminton on grounds. Lake swimming, golf, rock hunting, downhill skiing, hiking, canoeing nearby. Alcoholic beverages not served. Well-behaved pets welcome; however, advance notification is required and a fee is charged. No credit cards. Rosalie and Barbara Vanderzanden, Innkeepers.

Directions: From Maine Tpke.: use Exit 11, follow Rte. 26 north approx. 28 mi. into Norway, then on Rte. 118 west for 8 mi. to Rte. 37 south (left turn). Go ½ mi., turn right at Springer's General Store, up the hill ½ mi. From Conway, New Hampshire: Rte. 16 to Rte. 302 east to Fryeburg, Me. Take Rte. 5 out of Fryeburg to Rte. 35 south, thence to Rte. 118, which is a left fork (with Rte. 35 going right). Continue on Rte. 118 east, past Papoose Pond camping area, then watch for right turn onto Rte. 37. Go ½ mi. to Springer's General Store. Take immediate right turn, ½ mi. up hill.

WHITEHALL INN
Camden, Maine (1973)

If ever an inn and a setting were made for each other, the Whitehall Inn and Camden are perfectly matched. The neoclassic buildings of the inn are connected by a large porch filled with plenty of comfortable wicker furniture. The inn sits back from the main street among huge elm and pine trees, and there are many window boxes and arrangements of summer flowers.

Ed and Jean Dewing left Boston with their family and came to Camden in the early 1970s to become innkeepers. Now there are several members of the family who keep this highly reputable village inn thriving.

On the first floor there are several parlors and a large lobby, all of which are furnished with Maine antiques. The lounge has sewing machines ingeniously converted into tables, chess sets that invite competition, and a large collection of unusual shells displayed under glass. Guest rooms are country style.

Ed Dewing says that most of the guests still are interested in the Edna St. Vincent Millay Room, designed as a tribute to her, with many volumes of her poems, along with memorabilia that would be of interest to her numerous admirers. It was here at the Whitehall Inn on a warm August evening in 1912 that young Edna first recited her poem "Renascence."

The inn is just a short, tree-lined walk from the center of the village. An excellent folder provided by the inn has dozens of suggestions about activities in and around this part of Maine, including golf, sightseeing, art exhibitions, boating, swimming, hiking, and fishing.

I believe that a major part of everyone's country inn experience is the food. In reference to the Whitehall Inn, here's a letter I have from a gentleman from Vermont: "Because I have been connected with the food industry most of my life, I instinctively notice the small considerations that lift an establishment head and shoulders above the rest. During the past few years, we have enjoyed quite a few meals at the inn, and this year we were guests for a delightful week. The food is certainly exceptional."

Ed recently sent me a copy of a letter written to him by an eight-year-old boy who had been a guest at the inn. "Thank you very much for the hospitality you showed our family on our visit to Camden. Thank you, too, for the lobster buoy. It is hanging in my room. It will be a nice remembrance of our trip to New England. I will always remember putting that old wooden puzzle together."

Well, even if the young man's mother gave him a little assistance with words like "remembrance," I'm sure we will agree that he caught the Whitehall spirit.

Many guests comment on the fact that seven members of a family can work together in such harmony. This means there is always a Dewing on the scene at the Whitehall.

As Ed says, "After sixteen years filled with ups and downs, Jean and I are still glad we chose this way of life and already look forward to our seventeenth season in 1987. We promise the same beautiful sunrises and sunsets, crisp, clean air, brilliant fall foliage, friendly neighbors, a bountiful table, and lots of people who look out for everybody's comfort and well being."

WHITEHALL INN, Camden, ME 04843; 207-236-3391. A 38-guestroom village inn in a Maine seacoast town, 75 mi. from Portland. Modified American plan omits lunch. Bed and breakfast offered in Maine House and Wicker House. Breakfast and dinner served daily to travelers. Open May 25 to Oct. 15. Tennis, bicycles, shuffleboard, arrangemens for harbor cruises on grounds. Golf, hiking, swimming, fishing, day sailing nearby. No pets. The Dewing Family, Innkeepers.

Directions: From Maine Tpke. take Exit 9 to coastal Rte. 95. Proceed on Rte. 95 to Rte. 1 at Brunswick. Follow Rte. 1 to Rte. 90 at Warren, to Rte. 1 in Camden. Inn is located on Rte. 1, 1/2 mi. north of Camden.

"European plan" means that rates for rooms and meals are separate. "American plan" means that meals are included in the cost of the room. "Modified American plan" means that breakfast and dinner are included in the cost of the room. The rates at some inns include a continental breakfast with the lodging.

HARTWELL HOUSE
Ogunquit, Maine (1981)

My first glimpse of the Hartwell House on Shore Road, leading back to the center of Ogunquit, was most favorable. It was a two-story, pleasantly designed building with a facade of many Moorish arches. There were some gardens in the front and what appeared to be some considerable grassy acreage in the rear.

The unusually large and attractively decorated front porch area had beautiful summer furniture with lighthearted slipcovers. There were several groups of comfortable chairs and sofas, stacks of books and magazines, and many varieties of flowers. Four houseguests were playing bridge. It had the kind of atmosphere that invited me to sit down and feel at home.

There are nine guest rooms at Hartwell House, including two efficiency apartments and two studios with full-sized kitchens. A complimentary breakfast is served either on the patio or in the elegant dining room.

HARTWELL HOUSE, 116 Shore Rd., Ogunquit, ME 03907; 207-646-7210. A 9-guestroom (private baths) inn providing a very compatible atmosphere for a limited number of guests (4 rooms may be rented as a complete apartment). Rates include breakfast. Open year-round. The Whistling Oyster, the ocean, Perkins Cove, the Marginal Way, Ogunquit Playhouse, and churches all within walking distance. Fishing, golf, swimming, bicycles, sailing nearby. Tennis, swimming pool, and golf privileges available at Cliff Country Club. Not suitable for children under 14. No pets. Trisha and Jim Hartwell, Innkeepers.

Directions: Follow I-95 north through New Hampshire into Maine; take last exit before Maine toll booth; north on Rte. 1, 7 mi. to center of Ogunquit. Turn right on Shore Rd. approx. 3/4 mi. Hartwell House on right.

THE WHISTLING OYSTER RESTAURANT
Ogunquit, Maine (1969)

A balance of traditional New England fare and Continental-American cuisine best describes the luncheon and dinner menus at this most picturesque restaurant on Perkins Cove. Innkeeper John Parella is particularly proud of the fine fresh fish, meats, and other ingredients and the presentation and preparation that vary frequently. The menu especially features foods that are in season.

All of the baking is done on the premises, and the Whistling Oyster chefs make their own ice creams, often with fresh fruits.

While feasting on such offerings as fresh baked haddock amandine, tenderloin of beef with forest mushrooms, casserole of fresh Maine crabmeat, and roast duckling with fruit sauce, guests may enjoy the especially appealing view of the waterside ambience and the ebb and flow of the fishing village water traffic.

After a pleasant meal, guests often visit the gift shop, filled with elegant and often exclusive items such as imported china and crystal, gold and sterling jewelry, and two gourmet food lines. A popular item has been gift certificates for the gift shop or restaurant.

THE WHISTLING OYSTER RESTAURANT, Perkins Cove, Ogunquit, ME 03907; 207-646-9521. A waterfront restaurant and gift shop in Perkins Cove at Ogunquit. Lunch and dinner served daily. Open throughout the year. Reservations advisable. No lodgings, but nearby CIBR overnight lodgings can be found at the Hartwell House, Ogunquit (207-646-7210). John Parella, Innkeeper.

Directions: From the south, take the York exit from I-95. Turn north on Rte. 1 to Bourne Lane. Turn right on Shore Rd. for about 1 mi. to Perkins Cove turnoff.

THE BIRCHWOOD INN
Temple, New Hampshire (1986)

"We as a young nation of Americans are really just developing a true nostalgia of our own. Just since the Bicentennial has this craving grown tremendously, and an old country inn allows guests to turn back the clock and immerse themselves almost totally in an atmosphere of the roadside travel of the 18th and 19th centuries in America."

Judy and Bill Wolfe and I were enjoying a quiet moment in the back parlor of the Birchwood Inn, and I could see by the light in his eye that Bill was most enthusiastic about being an innkeeper.

The Birchwood Inn, sitting on one corner of the village green, is listed on the National Register of Historic Places and is believed to have been in operation since 1775. The present Federal-style brick building, along with the adjacent barn, was probably built about 1800, and the records document a history of changing uses that mirror the evolution of the small-town tavern in New England.

The small village of Temple has no telegraph wires in the center of the town, and it's pretty much the same as it's been for two hundred years, with the Grange Hall, Congregational Church, village store, Revolutionary cemetery, and old blacksmith shop.

In 1965, probably the most interesting and prized feature of the inn was discovered when some early wall murals were uncovered under layers of old wallpaper. The paintings proved to be the work of the well-known muralist Rufus Porter, painted between 1825 and 1833. Fortunately, they were restored and are now being carefully preserved by Bill and Judy.

Today, the inn is characterized by comfortable furniture, a Steinway square grand piano, wide floorboards, checked tablecloths of yellow, red, brown, and blue, music in the background, and many tiny little areas where guests can enjoy a tête-à-tête. On the other hand, there is much opportunity for sociability. Judy said, "We have developed countless friendships with lovely people from all over the world without ever leaving the comforts of our little inn. The opportunity to reach out to people of all interests is a rare privilege afforded to both innkeepers and their children alike." The Wolfes find that their three children enjoy being involved with inn activities.

There are eight most original guest rooms sharing three bathrooms. Each of them has its own theme. For example, the Seashore Room has a lobster trap and shore pictures; the Music Room is decorated with old instruments, including a violin lampstand; the Train Room reflects the fact that Bill is a train buff; and the Editorial Room has a collection of framed original front pages of newspapers with headlines about the moon walk and "Nixon Quits."

The kitchen is handled in an interesting way because Bill does the cooking. Judy bakes breads and desserts, including blueberry-lemon bread, blueberry cobbler, chocolate cake, and various pies and tortes. The evening menu is on a slate blackboard, and on the night of my visit included broiled lamb chops and scallops kabob.

Bill remarked, "Serving meals as innkeepers is like hosting a dinner party each evening, except it's a lot easier since you don't have to sit down with the guests. By the time they're finished, you're nearly finished as well."

Temple is sort of tucked out of the way on a paved back road, and I don't think I would have ever found it on my own, but thanks to one of my readers, I'm glad I did.

THE BIRCHWOOD INN, Rte. 45, Temple, NH 03084; 603-878-3285. A 8-guestroom (3 baths) village inn in southern New Hampshire. Open year-round. Dinner not served on Sun. or Mon. Hiking, xc skiing, hayrides, summer theater, ice skating, superb backroading, and numerous historic houses nearby; also the Cathedral in the Pines. No credit cards. Judy and Bill Wolfe, Innkeepers.

Directions: Take Rte. 3 north to Nashua. At Exit 7W follow Rte. 101 west through Milford to Rte. 45. Turn left 1 1/2 mi. to Temple. From I-91 at Brattleboro take Rte. 9 east to Keene to Rte. 101 through Peterborough, over Temple Mtn. to Rte. 45. Turn right, 1 1/2 mi. to Temple.

COLBY HILL INN
Henniker, New Hampshire (1974)

Following Don Glover's suggestion, I turned off Route 202 just outside Hillsborough, following the sign that says "West Henniker." One of the interesting things about this road is that at one point there are two bridges across the river almost side by side. They are both two-way bridges and I couldn't for the life of me figure out why anyone would want two bridges across the same river at the same point. Later, while standing in front of the long window in the dining room, overlooking the barns shown in Jan Lindstrom's sketch, Don laughed and said that the early inhabitants of New Hampshire certainly had some most interesting ideas.

This dining room has seen the major change at Colby Hill in recent years, with additional space providing more tables. The atmosphere is enhanced by wide pine floorboards, and the pine furniture causes me to run my hands over the tabletops and backs of chairs. The wood-chunk stove provides comfortable and welcome warmth when needed.

"Oh, I see you're watching our birds," Don said. "Many of our guests are confirmed bird watchers. Yesterday, one of them said that he saw a bobolink—I haven't seen one for many years. The new wider window really provides a much more intimate view of the birds."

This classic New Hampshire inn is on the outskirts of the small village of Henniker, the home of New England College. About ten years ago, two Bucknell University friends of mine, Don and Jane Glover, along with their son, Don Glover, Jr., and his wife, Margaret, acquired the inn. During the summer of 1986, Don and June decided to retire permanently to Avalon, New Jersey, with occasional visits to Henniker to give Don,Jr., and Margaret a little vacation.

The ceilings of the inn are low, the walls are hung with old paintings and prints, and the furnishings are country antiques. A grandfather clock ticks away in one corner. There are birds during all seasons and a gorgeous flower garden during spring and summer. In earlier times, the living room fireplace was used for baking bread.

Guest rooms at the inn are typical country New England. Many have candlewick bedspreads, hooked rugs, and old bowl-and-pitcher sets, reminiscent of the days when water was brought in from the outside. They all have that wonderful "old home" feeling.

"This is great cross-country skiing terrain," commented Don. "There are forty miles of trails in this vicinity and a great many of our guests, including the children, come up for long weekends, or even, when possible, during the week."

At that moment, I caught the aroma of freshly baked bread coming from the kitchen, so Don and I wandered back there. "We serve chicken

Colby House," he said, "and this, along with our fresh seafood, has been received very well. We have specials almost every day and usually a fresh fish of the day." Breakfasts are prepared by Sue, who is now in her tenth year at the inn. Sourdough pancakes with fresh blueberries, eggs, cereal, homemade wheat and graham toast, and corned beef hash, as well as coffee cakes and cinnamon buns are among her specialties.

One of my favorite things at this inn is a delightful swimming pool sheltered by an ell, formed by the two huge barns adjacent to the inn. It is most welcome on the hot days of the southern New Hamsphire summer.

This inn is enjoyable in many seasons because this section of New Hamsphire has lakes, state parks, golf courses, summer theaters, and antique shops that add to the attraction for vacationers or weekenders.

COLBY HILL INN, Henniker, NH 03242; 603-428-3281. A 12-guestroom (mostly private baths) inn on the outskirts of a New Hampshire college town. European plan. Breakfast served to houseguests only. Dinner served to travelers Tues. through Sun., except Thanksgiving, Christmas, and New Year's Day. Open year-round. Swimming pool on grounds. Tennis and xc skiing one short block; alpine, 3 mi. Golf, canoeing, hiking, bicycling, and fishing nearby. No children under 6. No pets. The Glover Family, Innkeepers.

Directions: From I-89, take Exit 5 and follow Rte. 202 to Henniker. From I-91, take Exit 3 and follow Rte. 9 through Keene and Hillsborough to Henniker. From the blinking light in town center, go west ½ mi. on West Main St. (Western Ave.) to the Oaks. Inn is on the right.

THE CORNER HOUSE INN
Center Sandwich, New Hampshire (1987)

It had been a long day filled with surprises and a few disappointments. I had been wandering around New Hampshire, visiting inns that I have never seen before, looking for possible new additions to the pages of this book, and I must confess that up to this point there had been more disappointments then surprises.

Then I came to the intersection of many roads in a small village called Center Sandwich, complete with a very nice village green, a library, a shop run by the New Hampshire League of Artists and Crafts since 1925, and many vintage white houses, fences, and several beautiful churches. Best of all, there before my eyes was a village inn called "The Corner House Inn."

Walking in the main entrance, I stepped into a common room where the decorations and furnishings were all in a true New Hampshire country-inn style. There were shining floors, appropriate country furniture, a checker game going on in one corner, and lots of paintings and some quilted wall hangings, along with decorative quilts on the walls.

I soon made the acquaintance of Jane Kroeger and chef Don Brown, the owners and keepers of this inn. I knew immediately that this was going to be a delight and not a disappointment. And I was right.

Naturally, we took a quick tour of the inn, walking up the front hallway where there is an old spinning wheel, a highchair, and a clothes tree. Around the top of the wall is a stenciled border. All of the guest rooms are immaculate, and furnished in a clean, country-inn style. The front bedroom has a very nice, light feeling with twin beds and posters advertising Renoir and Matisse gallery showings. Another of the four bedrooms has an antique painted headboard and a Monet poster. The back bedroom has a double and a single bed, a wicker rocker, and its own private bath. The fourth bedroom has a brass bed and a post-Impressionist poster. All the wallpapers are different, and the feeling of each guest room is quite different.

I had dinner in the bay window area of one of the four dining rooms. To my delight, I was joined by Fred and Ramona Stafford of Stafford's in the Field Inn. Ramona was extremely enthusiastic about Don's cooking, and we had lots of fun tasting each other's dinners. Later on, both Jane and Don joined us. Incidentally, on that evening I had brandied peach duckling. Other main dishes included such items as lobster and scallop pie and sautéed shellfish. Don pointed out that the seafood is always the freshest available. The breads and desserts are made daily in the Corner House kitchen.

The Corner House Inn has a great lunch menu, served every day, with lots of different kinds of soups and quiches, including a spinach and cheese variety. It's quite unusual to find an inn that also serves lunch, with a bill of fare that looked very, very tempting to me.

"Center Sandwich has one of the largest populations of artists and craftsmen in New Hampshire," Jane remarked. "Our guests can swim in Sandwich Bay on Squam Lake. And, oh yes, that's the very same lake on which *On Golden Pond* was filmed."

Indeed, the Corner House Inn is a great delight! We are happy to welcome it to the pages of *Country Inns and Back Roads* for the first time in this edition.

THE CORNER HOUSE INN, Box 204, Center Sandwich, NH 03227; 603-284-6219. A 4-guestroom (private and shared baths) village inn. Lunch and dinner served every day. Breakfast is included in room rate for houseguests. Open year-round. Art galleries, weaving designery, antique and crafts shops, historical museum, tennis, hiking, xc and downhill skiing all available. Not convenient for young children. Jane Kroeger and Don Brown, Innkeepers.

Directions: From I-93, exit at Ashland and follow Rte. 3 to Holderness; then Rte. 113 to Center Sandwich.

THE DARBY FIELD INN
Conway, New Hampshire (1981)

There's a real sense of adventure involved in just making the last stage of the journey to reach Darby Field Inn. I turned off Route 16 and followed the Darby Field sign, plunging into the forest on a wonderful dirt road that seemed to climb ever upward. Following this road through the forest, again I had the great feeling of expectation that something would emerge at the top of the mountain that was going to be grand, and grand it is.

The Darby Field Inn has a most impressive panoramic view from its terrace dining room and many of the bedrooms. On this particular day Marc and Marily Donaldson, the innkeepers, took turns making sure that I saw all of the redecorating that had been accomplished in the inn, and we also had a chance to talk about the great view of the mountains.

"Over there is South Moat Mountain," Marc explained, "and that's Mount Washington just to the right. We can also see Adams and Madison and White Horse Ledge in the center."

The Darby Field Inn sits on the edge of the White Mountain National Forest, where guests can cross-country ski, snowshoe, and hike to nearby rivers, waterfalls, lakes, and open peaks. Fortunately, there's a very pleasant swimming pool on the terrace, providing guests with not only a cooling dip in the hot days of summer, but still another view of the mountains.

Marily and I did a short tour of the rooms. "Each room has its own country personality," she observed. "Some have four-poster beds, patchwork quilts, and braided rugs. Most of them have private baths and, as I'm sure you've noticed, many face our special view of the valley."

There is a cozy little pub, where both guests and Marc and Marily's friends can come together. This is adjacent to the living room, which has as impressive a massive stone fireplace as I have ever seen.

I was curious about the origins of Darby Field Inn. "Samuel and Polly Chase Littlefield first came up here in 1826, when it was hard work farming through all those generations of hard winters and long distances," she recounted. "Later on, the home took in summer guests, and it was then that the innkeeping tradition began. In the 1940s, a man from Boston and his family came here, and the original farmhouse became the living room section of what was to be known as the Bald Hill Lodge. The barn and blacksmith shop came down and in its place the dining room and kitchen section was built. The swimming pool was added and even a small ski lift for guests."

As one might expect, the menu is a bit on the hearty side with lamb chops, filet mignon, veal piccata, and roast duckling satisfying outdoor-oriented appetites.

Marc and Marily met in Venezuela, Marily's homeland, and came to Darby Field in 1979. They saw it as a country home for their children and an opportunity to meet guests from all parts of the world.

Many guests at Darby Field really enjoy going through the three volumes of scrapbooks containing brochures from inns all over New England. They provide a very pleasant few hours of relaxation in the living room in front of the big fireplace, and invariably lead to making new acquaintances among other guests.

As Marc and Marily walked me out to the car, she said, "We can't let you go without pointing out our garden where we get so many of the good things we serve at the inn, including snow peas, peppers, cabbage, corn, lettuce, and brussels sprouts."

THE DARBY FIELD INN, Bald Hill, Conway, NH 03818; 603-447-2181. A 17-guestroom White Mountain country inn, 3 mi. from Conway. Modified American plan. Open all year. Bed and breakfast offered at various times and I would suggest checking with the inn in advance. Within convenient driving distance of all of the Mt. Washington Valley cultural, natural, and historic attractions, as well as several internationally known ski areas. Swimming pool and carefully groomed xc skiing trails on grounds. Tennis and other sports nearby. Marc and Marily Donaldson, Innkeepers.

Directions: From Rte. 16: Traveling north turn left at sign for the inn (½ mi. before the town of Conway) onto Bald Hill Rd., and proceed up the hill 1 mi. to the next sign for the inn and turn right. The inn is 1 mi. down the dirt road on the left.

DEXTER'S INN AND TENNIS CLUB
Sunapee, New Hampshire (1978)

What a day! The sky was the bluest of skies, the sun was the sunniest of suns, and New Hampshire during the last week in June was really showing off for the rest of the world. I crested the hill and found Dexter's Inn basking in all of this glory, its bright yellow paint and black shutters blending well with the black-eyed Susans, Queen Anne's lace, and other summertime flowers and the green trees in the background.

After parking my car, I strolled up the granite steps, and stepped into the entrance, over which was the date 1804. Here again was the comfortable library-living room with the handsome antique desk and some appropriate paintings of New Hampshire mountains and countryside. The furniture had been brightly slipcovered, and the room was wonderfully cool after the midday heat. I took a moment and stepped out to a screened-in porch with white wicker furniture and a ceiling painted to look like a canopy. It looked like a wonderful place to spend an evening.

Now I opened the door to the side terrace with its round tables and bright yellow umbrellas, remembering that I first sat here perhaps ten years earlier. There were tennis courts on both sides of the broad lawn and some tennis players were having a lively game. I could hear guests splashing in the swimming pool.

Suddenly, innkeeper Frank Simpson appeared, and true to his promise, recorded in the last edition of the book, he had a pitcher of lemonade. We sat and had a long conversation about innkeeping, including a word or two about Norman Arluck, who at eighty-two was spending his thirteenth consecutive year at Dexter's.

"Of course, our daughter, Holly, and her husband, Michael, have really taken over much of the really demanding work of the inn," Frank said. "It has made a tremendous difference to both Shirley and me to have two such enthusiastic innkeepers on board."

Now I heard the reassuring sounds of lawnmowers—lawnmowers always sound wonderful unless you're pushing them yourself, and it's a sound that perhaps a great many city folk don't hear very often. Frank continued about Holly. "She's added some very nice main dishes to our menu, including brandied chicken, artichoke hearts and shrimp, puffed pastry with steak Florentine, and Southern fried chicken, which we pass on a platter on Sunday."

Frank was called to the phone and I took a look at the bulletin board. It's small wonder that this part of New Hampshire is so popular with country-inn guests because there is always something to do, including a regular series of band concerts in nearby Sunapee, horseback riding, and drama and music at the Dartmouth Hopkins Center and the Barn Theater in nearby New London.

Frank returned, and we went to see some of the guest rooms in the main house, which are reached by funny little hallways that zigzag around various wings, and also the more rustic guest rooms in the barn across the street. Everything looked tiptop.

Well, my summer idyll at Dexter's was over, but even now I can hear Frank saying as I disappeared back down the hill, "Remember, we'll have another pitcher of fresh lemonade waiting next year."

DEXTER'S INN AND TENNIS CLUB, Box R, Stagecoach Rd., Sunapee, NH 03782; 603-763-5571. A 17-guestroom resort-inn in the western New Hampshire mountain and lake district. Mod. American plan; European plan available in late June and Sept. only. Breakfast, lunch, and dinner served to travelers by advance reservation; closed for lunch and dinner on Tues. during July and Aug. Lunches served only July, Aug. Open from early May to mid-Oct. Three tennis courts, pool, croquet, and shuffleboard on grounds. Lakes, hiking, backroading, and championship golf courses nearby. Limited activities for children under 12. Pets allowed in Annex only. No credit cards. Frank and Shirley Simpson, Innkeepers; Michael Durfor, Manager.

Directions: From north & east: use Exit 12 or 12A, I-89. Continue west on Rte. 11, 6 mi.—just 1/2 mi. past Sunapee to a sign at Winn Hill Rd. Turn left up hill and after 1 mi., bear right on Stagecoach Rd. From west: use Exit 8, I-91, follow Rte. 103 east into NH—through Newport 1/2 mi. past junction with Rte. 11. Look for sign at "Young Hill Rd." and go 1 1/2 mi. to Stagecoach Rd.

The date in parenthesis in the heading represents the first year the inn appeared in the pages of Country Inns and Back Roads.

HICKORY STICK FARM
Laconia, New Hampshire (1983)

I'm going to share a letter I received from one of our readers about her trip to Hickory Stick Farm:

"Vacationing by car in Vermont and New Hampshire last month was a great experience, but by the time we reached the resort area of Lake Winnipesaukee, my friends and I were ready for a change of pace from fast motorways, motels, and coffee shops.

"One evening we saw a sign pointing off the main road to 'Hickory Stick Farm' with a carved duck decoy underneath. Turning off into the woods we were immediately in a different world of unbelievable peace

and quiet, and we drove 1½ miles of winding roads. 'Round a bend in the road could be seen a picture-perfect red farmhouse on a hill overlooking a splendid panorama. The sun was still shining on the valley and Ragged Mountain in the distance was a misty purple.

"Entering the converted farmhouse was like entering the house of a dream grandmother. We were shown into the living room, which is used as a waiting room, while the hostess checked on the availability of a table for dinner. During the short wait we admired the antiques in the living room, including a spinning wheel, and enjoyed visiting the Gift Shop, where many locally made gifts were for sale.

"Scott Roeder, the innkeeper, introduced himself and recounted the history of the farm, which dates back a number of years when his mother and father first bought it.

"The atmosphere in the dining room was relaxed and happy, surrounded by antiques and pewter and red accessories. Our waiter, a student from Boston, suggested we order the famous roast duckling, available in one quarter-pound, one half-pound, or a whole duck that is carved at the table. I have never enjoyed such a tender and delicious duckling, and Mr. Roeder explained the very special way he has of cooking them so that they have a brown, crisp skin and tender, moist meat. It was served with an orange sherry sauce, stuffing, wild rice, and delicious vegetables.

"After a leisurely dinner Mr. Roeder happened to mention that he had room cancellations for the following night, so we immediately booked the rooms and returned to the farm on the following late afternoon. Our rooms were a welcome sight.

"The Rose Room had a queen-sized cannonball bed and pretty flowered wallpaper. The Gold Room had twin-sized cannonball beds under the eaves, and a comfortable sitting area with antique furniture. Both rooms had large bathrooms with baths, showers, and dressing areas.

"Breakfast was served in a small dining area in the living room and Mary Roeder cooked the eggs, bacon, and french toast. They were both very friendly and we all parted most reluctantly."

Thank you, Dear Reader, for sharing your letter with us. I am always happy to hear from *CIBR* inn-goers.

HICKORY STICK FARM, R.F.D. #2, Laconia, NH 03246; 603-524-3333. A 2-guestroom hilltop country inn and restaurant 4 mi. from Laconia in the lake country of New Hampshire. Guestrooms and breakfast available most of the year. Please telephone ahead. Open from Memorial Day to Columbus Day; closed Mon. except July and Aug. Dinners served from 5:30 to 9 p.m. Sun. dinner served all day from noon to 8 p.m. Extended hours during fall foliage season—call ahead. The Shaker Village in Canterbury is nearby, as well as the Belknap recreational area (10 mi.) with crafts and antique shows, concerts, Oktoberfests, alpine and xc skiing, and other New Hampshire attractions. Scott and Mary Roeder, Innkeepers.

Directions: Use Exit 20 from I-93. Follow Rte. 3 toward Laconia approx. 5 mi. over bridge over Lake Winnisquam. A short distance past this bridge, turn right on Union Rd. immediately past Double Decker, a drive-in restaurant, and follow Hickory Stick signs 1½ mi. into the woods. If you do not turn onto any dirt roads, you are on the right track. From Laconia, go south on Rtes. 3 & 11 (do not take Rte. 106) and turn left on Union Rd. (about ½ mi. past the Belknap Mall) and follow signs.

I do not include lodging rates in the descriptions, for the very nature of an inn means that there are lodgings of various sizes, with and without baths, in and out of season, and with plain and fancy decoration. Travelers should call ahead and inquire about the availability and rates of the many different types of rooms.

THE INN AT CROTCHED MOUNTAIN
Francestown, New Hampshire (1981)

Once again I turned off Route 202 at Bennington, New Hampshire, and followed Route 47 towards Francestown. I noticed that an unusual number of beaver dams had been built by our industrious friends. Admiring the farms on both sides of the road, I wound my way ever upward through the grove of trees, coming once again to the Crotched Mountain Inn, just a few paces from the base of a ski area.

The brilliant sunshine of the day glittered in the waters of the swimming pool and intensified the radiant hues of the uncountable iris. I stopped for a moment to admire the view. One of the intriguing things about this view is that it gets better with each visit.

Rose Perry came around the corner of the inn, and after warm hellos we wandered across the broad back lawn. The subject of how many years the inn had been included in *CIBR* came up. The first entry was in the 1981 edition. Interestingly, some of the things I mentioned then were still true today. I had visited Crotched Mountain early in June, when the late New England spring is most delicious with apple blossoms and lilacs, and I was smitten by the wonderful panorama stretching out for miles.

I made a second visit that year when the fall colors were as magnificent as only they can be in the Monadnock region, where occasionally the full range of color is reached before October 1.

It was during this second visit that I enjoyed a leisurely dinner and the opportunity to see John and Rose Perry and the inn in a different light. There was a glowing fire in the low-ceilinged parlor of the little pub, where after-dinner guests and other couples dropped in during the evening.

The inn was originally built as a farmhouse in 1822. The first owner constructed a secret tunnel from his cellar to the Boston Post Road, incorporating his home as a way station to shelter runaway slaves on the Underground Railroad. During the late 1920s, it was to become one of the most spectacular farms in New England, boasting an internationally recognized breed of sheep, champion horses, and Angora goats.

Unfortunately, the house was destroyed by fire in the mid-30s, rebuilt, and John and Rose came on the scene in 1976.

Rose is an attractive Indonesian woman. She is in complete charge of the kitchen, doing a great deal of the cooking. The menu includes roast duck with plum sauce, sautéed bay scallops, and Indonesian-style scallops with sautéed tomatoes, onions, pepper, and ginger.

Although several years have intervened, both Rose and John looked like the same fresh-faced young innkeepers they were at our very first meeting. I asked John what he thought was the most important thing

about innkeeping, and he unhesitatingly replied, "People." He went on to explain that it is really the returning guests who make innkeeping such a joy. "We have had people who have been back every year since we first took over," he said.

As I was leaving, Rose walked out to the car and said, "Do tell your readers that we love children to come here, and we have many things for them to do and see, and they always seem to have a good time."

THE INN AT CROTCHED MOUNTAIN, Mountain Rd., Francestown, NH 03043; 603-588-6840. A 14-guestroom (shared and private baths) mountain inn in southern New Hampshire, 15 mi. from Peterborough. European plan. Open from mid-May to the end of Oct., and from Thanksgiving thru the ski season. During winter, dinner is served on Fri. and Sat., and during holiday periods. Dinner is served from Tues. thru Sat. during the remainder of the year. Within a short distance of the Sharon Arts Center, American Stage Festival, Peterborough Players, Crotched Mt. ski areas. Swimming pool, tennis courts, xc skiing, volleyball on grounds. Golf, skiing, hill walking, and backroading in the gorgeous Monadnock region nearby. No credit cards. Rose and John Perry, Innkeepers.

Directions: From Boston, follow Rte. 3 north to 101A to Milford. Then Rte. 13 to New Boston and Rte. 136 to Francestown. Follow Rte. 47 for 2½ mi. and turn left on Mountain Road. Inn is 1 mi. on right. From New York/Hartford, take I-91 north to Rte. 10 at Northfield to Keene, N.H. Follow 101 east to Peterborough, Rte. 202 north to Bennington, Rte. 47 to Mountain Rd. (approx. 4½ mi.); turn right on Mountain Rd. Inn is 1 mi. on right.

THE INN AT THORN HILL
Jackson Village, New Hampshire (1987)

What a transformation! When I last saw Mount Washington from my guest room, it had been at sundown the previous day. The mountain's eminence had caught and reflected the last rays of the sun, until it finally disappeared in the ever-deepening hues of blue that marked a mid-September evening in northern New Hampshire.

This morning the top of the mountain was completely white! A six-inch snowfall had powdered several peaks of the Presidential Range, and Jack Frost had brushed some streaks of red, orange, yellow, and russet through the verdant greenery.

When I went down for breakfast there was excitement in the air, because here in this sometimes gulpingly gorgeous part of New England, the arrival of snow heralds an entirely new season. "Oh, it will be some time before we actually do any skiing," innkeeper Bob Guindon told me, "but we welcome it as a forerunner of great things to come. You know our village is really one of the most carefully planned cross-country ski areas anywhere in the world, and there are all kinds of trails, some of which cross our property, right from the center of town."

Bob and his wife, Pattie, are relative newcomers to Jackson, but they have plunged into the work and fun of innkeeping with great zest. Among Bob's former careers is that of a professional baseball player. Pattie, on the other hand, has been in the travel business and has taken many tours to other parts of the world. They have transformed what at one time was a sort of "ski dorm" into a glowing, year-round country inn.

Pattie has ingeniously divided the long living room into three separate areas, where guests can either enjoy a pleasant conversation or gather for tea or play at a game table.

Pattie loves stuffed bears. There are bears of all colors, sizes, and descriptions everywhere in the inn, and at least one bear in every guest room. There are even some seated at empty places in the dining room and in the wicker furniture out on the porch.

The gambrel-roofed main house, designed by Stanford White, is very Victorian and quite elegant, with all kinds of turn-of-the-century furnishings, gew-gaws, lace curtains, ivy hanging in the window, and carved wooden headboards, as well as oriental rugs. The Carriage House is on the rustic side, with maple furniture and a big living room with a fireplace where you can put your feet up on the coffee table and relax and enjoy the fire. Three little cottages provide a more secluded atmosphere, and one, according to Pattie, is excellent for an anniversary or a honeymoon.

The dinner menu was a surprise for me. I thought there would be hearty North Country offerings, but I found a definite creative flare in the

grilled quail, roulade of veal Tara (veal stuffed with lobster and spinach), and sirloin steak with green peppercorns and toasted pecans. Some of the appetizers are crabmeat ravioli and grilled brochette of swordfish with Japanese noodles. Breads, soups, and pastries are all homemade.

While winter sports here are great, it is also very enjoyable in the summer and fall, when guests lounge around the swimming pool or make the acquaintance of the ducks and the golden retriever, Albert, who can't swim. He sits in the nearby duck pond to cool off.

We are delighted to welcome the Inn at Thorn Hill to *Country Inns and Back Roads*.

THE INN AT THORN HILL, Jackson Village, NH 03846; 603-383-4242. A 20-guestroom (private baths) inn within sight of Mount Washington. Various package plans available for xc skiers. European plan. Breakfast and dinner served daily. Open all year. Jackson Touring Center within walking distance. Many cultural and recreational attractions nearby. Children over 6 welcome. Bob and Pattie Guindon, Innkeepers.

Directions: From Boston, take I-95, which becomes the Spaulding Tpke., and then Rte. 116. From I-93, cut over to the Kankamangus Hwy. and then to Bear Notch Rd., which comes out to Rte. 302. This route eliminates a great deal of traffic in Conway; however, Bear Notch Rd. is not plowed in the winter.

"European plan" means that rates for rooms and meals are separate. "American plan" means that meals are included in the cost of the room. "Modified American plan" means that breakfast and dinner are included in the cost of the room. The rates at some inns include a continental breakfast with the lodging.

THE JOHN HANCOCK INN
Hancock, New Hampshire (1971)

It was raining in Hancock, and the trees arching over the village streets provided a very welcome shelter for many of the umbrella-carrying villagers and visitors. There was a special gleam from many of the white narrow-clapboard Federalist homes. For instance, directly across from the John Hancock Inn there is a pleasant white clapboard with a Victorian porch and next to that is a typical New Hampshire double-galleried peak-roofed three-story house in white clapboard with white pillars on the front. The overhang of the third floor creates a sort of cavern effect.

The parking lot for the John Hancock was almost filled. As soon as I walked in the old front door, there was Pat Wells saying, "Oh, it's you!"

It was a busy morning for her, but we managed to have a few moments at the lunch table, and this time, with a choice of four different dining rooms, we decided on the one with the dried flower arrangements hanging from the exposed beams and overlooking the back lawn.

There was a display board showing the day's luncheon specials, and after looking at those and the luncheon menu, which included roast beef hash and poached egg, fried haddock, chicken shortcake, and other assorted unusual sandwiches, I decided on the roast beef hash.

Later, I went outside with Pat and Glynn while they discussed the new landscaping being done on the front of the inn. One of the interesting things about knowing them over these many years is that they always seem to be doing new things—building new dining rooms, redecorating, expanding the grounds, and making additions and improvements to the menu. Because, as Pat says, "You just cannot stand still; you have to move with the times and the circumstances."

When people interested in knowing more about country innkeeping come to visit me, I often suggest that they visit the John Hancock as an example of a certain type of inn located in a village. It is the continuing center for community activity and small enough so that villagers and visitors have the opportunity to get acquainted. It is New Hampshire's oldest continuously operating inn, and all of the guest rooms have been appropriately furnished. Many have double and twin canopied beds.

The inn enjoys the distinction of having murals, not by one, but by two itinerant 19th-century artists, Rufus Porter and Moses Eaton. Pat and Glynn told me Rufus Porter's works were discovered recently while they were doing some redecorating.

Our conversation, taking a circuitous route, arrived at their Sunday brunches. "Instead of having a buffet table, we prefer to offer our guests table service, and in many cases, our Hancock neighbors join with the out-of-town guests—it's becoming a regular stop-off after church or after the "morning-trip-out-for-the-paper."

As I drove away from the John Hancock Inn and my dear friends Pat and Glynn, whom I first met when they visited me in Stockbridge many years ago to talk about the possibility of finding a country inn to buy, I remembered the thought expressed by them a few years ago.

"I think that the whole business of innkeeping has been an act of faith for us. Back in 1972, the realization that we were going to be somewhere else was the controlling factor that led us to Hancock. God has been good these years. We believe that with His strength and guidance we can make the inn what it richly deserves to be—a haven for others, a source of pride for the town, and a deep and rich experience for our family. It is all that, I believe, but never could be without the faith that has supported us in every kind of problem."

THE JOHN HANCOCK INN, Hancock, NH 03449; 603-525-3318. A 10-guestroom village inn 9 mi. north of Peterborough, on Rtes. 123 and 137, in the middle of the Monadnock region of southern N.H. European plan. Breakfast, lunch, and dinner served daily to travelers. Sun. brunch. Closed Christmas Day and 1 wk. in spring and fall. Bicycles available on the grounds. Antiquing, swimming, hiking, alpine and xc skiing nearby. Glynn and Pat Wells, Innkeepers.

Directions: From Keene, take either Rte. 101 east to Dublin and Rte. 137 north to Hancock or Rte. 9 north to Rte. 123 and east to Hancock. From Nashua, take 101A and 101 to Peterborough. Proceed north on Rtes. 202 and 123 to Hancock.

LOVETT'S BY LAFAYETTE BROOK
Franconia, New Hampshire (1976)

Charlie Lovett was explaining his philosophy of innkeeping, which he has been practicing here at Lovett's for nearly forty years. "The whole idea is to run a comfortable inn. We think ours accommodates itself to the landscape."

Looking out over the striking White Mountains and then glancing back at the distinctive New England lines of this white clapboard building, I fully agreed with him.

"This is a mountain inn, and you know there are many reasons for coming to the White Mountains and especially to our little village of Franconia. We have antiquing, and flower shows and horse shows, summer theater, auctions, and country fairs. There also is the fall foliage, good winter and spring skiing, and cross-country skiing as well. I think that our guests like to escape from city life by visiting us.

"There are walks all over these mountains and all kinds of places to motor to," Charlie pointed out. "Most of the ski areas run their lifts during the summer and autumn. Shopping seems to intrigue our guests as well. We have several superior places right here in Franconia and a sprinkling of country stores and crafts shops throughout the mountains."

Charlie and I were in the sitting room with its deep couches, overhead beams, and woodburning stove. There is a painting of the inn showing Cannon Mountain in the background.

Lovett's has several country-inn-type guest rooms in the main house and in two nearby houses. There are more contemporarily furnished small chalets on the grounds with living rooms and mountain views, many of them with fireplaces. A few poolside chalets are also available.

An outdoor terrace faces Cannon Mountain on the south and great sunsets on the west.

With Lovett's impressive reputation for its food, it is difficult to make a choice from the tempting menu.

"We're particularly proud of our cold wild blueberry soup, hot mussel bisque, and curried fresh sorrel soup. The pleasure of three-course breakfasts is heightened by coffee made with Mount Lafayette's purest water," Charlie commented.

The nearby New England Ski Museum is the only ski museum I know of, and it has photographs and films of the early days of North American skiing, which had its beginning at nearby Peckett's Inn on Sugar Hill.

The establishment of the New England Ski Museum was one of Charlie's dreams. "It is for all the New England states and contains much memorabilia and history of some of the great early Austrian ski instructors such as Hans Schneider, who really provided the impetus that eventually resulted in the American ski industry. Lovett's was in on the early part of everything around 1930 and we had our own Swiss ski instructor here. He took the guests up on Cannon Mountain every day, and in those days you herringboned up the side of the mountain because there was no ski lift as there is now."

Winters in this part of New Hampshire are dominated by the presence of ski areas, principally Cannon Mountain, which looms in all of its snow-clad glory just a few minutes from Lovett's. Cannon is one of the principal downhill ski areas in New England, and its well-known tramway carries skiers to the top of the mountain for some really great skiing.

Lovett's is a sophisticated country inn with considerable emphasis on excellent food and service. It is well into its second generation of

one-family ownership and many of the guests have been returning for years. Their fathers and mothers came before them. There is a very definite spirit that pulls everybody together. As one guest remarked, "It's almost like a club."

LOVETT'S BY LAFAYETTE BROOK, Profile Rd.,Franconia, NH 03580; 603-823-7761. A 32-guestroom country inn in New Hampshire's White Mountains. Modified American plan omits lunch. Box lunches available. Breakfast and dinner served by reservation to travelers. Open daily from June 29 to Oct. 8 and from Dec. 26 to Apr. 1. Swimming pool, pond and streams for fishing, xc skiing, lawn sports on grounds. Golf, tennis, alpine skiing, hiking nearby. Mr. and Mrs. Charles J. Lovett, Jr., Innkeepers.

Directions: South of Franconia 2½ mi. on N.H. business loop, at junction of N.H. 141 and I-93 South Franconia exit; 2¾ mi. north of junction of U.S. 3 and 18.

THE LYME INN
Lyme, New Hampshire (1971)

On my most recent visit, Judy Siemons showed me the lovely new Lyme Inn notepaper, with a very delicate watercolor of the inn by a local artist, showing all four of the red brick chimneys and the four-plus stories of the inn itself. The second- and third-story open porches in the front of the building are plainly visible. Everything is set off by a trim white fence. It might be that in some future edition of *Country Inns and Back Roads* we would use this for our cover.

I was also pleased to discover the expanding crafts area on the second floor, with many delightful handcrafted gifts by mostly local artisans.

Judy was overflowing with news about the "Garrison stove in our third dining room. What a difference it makes, both in direct heat and warming up the atmosphere. We found a wonderful source of braided rag rugs, and have replaced many of our older rugs and covered previously bare floors with some of the nicest braided rugs I've ever seen. We've also added quite a few Hitchcock chairs and tables to our dining rooms."

The Lyme Inn is an antique-laden gem that sits at the end of a long New England common. The ten guest rooms with private baths and five rooms with shared baths have poster beds, hooked rugs, hand-stitched quilts, wide pine floorboards, stenciled wallpaper, and winged chairs. I feel certain that children would not be comfortable, because there is no entertainment particularly designed for them.

This inn is a treasure-trove of nostalgic memorabilia; one room displays old farm tools, and reminds us that this is good snowshoeing country. The house boasts a number of antique maps and salt-glazed pottery, and one of its bedrooms is outfitted in a rare suite of 19th-century painted "cottage" furniture, reminiscent of Eastlake.

My attention was drawn to the unusual collection of framed samplers on the wall of the dining room. "Oh, I am definitely into samplers," exclaimed Judy. "I am always anxious to know more about them and sometimes our guests are able to be of assistance.

"Samplers are a form of American folk art," she continued, "and I find that the real old ones are fast disappearing. A friend of mine who lives nearby does most of our framing and we are doing everything we can to preserve them, including using acid-free paper."

Breakfast, included in the room rate, features juice, fresh fruit in season, fried or scrambled eggs, french toast with local maple syrup, and blueberry muffins.

Chef Hans Wickert, trained in Germany and Switzerland, has introduced several Continental specialties, including hasenpfeffer. He offers a different menu for summer and winter, but always a veal dish and a shrimp dish, and always makes his own soups from scratch.

Guests are intrigued with the four sheep, two black and two white ewes. Judy says they are kept as added "lawn mowers." They're sheared every spring and she talked about possibly trading their wool for blankets at one of the crafts shops in the area. These sheep are kept in line by Duffy, the sheep dog, who is well known to almost every guest who stays at the inn. As Judy says of him, "He's just a people's dog and has never led a dog's life."

Although the village feels quite remote, it is nonetheless just ten miles from Hanover, New Hampshire, the home of Dartmouth College, and inn guests have the opportunity to enjoy some of the sporting and

theatrical events taking place there. It is just a few minutes from the Dartmouth Skiway, and there's plenty of cross-country skiing nearby. In fact, new snowmaking equipment at the Skiway has caused Fred and Judy to offer a midweek MAP special to take advantage of the uncrowded week days.

THE LYME INN, on the Common, Lyme, NH 03768; 603-795-2222. A 15-guestroom (10 with private baths) village inn 10 mi. north of Hanover on N.H. Rte. 10. Breakfast included in room rate. Dinner served daily to travelers except on Tues. Closed from Sun. following Thanksgiving to Dec. 26, and 3 wks. in late spring. Convenient to all Dartmouth College activities, including Hopkins Center, with music, dance, drama, painting, and sculpture. Alpine and xc skiing, fishing, hiking, canoeing, tennis, and golf nearby. No children under 8. No pets. Fred and Judy Siemons, Innkeepers.

Directions: From I-91, take Exit 14 and follow Rte. 113A east to Vermont Rte. 5. Proceed south 50 yards to a left turn, then travel 2 mi. to inn.

MOOSE MOUNTAIN LODGE
Etna, New Hampshire (1984)

Checking my own directions, I stopped at the Etna General Store and met a very attractive young woman who told me that I should take the second road on the right and follow the road up the mountain and the signs for the lodge. I set off for Moose Mountain Lodge with my heart high, reflecting that on my earlier visits it had been wintertime and sometimes necessary for Peter Shumway, the innkeeper, to come down to the bottom of the last steep incline to pick people up in his four-wheel drive. Up I went to the lodge and its fabulous view.

Moose Mountain Lodge is a rustic building high on the western side of Moose Mountain, built in the late 1930s, mostly of logs and stones gathered from the surrounding forests and fields. The broad porch extends across the entire rear of the lodge, and has foreground views of the rolling New Hampshire countryside and, in the distance, of famed Vermont peaks as far away as Rutland.

I passed through the new entryway and walked into the kitchen, as almost everyone does, joining Peter and Kay Shumway around the big table for a wonderful breakfast visit.

The kitchen is one of the centers of activity at Moose Mountain Lodge. "We run an open kitchen here," Kay said. "I like it when guests wander in and ask 'what's for lunch!' Incidentally, most of the time it's soup and salad." This was Kay's domain and it revealed her many interests besides cuisine, including flowers and plants. In the middle of the big butcher-block table was a copy of *Webster's New Collegiate Dictionary*. How can you go wrong in a kitchen that is also a haven for the intellectually curious!

There are twelve "lodge-type," rustic bedrooms with colorful quilts, lots of books and magazines, bunk beds and conventional single and double beds, and a rustic air that I seldom find these days.

"Many things are different here in the summer, including the menus," Kay remarked. "Summer meals have lots of fish and some meats with light sauces; all of the vegetables from the garden and all the fresh fruits that I can pick; sometimes cold soups. We have salads and home-made breads and generally fruit desserts.

"However, in the wintertime we serve stuffed squash, lots of potatoes and big roasts, and always a huge salad and all kinds of desserts. Everything is put out on the buffet table so guests can have whatever they want and they can sit wherever they wish."

In winter there are extensive cross-country ski trails everywhere, and the winter scenery is spectacular. It's great to come in after skiing and grab a cookie from the seemingly bottomless cookie jar.

A recent letter from Kay said, "It's a beautiful fall morning here on the mountain, and the fog is covering the floor of the valley below us, looking like a lake, with the hills like islands and the mountains like the far shore. Down in Hanover they don't know what a beautiful day it is going to be yet. The fall colors increase every day, and two days ago we had an early morning blizzard with two inches of snow on the ground for a while. I love this time of year and we feel so fortunate to be able to live here and share our mountain home with people who love it as we do."

MOOSE MOUNTAIN LODGE, Etna, NH 03750; 603-643-3529. A 12-guestroom (5 shared baths) rustic lodge a few miles from Hanover, New Hampshire. Closed April and May, and from Nov. 15 thru Dec. 26. Breakfast, lunch, and dinner served to houseguests only. Xc skiing for all abilities on grounds or nearby. Ski equipment available. Hiking, biking, walking, canoeing, backroading, and many recreational and cultural attractions nearby, including Dartmouth College. No pets. Peter and Kay Shumway, Innkeepers.

Directions: If arriving for the first time, stop in Etna at Landers Restaurant or the Etna Store and telephone the lodge for directions. The last mile up the mountain is steep, and when the road is icy, guests are met at the bottom parking lot with a 4-wheel-drive vehicle. Etna is on the map, a few miles east of Hanover.

I do not include lodging rates in the descriptions, for the very nature of an inn means that there are lodgings of various sizes, with and without baths, in and out of season, and with plain and fancy decoration. Travelers should call ahead and inquire about the availability and rates of the many different types of rooms.

PHILBROOK FARM INN
Shelburne, New Hampshire (1978)

I can't think of another inn in North America that has been under the ownership of the same family for 125 years. In 1986, that is exactly what Philbrook Farm Inn was celebrating—although they were so busy with their innkeeping that nobody remembered it until mid-1986. Then they had a party and invited about sixty guests who had been coming to the inn over many years. In some cases, their guests were members of families who have been coming there over *generations*.

Nancy Philbrook and her sister, Connie Leger, and Connie's son, Larry, have been joined by Larry's sister, Ann, and her friend, Madonna, which has swelled the family members of the staff considerably.

The main house of Philbrook Farm was built in 1834, and the first addition with the blue porch and old-fashioned door was put on in 1861. The east end was built in 1905, and the dining room, along with the "new kitchens" was added when the big barns burned in 1934.

The Philbrook Farm *is* New Hampshire. There are New Hampshire prints, paintings, and photographs, some of them really irreplaceable. There are some tints of old prints, hooked rugs, and many, many books about New Hampshire. A whole library of books is just on the White Mountains, some of them written by former guests of the farm.

In the kitchen there is a *ten-burner woodburning* range built by the McGee Furnace Company of Boston during the 1890s. "Yes," said Nancy, "we do almost all of our cooking and baking on this range. We only use the electric stove in case of emergencies or to keep things warm." Imagine a country inn where almost all of the cooking is done on a woodburning range!

Meals are New England-style home cooking. "It's all homemade with no mixes," said Connie. "There is one main dish each night, and the dinner usually consists of a homemade soup, some type of roast, such as

pot, pork or lamb. The vegetables are as fresh as possible, and we try to stay away from fried foods. Most of the guests enjoy roasts, because these days they are not served as much at home. All of the desserts are homemade. There's pie, ice cream, and pudding.

"For lunches, we serve salads, chowder, hot rolls, hash, macaroni and cheese, and things like that. On Saturday night we have a New England baked-bean supper,and we almost always have a roast chicken dinner on Sunday night. We always serve a full breakfast, and on Sunday morning we have New England fish balls and cornbread."

The latest news is that the old barn next door has been put into operation as a stable, and horseback riding, trail rides, instruction, and boarding for horses are now available.

The recently built swimming pool adds one more option to the summertime activities, which include hikes, picnicking, and nature walks on Mount Washington and the Appalachian Trail. In winter, there are cross-country trails on the 900-acre property and downhill skiing nearby.

Guests, friends, and family have been busily making cross-stitch door plaques with the names of many of the long-time returning guests, and another popular pastime is putting together one of the fantastic collection of ninety-eight jigsaw puzzles, all cut by Larry and Ann's great-grandfather and kept in a special cupboard.

Being an official Philbrook Farm "adoptee" (I am the proud posses- sor of a Philbrook Family Reunion T-shirt, having received it on the eve of one of their huge reunions), I must confess I am a little prejudiced in their favor. Once you've visited this delightful old New Hampshire inn, I think you will be, too.

PHILBROOK FARM INN, North Rd., Shelburne, NH 03581; 603-466- 3831. A 20-guestroom country inn in the White Mountains of northeastern N.H., 6 mi. from Gorham and just west of the Maine/N.H. line. Amer- ican, mod. American, and European plans available. Open May 1 to Oct. 31; Dec. 26 to Apr. 1. Closed Thanksgiving, Christmas. Swimming pool, shuffleboard, horseshoes, badminton, ping-pong, croquet, bil- liards, hiking trails, xc skiing, snowshoeing trails, horseback riding on grounds. Swimming, golf, hiking, backroading, bird watching nearby. Pets allowed only during summer season in cottages. No credit cards. The Philbrook and Leger Families, Innkeepers.

Directions: The inn is just off U.S. Rte. 2 in Shelburne. Look for inn direction sign and turn at Meadow Rd., cross R.R. tracks and river, and turn right at North Rd. The inn is at the end of the road.

ROCKHOUSE MOUNTAIN FARM INN
Eaton Center, New Hampshire (1978)

In past editions I have shared letters with you from Vicki Wille, who has been kind enough to write me about her adventures in visiting some of our CIBR inns. This time her letter is about a visit to Rockhouse Mountain Farm.

"Our confirmation letter read, 'maybe we can persuade you to stay an extra day, you'll love it here.' An understatement if ever there was one. No one wanted to go home! We couldn't have chosen a more wonderful place to take the children.

"Not only were we greeted by a smiling young lady who was busily at work in the kitchen—we were also greeted by the aroma of freshly baked onion bread, the smell wafting up the stairs along with us as we were shown to our rooms. As we turned to go up the stairs, we caught the view from the picture window in the living room—absolutely breathtaking, of mountains galore and fields full of wildflowers.

"Dinner was announced by a ringing bell, and the waitress informed us we would be seated at the sound of the second bell. By that time we were lined up at the door, dinner smelled so heavenly. And it was. The beef was so tender, the vegetables so fresh, and the peach pie for dessert was indescribable. The guests who shared the table with us kept us company as we wandered into the living room to enjoy the view and chat. Contentedly, we sat and watched the children having a wonderful time sliding down a hill across the road from the farm and taking turns following the leader back up the stony path to the inn. Yells and screams brought us all outside to enjoy the sight of the full moon as it rose from behind the mountain. . . .

"We tried to delay our departure as long as possible. We chatted for ages with friends we'd made during our brief stay, while the children

made the rounds, saying their goodbyes to the seven kittens they'd come to love. . . as well as to the geese who waddled around, proud to be a part of the farm, to the horses who grazed so quietly, to the cows they had a hand in milking for the cream and milk for breakfast and dinner. They also said long goodbyes to the friends they'd made in just a day.

"Then we heard a bell ring and turned to see Mrs. Edge waving goodbye to the guests from Texas. Now it was our turn to climb into the car—no more excuses left to stay on. However, Mrs. Edge was busy and I thought we might miss our turn at hearing the bell ring, but a newly made friend took hold of it and rang it as we drove slowly down the driveway. The only comforting thoughts we took with us were our reservations for the autumn and the same time next year at Rockhouse Mountain Farm."

In addition to the cows, horses, geese, and kittens mentioned above, there are turkeys, pheasants, peacocks, pigs, dogs, and chickens. Now, a new three-quarter-acre spring-fed pond will be the habitat for brook trout.

Rockhouse Mountain Farm is currently celebrating its fortieth year as a country inn, and many of their long-time guests have been returning to help the growing Edge family with their celebration. I join with everyone in saying how wonderful it is!

This is a good place to congratulate Johnny Edge on receiving the State of New Hampshire's Outstanding Co-Operator Award for accomplishment in the conservation of soil, water, and related resources.

ROCKHOUSE MOUNTAIN FARM INN, Eaton Center, NH 03832; 603-447-2880. An 18-guestroom (some private baths) country farm inn on 350 acres in the foothills of the White Mountains, 6 mi. south of Conway. Modified American plan. Open from June 15 through Oct. Farm animals; haying, hiking, shuffleboard; private beach on Crystal Lake with swimming, rowboats, sailboats, and canoes—canoe trips planned; stream and lake fishing; tennis and golf nearby. No credit cards. The Edge Family, Innkeepers.

Directions: From I-93, take Exit 23 to Rte. 104 to Meredith. Take Rte. 25 to Rte. 16, and proceed north to Conway and Rte. 153. Continue 6 mi. south on Rte. 153 to Eaton Center.

"European Plan" means that rates for rooms and meals are separate. "American Plan" means that meals are included in the cost of the room. "Modified American Plan" means that breakfast and dinner are included in the cost of the room. The rates at some inns include a continental breakfast with the lodging.

SPALDING INN & CLUB
Whitefield, New Hampshire (1976)

Many years ago the White Mountains in New Hampshire had numerous summer resorts where "mother and children" might come up early in the season and where "father" joined them for the last four weeks or so. These resorts were wonderful, gay places where everything that was needed for a long, complete vacation was either on the grounds or nearby. The lure of the mountains drew people in great numbers from Boston and New York.

Now, with few exceptions, all of these family-run resorts have disappeared, but not the Spalding Inn & Club, which is thriving under the ownership of William A. and Michael B. Ingram. Many of the amenities of earlier times are still preserved; for example, gentlemen wouldn't think of going to dinner without a jacket and tie. The inn is a focal point for the sports of lawn bowling and tennis, with several tournaments scheduled from mid-June to mid-September, including the U.S. National Singles and Doubles Lawn Bowling Championships.

The Spalding Inn & Club is an excellent example of entertainment and hospitality that can be provided for a family with many different preferences. For example, on the inn grounds there are four clay tennis courts, a swimming pool, a nine-hole par-3 golf course, two championship lawn bowling greens, and shuffleboard. Five golf courses are within fifteen minutes of the inn, and plenty of trout fishing and boating and enticing back roads are nearby. The Appalachian Trail system for mountain climbing is a short walk from the inn.

In addition to opportunities for a well-blended balance of vigorous outdoor activity, there are also facilities for quiet times, including an extensive library, a card room, and a challenging collection of jigsaw puzzles. Groves of maples, birches, and oak trees native to northern New Hampshire are on the inn grounds and there are over 400 acres of lawns, gardens, and orchards.

There are real country-inn touches everywhere. The broad porch is ideal for rocking, and the main living room has a fireplace with a low ceiling, lots of books and magazines, baskets of apples, a barometer for tomorrow's weather, a jar of sour balls, and abundant arrangements of flowers.

Those country-inn touches also include the traditional hearty menu items so satisfying after a day of outdoor activities in the White Mountains. Among other offerings in the air-conditioned dining room are delicious clam chowder, oyster stew, broiled scrod, poached salmon, pork chops, roast duckling, roast tenderloin, and sweetbreads. Children love the indian pudding. All of the pies, including hot mince, and the breads and rolls are made in the bakery of the inn.

Bill Ingram and his brother, Michael, have instilled a really fresh new spirit at this lovely inn. As Bill says, "We feel that this is a place that the younger crowd can enjoy, so we have added entertainment and dinner dances. With seventy guest rooms we are larger than the average inn in your book, but I'm sure our staff has a personal touch."

I agree.

SPALDING INN & CLUB, Mountain View Road, Whitefield, NH 03598; 603-837-2572. A 70-guestroom resort-inn in the center of New Hampshire's White Mountains. Full American plan includes lunch. Open early June to mid-Oct. Breakfast, lunch and dinner are served daily to travelers. Heated pool, tennis courts, 9-hole par-3 golf course, 18-hole putting green, 2 championship lawn bowling greens, and shuffleboard on grounds. Also Sunday night movies. Guest privileges at 5 nearby golf clubs. Trout fishing, boating, summer theater, and backroading nearby. William A. and Michael B. Ingram, Innkeepers.

Directions: From New York take Merritt Pkwy. to I-91; I-91 to Wells River, Vt./Woodsville, N.H. exit; then Rte. 302 to Littleton, then Rte. 116 thru Whitefield to Mtn. View Rd. intersection—3 mi. north of village. From Boston take I-93 north thru Franconia Notch to Littleton exit; then Rte. 116 thru Whitefield to Mtn. View Rd. intersection—3 mi. north of village. From Montreal take Autoroute 10 to Magog; then Autoroute 55 and I-91 to St. Johnsbury, Vt.; then Rte. 18 to Littleton, N.H. and Rte. 116 as above. The inn is situated 1 mi. west on Mountain View Rd.

STAFFORD'S IN THE FIELD
Chocorua, New Hampshire (1972)

I'd like to share a letter that was written about a visit to this inn. "I have just returned from the most fantastic experience at Stafford's in the Field, Chocorua, New Hampshire. It was almost unbelievable to me that in today's commercial world, it can still be possible to find a haven so well run by such a beautiful family.

"From the moment we left the highway and saw Stafford's, I knew this vacation would be something special. Fred and Ramona Stafford are incredible when it comes to hospitality. And, as you stated in your book, Ramona is a superb gourmet cook. Our stay brought back memories of visiting my grandparents long ago in their big old country home on the farm. This inn is an experience that I will long remember and I will make every effort to go back as soon as possible."

That letter was written in 1972, the first year I included Stafford's Inn in *CIBR*. Since that time, many things have been happening in this inn, which have made it an even more enjoyable experience.

For one thing, cross-country skiing is one of the big winter attractions. There are open fields and practice slopes for novices and marked trails for more accomplished skiers.

Today, as in 1972, still another side of Stafford's in the Field is Ramona's gourmet cooking. I hasten to point out that "gourmet" is a word I never use lightly, but my original conversation with her convinced me that she was not merely a good cook, but a dedicated searcher for true expression in the culinary art. Breads and pastries are home-baked, and there is a very generous selection of Russian, French, Italian, and German dishes with a knowledgeable use of herbs and spices. One of my favorite dishes is the spare ribs cooked in maple syrup.

All of this accumulated knowledge, experimentation, and years of preparing inn meals has culminated in the *Stafford's in the Field Cookbook*. "It has been a family project," declared Ramona. "Fred and our daughter, Momo, worked side by side with me, and even our sons made significant contributions."

Accommodations in the main house are comfortable rooms that have been furnished with country antique furniture. There are three new rooms, all with private baths. Other accommodations on the grounds are in cottages that are extremely suitable for families of all ages and sizes.

Fred and the guests sit together for the evening meal, and I think this is when the dinner party atmosphere is particularly enjoyable for everyone. Many guests enjoy a stroll through the open fields before dinner, walking down the shady paths in the woods surrounding the inn. Winter transforms these paths into ski trails and guests often spend the whole day out on skis.

In March, it's maple syrup time, and anyone who wants to help, can. I think it adds to the flavor of the blueberry waffles if one has had a first-hand knowledge of the source of the syrup!

The Staffords have a "freedom phone" that enables guests to receive telephone calls either in their room, the cottages, or in the dining room.

Stafford's in the Field is that inn "at the end of the road."

STAFFORD'S IN THE FIELD, Chocorua, NH 03817; 603-323-7766 (800-332-0355). A 14-guestroom (private and shared baths) resort-inn with 5 cottages, 17 mi. south of North Conway. Modified American plan omits lunch. Dinner is offered to the public with reservations. Open all year. Bicycles, square dancing, tennis, country golf, and xc skiing on grounds. Golf club, swimming, hiking, riding, and fishing nearby. No pets. The Stafford Family, Innkeepers.

Directions: Follow N.H. Rte. 16 north to Chocorua Village, then turn left onto Rte. 113 and travel 1 mi. west to inn. Or, from Rte. 93 take Exit 23 and travel east on Rtes. 104 and 25 to Rte. 16. Proceed north on Rte. 16 to Chocorua Village, turn left onto Rte. 113 and travel 1 mi. west to inn.

I do not include lodging rates in the descriptions, for the very nature of an inn means that there are lodgings of various sizes, with and without baths, in and out of season, and with plain and fancy decoration. Travelers should call ahead and inquire about the availability and rates of the many different types of rooms.

BIRCH HILL INN
Manchester, Vermont (1982)

Life takes some interesting twists and turns, doesn't it? For many, many years I used to drive north from Stockbridge on Route 7 to Manchester, Vermont, and then turn left at the Johnny Appleseed Bookstore, taking a shortcut around Manchester Center to reach Route 30 and continue on west to Dorset, and up the valley of the Mettowee through Pawlet on up to Lake St. Catherine.

I'm sure that almost every time I took this Manchester shortcut I was attracted to a very large, handsome white house that sat on a rise in a grove of trees. In the winter the snow would be shoveled out and piled high around the entrance, which was reached by a circular driveway. I used to imagine what kind of people lived in that house and what the interior was like.

In 1981 I learned that my lovely white house had indeed become an intimate inn. In the course of events I visited it and met Pat and Jim Lee, who were then new innkeepers, and I subsequently included it in the 1982

edition of this book. Pat's family has lived in that house since 1917, so the chances are I may have seen various members of the family outside as I passed to and fro en route.

The interior is every bit as attractive as the exterior. For example, there are windows on three sides of the living room, which has a wonderful warm feeling, aided by a low ceiling, a sizeable fireplace, a spinet piano, the ongoing, never-ending jigsaw puzzle, and innumerable books and magazines. Over the big fireplace is a print of George Washington's triumphal entry into New York City after the Revolutionary War.

For 190 years Birch Hill was a family home and today it has retained that same homelike feeling. It's obvious that the Lee family has a great deal of interest in art, music and history.

Accommodations are in five comfortable and cheerful guest rooms in the main house, all of which have views toward the mountains, farm, and pond. They are well decorated with paintings and furniture from the family home. A nearby cottage on the grounds has been converted into an ideal family-style accommodation as well.

Dinner is offered only to houseguests every night except Wednesday and Sunday, and I was most interested in what Pat Lee had to say about the "Beefalo" that she often serves. "Beefalo," she explained, "is a breed of cattle originally developed by the introduction of American bison (buffalo) genes into domestic cattle. Beefalo meat contains less than 15% of the fat of supermarket beef, and only 3% of the cholesterol.

"We have small steers and heifers here in the fields around the inn. They are always a great source of conversation among our guests."

One of the things that I enjoy at Birch Hill Inn is the custom of having the guests sit down around the big table together and really get acquainted. By the way, Pat serves a full breakfast every morning.

The well-groomed cross-country ski trails start out right from the inn's property and continue over hill and through the woods. These become excellent jogging or running trails at other times of the year.

In summertime there's good swimming and a trout pond, where the fish are reproducing at such a rate that guests can bring them back to the inn to be cooked for breakfast.

I think it's wonderful that my beautiful white house has become an inn that I can share.

BIRCH HILL INN, Box 346, West Rd., Manchester, VT 05254; 802-362-2761. A 5-guestroom (all private baths) extremely comforable country-home inn, with a family cottage, 5 min. from downtown Manchester Center. Breakfast included in the cost of the room. Dinners offered to houseguests only, every night except Wed. and Sun. Open after Christmas to mid-April, and May to late Oct.; 2-night minimum preferred (be sure to make reservations). Swimming pool, xc skiing, trout fishing, and walking trails on grounds. Alpine skiing at major areas nearby as well as tennis and golf facilities; great biking. Children over 6 welcome. No pets. No credit cards. Pat and Jim Lee, Innkeepers.

Directions: From Manchester Center, where Rtes. 7, 7A, and 30 meet, take Rte. 30 north 2 mi. to Manchester West Rd. Turn left on West Rd. and continue ¾ mi. to Birch Hill Inn.

BLUEBERRY HILL
Goshen, Vermont (1973)

I first visited Tony Clark at Blueberry Hill in midsummer of 1972, when the idea of opening up an inn exclusively for cross-country skiers was just taking shape in his mind. It became a reality the following year, and, as I guess all of New England knows, Tony was an innovator in what has become a very popular winter pastime. Today, most inns in New England, or in fact anywhere in the mountains, have some kind of cross-country skiing facilities on the premises or nearby.

In the meantime, Tony has continued to look for new paths to follow. Let me put it in his words:

"As you know, we are open for skiing from December through March. But, May through October, and especially summertime here in the Green Mountains is just fabulous. We're very popular with summer and fall backpackers and walkers. Many, many of our cross-country trails are used for walking and hiking, and it's possible to use the inn as a central point for such activities or to include it on an itinerary. We use our ski trails as nature and educational paths, providing all kinds of guides to help our guests learn the names of the trees and birds."

"Actually," he said, pronouncing it as only a native-born Britisher can, "we have a lot of other summertime activities here, including a kite-flying weekend during the second week in September. There are all kinds of kite contests, and with this wonderful open field immediately across from the inn, it's ideal for such activity. We also have a Mozart festival and a chamber music festival in the offing.

"I think the biggest attraction in summer is the peace, quiet, and fresh air. These are some luxuries that we sometimes take for granted—the luxury of fresh air, clean water, and no noise pollution—which are pretty special to people who live in cities."

Blueberry Hill is very definitely family style. Everyone sits around the big dining room table, and there is one main dish for each meal, cooked in the farmhouse kitchen. This main dish is likely to be something quite unusual, depending upon the cook's gourmet proclivities.

Bedrooms are plain and simple with hot water bottles on the backs of doors and handsome patchwork quilts on the beds. It is truly like visiting a Vermont farm.

In late July, to continue the summer saga, there has been an annual cross-country footrace and Blueberry Festival. The course covers ten kilometers on the paved and gravel roads, leading the runner down through the cool, shaded heart of Goshen, up a series of hills, and back through the woods and pastures, with beautiful views of the Green Mountains. Following the race, the Blueberry Festival, open to competitors and spectators alike, features a chicken barbecue with salads, homemade breads, and blueberry baked goods. An old-time square dance wraps up the festivities.

In June, Blueberry Hill hosts the annual Vermont croquet competition, and all competitors are asked to wear whites.

"As far as the cross-country skiing season is concerned, there is a ski touring center right across the road from the inn, which has a waxing area, repair shop, and an expert staff. There are seventy-five kilometers of trails with both challenging and moderate terrain."

Blueberry Hill is an unforgettable experience, whether it's early-morning coffee in the greenhouse, a day-long ski tour, or a romantic evening of relaxation in front of a roaring fire. There is great fishing, hiking, biking, and tennis nearby and always a refreshing dip in the pond.

Reservations for winter accommodations should be made as early as possible, as the inn is often booked solid for weeks at a time in winter.

BLUEBERRY HILL, Goshen, VT 05733; 802-247-6735. An 8-guestroom (private baths) mountain inn passionately devoted to xc skiing, 8 mi. from Brandon. Modified American plan for overnight guests. Open from May thru Oct and Dec. to March. Public dining by reservation only. Closed Christmas. Swimming, fishing, hiking, nature walks, and xc skiing on grounds. Much other recreation nearby. Tony Clark, Innkeeper.

Directions: At Brandon, travel east on Rte. 73 through Forest Dale. Then follow signs to Blueberry Hill.

BROOKSIDE FARMS
Orwell, Vermont (1987)

I cannot begin to tell you how many times in the last twenty years my imagination has been inspired when I've driven by the shimmering white Ionic columns and the neo-classic Greek revival buildings of Brookside Farms. Each time I've reflected on what a beautiful country inn it would make.

Then I discovered that Brookside indeed has now become just that. I immediately made an unannounced visit, and innkeepers Joan and Murray Korda couldn't have been more gracious. Joan is a very attractive woman, and her penchant for music and art is noticeable, not only in the interior decorations of the inn but also in her conversation. Not incidentally, she is also the cook. Murray Korda is an internationally known concert violinist, and when he's not sharing the innkeeping duties with Joan, he's giving concerts throughout the world, as evidenced by numerous posters and photographs that have publicized his many appearances.

Naturally, our conversation turned to the house. "There are nineteen Ionic columns, twenty-seven feet high around the front of the house," Murray told me. "Actually, there are two houses. The first house was built in 1789, and a second was built in 1843. You can see where the two of them were joined."

Elegantly furnished guest rooms are located in the main house. The restored 1810 guest house has a guest suite on the first floor, along with its own Keeping Room and parlor, and is an excellent example of a Federal farmhouse. On the second floor are four guest rooms of assorted sizes with authentic country wallpaper and appropriate country furniture.

"When our guests arrive we welcome them with a board of cheese and crackers and fresh fruit," Joan said. "We have a single entrée every night, and our main dishes include chicken grenadine, beef stroganoff, prime roast beef, and various Hungarian dishes because Murray is Hungarian. As far as breakfast is concerned, we'll prepare whatever our guests desire."

The talk drifted to things to do in the Orwell area, which is not far from Lake Champlain. "We have our own cross-country ski trails on 300 acres here," Murray said. "Some of our guests like to ski early in the morning, so Joan keeps a great big iron kettle with hefty soups in it all winter long. We also have hot cider and hot chocolate, and there's always a fire roaring in the fireplaces."

"Much time is spent right here in the dining room, because what Murray and I enjoy the most about innkeeping is getting acquainted with our guests," Joan told me. "Murray speaks seven languages fluently, and with his knowledge of Europe and his involvement in many things, including antiques, archeology, and history, along with our extensive travels, we have a variety of things to talk about."

There are wonderful old trees, some with nine-foot diameters; Hampshire sheep and Hereford cattle graze in the pasture, and two blue herons and many Canada geese sojourn on the 26-acre pond behind the 1810 barns.

There is so much more to tell about Brookside Farms; however, my main message is that this truly elegant, artistically oriented environment offers a really memorable country-inn experience.

We are happy to welcome Brookside Farms to *Country Inns and Back Roads* for the first time.

BROOKSIDE FARMS, Hwy. 22A, Orwell, VT 05760; 802-948-2727. A 6-guestroom (some shared baths) country estate in western Vermont near Lake Champlain. Breakfast included in room rate. Dinner available to houseguests only. Open year-round. Ski trails and antique shop on grounds. The Shelburne Museum, Morgan Horse Farm, Frog Hollow Crafts Center, Sheldon Museum, and Fort Ticonderoga nearby. Children welcome. No credit cards. Joan and Murray Korda, Innkeepers.

Directions: Rte. 22A is the relatively undiscovered highway that starts near New York City. Near Granville, New York, 22A continues in Vermont on the east side of Lake Champlain.

THE GOVERNOR'S INN
Ludlow, Vermont (1987)

What a perfectly splendid mid-September day for me to visit the Governor's Inn! The roads weren't crowded, and there were sudden bursts of orange, yellow, and red amid the backdrop of greenery covering the hills and valleys.

Deedy Marble met me at the front door of the inn, and as she showed me to my guest room on the second floor, she pointed out five generations of family photographs along the staircase. My bedroom had a beautiful brass head- and footboard that had been in Deedy's family for over 100 years. The furnishings and decorations were pure Victorian, with the exception of two watercolors by artist Virginia Ann Holt, which are also found throughout the inn.

Some of the amenities include the option of a morning tray of coffee and sparkling Mimosa delivered to your room, some special Governor's Inn chocolates, and in the hallway a "butler's basket" of necessities for guests who forgot toothbrushes, toothpaste, and the like. By the way, my bed was turned down at night and my towels had been changed.

"You've missed our complimentary three o'clock tea for our houseguests," Deedy scolded me, laughingly. "But that's your own fault. It is served on our beautiful Victorian silver service. We actually have second- and third-time guests who try to get here in time for tea. It's a wonderful way to begin a country visit. It gives you a chance to meet the other guests."

Although I missed tea, I was still in ample time to join the other guests in the "front room." Deedy introduced all of us and we were soon chatting away about what a wonderful time of year it was to be in upper New England. We were then individually escorted to our tables in the

candlelit dining room by one of the turn-of-the-century-clad waitresses. Deedy, who is an artist-cum-chef, described the six-course dinner. As each course was served, the dish was again described, in much the same way it is done at the Old Rittenhouse Inn in upper Wisconsin.

Whether there are five courses or six, dinner always begins with cream cheese and the Governor's sauce (the only recipe, incidentally, not included in the inn's delightfully refreshing cookbook). I don't see how any guest could leave the inn without a jar of this sauce, which is available for purchase.

Here are a few brief hints on the menu: Appetizers include mushroom strudel or marinated fish l'orange or steak strips with horseradish cream. Some of the main dishes are Lamb Gourmet, bluefish flambé, and Village Inn Steak Diane. These are augmented by intriguing side dishes. Desserts include chocolate walnut pie and peach ice with raspberry melba sauce.

If all of these seem to be a bit unusual it's because both Deedy and Charlie (he does the wonderful breakfasts) are passionately devoted to cookery. They have attended cooking schools in France, and their skills are evident in the menu.

Another of their innovations is the gourmet picnic hampers, for which the Governor's Inn has now become rather well known.

This brief account of the Governor's Inn has not done justice to this handsomely restored and preserved Victorian mansion, built by a governor of Vermont in 1890. It is beautifully furnished with family antiques and all the appointments and decorations are done with impeccable taste. However, I did want to leave sufficient room to say that there are many qualities about the Governor's Inn that will delight both confirmed and novice inn-goers. Among these are devoted attention to detail, dedication to making certain that guests' needs are met, and, perhaps best of all, a sincere, deep-rooted desire to bring loving care to everyone.

We are delighted to welcome the Governor's Inn to *Country Inns and Back Roads* for the first time.

THE GOVERNOR'S INN, 86 Main St., Ludlow, VT 05149; 802-228-8830. An 8-guestroom (private baths) village inn in central Vermont. Modified American plan includes dinner, breakfast, and afternoon tea. Open all year. Downhill skiing at Okemo Mountain and cross-country skiing nearby. Conveniently located to enjoy all of the rich recreational, cultural, and historical attractions in central Vermont. No facilities for small children or pets. Charlie and Deedy Marble, Innkeepers.

Directions: Ludlow is conveniently reached from all of the north–south roads in Vermont. It is located just off the village green, where Rte. 100 crosses Rte. 103.

INN AT SAWMILL FARM
West Dover, Vermont (1970)

It was mid-November. The southern Vermont sky was lowering, and all around me were signs and portents of snow. I was driving north from Dalton, Massachusetts, on Route 8A to the Mount Snow area in Wilmington, Vermont. This road goes through some most interesting northern Massachusetts and southern Vermont country with many villages. I was headed toward Sawmill Farm in West Dover, Vermont, and the reports on the radio indicated that snow was, indeed, on the way. Just imagine being snowbound at Sawmill Farm! Boy, oh boy!

With Wilmington behind me, I could now see the buildings of Sawmill Farm on my left. My last turn was over the bridge, which had been reconstructed since a previous visit.

I asked Rod Williams what he would do if all the guests were snowbound. "We would try to amuse them by getting everyone out to cross-country ski," he said. "If you can walk, you can cross-country ski. It's not like downhill. We can even start off with people who have never been on skis. Then we would organize picnics on the trails. We'd keep the fire in the fireplace going bigger and better than ever, and normally we would do tea at four o'clock, but on a snowbound day we start around one."

When Rod and Ione Williams made the "big break" from the pressures of urban life, they brought their own particular talents and sensitivities to this handsome location, and it is indeed a pleasing experience. There was plenty of work to do—a dilapidated barn, a wagon shed, and other outbuildings all had to be converted into lodgings and living rooms. However, over the years, the transition has been exceptional. The textures of the barn siding, the beams, the ceilings, the floors, and the picture windows combine to create a feeling of rural elegance.

Guest rooms have been both added and redecorated, and again I was smitten with the beautiful quilted bedspreads, the bright wallpaper and white ceilings, the profusion of plants in the rooms, and all of the many books and magazines that add to their guests' enjoyment. Lodgings are also found in outbuildings, including the Cider House Studio, which has a bedroom, dressing room, bath, and living room. The king-sized bed is in an alcove facing a fireplace.

In the living room of the inn there is a superb conversation piece that perhaps symbolizes the entire inn—a handsome brass telescope mounted on a tripod, providing an intimate view of Mount Snow rising majestically to the north.

Brill Williams, Rod and Ione's son, was a teenager when the family moved to West Dover. Now, he is the chef and officially one of the owners of the inn. The menu selection and quality of the food has been praised by many national restaurant and food reviewers. The menu changes with the seasons; for example, the fall menu includes grilled marinated duck breasts, backfin crabmeat, fillet of salmon, and a rack of lamb for two. Appetizers include clams Casino, backfin crabmeat cocktail, and cold poached salmon.

With a picture-book Vermont setting like this, accommodations like these, and an almost inexhaustible supply of ideas for sumptuous dining, the idea of being snowbound at the Inn at Sawmill Farm certainly had a great deal of appeal for me.

INN AT SAWMILL FARM, Box 8, West Dover, VT 05356; 802-464-8131. A 26-guestroom country resort-inn on Rte. 100, 22 mi. from Bennington and Brattleboro. Within sight of Mt. Snow ski area. Modified American plan omits lunch. Breakfast and dinner served to travelers daily. Closed Nov. 7 thru Dec. 7. Swimming, tennis, and trout fishing on grounds. Golf, bicycles, riding, snowshoeing, alpine and xc skiing nearby. No children under 8. No pets. No credit cards. Rodney, Brill, and Ione Williams, Innkeepers.

Directions: From I-91, take Brattleboro Exit 2 and travel on Vt. Rte. 9 west to Vt. Rte. 100. Proceed north 5 mi. to inn. Or take U.S. 7 north to Bennington, then Rte. 9 east to Vt. Rte. 100 and proceed north 5 mi. to inn.

THE INN AT WEATHERSFIELD
Weathersfield, Vermont (1982)

English hoteliers and innkeepers have a wonderful phrase that describes how they take care of their guests. It is "looking after." Isn't that a wonderful expression! Somehow or other it seems to summarize succinctly what inns are really trying to do, and which some inns accomplish with considerable grace.

The Inn at Weathersfield is a case in point. Ron and Mary Louise Thorburn are very models of innkeepers who "look after" their guests exceptionally well. The inn has a great many of the readily identifiable physical attributes—an ancient building that started as a farmhouse nearly two centuries ago, a history that includes a role as part of the Underground Railroad, an exceptional and bucolic setting in the Vermont mountains, seven fireplaces, and an 18th-century brick beehive bake oven in working order.

Of course, all of these are important, but it is really Ron and Mary Louise who draw people together and provide the generous dollops of congeniality and caring that make a Weathersfield stay so enjoyable.

Please allow me to share with you a translation from Elisabeth Szgeti's article in the French magazine *La Monde*, as a result of her visit a few years ago:

"Gourmet kitchen aromas, four shaggy dogs stretched all over the carpet at the entrance, a big wooden house where Mary Louise and Ron reign. They felt too young to retire and needed the fresh excitement of new faces and the daily accomplishments of a certain sophistication.

"Mary Louise said that spring at the Weathersfield starts around the twenty-first of April, and 'we begin to see a glimmer of bulbs coming through the ground. It's the beginning of the drama, with the trees coming into early leaf and soon after we have lilacs and daffodils and tulips.'

"I have on my mantelpiece in Paris a miniature ceramic picture created by Heather Thorburn, which I received, as do all the guests at Weathersfield, as I was leaving."

Those gourmet aromas mentioned come from Mary Louise's hand, and might be her duck breast in cranberry-orange sauce or pork tenderloin with white wine and mustard, among a long list of great dishes.

The inn is constantly growing and expanding, and the most recent addition is an aerobic exercise room with two stationary bicycles, a rowing machine, and a Nordic cross-country track exerciser. There is also a slant board, exercise weights, a barre, and a sauna. "This is to satisfy our many guests who enjoy the country but also like to continue on a regular exercise program," Mary Louise said.

There are many places for quiet conversation and reading in the inn, but my favorite is a little front parlor, with a whole corner bookshelf filled with all kinds of novels and books about interests and enthusiasms that I associate with country inn innkeepers and their guests—music, art, sports, theater, history, cuisine. While I was reading Gibbons, Mary Louise came in with a cup of hot cider.

Yes, guests are certainly "looked after" at the Inn at Weathersfield.

THE INN AT WEATHERSFIELD, Route 106 (near Perkinsville), Weathersfield, VT 05151; 802-263-9217. A 17-guestroom Vermont country inn a few mi. west of I-91 and north of Springfield. European plan, with breakfast and a high English tea included in the cost of the room. Dinner also served. Closed for dinner, Sun., Mon., and Tues. (although also available on those evenings during the high season). Horseshoes, badminton, croquet, billiards, sauna, exercise room, sleigh riding on grounds. Also a natural amphitheater with music and theater offered during the summer. Many footpaths and back roads. Bicycles available. Berry and apple picking, golf, downhill skiing (Ascutney and Okemo), xc skiing, horseback riding nearby. Children under 8 years old are not conveniently accommodated. No pets. Mary Louise and Ron Thorburn, Innkeepers.

Directions: Traveling north on I-91, use Exit 7 at Springfield and follow Rte. 106. Traveling south, take Exit 8 and follow Rte. 131 to Rte. 106 and turn south. From Boston, leave I-89 and follow Rte. 103 across New Hampshire west into Vermont, where it becomes Rte. 131, and then go south on Rte. 106.

THE INN ON THE COMMON
Craftsbury Common, Vermont (1976)

"We have doubled the size of our cross-country ski trail network. We now have a trail system that will link village–to–village to the Nordic Center. There are all types of terrain—something suitable for any level and a trail system big enough so that it will take the average skier many days to explore it."

Penny and Michael Schmitt of the Inn on the Common were enthusiastically outlining some of the improvements and additions at the inn, which is very close to the Nordic Center, a major cross-country ski center. "As of last fall, we have sixty kilometers of groomed and tracked trails, and an additional fifty kilometers of trails marked for back-country touring." This from Michael.

Penny and Michael Schmitt left New York City early in the 1970s and decided to start an entirely new way of life by opening an inn in Craftsbury Common, a beautiful Vermont hill-town, north and west of St. Johnsbury. They had been summering in this section of the state for many years, so the area was most familiar.

According to their brochure (please do not hesitate to write for one), the Inn on the Common is located in a beautiful, peaceful, unspoiled New England town. Each of the three inn buildings dates from the early 19th century and has been handsomely restored. The guest rooms are filled with antiques, folk art, original art, lovely wallpapers, hooked rugs, and custom quilts in wonderful colors. A complete turn-down service is provided, including a change of those big, fluffy towels.

At dinnertime guests are seated at three oval tables and, as the result of a very pleasant pre-dinner social hour, by the time the first course is served almost everybody is acquainted.

Guests get a choice at dinner of first courses and entrées. Penny told me that she has located a great deal of locally raised food. "In addition to vegetables," she said, "we now have quail and lamb raised for us as well as pheasant. A great deal of Provimi veal is raised in Vermont. Our fish supplier brings us superbly fresh fish, ranging from blue-fin tuna to frogs' legs. Among the choices are scallops with herbs and white wine and cream, and chicken served in a spicy wine and nut sauce garnished with shrimp and tomato."

Recognizing that more and more guests are enjoying longer stays, Michael and Penny have, in recent years, provided an expanding program of outdoor recreation that includes a swimming pool, tennis court, and English croquet in summer, and cross-country skiing and other outdoor sports in the winter.

For the guests who prefer a contemplative vacation, the bookshelves are most generously stocked with best sellers and mysteries, and the

guest lounge with a fireplace is equipped with a library of films on tape. There is also a lovely garden that I have written about many times in the past.

In talking about the inn, Penny said, "People feel good about the inn and good about themselves when surrounded by beauty. Our wonderful, experienced staff backs this up with super food and attentive, caring service. The net result of all this seems to be more and happier guests than ever before, and I think that is what this business is all about. One important plus to that—Michael and I still love our work."

THE INN ON THE COMMON, Craftsbury Common, VT 05827; 802-586-9619. An 18-guestroom resort-inn in a peaceful Vermont town, 35 mi. from Montpelier. Modified American plan omits lunch. Breakfast and dinner served to houseguests only. Open 365 days a year. Swimming, tennis, croquet, xc skiing, snowshoeing on grounds. Golf, tennis, swimming, sailing, horseback riding, canoeing, fishing, xc and downhill skiing, skating, hiking, and nature walks nearby. Attended pets allowed. Michael and Penny Schmitt, Innkeepers.

Directions: From the south take I-91 to St. Johnsbury exit. Take Rte. 2 west, to Rte. 15 west, to Hardwick. Then take Rte. 14 north for 8 mi., turn right and go 3 mi. up long curving hill to inn. From Canada and points north, use Exit 26 on I-91 and follow Rte. 58W to Irasburg. Then Rte. 14 southbound 12 mi. to marked left turn, 3 mi. to inn.

THE MIDDLETOWN SPRINGS INN
Middletown Springs, Vermont (1982)

My connections with the town of Middletown Springs go back at least forty years. At that time I made frequent visits to nearby Lake Saint Catherine, and it was part of the fun to drive over the Poultney hills and to take the lovely curving road that followed the tumbling brook to this sequestered Vermont village.

The Middletown Springs Inn is located on a picturesque green in the middle of this village. The green itself has a brave Civil War laddie on top of a pedestal and an American flag on a slightly bowed flagpole. These are protected by a cannon of some indefinite years. Around the square is the church and a nice Vermont home with a porte cochere, and across the way is a Federal-period brick house. The entire town is on the National Register of Historic Places.

The inn is an 1879 Victorian mansion, built at the time when Middletown Springs was quite a thriving place, mostly because of the springs that still bubble up. At one time the town's reputation for its water rivaled that of Saratoga Springs.

After a three-year search for an inn, Steve and Jane Sax are very happy with their choice. Jane showed me into the parlor with its impressive curved wall on the left of the central hall. This leads into the library, which is a little less formal, and then on into the large center music room with its grand piano.

A handsome carved stairway to the second floor reminds me of the one at the Mainstay Inn in Cape May, New Jersey. Again, there is a center hallway with antique-furnished guest rooms on either side. Terrycloth bathrobes are provided for rooms that have shared baths.

"We brought with us our collection of antique china, glassware, pewter, clocks, and furniture," Jane told me. "Even though the inn retained many of its antiques from previous owners, there was still enough room for our own treasures, including the pictures of my great-great-great-grandparents and their grandfather clock. We added two poster beds and some antique chairs and rockers."

"Our big country kitchen is the heart of the inn," Steve said, "where all our guests find their way in the morning or evening. I am the chef and I make freshly baked bread, blueberry muffins and bubbling homemade soups. We also serve beef Victorian, baked stuffed haddock, and chicken Roquefort. Jane prepares the desserts, with rum torte and English Trifle being the house specialties. A morning favorite is our country breakfast of fruit, cereal, spiced German pancakes and locally produced Vermont maple syrup. We treat all our guests like company.

"We're always delighted to assist in planning the day's activities, arranging bike rentals and sharing our favorite meandering routes. Actu-

ally, we're located near some of the best hiking, biking, skiing, and picture-taking in New England, and there's lots of jogging and running, and cross-country or downhill skiing."

I want to make particular note of the fact that the Christmas holidays at the Middletown Springs Inn are most unusual, with sleigh rides, treasure hunts, and gifts. Each evening features the food of a different country, and on the final evening, guests are encouraged to join the innkeepers in wearing Victorian costume.

THE MIDDLETOWN SPRINGS INN, Middletown Springs, VT 05757; 802-235-2198. A 10-guestroom (5 with private bath) Victorian mansion on the green of a lovely 18th- and 19-century village. Modified American plan includes full breakfast and dinner. Other travelers served by prior reservation. Open year-round; however, call in advance for reservations. Within easy driving distance of all central Vermont summer and winter recreation. Mt. Killington, state parks, summer theater, trout fishing, hiking, xc and alpine skiing, bicycling, horseback riding, swimming, golf, tennis nearby. Not suitable for young children. No pets. Jane and Steve Sax, Innkeepers.

Directions: From Manchester Center, Vt., follow Rte. 30 to Pawlet and turn north on Rte. 133 to Middletown Springs. From Poultney, Vt., follow Rte. 140 to East Poultney and on to Middletown Springs.

The date in parenthesis in the heading represents the first year the inn appeared in the pages of Country Inns and Back Roads.

MOUNTAIN TOP INN
Chittenden, Vermont (1987)

The first time I visited Mountain Top it was an exceptionally brilliant winter's day; the sky couldn't have been bluer, and the sun on the freshly fallen snow made the road up the mountain positively dazzling. As I pulled into the parking lot in front of the inn, I could hear the sound of sleigh bells, and, sure enough, along the country road came some guests in a horse-drawn sleigh, which was later to carry me to the maple sugar house, where the inn's syrup is boiled down. Particularly in evidence were the skating rink, toboggan hill, and cross-country ski facilities, where there were dozens of skiers of all ages.

On the occasion of my second visit, I went up this very same Vermont road, and the trees, which before had been delicately mantled in snow, now formed a green, arched canopy, and the farms and meadows blended into a midsummer's idyll.

Inside Mountain Top Inn, I gazed in wonderment through the two-story staircase window at the sweeping view of a beautiful lake, where inn guests were canoeing, sailing, and swimming.

"Mount Carmel is the high peak over there," innkeeper Bill Wolfe commented. "There are hiking trails, and that is a five-hole golf course you're looking at."

"We've enlarged things considerably," Bill told me. "Cross-country skiing has really come into its own, and we have 110 kilometers of trails and state-of-the-art grooming equipment, which makes them among the finest anywhere in the world. Our ski shop is in a former barn and has snowshoe furniture and woodburning stoves. We have an excellent staff of instructors also."

Bill and I continued our tour of the inn, and I noticed how nicely the "country inn" atmosphere comes across in the guest rooms, which have

reproductions of antiques, very pleasant quilts, quilted wall-hangings, and Shaker-style rockers.

Bill told me that the horseback riding program has been very popular. "We are the only resort that I know of with riding and cross-country skiing included in our rate."

Mountain Top is a deftly orchestrated example of how a country-inn experience can also include a great deal of entertainment and enjoyment for outdoor-minded guests of all ages. With fifty guest rooms it is somewhat larger than the average New England inn included in this book; however, thanks to innkeeper Wolfe, there is a good personal rapport among the staff and the guests.

The modified American plan offers truly gargantuan menus, most of which are very hearty country fare.

Among all the helpful literature is a booklet called "Get Lost in Vermont..." with maps and many suggestions for trips to nearby historic and natural attractions. Above and beyond all the possibilities for recreation and diversion, I think the chance to walk to secluded spots where beavers have built lodges in mountain ponds helps make Mountain Top a special place.

We are happy to welcome Mountain Top to *Country Inns and Back Roads*.

MOUNTAIN TOP INN, Mountain Top Rd., Chittenden, VT 05737; 802-483-2311 or 800-445-2100. A 50-guestroom (private baths) four-season resort-inn located in the Green Mountains, between Middlebury and Rutland. Cottages and chalets nearby. Various guestroom categories. Modified American plan. Open year-round. Sailing, canoeing, fishing, swimming, horseback riding, tennis, golf, walking, hiking, xc skiing, ice skating, toboggans, horse-drawn sleigh rides, and lawn games all available at no additional cost. Many nearby historical and cultural attractions. Special attention for children. William Wolfe, Innkeeper.

Directions: Chittenden is north of Rte. 4 and east of Rte. 7. After arriving in the village, turn left at the little bridge and stay to the right of the war monument. This is Mountain Top Rd.; follow it up the mountain and to the inn.

NORTH HERO HOUSE
North Hero, Lake Champlain, Vermont (1972)

Once again I was sitting on the front porch of the North Hero House, looking east across Lake Champlain into Vermont, where Mount Mansfield seemed almost close enough to walk to. The sun was just at the right angle to reflect the beautiful blue waters of the lake. It was one of those wonderfully great, dreamy summer days, and I left the porch to walk over to the grassy area where there were very comfortable chaise lounges that invited sunning and chatting, and particularly reading. I have never seen anything that is quite as attractive in its own way as this dock area with its green grass.

In looking over the accounts of my sixteen visits to the North Hero House, I find that almost without exception they start from the perspective of my rocking on the front porch of the inn, looking out over Lake Champlain and Mount Mansfield in Vermont.

This time, however, in addition to Caroline and Roger Sorg, longtime innkeepers, and their daughter, Lynn, a new and very important principal has been added to the cast—John Apgar, the new innkeeper. John is also associated with David Sorg, the son of Roger and Caroline, at a restaurant in Randolph, New Jersey, called Old Timbers.

John was particularly generous in his praise of Lynn, who is responsible for the kitchen. Monterey chicken and roast pork with cider gravy and fresh apple fritters are a couple of the temptations.

I should explain that Roger and Caroline were on hand for the summer of 1986—and will also be at the inn during 1987.

The main house of the inn, a substantial three-story wooden frame building, was built in 1891. It sits on a slight rise overlooking the lake. The inn and the beach catch the early morning sun. The comfortable guest rooms are especially appealing to guests who appreciate traditional inn attributes, as well as modern conveniences.

Additional accommodations are available at other lakeside dwellings that have been adroitly converted into comfortable guest rooms, many directly on the water.

The North Hero House provides guests with the opportunity to enjoy many wonderful adventures nearby. It is just an hour and fifteen minutes from old Montreal, Canada; forty-five minutes from the famous Shelburne Museum, with its impressive collection of early Americana; and only a short distance from Mount Mansfield and Stowe to the east, which can be reached entirely by back roads.

For those people with boats, North Hero Island can be reached by water, as it is part of the inland waterway stretching from Key West, Florida, to the St. Lawrence Seaway.

For the second year in a row, the North Hero House will stay open through October 31, offering everyone a chance to experience Vermont's most colorful time. If you are planning to visit, make your reservations as early as possible.

NORTH HERO HOUSE, Champlain Islands, North Hero, VT 05474; 802-372-8237. A 23-guestroom New England resort-inn on North Hero Island in Lake Champlain, 35 mi. north of Burlington and 65 mi. south of Montreal. Modified American plan. Breakfast, lunch, and dinner served daily to travelers. Open from June to Oct 31. Reservations highly recommended. Swimming, fishing, boating, waterskiing, icehouse game room, sauna, bicycles, and tennis on grounds. Horseback riding and golf nearby. No pets. No credit cards. John Apgar, Innkeeper.

Directions: Travel north from Burlington on I-89; take Exit 17 (Champlain Islands) and drive north on Island Rte. 2 to North Hero. From N.Y. Thruway (87 north), take Exit 39 at Plattsburg and follow signs "Ferry to Vermont." Upon leaving ferry, turn left to Rte. 2, then left again to North Hero. Inn is 15 min. from ferry dock on Rte. 2. By water: follow sectional maps to North Hero–City Bay. Enter bay and proceed in westerly direction to North Hero House.

I do not include lodging rates in the descriptions, for the very nature of an inn means that there are lodgings of various sizes, with and without baths, in and out of season, and with plain and fancy decoration. Travelers should call ahead and inquire about the availability and rates of the many different types of rooms.

OLD NEWFANE INN
Newfane, Vermont (1981)

I've got a wonderful job, and I'd be the first to admit it. This time my wonderful job was taking me down a great road that followed a river through the Vermont green-clad mountains. From Route 11 near Stratton Mountain, I continued on Route 30 through Jamaica and Townshend, down to Newfane. This road is one of the crisscross ways of journeying through Vermont.

Townshend is worth special mention for its impressive village green and all the New England white clapboard houses and other very handsome homes.

The Old Newfane Inn is right on the corner of Route 30 and the common, next to the red brick Vermont National Bank. The entrance is on the side, and it is right across the street from the handsome Windham County Courthouse, which was moved from the top of Newfane Hill in 1825, the same year the inn was built.

In mid-July, the vines around the windows of the inn on the first floor and porch were in high profusion, as were the flowers. Befitting Eric and Gundy Weindl's European heritage, both the luncheon and dinner menus are posted outside, giving visitors a preview of the cuisine. There is an extensive menu for both meals.

I was escorted on a tour through every one of the ten meticulously decorated and furnished lodging rooms. It was like visiting a Vermont farmhouse of a hundred years ago. There were elaborate samplers and wall hangings such as I have never seen before. The second-floor rooms, at one time part of a ballroom, are light and airy, and there's a very pleasant little side balcony overlooking the green.

Speaking of the menu, Eric, who was trained as a chef in one of the best hotels in Switzerland, said, "I think we could be characterized basically as Swiss–Continental. Our maitre d' does such dishes as

chateaubriand or one of several flaming specialties at the tableside, which is always an extra treat."

"This I can tell you," Gundy said, "Eric is a very good-natured man who loves good fun, but he takes cooking very seriously and is most particular about everything on the menu, including frogs' legs, shrimp scampi, lobster, tournedos of beef, and medallions of veal. He is too modest to say this, but people drive for many, many miles just to enjoy dinner with us. You see, I'm the hostess, so I meet them all."

Dinner was served in the low-ceilinged dining room, with its mellowed beams overhead and windows along one side. The floorboards of varying widths were highly polished and there were pink tablecloths with white undercloths, candles on the table, and pistol-handled knives. The maitre d' was wearing an elegant-looking tuxedo, and the waitresses were in black uniforms trimmed with white.

I was entranced with the salad, which was very simple and served with one of the most extraordinary, but simple, dressings I have ever tasted—just my preference for salads. I've never tasted better calves' liver, served in a Tyrolean sauce, and I had the opportunity to sample the medallions of veal served with creamy mushrooms that were delicious. Everything could be cut with a fork.

Because both Eric and Gundy are highly involved throughout the day with food and dining room preparation, casual visitors cannot be accommodated for tours of the inn. If you have a reservation and find the front door locked, ring the bell and they will be delighted to show you to your room.

OLD NEWFANE INN, Court St., Newfane, VT 05345; 802-365-4427. A 10-guestroom village inn 12 mi. west of Brattleboro, on Rte. 30. European plan. Lunch and dinner served to travelers during summer. Closed for rooms on Mondays. Open mid-Dec. to first of April; May to end of Oct. Closed Thanksgiving, Mother's Day. Near many downhill ski areas, Marlboro Music Festival. Backroading, tennis, swimming nearby. No facilities for children under 7. No credit cards. Eric Weindl, Innkeeper.

Directions: From New York, follow 684 to 84 to Hartford; I-91 to Brattleboro, Exit 2. Follow Rte. 30 for 12 mi. to Newfane. From Boston, follow Rte. 2 to Greenfield. I-91 to Brattleboro, Exit 2; follow Rte. 30 to Newfane.

ROWELL'S INN
Simonsville, Vermont (1985)

"How do you make apple pie?" It was a natural question because as soon as I walked through the front door the delicious aroma of baking apples had enticed me through the downstairs hallway and the dining room, with its alternate floorboards of cherry and maple, and into the kitchen where Beth Davis was taking three more pies from the oven.

Without missing a beat, she said, "I make it with a crumb crust, and the filling is my grandmother's recipe. Maybe we can have a piece a little later on."

What an inn kitchen! It's just the kind of a place that guests cannot resist. Fortunately, Beth enjoys their company and is still able to perform all of her varied culinary tasks. There were cookies in a cookie jar, bread cooling, a jar of cinnamon sticks, a long string of pepper pods, bunches of garlic, a little sign that says "Kiss the Cook," an old cabinet with many cookbooks, a big old refrigerator with four doors and jars on the top that said "Apple butter," "Relish," and "Jam." There was everything the accomplished cook needs, within arm's length.

Meanwhile, Lee Davis came down from the second floor where he had been finishing redoing the guest rooms, and we stepped from the kitchen into the Tavern Room, which has all kinds of wonderful things on the walls and tables. There was another old-fashioned refrigerator, not with ice in it, but jampacked with books. There were dried flowers, duck decoys, a moose head, a piano, a mounted fish, all kinds of magazines, a checker game, a big copper pot for holding firewood, and a shoeshine chair. I made a mental note to ask Lee where it came from. There was a present-day cast iron stove, which was radiating heat all over this room and adjacent rooms. The Tavern also has an old-fashioned soda fountain

and a collection of syrup dispensers. There's a big tray of peanuts for shelling. Isn't it interesting that one never forgets how to shell peanuts?

I went back into the kitchen and asked Beth, "What's for dinner tonight?" She said, "We're going to start out with mushroom strudel, potato and leek soup, orange and grape salad on fresh greens with a homemade dressing, our own bread, beef tenderloin, new potatoes with dill sauce on them, broccoli and cheese—we use a Vermont cheddar. The dessert will be that apple pie with ice cream. We always have a five-course dinner."

Rowell's Inn is an authentic historic inn, built for that purpose in 1820 by Major Simons, who was the founder of the village, located at a bend in Route 11, across from Lyman Brook. This handsome red brick building, with the highly distinctive wooden porches added to the front, is on the National Register of Historic Places. The five guest rooms are furnished in the tradition of the inn's prosperous past, as are the front parlors.

Lee was very proud of the new sun room, just off the dining room and the kitchen. "Our guests will be able to enjoy sitting by the fire on a cool morning and yet feel the warmth of the sun while they enjoy coffee or, in the late afternoon, have a cup of hot chocolate or another refreshing drink. They'll be able to look out the windows and see all the natural beauty."

As I was leaving, I asked Beth about Christmas at Rowell's Inn. "Well, we start pretty early, along about the 11th or 12th of December, when our inn guests come, and the men go out and cut the trees and the women stay home and pop popcorn and string cranberries. We decorate both trees, one for the sun room and one for the living room. We don't have guests on Christmas Eve, but we do leave the Christmas decorations up through Valentine's Day at the request of our guests."

Everybody was gathered on the porch saying goodbye and I tiptoed back into the kitchen, and as quiet as a mouse I opened the cookie jar and took out one delicious sugar cookie.

ROWELL'S INN, RR 1 Box 269, Simonsville, VT, 05143; 802-875-3658. A 5-guestroom (private baths) inn in the mountains of central Vermont. Mod. American plan with 2-day minimum on weekends. Bed and break-fast also available midweek. Breakfast is included in the room tariff. Dinner is served by request to houseguests only. Open all year. Conve-nient to all the cultural, recreational, and historic attractions in the area, including, hiking, biking, trail riding, golf, tennis, fishing, theat-ers, downhill and xc skiing. Children over 6 welcome. No pets. No credit cards. Beth and Lee Davis, Innkeepers.

Directions: Rowell's Inn is between Chester and Londonderry on Rte. 11.

SHIRE INN
Chelsea, Vermont (1986)

If the word "idyllic" had not already been created, I would certainly have invented it myself just to describe this bucolic scene.

Standing on a sturdy wooden bridge immediately behind the Shire Inn, gazing down on a branch of the White River below, I caught the flash of a trout slipping through the cool, rushing waters. Some early owner of the house so appreciated this scene, he placed a bench long enough to hold eight people here on the bridge.

I had just driven through some exceptionally beautiful Vermont country, following Route 14 north from Lebanon, alongside the White River, to Chelsea. The village is listed on the National Register of Historic Places, and has two commons and several early-18th-century homes and buildings.

Built of Vermont brick in 1832 and surrounded on all sides by gardens and lawns, the Shire Inn, with its fanlight doorway and black shutters, is certainly one of the most attractive of these historic homes.

The entrance hallway is dominated by a handsome circular staircase. On one side of this hallway is a most comfortable living room with deep chairs and sofas, as well as lots and lots of books. "This is the gathering room for our guests," remarked Mary Lee Papa, who with her husband, Jim, is the innkeeper.

"We're open year around," Jim told me, "and it's a good base from which guests can explore the variety of recreational and cultural opportunities that abound up here in this area. We've got good cross-country skiing here in Chelsea—actually, right from our own backyard. There's also downhill skiing at the Sonnenberg Ski Area near Woodstock, and there's hiking and bicycling in fair weather, as well as swimming and boating in the summer, and skating in the winter on Lake Fairlee. Of course, everybody enjoys going over to Hanover, New Hampshire, where there are art galleries, theater, cinema, and many other attractions."

The six guest rooms are most attractively furnished and four of them have working fireplaces. Mary Lee referred to the one on the right side of the entranceway as "our toasty room, because the boiler is just underneath." Upstairs, there are two high-ceilinged rooms with fireplaces on the front, one with a delightful canopy bed. Each has a little sign that says, "Good night, rest well. Breakfast at 8:30." Another has a spool bed and ruffled curtains. Very pleasant country bedspreads and comforters are found in each of the guest rooms, and all the beds have triple sheets. The beautiful "pumpkin pine" floorboards have been brought back to their lovely natural finish. All the guest rooms, named after Vermont counties, have a bountiful supply of books and magazines, but each has its own distinctive quality.

Breakfasts are really almost beyond description. There are three courses, and the emphasis is on fruits of all kinds, including baked fruits, as well as all kinds of pancakes and homemade breads. There is also a cream cheese omelet, now and then, served with mint.

Dinner could include scallops in a caraway sauce, veal in vermouth sauce, chicken in a spice or curry sauce, pork chops with caraway stuffing, or fillet of sole in wine. For dessert there might be fresh blueberry pie or an amaretto mousse, chocolate-brandy cake, a grasshopper mousse, or chocolate cheese cake.

You will, as I did, have some fun getting there and after you arrive, I hope you'll agree with me that Chelsea and the Shire Inn have just the kind of "withdrawn New England" atmosphere that you hoped to find.

SHIRE INN, Chelsea, VT 05038; 802-685-3031. A 6-guestroom (2 with private bath) village inn in a beautiful central Vermont setting. Open all year with a vacation break in Nov. and Apr. Breakfast included in room rate. Evening meal available by advance reservation. The Justin Morgan horse farm, the Joseph Smith memorial, xc and downhill skiing, fishing, swimming, boating, walking, and bicycling are all available. No children under 8. No pets. No smoking. Jim and Mary Lee Papa, Innkeepers.

Directions: From I-89 use Exit 2, proceed west on Rte. 14, then northward on Rte. 110 to Chelsea. From I-91, take Exit 14 and turn left on Rte. 113 proceeding northwest to Chelsea. Both of these roads are extremely picturesque.

THREE MOUNTAIN INN
Jamaica, Vermont (1982)

I have to tell you that I am again smitten with still another daughter of Charlie and Elaine Murray. A few years ago I met Claire, when she was about fourteen and taking care of the inn on a morning when Charlie and Elaine were otherwise engaged. She showed me around the inn and told me all about what it's like to grow up in the inn business. Now, Claire is a young woman with a year in Siena, Italy, behind her and a possible future in international affairs.

Then, incredibly, here I was once again sitting on that very comfortable couch in front of that tremendously impressive huge fireplace at the Three Mountain Inn, talking with another fourteen-year-old Murray beauty. This one is Sarah, and, like Claire, she was full of news and impressions, and bubbling over with enthusiasm about things that were going on at Three Mountain Inn.

"Well, what I'm doing now is mostly serving here at the inn, but I help out in other areas. I'm a lifeguard, I'm a tour guide in the state park, and I can arrange tennis games, but I don't really play all that well yet myself. You know we're having the Volvo Tournament again this summer, which means that Jimmy Connors, Ivan Lendl, and John McEnroe will be in the vicinity," she chatted. "Would you like to see some of the things that we've been doing?"

Well, I'll confess I would have walked all the way to Manchester, Vermont, just to keep her company. We walked next door to Robinson House, which Elaine and Charlie have purchased and renovated for additional guest rooms. "The lady who owned it was an antique dealer so the house is lovely inside. Don't you agree?" I agreed.

"I get to go on antique trips, which I am very interested in," she said. "I think I've convinced my parents to let me decorate one of these guest rooms. I like pastel colors because I think that would give the room a gayer touch."

She continued, "Oh, I know something that you will like. On Christmas Eve we're going to have a Christmas party for all our guests, with tree trimming and everything. Normally, we just have our family here, but everybody thinks this will be great fun."

The main house at Three Mountain Inn was built in the 1780s. It's a small, beautifully restored Colonial inn with wide planked pine walls and floors and an original Dutch oven fireplace. It has a wonderful library as well, which is very good for long weekends. Sage Hill House, a small farmhouse across the street, is also part of the inn. With kitchen facilities, it is often used by families.

The inn's location in Jamaica, a very small mountain village, makes it just a short drive from three ski areas—Stratton, Bromley, and Magic

mountains—and also within walking distance of hiking, cross-country skiing, and ice skating.

"I hope that you'll mention the fact that we have very good jogging and running here in the mountains. I ran around the University of Virginia campus in Charlottesville when we were there on vacation, and when I graduate from Cushing Academy, I think I would like to go to college there. I like to run and I hope to go into competition next year—at least I'm going to try."

Sarah and I put our heads together over the menu, and she was glowingly complimentary about her mother's cooking, which features freshly baked breads and desserts, as well as Elaine's own salad dressing. Some menu favorites are trout amandine, scallops maison, chicken paprikash, carrot vichy soup, and butter pecan ice cream pie with hot caramel pecan topping.

Sarah was pretty proud of both her parents. "After all," she said, "Kelley, my oldest sister, and Claire and I all turned out pretty well, don't you think?"

You bet I did.

THREE MOUNTAIN INN, Rte. 30, Jamaica, VT 05343; 802-874-4140. An 18-guestroom inn (some rooms in adjacent houses) located in a pleasant village in southern Vermont. Modified American plan (rates include breakfast and dinner). Dinners also served to travelers nightly except Wed. Closed Apr. 15 to May 15; Labor Day to Sept. 10. Swimming pool on grounds. Tennis, golf, fishing, horseback riding, nature walks and hiking trails in Jamaica State Park, downhill and xc skiing, Marlboro Music Festival, Weston Playhouse, all within a short drive. No pets. No credit cards. Charles and Elaine Murray, Innkeepers.

Directions: Jamaica is located on Rte. 30, which runs across Vermont from Manchester (U.S. 7) to Brattleboro (I- 91).

THE VILLAGE INN
Landgrove, Vermont (1977)

Don Snyder was telling me about Christmastime at the Village Inn while he whipped up some of his special blueberry pancakes. "Yes," he declared, "there is a berry in every bite." Then he deftly flipped over one of the beauties on the hot grill.

"Well, you know we're really set up to have lots of children here at any time," he told me. "However, at Christmas it's particularly appropriate. The Christmas tree is decorated on Christmas Eve. All the ornaments are put on the table, and everyone has fun decorating the tree. Of course, it's a school holiday then, so we have lots of families here for

skiing, and both grown-ups and kids help decorate the tree. There are small trees available for individual guest rooms, and some of our guests have Christmas right in their own rooms. However, we have gifts under the tree, and guests can hang their own stockings. As you might imagine, on Christmas Day we serve a great big Christmas dinner at noon."

The inn is a really family affair, with Don presiding in the kitchen and Else at the front desk. Norma Quinn also helps to serve breakfast, greet guests, and do duties with Else. She tells wonderful stories. Jay and Kathy Snyder and their daughters, Kim and Heidi, who are fast growing up, are also at the inn during the summertime.

In the winter, there are lots of things to amuse guests of all ages and predilections. There is cross-country skiing, right from the inn's back door, as well as downhill skiing at several very prominent ski areas nearby. There is also paddle tennis. In summer, there is tennis on the inn's own court, pitch and putt golf, volleyball, and lots of wonderful trails to hike. The Alpine Slide at the Bromley ski area is very popular with kids of all ages.

Horse-drawn sleigh rides on the snowy roads are offered during the winter and usually start off at sunset, getting back in time for dinner. It's a nice country experience. The inn has some midweek package plans, all of which include various combinations of alpine and Nordic skiing, and skiers particularly find the hot tubs most inviting.

With all of this outdoor activity, as one might imagine, the food is a very important attraction, and among the main dishes are steak with bordelaise sauce, leg of lamb, pot roast, roast beef, chicken, and turkey. Dinner is not served on Wednesdays during the summer. Incidentally, breakfast is included in the rate in the summer, and dinner is an extra charge. In winter, guests are under the modified American plan, and no lunch is served.

I've always been intrigued by the big couch in the living room that holds at least twelve people at one time. It is also known as "the seducery." It's particularly popular with everybody during the winter.

While children find it good fun to be at the Village Inn, adult activities abound, including summer theater in nearby Weston, which is reached by a most agreeable dirt road. In 1986, they did such popular plays as *Brighton Beach Memoirs*, *You Can't Take it with You*, and *Chorus Line*.

THE VILLAGE INN, Landgrove, VT 05148; 802-824-6673. A 21-guest-room rustic resort-inn in the mountains of central Vermont, approx. 4½ mi. from Weston and Londonderry. Complimentary breakfast in summer. Modified American plan in winter. Dinner served to travelers by reservation during the summer except Wed. Open from Nov. 23 to Apr. 15; July 1 to Oct. 17. Swimming, tennis, volleyball, pitch-and-putt, paddle tennis, xc skiing, fishing on grounds. Downhill skiing, riding, indoor tennis, antiquing, backroading, Alpine Slide, golf, summer theater nearby. Children most welcome. No pets. Jay and Kathy Snyder, Innkeepers.

Directions: Coming north on I-91 take Exit 2 at Brattleboro, follow Rte. 30 to Rte. 11 and turn right. Turn left off Rte. 11 at signs for Village Inn. Bear left in village of Peru. Coming north on Rte. 7, turn east at Manchester on Rte. 11 to Peru. Turn left at signs for Village Inn. Bear left in village of Peru.

"European plan" means that rates for rooms and meals are separate. "American plan" means that meals are included in the cost of the room. "Modified American plan" means that breakfast and dinner are included in the cost of the room. The rates at some inns include a continental breakfast with the lodging.

WEST MOUNTAIN INN
Arlington, Vermont (1984)

Wes Carlson lovingly handed me a potted African violet and said, "This needs bright but never direct sunlight. It prefers temperatures from about 65 to 75 degrees and high humidity. As the air is very dry during the winter months, the violet would benefit from frequent light mistings, but never allow the water to bead up on the leaves or collect around the stems. Water it whenever the soil is dry to the touch with tepid water and a weak mixture of African violet food. Never let the pot sit in water for more than a few minutes; it will rot the roots. You can, however, to provide humidity, place the pot on pebbles with water beneath. Your violet hates drafts and loves classical music and polite conversation."

I think that Wes's advice typifies, if anything could, the real spirit at the West Mountain Inn. In the first place, guests are presented with these precious flowers as they depart. An African violet is put in each bedroom, and the guests may take them home. Is there a more appropriate symbol of hospitality?

Both Wes and Mary Ann personify the very highest spirit of innkeeping. As Mary Ann explained it to me while we were walking through the snow to see some of the animals: "I think we are all gathered together as one people living on a beautiful planet and we would like to share our part of it with other people.

"Wes likes to feel that he is involved in international peace and love, so our animals are from all over the world. There are dwarf rabbits from

the Netherlands, African pigmy goats,and Peruvian llamas. We also have assorted artifacts, including nutcrackers from Germany and Holland, a Norwegian collection of trolls, and a small African collection of crafts in our library area. We like to think of ourselves as including everyone and wanting everyone to be here."

As we walked back across the snow, I noted the wonderful view, looking right down to the Battenkill River, out through the valley, and over to the Green Mountains. Mary Ann told me more than twenty-five species of birds visit here throughout the year, and I enjoyed seeing the birds fluttering around the many bird feeders.

There is a wide variety of outside diversions on the 150 acres of meadows and hills, where wilderness trails abound. The cross-country ski trails have been extended considerably, especially with the novice skier in mind. The area is famous for its fishing, and there is canoeing on the Battenkill.

The guest rooms are in many sizes and shapes: some with outside porches, one with a working fireplace, one with a bedloft for children, two with high, pine-paneled cathedral ceilings, and all attractively and comfortably furnished. There is a room on the first floor equipped for disabled persons.

"We've named our guest rooms for Robert Frost, Norman Rockwell, and Rockwell Kent," Mary Ann told me. "These, and others, are people who lived in the area or had some significance here. We have rooms named after Governor Chittenden, Ethan and Ira Allen, and Dorothy Canfield Fisher, a wonderful authoress. We have a room with about fifty of her books. There is also a room named after Carl Ruggles, a wonderful gentleman who lived here in the fifties. He was an avant-garde composer, and not too many people played his music because it was discordant. There's a wonderful story I'll tell you later about why we named one of the rooms for Booker T. Washington."

There's more to a good inn than food, facilities, and atmosphere. The West Mountain Inn has all of these plus a highly commendable *esprit*.

WEST MOUNTAIN INN, Arlington, VT 05250; 802-375-6516. A 13-guest-room (private and shared baths) comfortable hilltop country estate with a view of the Green Mountains. Mod. American plan. Breakfast and dinner served to travelers daily; a Sun. brunch served 9 to noon. Open year-round. Swimming, canoeing, hiking, fishing, nature walks, xc ski-ing, and tobogganing on grounds. Special weekend programs from time to time; call for information. Children welcome. No pets. Mary Ann and Wes Carlson, Innkeepers.

Directions: Take Historic Rte. 7 to Arlington. Follow signs for West Mountain Inn, ½ mi. west on Rte. 313; bear left after crossing bridge.

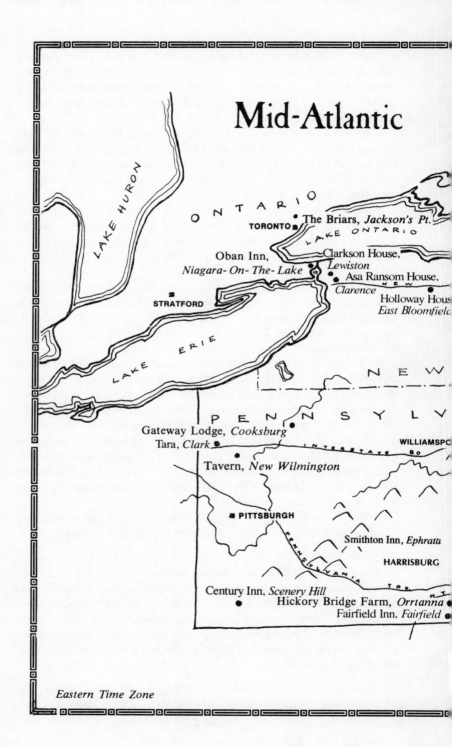

Mid-Atlantic

LAKE HURON

ONTARIO

TORONTO ● The Briars, *Jackson's Pt.*

LAKE ONTARIO

Oban Inn, *Niagara-On-The-Lake*

Clarkson House, *Lewiston*

Asa Ransom House, *Clarence*

STRATFORD

Holloway House, *East Bloomfield*

LAKE ERIE

NEW

PENNSYLV

Gateway Lodge, *Cooksburg*

Tara, *Clark*

INTERSTATE 80

WILLIAMSPO

Tavern, *New Wilmington*

■ PITTSBURGH

Smithton Inn, *Ephrata*

HARRISBURG

PENNSYLVANIA TPK.

Century Inn, *Scenery Hill*

Hickory Bridge Farm, *Orrtanna* ●

Fairfield Inn, *Fairfield* ●

Eastern Time Zone

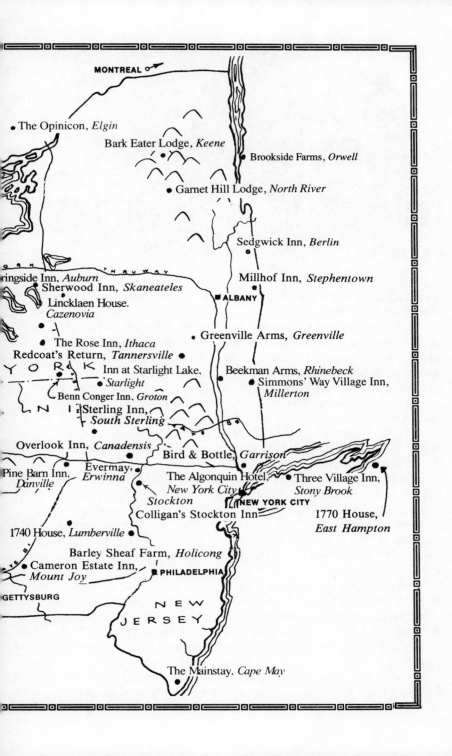

COLLIGAN'S STOCKTON INN
Stockton, New Jersey (1983)

"Yes, I know that we are very well known as the inn said to have inspired the song 'There's a Small Hotel,' but I think that a great many of our guests are returning because of all of the additional features and attractions that we continually offer throughout the year."

I was talking with Todd Drucquer as we strolled through the many dining rooms and accommodations at Colligan's Stockton Inn. He was—as is his wont—waxing very enthusiastic. "We have a cabaret every Friday in the Garden Room and we have jazz every Saturday in Colligan's Silver Dollar Bar," he said. "On every Sunday we have a brunch that would knock your eyes out."

Coming across the bridge from Pennsylvania to New Jersey, you can see the double gallery of Colligan's Stockton Inn. There are old stones, white pillars, and a mansard roof on the third floor. Evidently, there's been an accommodation here since about 1790, although the present building, or most of it, dates back about 150 years. The stone walls have the wonderful weathered look that comes with Pennsylvania–New Jersey stone.

We passed through the dining room that has the unusual murals that have been there for years. "These were painted on the plaster walls and depict the countryside as it was during the early part of the 19th century," Todd said. "As you see, we have carefully restored some of them. These murals are the very first things that attracted me when I visited for the first time."

I asked him about some of those events that made the inn desirable for revisits. "Well, for one thing we have two-night midweek getaways," he told me. "These have been augmented by the introduction of a 'romantic overnight' as well. We also make special events out of Veteran's Day weekend, Election Day, and the Fourth of July. You know my family, and you know how enthusiastic we are about things that bring families together.

"There's also the antique show and sale at Prall's Mill during August, as well as the New Hope Auto Show. We also have ethnic dining on Fridays throughout the winter months."

By this time we had visited all of the guest rooms, including those in the main inn, the Carriage House, the Wagon House, and the Federal House. Most of the guest rooms are suites with fireplaces, but they are all handsomely furnished and most comfortable.

We ended our stroll in the tavern. "This has been here for the entire life of the inn," Todd said. "It's where the local townspeople come at the end of the day, and we don't want to change it very much because we think it's lovely just the way it is. It belongs to the town, and like an Englishman's pub, it's 'their' place."

There's a good-sized menu at the inn, with at least a dozen entrées. Besides the deviled crabcakes, for which it is famous, there's also sole in parchment and something that I like very much—boneless roast strawberry duck.

With Bucks County, Pennsylvania, just over the Delaware River, it's no wonder that a great many of the inn guests return to the small hotel with the wishing well.

COLLIGAN'S STOCKTON INN, Route 29, Stockton, NJ 08559; 609-397-1250. An 11-guestroom (mostly suites) traditional inn in a Delaware River village. Lunch and dinner served every day. Open all year except Christmas Day. Weekend minimum 2-night stay; holidays, 3 nights. All of the scenic, historic, and cultural attractions of nearby Bucks County, Pa., and New Jersey are within a very short distance. No pets. Todd and Penny Drucquer, Innkeepers.

Directions: From New York City: Take New Jersey Tpke. south to Exit 10, then follow I-287 north of Somerville, exiting to Rte. 22 west. Go 2 ½ mi. and then take Rte. 202 south, past Flemington to the Delaware River. Use the last exit in New Jersey, marked "Rte. 29, Lambertville and Stockton." Go 3 mi. north on 29 to Stockton. From Philadelphia: Follow I-95 north to the Delaware River. Cross the Delaware to the first exit in New Jersey, marked "29 Trenton/Lambertville." Follow 29 north through Lambertville, approx. 17 mi. to Stockton.

THE MAINSTAY INN & COTTAGE
Cape May, New Jersey (1976)

"What is Renaissance Revival?" I inquired of Tom and Sue Carroll as we were sitting on the side porch of the Mainstay Inn having a cup of tea in the afternoon.

"It's interesting that you should mention that," remarked Sue, "because our furniture here is almost all Renaissance Revival. It's flowing to the eye with graceful curves. Walnut was used extensively during the 1870s, and there are very tall mirrors, tall headboards and wardrobes. They're a shock compared to things today. I think the fun of staying here is that you are seeing furniture that would probably never go in your house, and it can be very exciting."

While we were chatting, I noticed an occasional horse and carriage clip-clopping by the inn. "Oh, yes," Sue said, "Cape May has regular horse-and-carriage and antique auto tours of the town."

In a community that has gained a great reputation for Victorian restoration and revival, the Mainstay Inn is an outstanding example. It was built in 1856 by wealthy Southern planters as an elegant gambling club. The first operator of the club, a Mississippi showboat minstrel, employed a lady to rock on the front porch, watching for the police. If she rocked violently, the gamblers inside would quickly stash their evidence, and when the police arrived, they would be having a harmless musicale.

Today, the Mainstay is a lovely guest house in one of the most unusual remaining Victorian environments: the town of Cape May, New Jersey. Tom Carroll had pointed out to me that there are over 600 Victorian buildings in Cape May in various stages of restoration and preservation.

The drawing room has Victorian wallpaper, which can be seen in the Bradbury & Bradbury wallpaper catalog and also in some of their advertising. This is a carefully researched, authentic Victorian reproduction.

Tom and Sue have created one of the most dramatic Victorian hallways in the country, with ceiling decorations, stenciling, oriental carpeting with brass rods on the staircase, and gold cording as a rail. They've refinished floors, repaired wood, and found old brass hinges, among other things.

Upstairs, the guest rooms have such dramatic furnishings as ten-foot mirrors, ornately carved headboards, and marble-top dressers. Under some of the beds are chamber pots that roll out on wooden trays, and other beds have the original mosquito nets attached to small pulleys in the ceilings.

The only meal served at the Mainstay is breakfast, offered in warm weather on the broad veranda, and on cool mornings in the Grand Dining Room. The house tour is conducted every day at 3:30 p.m. for both

houseguests and interested visitors. Everyone is invited for tea after the tour.

Tom and Sue have renovated the beautiful old house next to the Mainstay, and now provide a total of twelve guest rooms in the two houses. They are all decorated in the Victorian manner and named for famous Americans who visited Cape May.

I'm happy to report that Tom's plans to open the Cape May lighthouse to the public will be fullfilled very shortly.

THE MAINSTAY INN & COTTAGE, 635 Columbia Ave., Cape May, NJ 08204; 609-884-8690. A 12-guestroom inn in a well-preserved Victorian village just one block from the ocean. Breakfast served to houseguests. Open every day from Apr. to Dec. 10. Open in Dec. for Christmas house tours. Boating, swimming, fishing, bicycles, riding, golf, tennis, and hiking nearby. Not suitable for small children. No pets. No credit cards; personal checks accepted. Tom and Sue Carroll, Innkeepers.

Directions: From Philadelphia take the Walt Whitman Bridge to the Atlantic City Expy. Follow the Atlantic City Expy. to exit for Garden State Pkwy., south. Go south on the Pkwy., which ends in Cape May. The Pkwy. becomes Lafayette St.; turn left at first light onto Madison. Proceed 3 blocks and turn right onto Columbia. Proceed 3 blocks to inn on right side.

A number of inns have nearby airports where private airplanes may land. An airplane symbol at the end of the inn directions indicates that there is an airport nearby. Consult inn for further information.

ALGONQUIN HOTEL
New York, New York (1971)

I have always had a great deal of fun writing about my experiences at the Hotel Algonquin in New York City.

The first time I mentioned it was in the 1971 edition, when it had come to my attention that many people following *Country Inns and Back Roads* felt the need of a place to stay in New York City. Someone recommended the Algonquin, and after a long visit, I agreed that it was the closest thing to a country inn I'd yet found in New York.

In the 1972 edition I spoke about seeing a well-known French movie actor having tea in the lobby, and about riding up in the elevator with a famous stage actress who announced in the glorious tones of a French horn, "Fifth floor, please."

Andy Anspach, the innkeeper, commented that people like actresses, diplomats, and internationally famous figures deserve a private life, and the Algonquin attempts to provide it while they are in New York. As he said, "We are terribly conservative by inclination. We've tried not to change too many things around here since the early 1920s, when it was famous as a meeting place for the Algonquin Round Table wits. People seem to enjoy our accommodations, which include oversized bathtubs and meticulous room service."

In 1974 I spoke at length about the friendliness of the staff and how guests are quite likely to be remembered even though the Algonquin is, in truth, a very busy place.

In 1975 I did a long piece on the late evening supper buffet where guests come in after the theater, the opera, the basketball or hockey games to enjoy Welsh rarebit, lobster Newburg, salad, fluffy cakes, apple pie, and ice cream.

It is possible to enjoy a delightful repast every evening of the week, including Sunday.

In 1976 I luxuriated with breakfast in bed at the Algonquin, and described the browned corned beef hash with a poached egg, warm dutch coffee cake, and above all, the superb Algonquin hot chocolate.

The story of the celebrated Algonquin Round Table is being made into a one-hour documentary for National Public Television, and a book, charmingly titled *The Ten Year Lunch,* based on the two years of research that went into that TV project, has been published. It is the eighth book published about the Algonquin over the many decades since its doors opened in 1902.

The book *Algonquin Cats* is now in paperback.

After-theater entertainment has featured any number of well-known artists, including Steve Ross, Julie Wilson, Michael Feinstein, and Margaret Whiting. It's all in the country inn tradition, even in the city!

ALGONQUIN HOTEL, 59 W. 44th St., New York, NY 10036; 212-840-6800. A 200-guestroom quiet, conservative inn in the heart of Manhattan. Convenient to business, theaters, and shopping. Breakfast, lunch served every day. Dinner is served Mon. through Sat., and a Sun. supper is served on Sun. from 5:30 p.m. The late supper buffet is offered Mon. through Sat. at 9:30 p.m. Open year-round. Very near bus, rail, and air transportation. Garage directly opposite entrance, with complimentary parking for weekend visitors arriving after 5 p.m. Fri., for minimum 2-night visit. No pets. Andrew Anspach, Innkeeper.

Directions: 44th St. is one-way from west to east; 43rd St., from east to west. Garage is accessible from either street.

"European Plan" means that rates for rooms and meals are separate. "American Plan" means that meals are included in the cost of the room. "Modified American Plan" means that breakfast and dinner are included in the cost of the room. The rates at some inns include a continental breakfast with the lodging.

ASA RANSOM HOUSE
Clarence, New York (1976)

The letter was typical of several I have received from readers who have stayed at the Asa Ransom House: "A delightful surprise; we didn't realize that such a wonderful old place existed near Buffalo. Here we were treated as personal guests. Our bedroom was really beautiful, furnished with old pieces and decorated with exquisite taste. The bathroom was one of the prettiest and cleanest I have ever seen. The dining room was crowded, but our table was kept for us until we arrived and then we sat down to one of the finest meals I have had for years. The next morning a complimentary breakfast was served because we were remaining overnight. Everything seems to be homemade and from organically grown produce. We intend to return."

As long as I am at it, let me quote still another reader's letter: "Driving down the main street of Clarence at dusk on a December day my spirit was brightened when I saw the warm glow of the lights of the inn reflected on the snow. I could see through the windows that everyone was thoroughly enjoying themselves. Upon entering I was greeted by Judy Lenz who showed me to my bedroom and gave me a bowl of fruit.

"I had a real treat on the first night of dinner. It was fillet of sole in parchment, which is a sole with mushroom stuffing and wine sauce, baked in parchment. It was most unusual.

"An evening by the fire near the Franklin stove and a good book was a change of pace (without television) and most enjoyable. While I was reading, one of the waitresses asked if she could bring me some tea or coffee."

The unique printed menu also includes the Asa Ransom News, which provides interesting historical and gastronomic observations. Be-

sides an impressive assortment of main dishes, such as fresh Boston scrod, seafood soufflé, and country inn veal, the dinner includes steaming soup from the kettle, tossed garden greens, fresh vegetables, and freshly baked bread and muffins.

The inn has two distinctly different dining rooms and four totally different guest rooms. Each has a name to suit its own personality. An 1825 cannonball double bed proudly presides in the Red Room. The larger Gold Room is outfitted with twin iron-and-brass beds with coordinated patchwork coverlets, and originally designed stenciling on the upper walls, whose theme is old-fashioned American hospitality. The Green Room has two double beds, a sitting area with a love seat, a bookcase, and a view of the herb garden.

Each of the two dining rooms has its own decorative theme, and one room is set aside for non-smokers.

The Asa Ransom House menu reflects the Lenzes' innovative flair, as well as some deep convictions about their life. For example, their religious persuasion prohibits serving pork and shellfish. As a pork substitute, "one of our favorite dishes," Bob comments, "is chicken breasts with raspberry sauce. This was discovered last winter on one of the gourmet nights held frequently during the winter season."

Breakfast for houseguests consists of fresh fruit, muffins, and a beverage, as well as Judy's special breakfast egg pie.

The Asa Ransom House is closed on Fridays and Saturdays because of the religious beliefs of Bob and Judy, who are members of the Church of God. Friday provides them with the opportunity to spend time with their families or to set off with their daughters for some point in western New York or southern Ontario to enjoy many scenic attractions. As Bob says, "We frequently end the day with a fine dinner at an old favorite or sometimes discover some new country inn."

ASA RANSOM HOUSE, Rte. 5, Clarence, NY 14031; 716-759-2315. A 4-guestroom village inn approx. 15 mi. from Buffalo near the Albright Knox Art Gallery, the Studio Arena Theatre, the Art Park, and Niagara Falls. European plan. Dinner served on Mon. through Thurs., 4:00 to 8:30 p.m.; Sun., 12:00 to 8:00 p.m. Jackets required. Lunch is available on Wed. only. Closed Fri. and Sat. Tennis, golf, fishing, swimming nearby. Limited amusement for children under 12. No pets. No credit cards. Bob and Judy Lenz, Innkeepers.

Directions: From the New York Thruway traveling west, use Exit 48A-Pembroke. Turn right to Rte. 5 and proceed 11 mi. to Clarence. Traveling east on the N.Y. Thruway, use Exit 49; turn left on Rte. 78, go 1 mi. to Rte. 5 and continue 5 1/4 mi. Coming from the east via Rte. 20, just east of Lancaster, N.Y., turn on Ransom Rd., go to end and turn left.

BARK EATER LODGE
Keene, New York (1985)

The most welcome comment I can receive about this book is, "The inn was exactly the way you wrote about it." I try to do that in every inn-stance (little play on words, there). In this case, I'm going to let Joe-Pete Wilson and Harley McDevitt describe Bark Eater themselves.

"The lodge is a modest, 150-year-old farmhouse, preserved to give the guest a true feeling of 'life back when.' We offer good home cooking, sometimes done on our wood stove, informal family-style meals, and relaxed evenings with good conversation around the fireplace. Occasionally, we schedule talks and advice on ski waxing, mountain safety, or skiing technique.

"We maintain several miles of cross-country ski trails; some to entice the beginner, others to challenge the expert. We have certified instruction, tours, and rentals or sales from our own ski shop. We also have moonlight tours, citizen races, and guided picnic trips into the wilderness.

"In summer, we switch to exploring the great outdoors on foot or horseback, mountain or rock climbing, or just strolling around nearby country roads or trails. There is great trout fishing nearby and plenty of opportunity for swimming, canoeing, sailing, tennis, golf, and other sports.

"We have twenty-seven horses and we offer picnic trips, trail rides, and lessons. Our horses range from good-looking easy trail horses to well-trained English riding horses.

"A visit during the Adirondack autumn, with its spectacular colors, is unbelievable."

Bark Eater Lodge is a year-round country inn specializing in cross-country skiing in the winter, and enjoyment of the outdoors in all seasons of the year. It is situated on sixty acres of beautiful rolling meadow with a delightful pond, in the High Peaks region of the Adirondacks.

It is homey and informal, and at the same time, eclectic. The magazines and newspapers include the *New York Times, Architectural Digest, Natural History, Backpacker,* and *Gourmet,* to name a few. There are stacks of books on a wide diversity of subjects. I've always been able to tell a great many things about an inn by the nature of the books that are available to the guests.

The kitchen is wide open for everyone to enjoy. There are a couple of old-fashioned stoves and modern ones, as well. Guests are welcome to sit down at the table and talk with Harley while dinner is being prepared. By the way, these dinners are a feature of the inn and, because of the great outdoor activities, are often very hearty. Everybody sits down about seven o'clock in the evening around the big table.

Guest rooms have rocking chairs, many old-fashioned wash stands, double and single beds, over and under bunks, wooden chests, and a wonderful old-fashioned feeling.

New guest rooms with private baths have been added in the Carriage House next to the inn. They have been most tastefully designed by Harley with a more modern flavor.

Bark Eater is on a special "inn-to-inn" program, described in a special folder, that begins with the Greenville Arms in the Catskills and continues north to Garnet Hill Lodge in the Adirondacks. All three of these inns are in *CIBR*, and full details are available at any inn.

To illustrate just how "up country" Bark Eater is, if you don't succeed in making a telephone connection on the first try, keep trying. It's a real country telephone system.

When you visit Bark Eater Lodge, bring a great sense of expectancy.

BARK EATER LODGE, Alstead Mill Rd., Keene, NY 12942; 518-576-2221. A 12-guestroom (some with shared baths) rustic mountain inn in the Adirondacks. Rates include a full country breakfast. Open all year, but check in advance during April. Dinners served. A wide variety of mountain recreation available at the inn or nearby, including High Peaks climbing, Hudson River Gorge whitewater rafting, and self-guided hiking tours. Horseback riding, swimming, tennis, golf, canoeing, sailing available nearby. Children welcome. No credit cards. Joe-Pete Wilson and Harley McDevitt, Innkeepers.

Directions: From the Northway take exit 30, follow Rte. 73 for 1 mi. past the village of Keene and turn right on Alstead Mill Rd. Inn is 1/2 mi. beyond.

BEEKMAN ARMS
Rhinebeck, New York (1967)

"I've heard lots of explanations for the name 'Rhinebeck' or 'Rynbeck,'" said Chuck LaForge, as we sat down for dinner in the low-ceilinged Tap Room of the Beekman Arms, "but recently I learned that on the same ship with Peter Stuyvesant was a German, William Beckman, who originally came here from the Rhine Valley. His son received a land grant here in 1703 from Queen Anne of England, and he named the property Rhinebeck. 'Beckman' could have been changed to 'Beck' through a clerical error in later years."

By 1769, the Beekman Arms, which started from rather humble beginnings in 1700, had increased in size to two full stories with a roomy attic that later became a ballroom. When trouble arose with the Indians in the area, the entire community would take refuge within the inn's walls.

During the Revolution, George Washington and his staff enjoyed the fare of the inn, and the window from which he watched for his couriers is still in place. Those were anxious days also for Lafayette, Schuyler, Arnold, and Hamilton, who spent many hours at the inn. In fact, over the years hundreds of men who have helped fashion the destiny of our nation partook of the inn's hospitality.

Tonight, the light from the flickering candles was reflected in the varnished tabletops and overhead beams. The walls were hung with ancient documents and prints and sabres and muskets, many of them dating back to the days of the American Revolution. This was the same place where pioneer families and early tradesmen enjoyed a roaring fire and perhaps took a pipe similar to the white clay pipes that also adorned the walls.

While earlier Colonial Beekman Arms menus probably included such items as roast beef, venison, bear steak, pheasant, quail, and turkey,

tonight chef Kathy Shepard's menu had varieties of boned roast duckling (raspberry sauce or hunter's style), fresh seafood, scrumptious veal preparations, as well as a few select recipes from other inns featured in *CIBR*. Casual but elegant country dining is the fare.

During most of the more than twenty years I have visited the Beekman Arms, Chuck has been kind enough to share news of the ongoing new developments with me. These have included the creation of a greenhouse dining area in the front of the building, the Antique Barn with thirty shops, and the growth of still another adjunct to the Beekman Arms—the Delameter House, built in 1844.

Chuck suggested that we take a stroll to the Delameter House to see all of the recent developments. "This is the Delameter courtyard," he commented, as we walked into an open-ended square area. There were buildings on three sides, including one that had been there earlier and a Federal house of batten-and-board design similar to the original Delameter House, which had been moved from another point in the village.

The guest rooms in this section are furnished with a very pleasant restraint; each has a four-poster bed and a fireplace, and there is split wood for the fire. Each of them has its own little refrigerator. There are thirty-one rooms in this complex.

"I think that these rooms add a completely new dimension to what we offer at the Beekman Arms," Chuck declared, as we walked back through the courtyard past the Carriage House, which also has some additional attractive guest rooms. "We have attempted to emulate the early designer, Alexander Jackson Davis, as much as possible."

The Beekman Arms today is more than a historic inn where thousands of guests enjoy its fascinating and authentic Colonial decor and menu; like many other country and village inns, it is still the community meeting place. Decisions great and small have been made within its walls for almost three hundred years.

BEEKMAN ARMS, Rhinebeck, NY 12572; 914-876-7077. A 12-guest-room village inn with an additional 31 rooms and 2 suites in nearby guest houses. European plan. Breakfast, lunch, and dinner served to travelers daily. Open year-round. One mile from Amtrak station at Rhinecliff (2-hr. train ride from Grand Central Station). Short drive to Hyde Park with F.D.R. home and library, Rhinebeck World War I Aerodrome, and Culinary Institute of America. Golf, tennis, swimming nearby. No amusements for young children. Chuck LaForge, Innkeeper.

Directions: From N.Y. Thruway, take Exit 19, cross Rhinecliff Bridge and pick up Rte. 199 south to Rte. 9. Proceed south on Rte. 9 to middle of village. From Taconic Pkwy., exit at Rhinebeck and follow Rte. 199 west 11 mi. to Rte. 308 into village.

BENN CONGER INN
Groton, New York (1983)

"That is the world's greatest rocker." I'll admit that I was somewhat skeptical about Mark Bloom's adamant statement. It looked like a lot of other rockers I had seen. Well, maybe it was a bit more sturdy and perhaps wider, but beyond that it looked like your everyday rocking chair. Mark and his wife, Pat, and I were seated in the library of the Benn Conger Inn. They were telling me of their adventures in finding the Benn Conger, and also how they happened to have made such a good reputation in a relatively short time. "In 1981 Mark took a job as the head chef at a very fine restaurant in Chicago's Lincoln Park. We were already married and had begun to dream of owning our own country inn. We scouted many places, and then in 1984 we saw the real estate listing for the Benn Conger Inn, came East to take a look at it, and immediately fell in love with it." This from Pat.

"We worked long and hard just to get things open and going," Mark said, "and the inn is furnished with a combination of our furniture and treasures we've found at antique shops. It's our home and we're happy to share it with our guests."

Pat continued, "Mark does all the cooking, baking, and kitchen management, and he's terrific. His food is made with the finest ingredients and prepared with real style. We think of ourselves as a European *auberge*—we specialize in the country cooking of France and Italy. Mark makes stews and roasts that taste like heaven in a bowl. Our guests tell us that our food is different, and we've developed a sizable following."

While we were chatting, a black Labrador retriever named Riff, who was about the size of a small pony, came in the library. "He's not allowed in during the dinner hour, but he is around among the guests at other times and he's very lovable. We also have a big calico cat who has become a pet of the guests, too. She's unpredictable and saucy."

The Benn Conger is a stately Greek Revival mansion, built in 1921, overlooking the village of Groton. There are eighteen acres of rolling land, great for cross-country skiing and nature walks. Extensive plantings complement the front entrance. I noticed marigolds, snapdragons, asters, primroses, roses, Canterbury bells, red salvia, purple and green basil, pansies, and Johnny-jump-ups.

The first thing a guest sees upon gaining entrance to the impressive front hallway is a sweeping, curved staircase that leads up to the second floor, where, among other things, there's a spacious window seat, perfect for reading a good book. This nook has a group of video cassettes, including some of those movies you thought you'd never be able to see again, like *Casablanca* and *The Maltese Falcon*.

The guest rooms are furnished with antique wood and brass beds, flannel sheets, warm comforters, and period furniture. "We wanted it to be comfortable, more elegant than a home but not museum quality," Pat told me.

Whether by chance or design, I think that Mark and Pat have caught the spirit of the 1920s in portions of the interior decorations of the inn. The use of period posters from various art museums, as well as some other selective original works of art, placed with care and taste, have recreated a certain ambience of the 1920s and 1930s.

"Well, so far, all you've done is to look at the 'world's greatest rocker.' Why don't you try it?" I did and they were absolutely right. It is the world's greatest rocker.

We're pleased to welcome the Benn Conger Inn back to the pages of *Country Inns and Back Roads* in 1987.

BENN CONGER INN, 206 West Cortland St., Groton, NY 13073; 607-898-5817. A 4-guestroom (private and shared baths) village mansion in a quiet community in the Finger Lakes District. Complimentary full breakfast. Dinner served nightly except Mon. Open Apr. thru Feb. Cornell and Ithaca Universities nearby, as well as golf, tennis, swimming, downhill and xc skiing, and backroading. No entertainment for children under 10. Mark and Pat Bloom, Innkeepers.

Directions: From I-81, take Exit 12 (Homer), turning south on Rte. 281 for 3 mi., and west (right) on Rte. 222. Continue 10 mi. to Groton, crossing Rte. 38 and making no turns. The Benn Conger is up the hill on the right.

BIRD AND BOTTLE INN
Garrison, New York (1972)

I had awakened to the joyous sound of the birds and had lingered under the covers at the Bird and Bottle for just a few more minutes, noting with appreciation the handsome overhead beams made of mellowed, weathered barnboard and the rest of the furnishings in my room in one of the outbuildings of the inn. Out the window I could see the high spreading branches of one of the huge old trees against the blue spring sky, with just a wisp of a white cloud.

There was much to do that day, so a few minutes later I ambled over the red brick walk to the main building of the inn for breakfast. Some birds flew overhead and one of them landed on the chimney of this yellow clapboard house that has played host to so many travelers and guests over the years. I opened the Dutch door with its heavy cast-iron hardware and stepped into the main reception area where the polished, wide pine floorboards seemed almost to reflect an oil portrait of a young lady dressed in Colonial costume.

To my right was the low-ceilinged dining room, where the previous night there had been gleaming white napery with candles and many diners seated side by side—a very romantic idea, indeed. The menu on the blackboard had announced that there was ratatouille au froid, also smoked trout, french onion soup, and then a supreme of chicken, roast duckling Bigarade, and rognon de veau moutarde. Dinners are *prix fixe*.

For breakfast, innkeeper Ira Boyar suggested the small dining room with a crackling fire against the chill of the early spring morning. There were fresh flowers on the table.

I had selected my breakfast order the night before from a menu that included all kinds of eggs, sausage, and fruit juice. I chose scrambled eggs and sausage and noticed some other houseguests were having beautiful french toast served with syrup or honey. We soon began to talk with one another because it's that kind of atmosphere.

Breakfast completed, I leaned for a moment on the window overlooking a little terrace and stream, where a light spring rain was making punctuation points in the small puddles. The trees were in early bud and I could well imagine what magic the entire scene would reveal in another two or three weeks.

Ira suggested that I might like to see more of the bedrooms in the main building, and as I walked up the stairs I realized that I was looking at the same Colonial wallpaper that I have in my own dining room. However, it seemed much more appropriate in this setting, here on the second floor where the floorboards creaked a little and were slightly aslant.

All of the bedrooms are furnished in Early American antiques and

have either a canopy or a four-poster bed. All have private baths and woodburning fireplaces. There are two double rooms and a suite which includes a cozy sitting room.

The Bird and Bottle goes back to the mid-1700s, when it was a stagecoach stop on the New York to Albany route. Its nearness to West Point undoubtedly made it a meeting place for Benedict Arnold's emissaries to the British, prior to his defection.

Today, the Colonial atmosphere is preserved with narrow clapboards (quite unusual), low ceilings, and rich paneling. The inn is beautifully decorated with many duck decoys, period wallpaper, pewter, old paintings, and many wooden accessories. It is indeed like stepping back into an earlier time.

BIRD AND BOTTLE INN, Garrison, NY 10524; 914-424-3000. A 4-guest-room country inn, rich in antiquity, located on Rte. 9, a few miles north of Peekskill, N.Y. MAP rates include both a full breakfast and dinner. From April 1 to Nov. 1 lunch and dinner served daily. From Nov. 1 to April 1 dinner served Wed. thru Sun. Sunday brunch served year-round. A short distance from Boscobel Restoration, U.S. Military Academy at West Point, and Sleepy Hollow Restorations. Ira Boyar, Innkeeper.

Directions: From NYC: cross Geo. Washington Bridge and follow Palisades Pkwy. north to Bear Mtn. Bridge. Cross bridge and travel on Rte. 9D north 4½ mi. to Rte. 403. Proceed on Rte. 403 to Rte. 9, then north 4 mi. to inn. From I-84, take Exit 13 and follow Rte. 9 south for 8 mi.

GARNET HILL LODGE
North River, New York (1980)

September in the Adirondacks! It's hard to imagine a more gorgeous place. I was having a morning cup of coffee on the balcony of my bedroom, one of the six recently remodeled guest rooms at Garnet Hill. All of them have an excellent view of Thirteenth Lake, below the ridge on which the lodge sits.

I thought of my last visit in late March, when I had joined George and Mary Heim and a group of CIBR innkeepers for a meeting and some of the last cross-country skiing of the season. Now it was early September and one of the best times to travel, when the weather is marvelous with just a slight chill in the air.

I reluctantly left my vantage point, collected my tape recorder and camera, remembering that George had told me that all of these rooms in the Log House have private baths and are finished in a nice combination of original pine paneling and wallpaper. There were also fresh flowers adding a pleasing touch.

Garnet Hill Lodge is an all-season resort-inn. The Log House was built in 1936, and it is a true rustic lodge, with a big combination living/dining room of varnished Adirondack white pine in a post-and-beam construction—the bark has been left on in many cases. Guests gather around the big fireplace for some good conversation and fun.

Even on rainy days there are things to do in this lodge, including watching movies, television, or the VCR, or playing games. And there are books and books and books. The room is big enough to accommodate several different groups comfortably.

While we were taking a short tour of the property, George and Mary expressed great pride in the new nature trail. "All the trees have been

carefully marked," Mary told me, "and one of the trails is used for skiing in the winter."

Besides walking and hiking, there is canoeing and fishing. Among the many other outdoor activities are white-water rafting trips on the upper Hudson River through a fifteen-mile gorge, which has some of the most spectacular rapids and scenery in the Adirondacks. "Fishing is another big thing here," George commented. "We have land-locked salmon and brook trout right here on the lake, and the nearby lakes and streams have lake trout, rainbows, brownies, bass, walleyes, and pickerel.

"I'd say we have two faces up here on the mountain," George said. "Our wintertime face is cross-country skiing. The Adirondacks offers some of the best snow in the East. We get over 125 inches here, and there is downhill skiing at Gore, Whiteface, and Lake Placid. Our own cross-country skiing includes forty kilometers of scenic, groomed trails, and we have a well-equippped ski shop with an experienced staff for lessons and tours."

Winter or summer, the evening meal is a big event at Garnet Hill Lodge. The menu includes a sizeable group of appetizers—paté, shrimp cocktail, and soups. Entrées might be fish, shrimps, scallop Provençale, baked stuffed shrimp, fillet of tenderloin, chicken in many different forms, or center-cut pork chops broiled and then sautéed in a savory brandied apple sauce.

I asked George about the animals one might see on a walk in the woods. "Well, we have black bear, although they are very seldom seen; however, you can see white-tailed deer, red foxes, minks, an occasional beaver, and the other day a coyote came right up on the ski trail. You don't see them very often, but they're out there."

GARNET HILL LODGE, l3th Lake Rd., North River, NY 12856; 518-251-2821. A 20-guestroom rustic resort-inn high in the Adirondacks, 32 mi. from Warrensburg. Mod. American and European plans available. Breakfast, lunch, and dinner served to travelers. Open year-round except 2 wks. in June and Nov. Swimming, boating, hiking, fishing, and xc skiing on grounds. Downhill skiing, long-distance hikes, Hudson River white-water rafting trips, and beautiful Adirondack drives nearby. The area has many museums, arts and crafts centers, and historical points. No pets. No credit cards. Taxi service provided to bus stop 30 mi. away. George and Mary Heim, Innkeepers.

Directions: From the Northway (I-87) take Exit 23 and follow Rte. 8 north 4 mi. Take left fork (Rte. 28) 22 mi. to North River. Take second left (l3th Lake Rd.) 5 mi. to lodge. For more explicit directions, write for brochure.

GREENVILLE ARMS
Greenville, New York (1975)

To me one of the most exciting things about my visits to country inns for the past twenty-two years is the spirit of innovation expressed at many inns. This is particularly true at the Greenville Arms in the northern Catskills. Besides having a family tradition of innkeeping extending at least forty years into the past, for the past few summers the inn has been hosting special painting workshops, which I'll discuss in just a moment.

A Victorian country mansion with several interestingly fashioned porches, cupolas, gables, and corners, the inn is well shaded with tall trees and beautifully landscaped with bushes and shrubs. Throughout, the atmosphere could best be described as "homey and inviting."

Another dimension to be found at the Greenville Arms is its role as a very comfortable resort-inn. Behind the main house, with its several bedrooms with private and shared baths, is the Carriage House, where there are more contemporary rooms, all with private baths. There is a large, beautiful lawn with shuffleboard, ping-pong, horseshoes, badminton, lawn bowling, and a swimming pool.

The innkeepers at Greenville Arms are two sisters, Barbara and Laura Stevens. They are carrying on the family tradition, since Greenville Arms was originally owned by their mother; their aunt and grandmother still own inns in the Catskill Mountains.

The main house at the Greenville Arms was built in 1889 and has the feeling of being almost frozen in time, with the same type of furniture, decorations, and lifestyle. There are even button switches for some of the lights. One of the most delightful things for me was the many different types of bedspreads. Off the second floor is a porch that you always wanted and never had.

Dinner is single entrée and is really typical Catskill Mountain home-cooking with lots of turkey, baked ham, roasts, and fresh vegetables from the garden.

Greenville Arms is located in a region rich in history and resplendent with natural beauty. The northern Catskill Mountains, the Hudson River, and the rural farmland in the valleys between have attracted travelers and inspired artists for generations. This is the land of Thomas Cole, Frederick Church, and the renowned Hudson River school of art.

I had the opportunity to attend for a brief time one of the art classes being conducted by Sygmund Jankowski. While I didn't have the opportunity to take any lessons, I talked to some of the students, all of whom were most enthusiastic about not only the instructor but the opportunity to take advantage of the limitless subject matter in the area and to work one-on-one with such a splendid communicator. As one student told me, "He said, 'I'll walk with you along every step of the way.' And he did. I found it fascinating."

For a special brochure with all the details about the Hudson River Valley painting workshops call either Laura or Barbara. I have seen the schedule for 1987, and also the list of the artist-instructors and, believe me, nothing would give me more pleasure than to be able to take an entire week and participate myself.

One other note: the Greenville Arms has joined with Garnet Hill Lodge and the Bark Eater Lodge, both *CIBR* inns located in the Adirondacks, in a special "inn-to-inn" program.

GREENVILLE ARMS, Greenville, NY 12083; 518- 966-5219. A 20-guest-room Victorian country inn in the foothills of the northern Catskill Mountains, 25 mi. south of Albany, 120 mi. north of New York City. Modified American plan rates include a hearty breakfast and a specially prepared single-entrée country dinner. Bed-and-breakfast rates also available. Open mid-April to mid-Nov. Pool and lawn sports on grounds. Antiquing, country auctions, historic sites, horseback riding, golf, tennis nearby. Children are welcome. Pets accommodated in nearby kennels. No credit cards. Laura and Barbara Stevens, Innkeepers.

Directions: Exit N.Y. State Thruway at 21B (Coxsackie–New Baltimore). Turn left on 9-W south 2 mi. to traffic light. Turn right on 81 west, 13 mi. to Greenville. Turn left at traffic light on 32S. You will see Greenville Arms on the right. Via Taconic Pkwy.: Exit at Ancram on Rte. 82W, over Rip Van Winkle Bridge and follow Rte. 23W to Cairo. Turn right on 32N, 9 mi. to Greenville.

LINCKLAEN HOUSE
Cazenovia, New York (1968)

If an old-time stagecoach driver were to pull up his team in front of the Lincklaen House today, he would find the hotel looking almost the same as it did in 1835, at least outwardly. The locally made brick, the fine chimneys, the broad front steps, and the columns flanking the doorway were built to last—and they have. Twenty or more stagecoaches passed through Cazenovia each day traveling over the Third Great Western Turnpike, and the snap of the drivers' whips was a familiar sound. The stages carried the mail and as many as fourteen passengers, and the Lincklaen House must have been a welcome respite from hours spent in those lumbering horse-drawn conveyances.

Guests staying at the Lincklaen House and meeting innkeeper Helen Tobin for the first time, frequently say, "Oh, I feel as if I have known you for a long time." This is because Helen has genuine warmth and consideration, and the Lincklaen House reflects this feeling. She insists on fresh flowers, crisp vegetables, hot popovers, hearty portions, lots of bath towels and, above all, a feeling of rapport with her guests.

"I try to visit with everyone while they're here," she said. "Many become good friends and stop off many times. We always get lots of Christmas cards from them.

"We have been working for the past year repainting and stenciling as many guest rooms as possible. We've also refurbished the front of the building with fresh paint. As a matter of fact, I think we look quite 'spiffy.' "

The Lincklaen House has been called one of the best examples of early 19th-century architecture in central New York State. Its Greek Revival lines are in harmony with other buildings in this college town. The inn was named after the founder of the village, and over the years, many famous guests have enjoyed its hospitality.

Cazenovia is one of the attractive towns along Route 20 in central New York State. This road, by the way, is a very interesting alternative to traveling across the state entirely on the Thruway, just a few miles to the north.

"We are getting to be a very special-event-minded community," Helen remarked. "We have the winter festival every February; the Lorenzo needlework exhibit the whole month of June; arts and crafts on our village green; plus a parade and fireworks over the 4th of July; the Lorenzo driving competition, which takes place in July; the Franklin car reunion each year in August, and our own events here at the Lincklaen House at Christmastime.

Cazenovia provides a wide variety of sports and diversions. Swimming, fishing, sailing, waterskiing, and in winter ice skating and ice fishing are available on the lake, and there is also tennis, horseback riding, and skiing nearby. A small folder outlines five lovely motor tours in the vicinity of the town, and eventually all roads lead back to the Lincklaen House for afternoon tea.

"We serve afternoon tea every day," Helen told me, "and it's the one time of the day that I make every effort to be back here to meet my guests and introduce them to each other. It's one of the nicest times of the day at the Lincklaen House, when we are all sitting around the fire or in the courtyard."

LINCKLAEN HOUSE, Cazenovia, NY 13035; 315-655-3461. A 27-guest-room village inn, 20 mi. east of Syracuse. European plan. Modified American plan upon request. Breakfast, lunch, and dinner served to travelers daily. Open year-round. Near several state parks, the Erie Canal Museum, and the Canal Trail. Tennis, golf, bicycles, alpine and xc skiing nearby. Helen Tobin, Innkeeper.

Directions: From west on NY Thruway, take Exit 34A, follow Rte. 481 south, take Exit 3E and follow Rte. 92 east to Cazenovia. From east on NY Thruway, take Exit 34 and follow Rte. 13 south to Cazenovia. From Rte. 81, take Exit 15 (Lafayette) and follow Rte. 20 east, 18 mi. to inn.

MILLHOF INN
Stephentown, New York (1979)

I was speeding across Richmond Mountain in Massachusetts headed toward Route 22 in New York State to make my annual visit to the Millhof Inn and the Tallet family.

I'd been looking forward to this twenty-mile trip from Stockbridge to Stephentown, because I knew there are always some new and exciting things to share with Ronnie and Frank, and with their three rapidly-growing-up children. Debbie has now graduated from college with a degree in hotel management and tourism and is now in the hospitality world; Lisa

is in her third year at college; and young Gregory, with whom I have toured the Millhof several times in the past, is growing like a weed and is a great help around and about the inn.

The word "millhof" really means millhouse, and this building was actually used as a sawmill for many years. Frank and Ronnie have made numerous alterations and additions, but the basic structure remains the same. It is the colorfully decorated, handcarved railings and window shutters that make it similar to many European inns I have visited.

Frank is from a French background and Ronnie was born in Yugoslavia. Many of the furnishings and decorations are from the old country. Ronnie is quite an accomplished artist and has done a number of the paintings displayed at the inn.

The European alpine theme extends throughout the inn and particularly to the lodging rooms, each one of which is individually decorated and furnished with plants, books, fresh flowers, and magazines. Frank has done almost all of the decorating and redesigning, and he also constructed the very attractive garden deck where breakfast is served in the summertime.

"Guests love our breakfasts," Ronnie said. "There is always homemade jam, oatmeal, sunflower seed home-baked bread, and, your favorite, blueberry wheat pancakes." Afternoon tea is served at the Millhof and this is especially appreciated by guests who arrive after a long drive.

The Tallets are very proud of the twin-, double-, and queen-bedded rooms and suites with fireplaces for those wanting to cuddle up on their own hearth. "They are our most popular," Ronnie said.

The Millhof has what I consider to be a most commendable policy that restricts smoking to the downstairs common area. "This seems to be sufficient for almost all of the smokers," she said.

The ever-growing and increasing gardens are a most engaging feature at the Millhof, including the rock garden by the swimming pool, where there are some gorgeous day lilies and clumps of lavender. This pool area is particularly popular with guests at the end of the day.

"We're attracting people who want a quiet place, a place to relax," is the way Ronnie summed up the pleasant evolution of the Millhof Inn. "We try to make things as comfortable and as pleasant as possible, and the result is that guests are coming for longer stays. One couple actually got married here.

"These have been wonderful years for us. Although we are quite close to Tanglewood, where the Boston Symphony plays every summer, and Williamstown, with its summer theater, many of our guests find the atmosphere of rest and relaxation very pleasing."

MILLHOF INN, Route 43, Stephentown, NY 12168; 518-733-5606. A 10-guestroom middle-European-style country inn, 14 mi. from Pittsfield and 12 mi. from Williamstown. A pleasant drive from both Tanglewood in the summer, and Jiminy Peak and Brodie Mountain in the winter. European plan. Full breakfast menu served daily. Afternoon tea served to guests. Many fine restaurants nearby. Open every day from May 26 through March 31. Swimming pool on grounds. Hiking, skiing, backroading, and all of the famous Berkshire recreational and cultural attractions nearby. No pets. Frank and Ronnie Tallet, Innkeepers.

Directions: From New York: exit the Taconic Pkwy. on Rte. 295. Travel east to Rte. 22, making a left turn and continuing north to Rte. 43. Turn east (right) on Rte. 43 toward Williamstown. The inn is 1 mi. on the left. From Boston: exit Mass. Tpke. at New Lebanon. North on Rte. 22 to Rte. 43, as above.

A number of inns have nearby airports where private airplanes may land. An airplane symbol at the end of the inn directions indicates that there is an airport nearby. Consult inn for further information.

THE REDCOAT'S RETURN
Tannersville, New York (1977)

I think it's fair to say that every inn I have written about in my books is unique. Each has its own personality and its own particular brand of hospitality. However, I have noticed certain similarities among various inns. In the case of Redcoat's Return, I am reminded of some British inns. One is the Royal Oak in Yattendon, another is the Collin House in Broadway in the Cotswolds, and still another is the Pheasant in the English Lake District.

I suggest that one of the reasons I see similarities is that Tom Wright, who with his wife, Peggy, is the innkeeper at Redcoat's Return, is a true Britisher. He was brought up in England, apprenticed at the Dorchester Hotel in London, and was at one time with the Cunard Line as a chef on the Queen Mary.

The furniture and decorations at Redcoat's, as it is familiarly known, could well be at home in many English pubs. For example, the paintings in the pub room include a bravura treatment of the Battle of Waterloo and

an oil painting of a young boy coming home with a mess of fish and a fishing pole over his shoulder. Another oil painting could well be a thatched cottage in the Cotswolds. Adding to this wonderful "hands across the sea" feeling is a family room with a solarium and a group of Hogarth prints.

For regular readers and followers of Redcoat's progress there is good news and bad news. First of all, the new dining room and deck has been very successful, and, as Peggy Wright points out, the air conditioning is certainly a blessing during the summer. The room faces west towards some beautiful sunsets, and the deck is very popular as a gathering place in the summer, and for an occasional wedding as well.

The bad news is that Rex, the Irish setter who loved to take Redcoat's guests on hikes, is no longer at the inn. However, his place has been taken by Humphrey, a Swiss mountain dog, who is learning the routes already.

There are twelve guest rooms in the inn, all with wash basins and several with private baths. "We've tried to preserve the best of what is really appropriate for the building," Tom says, "and have made a few major changes that will provide more bathrooms." These guest rooms are rather small and cozy and definitely of the country inn variety.

The Wrights' preoccupation with things artistic also includes their sign in front of the inn, on one side of which is a red-coated soldier, looking surprisingly like Tom, and on the other side, a pretty woman in a period costume, who looks surprisingly like Peggy.

The British thing includes the menu, where steak-and-kidney pie is one of the most popular items, along with prime ribs of beef, usually served on the weekends. Beef stroganoff is another hearty favorite, as is the duckling.

The inn is built at an elevation of 2,000 feet, and there's plenty of both downhill and cross-country skiing nearby, particularly at Hunter Mountain. This is the kind of countryside that creates hearty appetites.

Whenever I visit Redcoat's, I like to sit down in front of the fireplace and soak up some of the atmosphere. I also positively have to go look at my favorite painting of the Indian maiden with a headband and a coy look, wearing an Indian costume that includes knee-length stockings. "That's one of our prize possessions," Peggy says. "She's a kind of Hiawathan Betty Boop."

THE REDCOAT'S RETURN, Dale Lane, Elka Park, NY 12427; 518-589-6379. A 12-guestroom English inn approx. 4 mi. from Tannersville, N.Y., in the heart of the Catskill Mts. European plan. Lodgings include breakfast. Dinner served daily except Thurs.; no lunches served. Open from Memorial Day to Easter. Closed 1 wk. in early Nov. Please call for details. Within a short drive of several ski areas and state hiking trails. Nature walks, trout fishing, croquet, skiing, swimming, ice skating, riding, tennis nearby. No pets. Tom and Peggy Wright, Innkeepers.

Directions: From the New York Thruway, going north, use Exit 20; going south, use Exit 21. Find Rte. 23A on your map and follow it to Tannersville; turn left at traffic light onto County Rd. 16. Follow signs to Police Center, 4½ mi. Turn right on Dale Lane.

THE ROSE INN
Ithaca, New York (1986)

Perhaps it is because I am so attuned to the characteristics of Central New York State that the flat-topped cupola of the Rose Inn attracted my eye. Many 19th-century homes have such cupolas. I was driving north from Ithaca along the shore of Cayuga Lake, and there on top of a small hill was a gorgeous mansion with the easily recognizable, graceful lines of a mid-19th-century Italianate home. Innkeeper Charles Rosemann met me as I was parking the car, and together we started on a lovely tour of the inn.

About the first thing I learned is that the Rose Inn is known locally as "the house with the circular staircase."

As Charles explained, "The house is a gem of woodcraft, built of heavy timbers with large, heavy handcut doors of oak. The floors are laid with quarter-sawed oak, inlaid in parquet fashion. It was built and completed in 1851, with the exception of a center staircase that would have led to the cupola. No one capable of completing it could be found. Hundreds of feet of priceless Honduras mahogany were stored for over half a century. In 1922 a master craftsman appeared, and he worked for two years building a circular staircase of that solid mahogany, which extended from the main hall through two stories to the cupola."

The inn displays the ambience of its period. High ceilings, the warm glow of woods from indigenous American trees long gone, marble fireplaces, and period antiques provide an elegant but surprisingly comfortable setting. Sherry Rosemann said, "Telephone callers sometimes ask us what the atmosphere of the inn is like, and we tell them that we have an elegant country mansion that is at the same time intimate and relaxed. To illustrate the point, guests feel as comfortable coming down for dinner casually dressed as they do in formal attire."

Because I have a space limitation, please take my word for it that all of the guest rooms are done in the same beautiful but comfortable fashion. Several new guest rooms have been added, and all have the same high ceilings and fine millwork found throughout the inn.

Dinner is something special. Sterling silver settings and candlelight set the mood for such four-course, single-entrée dinners as rack of lamb with an herbed sauce or scampi Mediterranean, cooked in a light curry and cream sauce. For larger parties there is chateaubriand grilled over charcoals. Eclectic and ethnic meals are also available, and since dinners are served only with advance reservations, the innkeepers have a chance to create something quite different.

My visit was true to form and I was delighted. At breakfast (Sherry cooks the evening meal and Charles cooks breakfast), Charles explained, "We like to give our guests a good start, and so we have full breakfasts,

including hand-squeezed orange juice, our own blend of coffee, home-made jams and jellies, along with fresh fruits, German apple pancakes, french toast, or eggs Benedict."

There are many, many more things to share about the Rose Inn, but I think the best way for such sharing is a visit to the inn itself. It may be known as the inn with the circular staircase, but I think the second most wonderful thing is that Sherry and Charles Rosemann appeared on the scene—just the right people to maintain this beautiful building and permit those of us who love inns to enjoy its hospitality.

THE ROSE INN, 813 Auburn Rd., Rte. 34—P.O. Box 6576, Ithaca, NY 14851; 607-533-4202. A 10-guestroom (9 baths) elegant New York State mansion just a few moments from Cornell University. Breakfast included in room rate; dinner offered by advance reservation except Sun. and Mon., unless it's a holiday. Open all year. Conveniently situated to enjoy the beautiful Finger Lakes scenery and attractions, including Cayuga Lake, wineries, and college campuses. No facilities for children under 10. Arrangements can be made for pets. No smoking anywhere in the inn. Charles and Sherry Rosemann, Innkeepers.

Directions: From N.Y. State Thruway take Exit 40 and Rte. 34 south about 36 mi. The inn will be on your left before arriving in Ithaca. From I-81 use Exit 11 (Cortland) to Rte. 13 to Ithaca. Take No. Triphammer Rd. right, 7.4 mi. to inn.

THE SEDGWICK INN
Berlin, New York (1985)

There is a small but cleverly contrived booklet on each dining room table at the Sedgwick Inn. It not only contains an extensive list of the appetizers, soups, entrées, and desserts that are frequently offered, but its pages also have some extremely unique Victorian-style cartoons and some quotes from various food writers and travel authors who have found Bob and Edie Evans' establishment noteworthy.

As I have written (and they quoted me): "Mr. Currier and Mr. Ives would have loved the Sedgwick Inn. It has beckoning windows framed by wooden shutters and the traditional white clapboard walls reminiscent of homey farmhouses and buildings seen so often in Currier and Ives colored prints. Although the central part of the building was constructed in 1791 during the Colonial period, the principal architecture is Victorian."

On this particular evening in late October, Virginia Rowe, the editor of this book, and I had driven the short hour over from the Berkshires. The colors were still holding because as yet there had not been a killing frost. Berlin nestles in a valley, which has a wonderful patchwork quality, between two ranges of respectably high hills. The trim little houses looked very neat and comfortable. Many of the farmhouses had flowers in their yards as well as pumpkins and cornstalks on the porches. This was just a few days before Halloween.

Again approaching the Sedgwick Inn, I was struck by the feeling of brightness and vitality. The windows of the Coach Room Tavern revealed a scene resembling a Dickens party. The low-ceilinged room, with its antique chairs and tables, was filled with diners. The candles, flickering in their solid brass holders, created a warm, intimate glow.

The Sedgwick Inn is located on one of the main roads between New York and Montreal. The building once served as a stagecoach stop, a summer house for a prominent New York City family, and for many years had a good reputation in the area as a restaurant. Bob and Edie have added a considerable dimension to the establishment. They've created some excellent Victorian country inn guest rooms in the main house, and there is an antique shop housed in a beautiful one-room building with a historic designation. This was once used as a Civil War recruiting station and had later lives as a dentist's office and a feed store. An art gallery in an old converted carriage house displays old prints and modern paintings, as well as some of Edie's sculptures. There is also a gift shop featuring carefully selected gifts and jewelry.

On this evening the menu on the blackboard offered three different kinds of soups, including apple pumpkin, which I tried, and it was super delicious. Appetizers included Scotch eggs, Baltimore crabcakes, and

stuffed mushrooms. The choices for entrées were fillet of sole Picasso and veal Vulpera, orange shrimp tempura, chicken in plum sauce, and filet mignon. The desserts were key lime pie, apricot almond crêpes, frozen chocolate mousse pie (sinful), and a selection of coffees and teas. These are all listed in the booklet that I mentioned earlier, and the list is most impressive. The menu changes weekly, beginning on Thursday. Tables are reserved for the entire evening.

After dinner, we had a chance to see the newest bedroom in the inn, furnished in a Victorian style and featuring a lovely stenciled bedboard. It has its own private stairway leading down to the dining room.

One final note: On the last page of the little booklet, Bob and Edie display their puckish sense of humor by quoting the last words of Union Army General John Sedgwick during a battle in the Civil War. When his officers urged him to duck behind a parapet, the general ignored the warnings. "Nonsense," he declared. "They couldn't hit an elephant at this dist. . ."

THE SEDGWICK INN, Rte. 22, Berlin, NY 12022; 518-658-2334. A 6-guestroom (private baths) country inn almost midway between Tanglewood, Shaker Village, and Williamstown. European plan. Breakfast, lunch, and dinner served daily, except Mon. Open all year. Conveniently located to enjoy all of the recreational and cultural activities of the Berkshires. Motel accommodations also available. Bob and Edie Evans, Innkeepers.

Directions: The inn is located on Rte. 22 between Petersburg and Stephentown, New York.

1770 HOUSE
East Hampton, Long Island, New York (1980)

"Acquiring the 1770 House was part of a longtime dream for us," recounted Sid Perle. "We spent many months searching outer Long Island for just the right place for the ideal country inn." Sid and I were seated in the main living room of the inn, where some of the most recently acquired pieces are from the old Easthampton Post Office. They have been used very cleverly. There was one window labeled, "General Delivery." Another one for money orders now has a tiny television set that disappears completely, if necessary.

We were joined momentarily by Miriam Perle, who is the chef at the inn. She formerly ran a cooking school in Great Neck for twelve years and studied earlier at the Cordon Bleu in Paris.

The menu changes weekly and, with the exception of desserts, it is a complete meal. There are such appetizers as spaghettini with a robust fresh tomato sauce, fresh poached salmon served with three sauces, stuffed artichoke Siciliano, crabcake Edna Lewis—lump crabmeat cake sautéed in a butter and mustard dressing. The salads are different every week, as are the salad dressings.

I asked Miriam about the main dishes. "Well, as you know, we're here on the end of Long Island, where there is lots of fresh fish available. So, our entrées very frequently include stuffed fresh swordfish, lobster creole, and other fish dishes. Tonight, we also have stuffed filet mignon, rack of lamb, roast loin of pork with a lemon-garlic marinade, and your favorite, roast duck with a lingonberry glaze." She knows my great love of roast duckling and knew that she had, indeed, made a conquest.

Downstairs in the Tap Room there is a beautiful beehive fireplace, and many old trivets and other artifacts on the wall. The atmosphere is quite similar to an English pub.

"Your readers might be interested in the fact that on Thanksgiving we have hors d'oeuvres and soup in the Tap Room, then everyone goes upstairs to the main dining room for dinner, and dessert is offered in the library—but not until we have all had a walk in the village!"

The bedrooms are delightful. Several of them have canopied beds and combinations of French and American Victorian antiques, including several bedside tables with marble tops. They are all very romantic, and one in particular on the ground floor overlooking the garden struck my fancy as being an ideal honeymoon suite.

Incidentally, guests at the 1770 House can also be booked at the Mill Garth in Amagansett, just a short distance away. It has fetching rustic cottages, some of which have their own cooking conveniences.

Sid said there have been several references to my quotation from Owen Meredith, which is occasionally used on their menus:

We may live without friends, we may live without books, but civilized man cannot live without cooks.

Sid put an arm around Miriam. "I always tell them that I'm the luckiest guy in the world because I'm married to one of the world's great cooks."

1770 HOUSE, 143 Main St., East Hampton, Long Island, NY 11937; 516-324-1770. A 6-guestroom elegant village inn near the eastern end of Long Island. Open all year. Dinner served Friday through Tuesday during the summer months. During the off-summer months, dinner served Saturday only. During July and August, weekend reservations made for 4 days only and mid-week reservations for 3 days only. Convenient to many cultural and recreational diversions, including antiquing and back-roading. Not comfortable for children under 14. No pets. The Perle Family, Innkeepers.

Directions: From New York City, take the Long Island Expressway to Exit 70, and then turn south to Rte. 27 East, the main street of East Hampton. The inn is located diagonally across the street from Guild Hall.

THE SHERWOOD INN
Skaneateles, New York (1979)

Skaneateles is a pleasant village oriented to the lake of the same name, with several impressive old buildings whose integrity has been preserved, although the town has been modernized. The center of activity is undoubtedly the Sherwood Inn.

Talk about a clear day! I stood on the front steps of the Sherwood, looking as far down the lake as I could see. There were a few early-morning fishermen and, even as I watched, a couple of swimmers came to the beach, right in front of the inn. A beautifully restored 26-foot mahogany Chris Craft was moored just a few paces from the front of the inn. Known to owner Bill Eberhardt, as well as to the staff of the inn, as the "The Boat," it is one of the amenities offered at the Sherwood, and is available for rides on the lake.

The porch of the inn was ablaze with blooming plants. Tiny pots of pink begonias graced each table, and hanging purple geraniums and baskets of petunias were everywhere.

This morning I returned to the lobby to find a very unusual display of crafts, all made by craftspeople from Skaneateles and the vicinity. For example, there was a display of wooden blocks put together to form a small village. This is part of the Sherwood's continuing effort to bring area crafts and arts to the attention of the traveling public.

In one corner of the lobby, the continental breakfast for inn guests was laid out with orange juice, some tempting sweet rolls, and pots of coffee. On the piano, a print of the inn was displayed.

Many of the sixteen lodging rooms and three apartments have a view of the lake, and almost all of them were completely redecorated within the past year. A community open house was held to show off these rooms and over 350 people attended! Skaneateles is certainly proud of its inn, which is now sporting a new coat of exterior paint.

Like many other New York State hostelries, the Sherwood Inn started its life as a stagecoach tavern and, after several ups and downs, has finally achieved an even greater reputation as a village inn and vacation destination.

Christmas is very colorful and rewarding here. The town itself has more than the usual display of colored lights and wreaths, and the inn is ablaze with a joyous Christmas spirit. It so happens that the lobby lends itself very well to an unusually tall Christmas tree that, along with three others, creates a very festive setting for the many community activities and Christmas parties held at the inn. The local garden club decorated the lobby for Christmas, and the members were entertained with a high tea at the inn. During the holiday season out-of-town guests think they are in some kind of make-believe village.

A recent edition of *Travel and Leisure* featured the village of Skaneateles. The Sherwood Inn received prominent coverage, with particular attention to the inn's Federal-period antiques, oriental rugs, pegboard pine floors, and a special mention of the antique dollhouse and the fireplaces that send a warm glow into the lobby during the late fall and winter.

Skaneateles is in the heart of New York State's scenic Finger Lakes area, and the inn makes an ideal touring center for a stay of several days while visiting the many other lakes in the area, as well as the nearby vineyards and other western New York places of interest, such as Ithaca, the home of Cornell University. It is also possible to visit other *CIBR* inns in the area for lunch or dinner.

THE SHERWOOD INN, 26 West Genessee St., Skaneateles, NY 13152; 315-685-3405. A 16-guestroom village inn on the shore of Lake Skaneateles in the Finger Lakes district of New York State. Continental breakfast included in room tariff. Lunch and dinner served daily to travelers. Open every day except Christmas. Tennis, swimming, golf, and indoor winter ice skating available nearby. Near Everson Museum, Barrow Art Gallery, and William Seward House. William Eberhardt, Owner; Ellen Seymour, Innkeeper.

Directions: From New York State Thruway use Weedsport exit and follow Rte. 34 south to Auburn (6 mi.). Turn east on Rte. 20, 7 mi. to Skaneateles. From the south use Rte. 81 to Cortland, then Rte. 41 to Skaneateles, turning left on Rte. 20 for about 1 mi.

SIMMONS' WAY VILLAGE INN
Millerton, New York (1986)

"We are actually only two hours from Manhattan! Just take the Sawmill River Parkway to Route 684, then Route 22, and on up to Millerton, and here we are."

Robert and Carol Sadlon and I were seated in the Tearoom at Simmons' Way Village Inn. I had just finished a most sumptuous dinner, and we were talking about this new room, which had been completed since my last visit. "We serve afternoon tea here—inspired by the Village Inn in Lenox—and it is also a great place for guests at the inn to congregate and to have some cappuccino, a snack, or some refreshments." The windows in the Tearoom look out over the porch of the inn which, in turn, has a view of the broad lawn that sweeps down to the village street. There are some old-fashioned street lamps along the driveway. The inn sits right next to a church, sharing some gorgeous trees.

The inn, a comfortable, old majestic Victorian, is highly photographable, with a porte-cochere, a third floor, and several balconies and porches.

The inn's interior, almost completely renovated, has been done over with great *panache*.

The front doorway leads into a center hall, and on the left is a very cozy parlor with a fireplace and twin couches. In this room, as in all of the other public rooms and guest rooms, the finish has been taken down to the original wood, resulting in some most remarkable colors and hues. The Sadlons' interest in art is reflected throughout the inn with handsome prints and paintings.

Access to the guest rooms is up a twisty little paneled-oak staircase that has two stained-glass windows. In the guest rooms there are spool beds, brass beds, four-poster beds, beds with draped canopies, down pillows, plush linens, handsome wardrobes, beautifully refinished tables and chests of drawers. There are sitting areas and some fireplaces, and each room has a private bath. It is a most romantic environment with a traditional European touch. Each of the guest rooms has its own distinctive color and a wonderful light, airy feeling.

The dinner menu leads off with some uncommon starters, including Icelandic Gravlax, a sugar-cured salmon served with a mustard sauce. Main dishes include creole eggplant stuffed with shrimp and crabmeat, Cajun blackened steak, and roasted crispy duck served with strawberry-ginger sauce.

Mention has to be made of the fact that the Sadlons are also the proprietors of the Movie House, right across the street from the inn. There are actually two cinemas available: one on the first floor shows more-or-less conventional films, and a second-floor cinema offers foreign and art films. Cappuccino and light refreshments are offered in the second-floor art gallery. Actually, the Movie House is well patronized by inn guests as well as by local people. As Carol says, "We introduced cappuccino to Millerton four years ago, and our little café has become an important social endeavor in the village today."

For me one of the memorable things about the Simmons' Way Village Inn is that it is indeed a *village* inn. Millerton is a very pleasant and peaceful little community and the inn is the center of social activity there. Furthermore, it is in a perfect place for parents to make private school visits with their children, since there are at least a half-dozen private schools within a very short distance.

And all of this just two hours from Manhattan!

SIMMONS' WAY VILLAGE INN, Main St., Rte.44, Millerton, NY 12546; 518-789-6235. An 11-guestroom village inn in a pleasant rural community on the Conn./N.Y. border. Open year-round. Dinner is served Wed. thru Sun. during the winter. Sunday brunch. Starting in Apr. lunch and dinner served every day and afternoon tea on weekends. Convenient for much recreational and cultural activity, including the Sharon Playhouse, Music Mountain, Lime Rock Race Track, Rudd Pond State Park with walking trails, antiquing and shopping. Just a few miles from the mansions along the Hudson River. Robert and Carol Sadlon, Innkeepers.

Directions: From New York City take Henry Hudson Pkwy. to Sawmill River Pkwy. to Rte. 684 north and follow Rte. 22 to Millerton.

SPRINGSIDE INN
Auburn, New York (1971)

Once again the familiar red clapboards of the Springside Inn, with beautiful hanging flowers on the front porch and more hanging flowers on the little lamps flanking the graceful drive that circles the broad lawns, came into view. It occurred to me that with all of these flowers, plus those in the window boxes, in the gardens, and in the various dining rooms, this could be known as "the inn of the flowers."

I had driven across New York State on Route 20, after a short visit with Helen Tobin at the Lincklaen House in Cazenovia and Bill Eberhardt at the Sherwood Inn in Skaneateles. Nearing the center of town, I kept my eye out and turned left on Route 38, proceeding to the traffic circle and then down the west shore of Owasco Lake.

Many years ago when I was about eight years old, my father and mother drove from where we lived in Elmira, New York, to this very spot on the shore of the lake, where there was a wonderful amusement park. What a great day that was to ride the then world-famous roller coaster. The park is no longer in existence, and I must say I really haven't enjoyed roller coasters since.

Bill Dove, who said he had been keeping a weather eye cocked for me, was waiting on the porch and suggested that it would be time to have some "breakfast in a basket" fruit and homemade muffins, offered to every Springside Inn guest as a part of the room rate. "The first person down plugs in the coffee pot," he said with a smile. "Norm, you'd be surprised at how many guests send us thank-you notes for this breakfast."

Springside Inn is in the heart of New York State's Finger Lakes District. I've been visiting it for many years, and each time Bill has some more news for me about activities at the inn.

"My family and I have done a few things to improve the atmosphere and lovely grounds we have here," he told me. "We have installed

carpeting throughout all our guest rooms, giving them a sense of warmth and color. We also have followed your suggestion of leaving a couple of rooms open for viewing by our guests.

"One project still tucked away in our minds is a gazebo. This would be ideal not only for wedding ceremonies, but also for entertainment. Our dinner theater, begun at least fifteen years ago, has been increasingly popular every year. The current production is *George M*.

"I'll tell you who's been doing a wonderful job here, and that's Abe Eberhardt, my daughter Missy's husband. He is a real 'jack-of-all-trades' and is a great asset to the inn. He can fix everything from leaky faucets to refrigeration units. During the busy summer months, he works in the kitchen behind the broiler."

Our breakfast completed, we walked inside and up the red-carpeted stairway to the second floor to look at several of the guest rooms. Each of them is decorated to give a different feeling; one is in shades of pink, with a pink bedspread and matching curtains. There are friendly rocking chairs in front of the window overlooking the small pond and the lake beyond. Still another guest room has twin beds, Victorian furniture, and lamps with red bows. By way of contrast, the room on the top floor is done in shades of beige and yellow with formal valances on the windows, a Tiffany-type lamp, hooked rugs, and twin beds.

I noticed that there were small baskets of cheese and Finger Lakes wine in each of the guest rooms.

We wandered into the main dining room, the Surrey Room, and from my first visit I remember the authentic turn-of-the-century lamps that lend a pleasant feminine elegance to what otherwise might be considered a masculine room. By the way, the Sunday brunch and the family dinner, served for many years at the inn, still continue to be real culinary treats.

"You know, Norm, I'm always surprised and happy to see so many of our guests from Canada. Many of them come from Toronto and Montreal, and some have been coming back for years."

SPRINGSIDE INN, 41 West Lake Rd., Auburn, NY 13021; 315-252-7247. An 8-guestroom (some shared baths) country inn, 1 mi. south of Auburn with a view of Owasco Lake, in the heart of the historical Finger Lakes. Lodgings include continental breakfast. Open every day; however, may be closed during the month of Jan. Boating, swimming, bicycling, golf, riding, alpine and xc skiing nearby. The Dove Family, Innkeepers.

Directions: From N.Y. Thruway, take Exit 40 and follow Rte. 34 south through downtown Auburn to Rte. 38. Follow Rte. 38 south to traffic circle at lake and take 2nd exit right at west shore of Owasco Lake. Drive 1/4 mi. to inn.

THREE VILLAGE INN
Stony Brook, Long Island, New York (1972)

On a fresh August morning, I was sitting in one of the beach chairs under a tree on the terrace in front of my cottage at the Three Village Inn. Seagulls circled over the scene, which included the broad lawn leading down to the marina, with its many sailboats and cruisers, to the marshes beyond and the low cliffs on the northern shore of Long Island in the distance. A friendly robin lighted on the rustic fence and began poking his way through the entangled rambler roses.

The previous afternoon, I had taken the ferry from Bridgeport, Connecticut, to Port Jefferson, Long Island, a trip that took an hour and thirty minutes, and then followed Route 25A through one or two villages, arriving at Stony Brook just about six-thirty in the evening. Once again it

was Whitney Roberts, who has literally grown up in this inn, who greeted me with the news that his mother and father, Monda and Nelson, along with his brother, Larry, would be joining me for dinner a little later on.

The Three Village Inn is, at all odds, a Long Island institution and tradition in one of the most interesting and well-preserved towns on Long Island. The Roberts family has a background of innkeeping which began with Whitney's grandfather, who came from Rockland, Maine, and opened a restaurant called "The Maine Maid" in nearby Jericho, Long Island.

Originally, accommodations were found only in the main house of the inn, but since 1971, the year of my first visit, several cottages have been refurbished or built to accommodate guests, some of which face the yacht club and marina. These are furnished with Colonial reproductions, and some have fireplaces. Monda Roberts says that they are quite a favorite with honeymooners.

From my very first visit I realized that Nelson (he's the head chef) and Monda Roberts have placed great emphasis on the food. They are very particular about some things, including not using foil for baked potatoes, and baking them in rotation through the evening. Vegetables are fresh whenever they are available. The menu is quite extensive and includes a great deal of beef, pork, veal, and lamb, as well as the fresh seafood. The extra touch of serving sherbet with the main meal is something I have always enjoyed. Desserts include such things as apple crisp, homemade cakes, indian pudding, and delicious fruit pies and tarts. They are all made in the inn's kitchen.

In addition to walking along the sandy beach behind the inn and watching the boats from the marina, there are many things to do on the north shore of Long Island, which is rich in Colonial history. There's quite a gathering at twelve o'clock noon each day at the Stony Brook post office where an enormous carved wooden eagle with a twenty-foot wingspread slowly flaps its wings.

"In the off-season we have a lot of people from Manhattan come out for a restful weekend, because everyone is working at such a pace these days," Monda told me. "During the week visitors to SUNY at Stony Brook are frequent guests. By the way, it is possible to come from Kennedy Airport to the Three Village Inn by limousine for a relatively reasonable rate. We can make arrangements." The inn is about sixty miles from New York City.

Nelson and Monda Roberts and their sons have been at the Three Village Inn since 1946, and since 1978 they have been the innkeeper/owners. It's given me a great deal of pleasure to be visiting it since 1971.

THREE VILLAGE INN, 150 Main St., Stony Brook, L.I., NY 11790; 516-751-0555. A 9-room village inn with 23 adjacent cottage motel accommodations, 5 mi. from Port Jefferson, on Long Island's historic north shore. European plan. Lunch and dinner served to travelers daily. Closed Christmas. Near the museums of Stony Brook. Golf, swimming, and boating nearby. Special attention given to handicapped persons. No pets. Nelson and Monda Roberts, Innkeepers.

Directions: From L.I. Expressway, take Exit 62 and travel north on Nichols Rd. to Rte. 25A. Turn left on Rte. 25A and proceed to next light. Turn right onto Main St. and travel straight ahead to inn. Available from New England via L.I. ferries from Bridgeport during the summer. Ferry reservations advisable. (N.Y.: 516-473-0286; Conn.: 203-367-8571.)

THE CLARKSON HOUSE RESTAURANT
Lewiston, New York (1973)

Just a few minutes from Niagara Falls, the Clarkson House is very popular with regular diners who live as far away as Rochester and Toronto. Roast prime ribs of beef, New York strip sirloin, live Maine lobsters, baked white fish, fabulous baked potatoes, cherries Jubilee, Baked Alaska, and a puff pastry stuffed with ice cream and topped with hot fudge sauce are some of the menu treats to consider. Special children's items are available.

On the walls of the dining room there is a collection of tools and gadgets used more than one hundred years ago. "They haven't discovered the use for some of them!" said Marilyn Clarkson. There are old-fashioned kerosene lamps on the tables, and the walls have several good paintings interspersed with wall lamps.

Of great interest is the lobster tank that holds up to 200 lobsters in artificial sea water.

THE CLARKSON HOUSE RESTAURANT, 810 Center St., Lewiston, NY 14092; 716-754-4544. A country restaurant, 7 mi. from Niagara Falls and Olde Fort Niagara. No lodgings. Dinner served daily except Mon. Closed Christmas. Bob and Marilyn Clarkson, Innkeepers.

Directions: From I-190, exit at Lewiston and follow Rte. 104E for 1½ mi. Turn right on Rte. 18F and travel 2 blocks west to restaurant.

Favorite Back Roads

Our very favorite back road is one that we have shared with many, many guests. The destination is a small historic village nestled in the Helderberg Mountains. The eleven-mile drive is truly scenic, with lovely Catskill Mountain views all the way. The village itself was once a prosperous milling community. The beautiful homes and churches are a true find for anyone with an interest in 18th- or 19th-century architecture. My favorite reason for visiting the village is the State Preserve, located just at the end of town. The Preserve is like a well-kept secret! There are trails to walk leading to a quiet, peaceful lake, and an absolutely gorgeous waterfall that's perfect for walking under and up in the summertime! We like to direct people on alternate routes going and returning. Both routes offer antique shops and country stores that shouldn't be missed. One country store boasts an inventory of over 1,000 items—anything anyone could possibly want from fresh cut flowers to new snow tires!

Barbara and Laura Stevens
Greenville Arms
Greenville, New York

THE HOLLOWAY HOUSE RESTAURANT
East Bloomfield, New York (1976)

Doreen Wayne's letter was most welcome and filled with interesting news. "It's hard to believe that this is our twenty-fifth year at the Holloway House. What a lot has happened in that time. Our children have grown up and married, and we have all worked hard at maintaining and improving Holloway House.

"We are still doing all the things that are our specialties—Steve's wife, Dawn, is baking our Sally Lunn bread and rolls and pies; the summer Friday night buffet is popular and we've increased the number of our Sunday guests by offering a variety of lighter, full-course dinners."

Other entrées at the Holloway House include chicken, ham, lamb, steaks, scallops, flounder, and prime rib on a Saturday evening.

Holloway House is a real family adventure.

THE HOLLOWAY HOUSE RESTAURANT, Rtes. 5 & 20, East Bloomfield, NY 14443; 716-657-7120. A country restaurant 8 mi. west of Canandaigua, N.Y. No lodgings. Lunch served daily 12 to 2 p.m.; dinner—5:30 to 8:30 p.m., Sunday—12 to 7:30 p.m. Closed Mon. Open April 1 thru Thanksgiving. Sonnenberg Gardens, golf courses, and Finger Lake Racetrack nearby. Fred, Doreen, and Mildred Wayne, Innkeepers.

Directions: From N.Y. State Thruway, take Exit 45. Follow Rte. 96S 3 mi. to Victor, N.Y. At the third traffic light go south on Maple Ave., 5 mi. to Holcomb. Turn right at light and then take second left to Rte. 5 and 20.

BARLEY SHEAF FARM
Holicong, Pennsylvania (1982)

Ann Mills told me that I should not miss the pair of Canada geese who herd their four goslings in and out of the pond every morning. "The mother and father arrive every spring and stay long enough to produce the eggs and guide the family, and then a few weeks later they all fly away. The parents come back again every year."

Rather than disturb them, I sat on the terrace of Barley Sheaf Farm looking down across the lawns over the old stone fence, bordered by gorgeous spring flowers and covered with vines, into what could best be described as the next lower level of lawn, where the geese, the pond, and the swimming pool were.

Earlier that morning, lying abed in my room, which had been fashioned out of one of the original outbuildings of the farm, I became aware of the fact that Barley Sheaf was a series of foregrounds and backgrounds. For example, on the walls and window sills beside my brass bed there were several country artifacts. Then out of one of the windows, I could look over the red brick walks and farm fence in the foreground across the fields to the line of trees in the background. The

other window provided a wonderful view of the old barn on the property. This handsome building, which saw service on this property for most of the 19th century, if not longer, has the recognizable earmarks of an early Pennsylvania antiquity. The stone pillars and walls support the second and third floors, constructed of long plank siding. Meanwhile, the sounds of the mourning doves and busy birds filled the Bucks County morning air with their anticipation of another busy day.

Located in the heart of Bucks County, north of Philadelphia, Barley Sheaf Farm has been designated a National Historic Site; the original part of the farm dates back to 1740. There are chickens and horned Dorsets on the property, and the eggs that are eaten for breakfast are often straight from the nest. There are also beehives, and the wildflower honey they yield is often taken home by the guests. Almost everything comes from the farm and the bread is baked fresh every day.

The emphasis of Barley Sheaf Farm is more on hospitality than on farming. The living rooms and reception areas are adorned with impressive Early American oils and prints, and there's a decided interest by all the Mills family in Early American antiques.

Guest rooms indicate a continuous labor of love, as country antiques abound and personal touches, such as the international doll collection in one of the bedrooms, provide a homey feeling. Each room has its own distinct character and flavor; one has a mahogany sleigh bed with a Hitchcock dresser and still another has an antique iron bed with a very handsome quilt. There's an antique brass bed and a fireplace in the master bedroom suite, with a lovely view of the terrace.

The emphasis of Barley Sheaf Farm is more on knowledgeable hospitality than on farming. The living rooms and reception areas are adorned with impressive Early American oils and prints, and there's a decided interest by all the Mills family in Early American antiques.

Plans are afoot to put aside a corner of the old barn for antiques and local artwork to be enjoyed and purchased by guests.

Now, what about my Canada geese? I hadn't seen them yet. Could they have indeed flown off on the very morning of my arrival? Ah, I could now see a long graceful neck among the grasses along the edge of the pond and, sure enough, a four-gosling flotilla was heading out across the placid waters. Whatever else might happen today, the geese would be at Barley Sheaf Farm.

BARLEY SHEAF FARM, Box 10, Holicong, PA 18928; 215-794-5104. A 9-guestroom bed-and-breakfast inn, 8 mi. from Doylestown and New Hope, Pa. A full breakfast is the only meal served. Open Valentine's Day thru weekend prior to Christmas; weekends only mid-Jan. to mid-Feb. Minimum 2-night stay on weekends; 3-night minimum on holiday weekends. Near Delaware River, Bucks County Playhouse, George Washington's Crossing. Croquet, badminton, swimming pool, farm animals on grounds. Tennis, boating, canoeing, and horseback riding nearby. Near all of the natural and historical attractions of Bucks County, Pa. Recommended for children over 8. No credit cards. Don and Ann Mills, and Don Mills, Jr., Innkeepers.

Directions: Barley Sheaf Farm is on Rte. 202 between Doylestown and Lahaska.

CAMERON ESTATE INN
Mount Joy, Pennsylvania (1982)

Betty Groff was telling me about the history of the Donegal Presbyterian Church, which adjoins the Cameron Estate Inn property. We had been wandering around the parklike grounds of the inn and quite naturally gravitated toward this historic spot.

"Founded by Irish settlers prior to 1721, this is the church with the famous Witness Tree. On a Sunday morning in September, 1777, an express rider came to the church with the news that the British Army under Lord Howe had left New York to invade Pennsylvania. Challenged to show proof of their patriotism, they joined hands around the historic tree and declared their loyalty to the new cause of liberty and to the founding of a new nation."

As we walked beside a woodland stream, she pointed out the many trout darting about in it. "We stock this stream with trout, which our guests may fish for," she said. Standing for a moment on an old stone bridge, she continued the narrative. "As you know, Abe and I live right here in Mount Joy and we've been operating the Groff Farm Restaurant for quite a few years. But we've always wanted to own an inn and we had our envious eye for a long time on this estate."

Agreeing to meet for dinner later on, Betty and I separated at the front door of the inn, a most impressive red brick mansion, built in 1805, with attractive dormer windows on the third floor. I speculated mentally that the broad veranda running around three sides of the inn probably had been added later in the 19th century.

Stepping inside, I found the interior to be exactly what one would have expected in a mansion: large living rooms, a library, generous-sized bedrooms, some with canopy beds and a great many with fireplaces. There are many oriental rugs and period furnishings chosen by Abe and Betty to define the historical significance of the inn. These are fitting complements to the fine paneling and marble embellishments.

Dinner that evening in the main dining room was another baronial experience, with excellent service, delicate china, and fine silverware against pristine napery. The menu included roast Long Island duckling with a mandarin orange sauce; chicken sauté "Simon Cameron" served with ham and complemented by a wine-and-cheese sauce, and white asparagus; and a succulent Steak Diane. These are an interesting contrast to the family-style dinners offered at nearby Groff's Farm Restaurant, which specializes in Pennsylvania Dutch food. Inn guests also eat there.

Betty Groff is the author of two best-selling cookbooks: *Good Earth Country Cooking* and *Betty Groff's Country Goodness Cookbook*. She's also been seen on many TV programs and featured in magazine articles.

CAMERON ESTATE INN, R.D. #1, Box 305, Donegal Springs Rd., Mount Joy, PA 17552; 717-653-1773. An 18-guestroom (16 with private baths) elegant inn in a former mansion, 4½ mi. from Mt. Joy and Elizabethtown. Complimentary continental breakfast. Lunch and dinner served every day except Sun. and Christmas. Open year-round. Convenient to all of the attractions in the Pennsylvania Dutch Amish country, as well as the Hershey and Lancaster museums, art galleries, crafts shops, and theaters; halfway between Gettysburg and Valley Forge. No children under 12. No pets. Abram and Betty Groff, Innkeepers.

Directions: The inn is situated in the heart of the triangle formed by Harrisburg, York, and Lancaster. Traveling west on Pennsylvania Tpke. take Exit 21. Follow Rte. 222 S to Rte. 30 W to Rte. 283 W. Follow Rte. 283 W to Rte. 230 (the first Mt. Joy exit). Follow Rte. 230 through Mt. Joy to the 4th traffic light. Turn left onto Angle St. At first crossroads, turn right onto Donegal Springs Rd. Go to the stop sign. Turn left onto Colebrook Rd. Go just a short distance over a small bridge. Turn right, back onto Donegal Springs Rd. Follow signs to inn—about ½ mi. on the right. Traveling east on the Pa. Tpke. take Rte. 72 at Lebanon Exit to the Square in Manheim. Turn right on W. High St. This becomes the Manheim—Mt. Joy Rd. Follow directly into Mt. Joy. At the first traffic light, turn right onto Main St. Follow Main St. to the next traffic light. At light turn left onto Angle St. Follow above directions from Angle St.

CENTURY INN
Scenery Hill, Pennsylvania (1972)

"So this is a joggling board," I observed. "Yes," responded Skip Harrington, "we've had it here for a number of years and the guests really like it."

Skip, who is really Gordon Harrington, Jr., and his wife, Megin, and I were sitting on this great long, suspended board that "joggles," and that's all I'm prepared to say about it. "It's been tempering for at least seventy-five years," Skip said. "You just sit on it and it goes up and down."

Pointing to a magnificent black locust tree, he said, "Lafayette and Andrew Jackson probably passed under the branches of that tree. The Century Inn was built before 1794, and is the oldest continuously operating tavern on the National Pike, most of which is today's U.S. 40. Consequently, the inn has played an important role in the history of southwestern Pennsylvania. Lafayette stopped here on May 23, 1825, and Jackson was a guest twice, once on the way to his inauguration as President of the United States.

The inn remains what it has been for so many years: the pride of the community and a place sought out by true lovers of country inns. They've been coming for many years to enjoy stuffed pork chops, roast turkey, seafood, whipped potatoes, sweet potatoes, absolutely scrumptious cole slaw, and homemade pies.

As many times as I have visited the inn I always delight in visiting Room 5, which will probably never be occupied because it is jampacked with dolls of all sizes and descriptions.

Guests stopping at the inn today are attracted as much by the vast array of antiques as they are by the bill of fare. All of this restoration was started by Skip's mother and father, Gordon and Mary Harrington, who purchased the inn in 1945, and restored and furnished it with rare and valuable antiques collected during their lifetime.

I had arrived at high noon on a beautiful warm September day. There were generous flowers in the front of the inn and large potted geraniums interspersed with rocking chairs and benches on the porch.

The room on the right, off the main hall, has the Whiskey Rebellion flag, just as it was during the time of my first visit many years ago, when I met Gordon and Mary Harrington. We talked all through dinner and far into the night of the things that inn-seekers enjoy so much: history, music, art, and the lovely countryside.

"Let's go down the street and look at our new shop," Megin said. "There are twenty-three little shops in Scenery Hill, and we are gaining a wonderful reputation among people who like to have a personal shopping experience." Well, walk we did, and when I stepped into "It's Always

Christmas," the name of Megin's shop, I realized I was in a place where Christmas never ends. It has all kinds of Christmas everythings, including a Christmas tree hung with miniature dolls, a corner cupboard with more of the same, still another tree decorated differently, toys, paintings of ducks, and dozens of things one can mix with Christmas. Each of the little rooms of the shop, which is a former house, have been decorated differently.

After a chance to see a few of the other shops, we walked back up the street, returning to the inn to enjoy lunch in the Keeping Room, with its huge fireplace and truly astonishing collection of old tools and artifacts decorating the mantel. It's a cozy dining room, and many a lovely meal have I enjoyed in this pleasant atmosphere.

All of this and a joggling board!

CENTURY INN, Scenery Hill, PA 15360; 412-945-6600 or 5180. A 10-guestroom village inn on Rte. 40, 12 mi. east of Washington, Pa., 35 mi. south of Pittsburgh. European plan. Breakfast served to houseguests only. Lunch and dinner served to travelers daily. Open Mar. 16 to Dec. 23. No pets. No credit cards. Personal checks welcome. Megin and Gordon Harrington, Jr., Innkeepers.

Directions: From the east, exit the Pa. Tpke. at New Stanton. Take I-70W to Rte. 917S (Bentleyville exit) to Rte. 40E and go 1 mi. east to inn. From the north, take Rte. 19S to Rte. 519S to Rte. 40E and go 5 mi. east to inn or take I-79S to Rte. 40E and go 9 mi. east to inn. From the west, take I-70E to I-79S to Rte. 40E and go 9 mi. east to inn.

EVERMAY-ON-THE-DELAWARE
Erwinna, Pennsylvania (1982)

One of the subheads for an article in *Philadelphia Magazine* just happened to catch my eye. It read: "Evermay-on-the-Delaware: The crown jewel of Bucks County country inns." The author went on to praise the horses, sheep, geese, and the long-haired red Scottish West Highland cattle, and the beautiful lawns and impressive trees. Furthermore, it had a very apt description of the inn itself, its antique furnishings and its delicious breakfast, and dinners. I was quite in agreement with it.

Long before Ron Strouse and Fred Cresson discovered and explored the full potential of this lovely property, Evermay had existed as an accommodation as far back as 1871. The original part of the house was built in 1700 by a prominent family in the valley. A 1905 photograph in the parlor of the inn shows that it has hardly been changed since then.

A recent letter from Ron and Fred pointed out that the animal population has increased, but with a slightly different bent: "We now have two horses, Canton and Flow Blue, the two Scottish West Highland cows, Eunice and Flyn, and a host of sheep, as well as the peacocks and geese." Animals are an important part of Ron's life, and plants and flowers are important to Fred.

"Our 7:30 dinner, served on Friday, Saturday, and Sunday, has become a very special experience. It is now six courses. We begin with champagne and hors d'oeuvres, and then serve an appetizer, soup course, salad, entrée, cheese and fruit, and dessert. Some of the entrées include sautéed Muscovy duck on onion marmalade with lingonberries, and roast loin of veal with mushroom sauce. All of the desserts are homemade. There are a couple of dishes we would like to test on you when you visit next time. We also serve on Thanksgiving, Christmas Day, and New Year's Eve."

One of my favorite times at Evermay is very early in the morning, when I can watch the sun coming up over the river and hear the geese and other birds heralding the first streaks of daylight. This scene is especially available to rooms on the top floor facing the river. At that early hour there are few cars on the river road, and I feel as if I am very much in my own private world.

Beside the snug rooms on the top floor, Evermay has larger, second-floor, master-sized guest rooms, many with fireplaces. The views from the front of the inn include the Delaware River, but I find that the views from the rear are equally inviting. These include the meadows and gardens that Ron and Fred have developed, as well as the hills beyond. Additional guest rooms are now available in the recently remodeled carriage barn.

I think that readers might be interested in Ron's comment on his travels with Fred in Europe: "During the September lull, we traveled from Vienna to Venice and back, staying at some fine inns and hotels. I guess there are not really many new major ideas to be discovered as innkeepers travel to other inns, but there are a whole host of details and refinements to be discovered, many of which we hope to incorporate into Evermay. I guess, after five years here and ten years as innkeepers, there is an Evermay 'style' which will not change, but hopefully can always be enhanced and improved."

I actually visited Evermay before the first guest had been escorted to a guest room, and it's been a pleasure for me to see how Ron and Fred have made this such a wonderful country inn experience. It is a "crown jewel."

EVERMAY-ON-THE-DELAWARE, Erwinna, PA 18920; 215-294-9100. A 16-guestroom riverside inn in upper Bucks County. Breakfast and afternoon tea included in the room tariff. Box lunches available for houseguests. Dinner served Fri., Sat., Sun., and holidays at 7:30 p.m. by reservation. Open every day for lodging except Dec. 24. Convenient to all of the Bucks County natural and historical attractions, including handsome mansions, museums, and amusements for small children. No pets. Ron Strouse and Fred Cresson, Innkeepers.

Directions: From New York City, take Rte. 22 to Clinton; Rte. 31 to Flemington; Rte. 12 to Frenchtown. Cross river and turn south on Rte. 32 for 2 mi. From Philadelphia, follow I-95 north to Yardley exit and Rte. 32 north to Erwinna. There are several other routes also.

FAIRFIELD INN AND GUEST HOUSE
Fairfield, Pennsylvania (1976)

The Fairfield Inn is one of the most "country" inns in *CIBR*. It is the only inn that serves dinner in the middle of the day and supper at night. This is a definite offshoot of the predominantly agricultural nature of Fairfield Village and Adams County; those are the terms used by farm families to describe the two meals of the day.

Just to add further to the country feeling, my bedroom in the main inn (there are four more in the guest house just a few paces across the street) had ball-fringe curtains, a bed with a macramé canopy, fresh roses, and a growing fern. The shiny, varied-width floorboards have found a fitting complement in a beautiful oriental rug.

The main building of the Fairfield Inn is an impressive three-story Pennsylvania stone building with wood balconies on the front. Further country influences are the window boxes found in great profusion everywhere. The inn is famous not only for having extremely enjoyable country food and pleasant service, but also for being in every sense of the word a meeting place and a center of the social activity for the region. The Country Squire Gift Shop in the loft is drawing both local visitors and travelers.

The building began its long career as the plantation home of the Miller family, who settled here in 1755. The rear portion of the building dates from 1757, and the front stone section was built about the same time that Squire William Miller laid out the town.

The four bedrooms in the guest house across the village street are furnished mostly with original antiques. Some of the rooms look out over the village scene and others in the rear have a view of the mountains.

Innkeeper David Thomas was telling me about some of the inn activities. "The inn is a setting for many events throughout the year, including the Festival of Christmas. This is held on four weekends in December. Reservations are open the first Monday in November and are filled almost within hours."

The inn and the village are also the scene of the "Pippinfest," held on an autumn weekend, usually in September. This is a real apple harvest celebration, with cider pressing, apple butter, square dancing, an antique car display, an apple dessert baking contest, bonfires, old movies, and block parties.

Last October the Art Department of Gettysburg College featured the Fairfield Inn's collection of Pennsylvania coverlets. The exhibit was titled the "Great American Coverup in Pennsylvania." The show was open to the public and ran until mid-November. David presented a lecture on the collection, which includes approximately 50 examples and dates from the 1830s to the mid-1860s. I tried desperately to be there during

that time, but was unable to join in the festivities. Knowing David, I am sure that everything went off in tiptop shape. By the way, he is happy to talk about coverlets to his guests at any time.

Besides the specialty of chicken and biscuits, the menu of the Fairfield Inn also has country ham steak, which David describes as "the salty kind," scallops in wine sauce, roast prime ribs of beef, and baked seafood pie.

Bean soup is always on the menu, because it commemorates the occasion when the townswomen made bean soup in iron kettles to feed the starving soldiers after the battle of Gettysburg.

Speaking of Gettysburg, Fairfield is just eight miles west of Gettysburg and is an excellent place to stay during visits to the battlefield. Jeb Stuart is said to have stolen 700 horses from the valley to further the Confederate cause in 1862.

Yes, the Fairfield Inn is real "country," but David Thomas has added a few very sophisticated touches as well.

FAIRFIELD INN AND GUEST HOUSE, Main St., Fairfield, PA 17320; 717-642-5410. A 6-guestroom (shared baths) country inn and restaurant near Gettysburg. Breakfast, lunch, and dinner served daily. Closed on major holidays, Sundays, and first week in Sept. and Feb. Dinner reservations advised. Nearby region is rich in history, including Gettysburg Battlefield, Caledonia State Park, and Totem Pole Playhouse; 3 mi. from Ski Liberty. No pets. David W. Thomas, Innkeeper.

Directions: Fairfield is 8 mi. west of Gettysburg on Rte. 116.

GATEWAY LODGE
Cooksburg, Pennsylvania (1983)

In the past two editions I have begun the account of my visit to the Gateway Lodge by sharing a conversation I had with innkeepers Linda and Joe Burney about the black bears in Cook Forest. This time, as we were enjoying a candlelit dinner, we talked about the other animals in the woods. "Besides the bears," Joe said, "we also have bobcats, raccoons, porcupines, skunks, deer, turkeys, rabbits, chipmunks, grey squirrels, and an uncountable number of birds."

It had been a typical day for me on the road, starting with waking up at the Benn Conger Inn in Groton, New York, continuing on for an elaborate breakfast at the Rose Inn in Ithaca, and then arriving at the Gateway Lodge about four o'clock. After saying hello, I donned my bathing trunks for a dip in the new indoor swimming pool.

I must point out that since 1981 it has been the lodge's custom to allow the first caller who makes a dinner reservation to set the menu for that evening. The choices might include chicken Cordon Bleu, thick pork chops with bread stuffing, country-style barbecued spareribs, chicken and biscuits, or baked trout, among others. On that particular night the main choice, which had been chosen by an earlier telephone caller, was braised sirloin steak.

Gateway Lodge is a rustic country inn in Cook Forest, where the pine and hemlock may be seen in all their majesty, towering 200 and more feet above the pine-needle-carpeted forest. Hundreds of years of growth, untouched by human progress, has preserved for us some of the most magnificent forest scenery east of the Rocky Mountains. The pine and hemlock logs of the lodge suggest the ruggedness of our pioneer forebears.

The big living room of the main lodge has log walls and a beautiful big fireplace, with lots of deep, comfortable chairs gathered around it. The guest rooms have beds with chestnut headboards, and all have comforters and dust ruffles. Most rooms with baths "down the hall" also provide fluffy robes for the trip.

In addition to the rustic guest rooms in the main lodge, there are six cabins across the road in the forest, which require a minimum two-night stay. These cabins have kitchen conveniences, porches, and fireplaces, and are very snug with lots of firewood. Some guests decide to return to these for longer stays.

The Cook Forest really serves as the recreational motivation to visit this rustic hideaway. It has twenty-seven miles of hiking and over seventeen well-marked trails for good cross-country skiing. It's possible to fish for trout and warm-water fish in the Clarion River, and there are over ninety species of birds that have been identified in the park. Canoeing

and inner-tubing can also be enjoyed, as well as golf, horseback riding, swimming, superb backroading, and there's even a summer theater nearby.

After dinner I strolled down to the Mountain Greenery Gift Shop, a little rustic building just a few steps away, where there are all sorts of gifts, made mostly by local craftspeople. "It makes a very nice place for our guests to browse in both before and after dinner."

"Our winters are very active here," Joe commented, as we wandered back up to the front porch of the lodge. "We have all kinds of carefully maintained cross-country ski trails, ice skating, miles of snowmobile trails, and one of our new things is sleigh rides, starting right here from our front porch." "Yes," Linda chimed in, "as a matter of fact, winter is one of our busiest times."

Linda made a sign to me and put her finger to her lips. She pointed down the forest road to where three deer were crossing. "It happens all the time," she whispered, "but it always gives me a big thrill."

GATEWAY LODGE, Rte. 36, Cooksburg, PA 16217; 814-744-8017. An 8-guestroom (some private baths) rustic lodge in the heart of Cook Forest in western Pa. Cabins require 2-night minimum stay. Open year-round, except Wed., Thurs., and Fri. of Thanksgiving week and from Dec. 22 to 25. Indoor swimming pool. Beautiful backroading and many trails in forest. All types of seasonal outdoor recreation available. The Burney Family, Innkeepers.

Directions: Because Cooksburg is accessible from all four directions, locate Cook Forest State Park on your map of Pa., and find Rte. 36. The lodge is on Rte. 36, 15 min. north of I-80.

HICKORY BRIDGE FARM
Orrtanna, Pennsylvania (1978)

Once again I was taking the road from Fairfield to Orrtanna and Hickory Bridge Farm. It is one of my most favorite back roads.

There are great cornfields on one side and apple orchards on the other and, in the midst of all, a large farmstand with a wonderful collection of pumpkins out in front, and every imaginable type of the fresh farm produce that is abundant in this highly agricultural area.

I turned at the inn sign, passed over the railroad track, and was in sight of Nancy Jean and Doctor Jim Hammett's Hickory Bridge Farm. There were the big red barn, the many flower gardens, the old farmhouse, and the ever-growing collection of old farm machinery and carts. The newest addition was a natural swimming pond with a diving platform. All of this was set against the background of beautiful, swaying trees, which in late September were beginning to take on their autumnal colors.

Walking through the gate, I was greeted with open arms by Nancy Jean. We stepped into the house, where there was a beautiful, welcome fire in the huge stone fireplace, over which a musket was hung. Nancy Jean proudly pointed out the decorations in the dining room, done by her son, David, who now has full-time charge at a church just east of Gettysburg. Breakfast was well in progress, and on the sideboard was a selection of dry cereals, some hot oatmeal, granola, and orange juice.

As usual, Nancy Jean was overflowing with energy and exuberance. "The apple butter is made right here on the farm," she said. "The vegetables are from our garden, and the peaches, from our neighbor's orchard. We have honeydew melons and cantaloupes from our own farm, too."

The bedrooms in the main house are Pennsylvania farm bedrooms. Many have washstands and one even has an old-fashioned radio on the shelf. There are many additional touches, such as good country-type fixtures on the walls, that make the bedrooms very pleasant, including a rocking chair for two in one room.

The guests take breakfast out on the deck, overlooking the island and the covered bridge over the creek. "Sometimes they stay out here so long I have to shoo them out so that we can get the breakfast dishes done," Nancy Jean said. "This is a wonderful place for birders, and guests come out with their spyglasses."

We took a little tour around the grounds, ably assisted by one of the eight grandchildren. One of the points of interest is a country store museum, where there is penny candy, molasses, sarsaparilla, and apple butter for sale. However, it is basically a museum store, with an old post office money window, and it provides a great deal of amusement for guests.

Additional accommodations are in two cottages beside the brook in the woods. Plans are also in the works to build a guest lodge and garden breakfast room as an addition to the restaurant.

HICKORY BRIDGE FARM, Orrtanna, PA 17353; 717-642-5261. A 7-guestroom (private baths) country inn on a farm (with cottages) 3 mi. from Fairfield and 8 mi. west of Gettysburg. Open year-round except Dec. 20 thru Jan. 10. Deposit required. Full breakfast included in rates. Dinner served to public on Sat. evenings by reservation. Near Gettysburg Battlefield Natl. Park, Caledonia State Park, and Totem Pole Playhouse. Hiking, biking, fishing, and country store museum on grounds. Swimming, golfing, horseback riding and antiquing nearby. The Hammett Family, Innkeepers.

Directions: From Gettysburg take Rte. 116 west to Fairfield and follow signs 3 mi. north to Orrtana.

A number of inns have nearby airports where private airplanes may land. An airplane symbol at the end of the inn directions indicates that there is an airport nearby. Consult inn for further information.

I do not include lodging rates in the descriptions, for the very nature of an inn means that there are lodgings of various sizes, with and without baths, in and out of season, and with plain and fancy decoration. Travelers should call ahead and inquire about the availability and rates of the many different types of rooms.

THE INN AT STARLIGHT LAKE
Starlight, Pennsylvania (1976)

The orchestra was playing "Moonglow." The peepers were peeping and the sunset afterglow was lighting the western sky. I had wandered out on the front porch of the Inn at Starlight, speaking, as everyone else did, to the mother cat and her two brand-new kittens. I wandered down the steps through the little grove of trees next to the lake and out onto the long dock, off of which were moored boats and sailboats.

I turned around to look at the lights of the inn and could hear the voices of some of my innkeeping friends from Pennsylvania and New York, who had gathered here to enjoy the opportunity to exchange experiences, tell good stories, and perhaps lend encouragement and counsel to each other. The trees along the shore created lacy silhouettes against the darkening blue sky. Then I noticed that several other innkeepers had decided to take a walk along the shore of the lake to help digest the wonderful evening meal. The small orchestra changed to a bit more up-tempo with "String of Pearls."

My evening meanderings also brought me within sight and earshot of four ducks who had taken up residence in the lake near the inn. Three of them were feathered in beautiful hues and the fourth was an ordinary white barnyard duck. They all had names and, as Judy McMahon explained, they had "just sort of all arrived and never left. They are busy morning and night rooting in the lush green grass at the edge of the lake for some succulent tidbits, and then cruising energetically to this end of the lake, occasionally diving down into the depths after some elusive fish."

This inn is on a back road, overlooking beautiful Starlight Lake. It is a rambling, old-fashioned, comfortable place with an accumulation of furniture from over the years. The combination lobby/living room has a

fireplace in one corner, and there are reminders that the McMahons are originally from "show business." Besides the piano and the guitar, books of plays or sheet music may be found on the tables or on the bookshelves.

Guest rooms are in the main building and also in adjacent cottages that have been redecorated and winterized. The inn is on the modified American plan, meaning that dinner and breakfast are included in the room rate. Lunch is offered every day at an additional charge.

There's a TV room, a game room in the main house, and lots of outdoor activity, from canoeing, sailing, swimming, and bicycling to ice skating on the forty-five-acre lake and cross-country skiing on eighteen miles of marked trails. There is a very pleasant lakeside play area, and many lovely walks and dirt roads for backroading in the picturesque woods. By the way, the McMahons have a fabulous collection of old films.

Some of my favorite reading is country inn menus and this one is particularly extensive. There are several different beef dishes, including filet medallions Bordelaise and sirloin steak au poivre. One of several veal dishes is a really tasty Wiener schnitzel. Roast duckling always makes a hit with me, and there is fresh local trout from a trout farm just six miles away.

The newest feature is Starlight's occasional murder mystery weekend. I've been offered a small role in a future production—probably the victim!

Now I could hear Jack McMahon's high tenor voice wafting out from the living room and I knew it was time to go back for a very pleasant evening at the Inn at Starlight Lake. It's always a pleasure to visit.

THE INN AT STARLIGHT LAKE, Starlight, PA 18461; 717-798-2519. A 28-guestroom resort-inn, 5 mi. from Hancock, NY. Modified American plan. Breakfast, lunch, and dinner served daily between May 15 and Apr. 1. Closed Apr. 1 through Apr. 15. Swimming, boating, canoeing, sailing, fishing, hunting, tennis, hiking, bicycling, xc skiing, and lawn sports on grounds. Golf nearby. No pets. Judy and Jack McMahon, Innkeepers.

Directions: From N.Y. Rte. 17, exit at Hancock, N.Y. Take Rte. 191S over Delaware River to Rte. 370. Turn right, proceed 3½ mi.; turn right, 1 mi. to inn. From I-81, take Exit 62 at Tompkinsville. Follow Rte. 107 east 4 mi. to Rte. 247N and Forest City. Turn left on Rte. 171 (the main street), and continue 10 mi. north to Rte. 370. Turn right and go 13 mi. east to Starlight. Turn left, 1 mi. to inn.

THE OVERLOOK INN
Canadensis, Pennsylvania (1975)

Bobby and Lolly Tupper and I were seated in front of the fireplace having a "Pierre-popover" drenched with butter and exquisitely delicious. Lolly handed me a small sheaf of papers, saying, "These are what we give all of our guests. It shows the temperature, the date, has wonderful maps of the area, including a detailed map showing the stores in the nearby villages, the woods trails for cross-country skiing in the winter, and all of the necessary details that would make a stay here more enjoyable." It is a good example of just the kind of tender care provided by the Overlook Inn for their guests.

If Overlook had nothing else, the entrance into the inn itself would be worth a visit. It is through a handsome porte-cochere, over which is a large covered porch. This is a most interesting way to arrive at a country inn.

The porch is a most engaging feature, with one piece after another of absolutely splendid white wicker furniture. It's a nice broad porch where one could sit when it is raining and not get wet. All around are wonderful woods of evergreens interspersed with apple trees, and there is a beautiful red maple right in front.

And birds. We were there in the middle of spring; what is a happier sound than birds chattering and chirping, while caring for another bumper crop of birdlings. There's also a salt block for deer within sight of the porch. It's such a wonderful experience to see these wild creatures.

The Overlook Inn, kept by Bob and Lolly Tupper, is high in the Pocono Mountains in northeastern Pennsylvania. The fragrant pine, blue spruce, and locust forests stretch out in all directions, and the robins, cardinals, and quail find them as inviting as the rhododendron and mountain laurel.

I took another one of the popovers and asked for the jam. "I'm glad you are enjoying them," Lolly said. "Pierre and his staff really do a splendid job, and we feel that our food is superior. We have dinner guests coming from New Jersey, New York, and as far as Hazelton and Harrisburg. Pierre does lots of appetizers, and his entrées include rack of baby lamb, Idaho rainbow trout, Pocono Mountain brook trout, stuffed quail with wild rice, and rabbit with shallot cream sauce. His desserts are always delicious."

"I wish you would come here during the winter," Bob suggested. "Our cross-country trails are great and we have all of them well marked. Of course, you can always do some downhill skiing here, too."

The bedrooms and suites at Overlook are the kind that you hope you will find when you go to a country inn. They have books, original paintings, plants, colorful afghans, two pillows for every head, comfortable furniture, and some have walls of aromatic cedar shakes.

Ultimately, what sets the Overlook apart are Bob and Lolly Tupper themselves. They have a keen understanding and a wonderful rapport with their guests, and this is what is mentioned most frequently in letters I have been receiving since the first year the Overlook Inn was included in *Country Inns and Back Roads*.

THE OVERLOOK INN, Dutch Hill Rd., Canadensis, PA 18325; 717-595-7519. A 21-guestroom resort-inn in the heart of the Poconos, 15 mi. from Stroudsburg, Pa. Mod. American plan. Dinners served to travelers; jackets requested. Open year-round. Pool, shuffleboard, bocci, horseshoes, hiking on grounds; golf, tennis, antiquing, backroading, summer theater, downhill and xc skiing nearby. No children under 12. No pets. Bob and Lolly Tupper, Innkeepers.

Directions: From the north, exit from I-84 to Rte. 390 south thru "Promised Land" about 12 mi. to traffic light in Canadensis. Make right hand turn on Rte. 447 north—go 1/3 mi. to Dutch Hill Rd. and turn right—inn is 1 1/2 mi. up hill. Look for sign on right. From New York City, take Geo. Washington Bridge to I-80 west. Turn off at Pa. Exit 52. Follow Rte. 447 north—straight through Canadensis traffic light— about 1/3 mi., past light to Dutch Hill Rd. Follow above directions from Dutch Hill Rd. From Phila., Pa. Tpke. to Northeast extension to Exit 35. Follow I-80 East to 380 West to Mt. Pocono Exit 8. Turn right on Rte. 940 to dead end. Make right and quick left; you're still on 940. Follow 390. Make left. Follow 390 to traffic light in Canadensis. Make left 1/4 mi. to Dutch Hill Rd. Turn right 1 1/2 mi. up hill.

THE PINE BARN INN
Danville, Pennsylvania (1976)

From the very first edition of *Country Inns and Back Roads*, which I wrote in 1966, I've maintained that innkeepers and their growing families were every bit as important to me as the changes and developments in the inns themselves.

The Pine Barn Inn is a case in point. I've been visiting and writing about it now for many years and I've seen some interesting developments—originally in the concepts and new ideas shared by innkeepers Shube and Marty Walzer. Later on, as Shube more or less retired to Florida, Barbara Walzer entered the picture, saving Marty from complete dissolution by marrying him a few years ago.

The inn began life in the 1870s as a wonderful Pennsylvania barn and later served for a long time as a riding stable, and then as a private home. It was transformed in 1950 into the Pine Barn Inn, and in 1967 it was purchased by the Walzers, father and son. Today, it is an inn and restaurant of considerable reputation.

The residents of that area of Pennsylvania think most kindly of the Pine Barn as a restaurant, with its menu that includes roast beef and roast leg of lamb, as well as homemade pies, breads, and rolls. Travelers speak highly of the accommodations. Even though they are somewhat "motel" in style, the rooms are furnished with attractive cherry reproductions and have many thoughtful touches that I always enjoy finding in a country inn, such as plants and magazines and books for guests to read in each guest room.

I have shared Marty's yearly letter with readers for the past few years in which he brings us up to date on son Christopher: "I'm going to make a serious attempt not to dwell on the progress of a certain $5\frac{1}{2}$-year-old. We must not bore the reader, although after last year's edition, every time Christopher comes in for breakfast it seems everyone knows him and greets him by name. This, of course, pleases him no end and encourages him to become the dining room cut-up. The Pine Barn is really his second home, and it is a marvelous atmosphere for him.

"Barb finished redecorating one of our private dining and conference rooms with a library theme. Oak paneling and oak floor-to-ceiling bookshelves, with reproductions of old photographs of Danville, have given the room an all-new look and it's excellent for private parties.

"The inn looks wonderful even if we can't brag of any great additions. We're taking a breather right now and looking at our priorities. Flowers adorned the grounds despite my entire ignorance of horticulture. Craig, who heads our maintenance department and who Christopher says can fix anything, managed to keep everything seeded, watered, and growing.

"Chef Ralph Richardson with the able assistance of Larry Horne and Scott Smith has kept the menu varied and fresh. I am also ready to put forward to the scientific world a new law of physics, which is: 'No one can possibly lose weight as long as they are a patron of Rose's soups or Polly's pies.'

"Our proximity to Geisinger Hospital is a great convenience for our guests who are friends and families of patients. We are within walking distance."

And now, dear reader, thus endeth the yearly report on the Pine Barn Inn. I will mention one more thing: when you visit ask Marty to tell you about the time he swam against Johnny Weissmuller.

THE PINE BARN INN, Danville, PA 17821; 717-275-2071. A picturesque country restaurant with 45 attractive motel rooms in central Pennsylvania. European plan. Breakfast, lunch, and dinner served daily except Christmas, July 4, and Memorial Day. Near Geisinger Hospital and several colleges and historic sites. Golf, tennis, waterskiing, sailing, and canoeing nearby. Pets allowed in some rooms. Martin and Barbara Walzer, Innkeepers.

Directions: From Exit 33 of I-80, go south 3 mi. to Danville. Take a left at the first traffic light. Proceed 10 blocks and follow signs to Geisinger Medical Center. Pine Barn adjoins the Center.

"European plan" means that rates for rooms and meals are separate. "American plan" means that meals are included in the cost of the room. "Modified American plan" means that breakfast and dinner are included in the cost of the room. The rates at some inns include a continental breakfast with the lodging.

1740 HOUSE
Lumberville, Pennsylvania (1973)

As often as I have driven up the so-called River Road, in reality Route 32, on the Pennsylvania side of the Delaware, it never ceases to wonder me (as our Pennsylvania Dutch friends would say) just how beautiful it is. Especially visible before the trees are in leaf, are the hills sloping up from the road on one side, and on the other, the canal and long stretches of the Delaware River. The road has a roller coaster quality, lifting up to the top of the hills, and dropping down beside the river. The laurel is green and welcome at all seasons, and here and there in April I could see errant tufts of grass that enjoyed a little more sunshine than others beginning to push up along the river bank.

It is a small wonder that many years ago, my friend Harry Nessler, the innkeeper at the 1740 House, came to this section of Pennsylvania and saw the possibilities of opening what at that time was a rather remarkable phenomenon, a country inn in the cluster of barns and other farm outbuildings. Each of the bedrooms at the 1740 House has either a balcony or a terrace with a full view of the canal and the Delaware River beyond. The inn abounds with bushes, shrubs, flowers, trees, and birds. A portion of the building is covered with beautiful green ivy.

There is a sort of natural division between the buildings, separated by a very small swimming pool. As Harry has said, "It's just enough to get wet."

A typical menu at the 1740 House includes a choice of three appetizers—things like mushroom soup, herring in cream sauce, and fettucini Alfredo. Typical entrées are filet mignon, chicken Marsala, crab Imperial, broiled scallops, and a baked fish. Desserts usually include crème caramel and always ice cream. Although there are several restaurants in the area, many of the returning guests have found it most convenient and

quite enjoyable to have a quiet dinner at the 1740 House. It is most necessary to make reservations for that dinner in advance.

There is a bridge over the river in Lumberville—a single-passenger bridge—and it's possible to go across to New Jersey on the other side. There is also a preserved canal lock, which shows exactly how boats were assisted through the canals in the old days.

Of course, backroading is one of the favorite pastimes of visitors to Bucks County. The back roads here not only have a great deal of history connected with them, but they have the historic old buildings, homes, barns, and sheds that make it even more enjoyable. There is something about the quarried stone in this part of Pennsylvania that mellows and weathers in a most handsome way.

Harry pointed out that one of the additional sports guests may enjoy is canoeing and tubing on the river, and there are places where canoes and inner tubes are available for this purpose. "The Delaware during the time when the water would be warmest is a relatively placid experience," he said, "with none of the hair-raising elements that we hear about on other rivers."

1740 HOUSE, River Rd., Lumberville, PA 18933; 215-297-5661. A 24-guestroom riverside inn, 6½ mi. north of New Hope, in the heart of historic Bucks County. Lodgings include breakfast, served to houseguests daily; dinner served daily except Sun. and Mon. by reservation only. Open year-round. Weekend reservations must include 2 nights. Pool and boating on grounds. Golf and tennis nearby. Superb backroading in an area rich in American history. Harry Nessler, Innkeeper.

Directions: From N.Y.C., travel south on N.J. Tpke., and take Exit 10. Follow Rte. 287 north to another Exit 10. Proceed west on Rte. 22 to Flemington, then Rte. 202 south over Delaware Toll Bridge. After an immediate right U-turn onto Rte. 32N, drive 5 mi. to inn. From Pa. Tpke., exit at Willow Grove and proceed north on Rte. 611 to Rte. 202. Follow Rte. 202 north to Rte. 32 and turn north to inn. From Phila., take I-95 to Yardley–New Hope Exit, follow 32N through New Hope and 7 mi. to inn.

I do not include lodging rates in the descriptions, for the very nature of an inn means that there are lodgings of various sizes, with and without baths, in and out of season, and with plain and fancy decoration. Travelers should call ahead and inquire about the availability and rates of the many different types of rooms.

SMITHTON INN
Ephrata, Pennsylvania (1987)

"We want our guests to have a great Lancaster County experience. The people who live in this part of Pennsylvania are our forebears and it is an opportunity to see who our forebears were, because here their customs have remained unchanged. It's like being in touch with your own past."

I was to ponder that thought, expressed by Dorothy Graybill, many, many times during my visit to the Smithton Inn and the surrounding countryside at Ephrata, a predominantly Pennsylvania Dutch community.

"Unfortunately, the image of the Pennsylvania Dutch has been considerably distorted over the years, largely because of the efforts to commercialize some of the customs, language, and artifacts. We have developed a booklet with suggestions for touring and shopping that completely eliminates any of these places," Dorothy continued. "Both Allan and I make extensive and continuing trips throughout the countryside to make certain that our guests see the 'real' Pennsylvania Dutch life."

Dorothy was speaking of her associate at the Smithton Inn, Allan Smith, who is, among many other things, an excellent architect and woodcraftsman. We were having a chat in the truly handsome Great Room of the inn, and I couldn't help but feel that this room, with its fireplace, hooked rugs, comfortable furniture, and brightly polished hardwood floors, was an excellent place to start any adventure of this nature.

The inn is a pre-Revolutionary inn and stagecoach stop, built in 1763, and has been an inn for most of its many years. Each of the guest rooms has its own working fireplace and can be candlelighted during the evening hours. Beds have canopies, soft goosedown pillows, and bright handmade Pennsylvania Dutch quilts. Red flannel nightshirts are an amusing touch for guests to wear if they wish. All of the guest rooms have fireplaces or cast iron stoves. Allan is pleased to escort inn guests through the inn, pointing out many of the marvelously designed and constructed features, not only in the original building, but in the additions that are being made. He has a wonderful sense of history and an obvious affection for good craftsmanship.

"We serve a full country breakfast and a rather simple but nourishing evening meal at our guests' request," Dorothy told me. "It consists of an appetizer, soup, salad, and a meat pie. Dessert is a homemade ice cream with our exceptional chocolate sauce, which is a story in itself."

Allan and Dorothy can also arrange dinner at a real Pennsylvania Dutch farm home nearby for their guests. "These are very conservative, accommodating Old Order people, who've become our friends and also the friends of many of the guests we've sent to them." I'd suggest that you ask Dorothy about this when you make your reservations.

The well-known Ephrata Cloister, an 18th-century German Protestant monastic settlement, is situated just a few steps away. It is the scene of *Vorspiel*, a musical drama presented throughout the summer.

The entire area abounds in museums, crafts shops, antique shops, summer and winter theater, concerts, winery tours, art exhibits, and Renaissance fairs. Many are located in old mills, inns, historic hotels, and on Mennonite farms. There are several Pennsylvania Dutch restaurants.

I strongly suggest that our readers plan on staying at the Smithton Inn for a minimum of two nights and, if possible, three or more. The expert and caring guidance from the innkeepers provides every one with a "real Lancaster County experience."

We are delighted to welcome the Smithton Inn to *Country Inns and Back Roads* for the first time.

SMITHTON INN, 900 W. Main St., Ephrata, PA 17522; 717-733-6094. A 7-guestroom (private baths) pre-Revolutionary inn in Pennsylvania Dutch country near Lancaster. Breakfast included in room rate. Dinner served to houseguests by advance reservation. Open all year. Convenient to all of Lancaster County's cultural, historic, and recreational attractions. Ephrata Cloister nearby. Dorothy Graybill, Innkeeper.

Directions: From north or south, take Rte. 222 to Ephrata exit. Turn west on Rte. 322 for 2.5 mi. to inn.

STERLING INN
South Sterling, Pennsylvania (1974)

I could not resist it any longer—I had been listening to the gurgling waters of the Wallenpaupack Creek for about twenty minutes on a warm, lazy afternoon. I was sitting on a lawn chair about fifty paces from the back of the Sterling Inn, just two feet from the bank of the creek. The smell of the freshly-cut lawn mingled with the scent of the forest on the other side of the water.

I kicked off my shoes, rolled up my pants, and waded out to stand on the flat, smooth shelf of rock in the middle of the creek. The water was clean and cool. There was a little pool about twenty-five feet away, deep enough for someone to sit in and have the water come up to his chest. A flash of red and another of blue signaled a cardinal and a bluejay darting into the woods, deep in the Pocono Mountains of Pennsylvania.

I climbed back on the bank and was drying my feet, when one of the other guests came and plunked down on a nearby chair. "I think this is one of the best-kept, neatest places that I have ever visited," she said. "It's as American as apple pie and fresh vegetables. The rooms are so comfortable, and I'm very glad I came. Don't you just love it here?"

Even if her enthusiasm hadn't been catching, I would have had to agree.

This was the friendly and unpretentious atmosphere that Alice Julian had in mind over a half-century ago when she acquired the Sterling Inn. That is the way her daughter and son-in-law, Carmen and Henry Arneberg, kept it, and the same way that the present owners, Ron and Mary Kay Logan are keeping it today.

The Sterling Inn is on a back road in the Poconos. There are enticing hiking and walking trails on the inn property and nearby. One of them,

Ron told me, leads to a waterfall on the ridge behind the inn. There is a very pleasant nine-hole putting green, a swimming area with a sandy beach, and a little pond with willow trees and a few ducks.

Guest rooms are in several very attractive buildings, all beautifullly situated in the parklike surroundings. Some handsome new suites have been furnished with beautiful antiques, Franklin woodburning fireplaces, and decks overlooking the creek that I was wading in.

The menu includes such entrées as roast lamb, pot roast, and standing rib roast because, Mary Kay Logan says, "This is the kind of food that people serve only when they are having guests for dinner." All the baking is done in the warm, friendly kitchen.

In many ways this Pocono Mountain inn personifies the things that I find most delightful in country inns. For example, fresh flowers are on the dining room tables at all times, and there are books and magazines in all parlors and sitting rooms. When guests advise the inn of their arrival time, the inn automobile will meet buses and airplanes. Special diets can also be accommodated.

The inn is open year-round, and the setting is like a picture postcard. Winter activities include cross-country skiing and lessons, ice skating, sledding, winter hikes, and roasting chestnuts or marshmallows by the open fire. The horse-drawn sleigh rides are very popular.

In the blaze of autumn colors there are incredibly beautiful nature walks along Wallenpaupak Creek and hikes on woodland trails. Spring and summer at the Sterling Inn, of course, offer all sorts of outdoor enjoyment.

STERLING INN, Rte. 191, South Sterling, PA 18460; 717-676-3311. From Ct., N.Y., N.J., Md., Del., Wash., D.C.: 800-523-8200. A 60-guestroom secluded country inn-resort in the Pocono Mountains, 8 mi. from I-84 and 12 mi. from I-380. Mod. Amer. plan. Reservation and check-in offices close at 10 p.m. Breakfast, lunch, and dinner served to travelers daily. Jackets required for dinner. Open year-round. Swimming, putting green, shuffleboard, all-weather tennis court, scenic hiking trails, xc skiing and lessons, ice skating, and sledding on grounds. Golf courses, horseback riding, major ski areas nearby. Gift shop and print gallery. No pets. Ron and Mary Kay Logan, Innkeepers.

Directions: From I-80, follow I-380 to Rte. 940 to Mount Pocono. At light, cross Rte. 611 and proceed on Rte. 196 north to Rte. 423. Drive north on Rte. 423 to Rte. 191 and travel 1/2 mi. north to inn. From I-84, follow Rte. 507 south through Greentown and Newfoundland. In Newfoundland, pick up Rte. 191 and travel 4 mi. south to inn.

TARA
Clark, Pennsylvania (1986)

Inspired by the world's most renowned movie, *Gone With the Wind,* Jim and Donna Winner restored a beautiful antebellum mansion located midway between Cleveland, Ohio, and Pittsburgh, Pennsylvania. They named it "Tara."

When I first saw Tara from the rolling highways of western Pennsylvania I wondered if magically I'd been transported in time to the Old South of the early 1800s—the era before the Civil War, when grace and grandeur, honor, fine clothes, plantations, and Southern hospitality were the lifestyle.

The house was built in 1854 and is one of western Pennsylvania's most famous historic landmarks. The mansion, with its two-story Grecian columns, overlooks 4,000-acre Lake Shenango surrounded by rolling hills of maple and pine.

Incurable romantics, Jim and Donna knew from the first time they saw what was to become Tara that it should definitely be a country inn. They have made it their home and have lavishly displayed their entire collection of antiques, art, rare china, and crystal throughout, including crystal chandeliers from Austria and a hand-painted Dresden chandelier from Germany. An antique brass chandelier featuring Steuben shades graces the circular stairwell.

There are fourteen guest rooms, all with working fireplaces. Each room has been carefully decorated to reflect the personality of a character from the book. For example, "Miss Melanie's" room is all feminine and fluffy in yellow and pink, with bows and wicker furniture. Overlooking the lake, it boasts one of the best views in the house. "Rhett's" room is masculine and strong. Its focal point is a center-island bed with a canopy that rises to the nine-foot ceiling. The "Katie O'Hara" room has an 18th-century hand-carved bed and a hand-painted ivy floor. The "old maid's" stairwell descends to the lovely antique private bath below.

There are two main dining rooms plus a patio café for outdoor dining in clement weather. "Ashley's" is for formal dining, with such offerings as rack of lamb, an array of tantalizing desserts, and special gourmet coffees, all served on antique tables, one of which belonged to President James Buchanan and was used in the White House during his administration, just before the Civil War. The "Old South Room" is a true-to-life Southern-style dining room, serving fried chicken, smoked ham, grits, cornbread, and other Dixie favorites, all served family style.

Tara is just fun to browse through. There is an authentic, primitive slave kitchen, a primitive bedroom with a genuine rope bed, and a collection of antiques that date back to 1760. The library itself is most impressive, with both old and new books, and one can read on the veranda or in "Miss Pittypat's Parlor."

The day after Thanksgiving, 100,000 tiny white lights will be draped in the trees and bushes. The trees in the parlor are decorated in a Victorian mode, and those in the Old South Room will be done in an old-fashioned style. Bows and holly adorn the crystal chandeliers.

TARA, 3665 Valley View Rd., Box 475, Rte. 18, Clark, PA 16113; 412-962-3535. A 14-guestroom mansion, 8 hrs. west of New York and 8 hrs. east of Chicago. Breakfast, lunch, and dinner served. Open year-round. Croquet, bocci, boating, fishing, swimming, carriage rides, bicycling, backroading, xc skiing, and golf. Not suitable for children. No pets. Jim and Donna Winner, Innkeepers.

Directions: Just inside the Pa. border on I-80 take Exit 1N and follow Rte. 18 north for 8 mi. Tara is located on the east side overlooking Lake Shenango.

A number of inns have nearby airports where private airplanes may land. An airplane symbol at the end of the inn directions indicates that there is an airport nearby. Consult inn for further information.

I do not include lodging rates in the descriptions, for the very nature of an inn means that there are lodgings of various sizes, with and without baths, in and out of season, and with plain and fancy decoration. Travelers should call ahead and inquire about the availability and rates of the many different types of rooms.

THE TAVERN RESTAURANT
New Wilmington, Pennsylvania (1974)

Until her passing in 1986, my good friend Mrs. Cora Durrast kept the Tavern for almost fifty-five years. I'm happy to report that her daughter, Mary Ellen Durrast, has now become the innkeeper.

The luncheon menu has twenty-seven main dishes. This is real country fare, including creamed chicken on a biscuit, cabbage rolls, grilled smoked pork chops, ham steaks, and cheese soufflé with creamed chicken. Two warm honey buns with whipped butter are always served.

Dinners include most of the luncheon offerings, plus about twelve other main dishes. Often, there is the most unusual combination of the white meat of chicken and lobster tail served in a special sherry sauce.

New Wilmington is just a few minutes from I-80, the east–west highway that traverses northern Pennsylvania. It's about 240 miles from the Poconos.

THE TAVERN RESTAURANT, Box 153, New Wilmington, PA 16142; 412-946-2020. A bustling country restaurant on the town square with 5 sleeping rooms in a lodge directly across the street. European plan. Lunch and dinner served daily except Tues. Reservations required. Closed Thanksgiving and Christmas. Sports and cultural events at Westminster College nearby. No credit cards. No diversions for small children. Mary Ellen Durrast, Innkeeper.

Directions: From I-80, take Exit 1-S, and follow Rte. 18 south to Rte. 208. Proceed east on 208 to town square. From I-79, follow Rte. 208 west for 14 mi. to New Wilmington.

Favorite Back Roads

It is true that all roads leading to the Inn at Starlight Lake are back roads. It's impossible to get here without finding yourself on some little-traveled, curving, up-and-down-road. Pointing out a few: Coming from New York City or the northern New Jersey area, one can approach Hancock from NY Route 97, which snakes along the Delaware and passes the replica of Old Fort Delaware. The Delaware River is one of our national treasures. In its upper portion it has changed little, scenically, since the last century. The upper Delaware branches into two parts at Hancock and forms some wonderful areas to travel by. You could really arrive by canoe with a little planning.

Coming from the south through Pennsylvania, one could drive through Honesdale, a charming 19th-century county seat with several historic points of interest, and take either Route 191 N, or Route 670-247 N to Route 370 through miles of . . . well . . . just COUNTRY.

Coming from the north, one can take Route 92 S (NY) to Route 171 (Pa.), and, at Lanesboro, see a national engineering landmark, the Starrucca Viaduct, built in 1848, the oldest train bridge still in use in America. The area is filled with railroad lore for the true railroad enthusiast and the casual observer— Honesdale, site of the first steam engine and gravity railroad, and Susquehanna, site of the first railroad depot and hotel combined in America, now a restaurant. While people are here, we are always pleased to give them hand-out maps and route them along these byways. The roads, by the way, are great for cyclists, too.

Judy and Jack McMahon
The Inn at Starlight Lake
Starlight, Pennsylvania

LAKE

Old Rittenhouse Inn, *Bayfield*

MINNESOTA

Schumacher's Hotel, *New Prague*   Seven Pines Lodge, *Lewis*

MINNEAPOLIS/ST. PAUL   Lowell Inn, *Stillwater*

St. James Hotel, *Red Wing*

WISCONSIN

Midwest
Central Time Zone

ILLINOIS

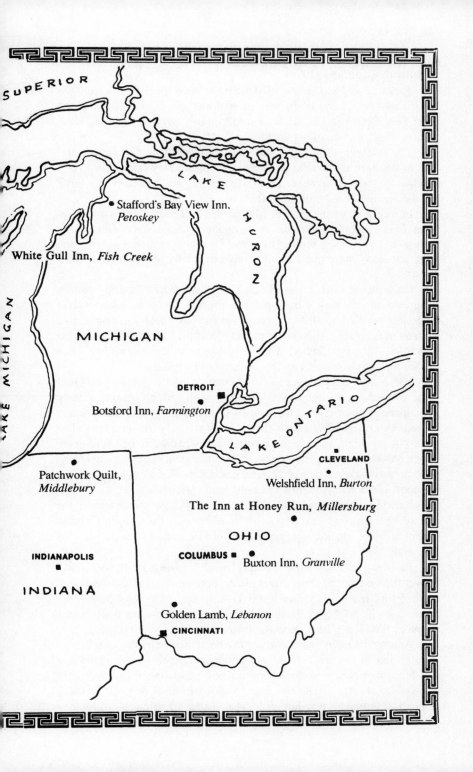

SUPERIOR

LAKE HURON

• Stafford's Bay View Inn, *Petoskey*

White Gull Inn, *Fish Creek*

LAKE MICHIGAN

MICHIGAN

DETROIT

Botsford Inn, *Farmington*

LAKE ONTARIO

CLEVELAND

Patchwork Quilt, *Middlebury*

Welshfield Inn, *Burton*

The Inn at Honey Run, *Millersburg*

OHIO

INDIANAPOLIS

COLUMBUS

Buxton Inn, *Granville*

INDIANA

Golden Lamb, *Lebanon*

CINCINNATI

PATCHWORK QUILT COUNTRY INN
Middlebury, Indiana (1971)

Almost every year since 1970 there has been special news from the Patchwork Quilt. I say 1970, because that was the year I first visited the Patchwork Quilt and met Arletta and Milton Lovejoy and Treva and Herb Swarm. First, a word of explanation:

The Patchwork Quilt is a real working farm in the rich agricultural area of northern Indiana, and has been in the Lovejoy family for over a hundred years. Five-course farm-style dinners are served in the large farmhouse in the center of the 260 acres.

In recent years the inn has offered bed-and-breakfast accommodations for overnight guests in three double guest rooms with shared bathrooms. However, thanks to some very cooperative local people, there are many more guest rooms available nearby for Patchwork Quilt guests.

On a recent visit, I stayed in a room called the "Treetop," which features a canopy bed, a hand-painted armoire, and a turquoise velvet chair. It is paneled in white and turquoise and has a beautiful print above a Franklin fireplace. Another room, known as the "Meadow," is paneled in wattled walnut hardwood. The Early American cannonball bed has a minicanopy made from an apricot quilted counterpane.

For many years the excellent reputation of the Patchwork Quilt came from the truly munificent evening meals, which include a zesty homemade soup or chilled fruit appetizer and a trip to the buffet that is loaded with many more salads than I could possibly mention here. The main course might include such offerings as herbed roast beef, open-hearth baked ham, burgundy steak, or Arletta's great prizewinning buttermilk-pecan chicken. The main course is accompanied by two vegetables, potatoes, hot homemade rolls and jams, and coffee or tea.

I always recommend that, if possible, dinner guests save room for one of the fantastic desserts—coffee-toffee pie, three-layer German chocolate cake, lemon meringue pie, old-fashioned custard pie...ad infinitum.

Besides the five-course evening meal I have partially described above, the Patchwork Quilt offers dining options. On Tuesday and Wednesday, luncheons are served from 11 a.m. to 2 p.m. and during the summer on Tuesday, Wednesday, and Thursday there are light dinner menus, called Early Bird Specials, from 4:30 p.m. to 6:00 p.m.

Among the many services that have been offered by this farmhouse-country inn is the Back Road Adventure package, which includes a five-hour back road tour and lunch, a five-course dinner, and overnight bed-and-breakfast. Arletta has also provided Patchwork Quilt Country Retreats at various times during the year. These are midweek, three-day

tours of the Amish community—meeting the Amish people, visiting in their homes and shops, and also enjoying dinners at the Patchwork Quilt.

Over the years the Patchwork Quilt has received much recognition in national magazines. Articles and stories have appeared in many different media. I guess the first real recognition came just about the time of my very first visit, when Arletta's famous pecan chicken recipe (still on the menu) won a national award.

I realize that I've been visiting the Patchwork Quilt Country Inn in Middlebury, Indiana, for almost three-quarters of the total of twenty-one years that there has been a *Country Inns and Back Roads*.

PATCHWORK QUILT COUNTRY INN, 11748 C.R. 2, Middlebury, IN 46540; 219-825-2417. A working farm restaurant and bed-and-breakfast inn about 20 mi. east of Elkhart. Dinner served by reservation only. Lodging rooms available only on Tues., Wed., Thurs., and Fri. evenings. Rates include continental breakfast. Closed Sun., Mon., Thanksgiving, Christmas, and New Year's. Thresher's Lunch served Tues., Wed., and Thurs. 11 a.m. to 2 p.m. during June, July, and Aug. No credit cards. Arletta Lovejoy, Innkeeper.

Directions: From east or west, exit Indiana Toll Rd. at Middlebury (Exit 107) and go north ¼ mi. to Country Rd. 2 and proceed west 1 mi. to inn. From Middlebury, follow Indiana Rte. 13 for 8 mi. north to Country Rd. 2 and west 1 mi.

BOTSFORD INN
Farmington Hills, Michigan (1969)

I go back a long time with the Botsford Inn, but not way back to 1836 when it was first built by Orrin Weston as a home, or to when the famous Botsford family took it over and converted it into an inn. But I have been visiting it for quite a few of the more recent years.

I can remember when I first heard of the Botsford Inn, my reaction was, "Who would expect to find a New England country inn in Detroit?" I soon learned that it wasn't really in Detroit, but Farmington Hills, and the people in Farmington Hills will tell you that there's quite a difference. It's a very pleasant residential town. The inn was a stagecoach stop on the road from Detroit, and, in fact, at one time the Grand River plank road followed an Indian trail that went on to Lake Michigan.

I strolled around the surprisingly spacious grounds and the rose garden, which was originally created by Mrs. Henry Ford, admiring the towering pine, maple, and elm trees. I realized that some of the more elegant features of the 19th century have been preserved at the Botsford, many by Mr. Henry Ford, who restored it in the 1920s. I think it is remarkable that such a valuable piece of property has not gone the way of the wrecking ball and bulldozer long before now.

One of the principal reasons for this must be attributed to the devotion of the present innkeeper and owner, John Anhut, who has a weakness for country inns. Following Mr. Ford's example, John has succeeded in holding back time. For example, in two sitting rooms there are many furnishings from Henry Ford's house, including a beautiful little inlaid spinet, a horsehair sofa, music boxes, inlaid mahogany tables, and spinning wheels.

The older sections of the inn have very low ceilings, huge beams, and handsome fireplaces with big andirons. One of the more celebrated features of the inn is the second-floor ballroom, where, at a country dance, long ago, Henry Ford first met the young lady who was to become his wife.

I'm certain that innkeeper Botsford and preserver Ford would approve of the contemporary changes that innkeeper Anhut has made, including tennis courts, air conditioning against the Detroit summer heat, and lodging rooms with reproductions of Colonial furniture.

It's also certain that the farmers, drovers, and traveling men of the past century would nod their heads in approval at the hearty offerings from the Botsford kitchen today. These include braised short ribs of beef with jardinière sauce, frogs' legs sautéed in chablis, Botsford old-fashioned chicken pot pie topped with flaky buttered crust, and roast prime rib of Western beef, au jus.

What appeals greatly to me about this inn is John Anhut himself. As busy as he is, he makes a concerted effort to meet every one of his guests. "Some of them have really become old friends to me," he said. "I think it's the best part of having a country inn."

The Botsford tradition of hospitality, begun during the Indian trail days, is continuing now with the Anhut family. In 1836, it was a day's journey from the banks of the river, where Detroit was a burgeoning city; today, it is just a short drive from the hustle and bustle of the Motor City. Worthwhile reminders of the past have been preserved and, best of all, the spirit of country innkeeping and community service is very much alive.

BOTSFORD INN, 28000 Grand River Ave., Farmington Hills, MI 48024; 313-474-4800. A 62-guestroom village inn on the city line of Detroit. European plan. Dinner served daily except Monday. Breakfast and lunch Tues. thru Sat. Sun. brunch. Closed Christmas and New Year's Day. Tennis on grounds. Greenfield Village, skiing, and state parks nearby. John Anhut, Innkeeper.

Directions: Located in Farmington Hills on I-96, easily accessible from major highways in Michigan.

The date in parenthesis in the heading represents the first year the inn appeared in the pages of Country Inns and Back Roads.

STAFFORD'S BAY VIEW INN
Petoskey, Michigan (1972)

"This," said Duff Smith, "is Hemingway country. Although he's associated with Paris and other glamorous places, actually this is the area where he spent 21 of his first 22 summers. He learned to hunt and fish here and this is where he was first married."

The aforementioned Janice Smith joined Stafford and me (Duff is really her pet name for him) and we walked a few paces from the inn across the railroad track and down to the shore of Little Traverse Bay, where I picked up a round, smooth stone and skipped it across the sparkling surface of the water. This was the same kind of stone Jan had pointed out to me a few years earlier, called the "Petoskey stone." It has many different colors, and I already have quite a few at home on my mantelpiece.

When we passed some young children who were out for a walk with their grandparents, it reminded me of some of the letters I have received from guests at Stafford's who are very pleased with the fact that guests of more advanced years are made so welcome at the inn.

"We just love them," said Janice. "They're wonderful. They mix so well with the very young; grandmothers and grandfathers always have patience with children and join in with the games. Lots of times I walk down to the tennis court area or the beach with them, and of course everyone knows that grandfathers know the best stories."

Stafford's, on the edge of the Bay View section of Petoskey, is a summer resort community that grew up around a program of music, drama, art, and religious lectures and services. The community began in the late 1800s, when people rode on the Grand Rapids/Indiana railroad or on lake steamers to reach this part of Michigan. The early residents built the Victorian homes that are scattered throughout Bay View today.

Stafford and Janice met in 1960, when he was the assistant manager of the inn and she was the hostess. Less than a year later he purchased the inn and they were married that same spring.

In 1986 there was a double celebration, the 100th anniversary of the Bay View Inn, and Stafford and Jan's twenty-fifth wedding anniversary. To help commemorate the event, the Smiths' children, Reg, Mary Kathryn, and Dean, presented their parents with a stained glass portrait of the inn, which is now hanging in the bay window of their family room.

The inn is a real Victorian experience, with its handsome mansard roof and cupola. Each of the bedrooms is furnished with period writing tables, rocking chairs, footed bathtubs, and antique beds. I like to think of it as an elegant antique lady. An elevator now goes to all three stories.

"Come on," said Janice. "Let's have a skipping contest, all three of us." Forthwith, we all searched for and found the best round skipping stones and pitched them far out, counting the skips on the waters of the lake. I'm afraid I was a poor third; the winner was Janice, of course.

STAFFORD'S BAY VIEW INN, Box 3, Petoskey, MI 49770; 616-347-2771. A 23-guestroom resort-inn on Little Traverse Bay in the Bay View section of Petoskey. Bed-and-breakfast plan includes full breakfast. Breakfast, lunch, and dinner served daily to travelers. Open daily May 18 to Nov. 1; Thanksgiving weekend; Christmas week, and long weekends during the winter sports season. Lake swimming and xc skiing on grounds. Historical Festival events, 3rd weekend in June. Bay View cultural programs in July and Aug. Golfing, boating, tennis, fishing, hiking, alpine ski trails, scenic and historic drives and excellent shopping nearby. Stafford and Janice Smith, Judy Honor, Innkeepers.

Directions: From Detroit take Gaylord exit from I-75 and follow Michigan Rte. 32 to Rte. 131, north to Petoskey. From Chicago, use Rte. 131, north to Petoskey.

I do not include lodging rates in the descriptions, for the very nature of an inn means that there are lodgings of various sizes, with and without baths, in and out of season, and with plain and fancy decoration. Travelers should call ahead and inquire about the availability and rates of the many different types of rooms.

LOWELL INN
Stillwater, Minnesota (1976)

This time I approached Stillwater from the north, following the course of the St. Croix River on Route 95. I began to understand why Art Palmer of the Lowell Inn was so enthusiastic about this part of the world. The rolling countryside, with its frequent glimpses of the river and the gentle touch of spring in the air, indeed creates a warm feeling for the generous gifts of middle America.

Just outside of Stillwater, the road drops down alongside the river, where there were dozens of watercraft, some of them already in use on the river here in late April.

Now the town of Stillwater came into view, dominated by a tall church spire, and a sign announced that this was indeed the birthplace of Minnesota in 1843. I passed the Washington County Historical Museum, and one block from the main street was the familiar building of the Lowell Inn with its Mount Vernon columns.

I stepped inside the reception area where all was quite serene. The grandfather clock told me that it was ten after one, and in the spacious George Washington Room on the right there were many people still enjoying lunch.

The lobby was bright and cheerful, with an oil painting of innkeeper Art Palmer's father over the mantel and a full-length painting of his beautiful mother on another wall. The Palmers have always been innovators—it runs in the family. It all started when Art's mother and father, who spent a great deal of their youth and young adulthood in show business, met here in Stillwater and were married. The opportunity arose to manage the inn, and so they stayed on and eventually became the owners in 1945. There's no doubt that the inn is a family enterprise, because there are several pictures of the Palmer family at various celebrations, including many weddings. There's a succession of growing children in a growing family.

The Palmer tradition of innovation is reflected in some of the unusual guest rooms at the Lowell Inn, some of which have circular bathtubs for two (if need be), a shower, and a jacuzzi. Each of the rooms is a true model of elegance. One has a circular glass standing shower and a washbowl of pink and white marble with very fancy fixtures. The bed with its decorator sheets and pillowcases looks almost too good to sit on. Each of the bedrooms has a small china cat carefully placed on each bed. "This is one of the most frequently mentioned of our ideas," smiled Arthur.

Barbara Cook, a very nice lady, came up and introduced herself to me. Barbara was here when Arthur's mother, Nelle, was here, and I was hungry for information about this very unusual woman. "Was she in evidence, was she here among the guests?" I asked. "Did she move among the tables and talk to people in the lobby?"

"Oh, yes. She always sat right in the dining room and watched everything. She was a very impressive woman."

"What are some of the things that are still going on here that she probably originated?"

"Well, our service. We've kept our service as it was when she was here, and she watched to make sure that it was always the best. I think it's wonderful that Mr. and Mrs. Palmer and the family have continued in that same tradition. She was a remarkable woman."

Barbara moved on to other duties and I sat down to lunch. I enjoyed the chicken livers that arrived in a small copper chafing dish and were kept warm by a lighted candle underneath, served with some absolutely smashing red cabbage and excellent chutney that went very well with liver.

As I passed through the lobby again, of course I looked up at that painting of Nelle on the wall. I felt as if I were getting to know her very well.

LOWELL INN, 102 N. Second St., Stillwater, MN 55082; 612-439-1100. A 22-guestroom village inn 18 mi. from St. Paul, near all the cultural attractions of the Twin Cities. European plan. Lunch and dinner served daily except Christmas Eve and Christmas Day. Open year-round. Canoeing, tennis, hiking, skiing, and swimming nearby, including 4 ski resorts within 15 mi. No pets. Arthur and Maureen Palmer, Innkeepers.

Directions: Stillwater is on the St. Croix River at the junction of Minn. 95 (north and south) and Minn. 36 (east and west). It is 7 mi. north of I-94 on Hwy. 95.

THE ST. JAMES HOTEL
Red Wing, Minnesota (1981)

The original St. James Hotel was built in the mid-1870s and according to the history of the hotel, was a very impressively designed and decorated building with various reception rooms, parlors, and a large ballroom, and was well known for its excellent food and service.

However, even at the top of its form it could not begin to approach today's *restored* St. James Hotel.

The entire project is a tribute to the fact that American ingenuity, capital, and know-how are able to reproduce successfully almost every type of furniture, ornamentation, decoration, and design of a hundred years ago, and still maintain the very best quality.

Almost all the furnishings in the St. James are copies of lamps, bureaus, tables, chairs, beds, and carpets originally manufactured during the Victorian era. All of this furniture is solid, well made, and sturdy, and doesn't have the rickety feeling that sometimes occurs. Even the small details have been considered, including brass soap holders, towel racks, doorknobs, hinges, and the like.

The hotel is a modern accommodation of today, but serves as a reminder of opulent days gone by. In addition to excellent reproductions, the photographs and prints taken in a bygone era are further reminders of the past. Many of the walls are hung with pictures of Red Wing, taken over a hundred years ago, both of the town and of the river steamers that made the town a regular stop.

What excites me most is that this small hotel in the heart of America could have been torn down and gone the way of so many others, but instead, it is making a contribution that bids fair to endure for at least another hundred years.

Turn-down bed service and the morning newspaper at the door are a couple of the niceties that add to the pleasure of a visit to the St. James. Bed linens and towels are of first-rate quality and the quilts for each bed were especially designed and made to harmonize with the furnishings and colors of the room. Many of the rooms look out upon the Mississippi River, where the unending flow of barges provides constant entertainment. An excursion boat is available for guests who would like a closer look at the river.

The Amtrak station is just across the street from St. James and many of the guests arrive in this most convenient fashion.

The lobby of the old original hotel has been restored, but it is not used as the lobby of today's St. James. Instead, it has been set aside for parties, banquets, and special occasions. Photographs of the original 1870s investors, who put up all of $60,000, look down upon today's travelers with a certain undisguised smugness.

A most unusual and fascinating history of the old St. James Hotel, recounted in the words of staff members who worked there in the earlier years of this century, has been compiled with great attention and loving care. Entitled *If Walls Could Talk*, the booklet has some wonderful photographs ranging from 1875 to 1980, and provides an interesting glimpse not only into the workings of a hotel, but also of life in days gone by.

The new–old St. James, always a familiar landmark in Red Wing, is making even greater strides in the 1980s.

ST. JAMES HOTEL, 406 Main St., Red Wing, MN 55066; 612-388-2846. A 60-guestroom restored country town hotel on the Mississippi River, 50 mi. from Minneapolis. Open all year. Breakfast, lunch, and dinner served to travelers. This is an in-town hotel with no sports or recreation on the grounds, but swimming, tennis, hiking, golf, bicycling, backroading, and river sightseeing trips are all very convenient. No pets. Gene Foster, General Manager.

Directions: From Minneapolis/St. Paul Airport take Hwy. 5 east, exit on Hwy. 55 to cross Mendota Bridge. Follow Hwy. 55 to Hastings where it joins Hwy. 61. Follow Hwy. 61, 22 mi. south into Red Wing. Accessible by Amtrak.

SCHUMACHER'S NEW PRAGUE HOTEL
New Prague, Minnesota (1979)

John Schumacher, who is one of the most energetic and cheerful people I've ever met, was telling me about some of the main courses at his inn. "Our game menu includes pheasant, quail, venison, and rabbit served in various ways. In addition, there is a full poultry menu, lots of fish and seafood, some Czech dishes, including sausages, and several veal dishes. As a matter of fact, I think there are about fifty-six main offerings on the menu.

"There's a special 'healthy heart cuisine' menu for people who are so inclined and also a menu for lighter appetites, including sauerbrauten sandwiches and a steak sandwich. Of course, the desserts will cancel out all of your good intentions."

John is a very innovative chef, having graduated first in his class from the Culinary Institute of America. He and Kathleen are young innkeepers who gain great satisfaction and personal fulfillment in running a country inn. As he says, "It's been a wonderful experience since I first came to New Prague a few years ago, and right from the start there were many things that had to be done, but it's been a highly satisfactory arrangement. Fortunately, I'm a chef and I feel that a great deal of our reputation centers around the fact that the food is something that I can control."

The building for Schumacher's New Prague Hotel was built in 1898 and originally was called the Broz Hotel. It was designed by Cass Gilbert, the same man who designed the George Washington Bridge, the Supreme Court building in Washington, and the State Capitol in Saint Paul.

If the menu and the food are impressive, then the inn's twelve guest rooms are equally so. Each is named for a different month and has an atmosphere and personality all its own. For example, January has "three-bear beds"—two beds put together to make a king-sized bed. Many of the guest rooms have a folk art theme; however, April departs and features an antique Victorian three-piece settee and a king-sized custom round bed with a mirrored headboard.

Wilkommen is stenciled on the floor of the entry for September, and the twin beds have red and white canopies, and wall coverings of red linen from Austria.

"We've been to Europe several times," John pointed out, "and I believe the decorations and cuisine here reflect my identification with Germany and Czechoslovakia. We have imported cotton-covered goosedown comforters and pillows, and there are many central-European decorative touches.

"We don't have any televisions or telephones in the rooms, but there are fresh arrangements of flowers and live plants, complimentary local newspapers, lots of books and magazines, and we even put candy under the pillows."

The latest news from John and Kathleen is that they are going to add additional rooms by remodeling the house next door.

New Prague is just thirty-five miles south of the Minneapolis/Saint Paul metropolitan area, and besides the fun of staying at Schumacher's, there is a surprising number of things to do nearby, including golf, tennis, and cross-country skiing. The Minnesota River is just nine miles away and is ideal for canoeing. The area is excellent for biking as well as running.

SCHUMACHER'S NEW PRAGUE HOTEL, 212 West Main St., New Prague, MN 56071; 612-758-2133. (Metro line: 612-445-7285.) A 12-guestroom (private baths) Czechoslovakian–German inn located in a small country town, approx. 35 mi. south of Minneapolis and St. Paul. European plan. Breakfast, lunch, and dinner served to travelers all year except 3 days at Christmas. Good bicycling and backroading nearby; also xc skiing, tennis, and golf. No entertainment available to amuse children. No pets. No credit cards. Kathleen and John Schumacher, Innkeepers.

Directions: From Minneapolis, take Rte. 494 west to Rte. 169 south to Jordan exit. Turn south on Rte. 21 for 9 mi. to New Prague. Turn left to Main St. at the stop sign, and the hotel is in the second block on the right.

THE BUXTON INN
Granville, Ohio (1976)

Ever since I learned about the connection between Granville, Massachusetts, and Granville, Ohio, on my first visit to the Buxton Inn in 1975, I've been fascinated by it. The fact is that Granville in western Massachusetts, just above the Connecticut border, is a very attractive town that happens to be well known in the area for having exceptionally fine cheese.

Granville, Ohio, the home of the Buxton Inn, has been called "Ohio's best kept secret." "It was founded in 1805 by a mass migration from Granby, Connecticut, and Granville, Massachusetts," Orville Orr told me. "The community is laid out like a typical New England village, as you can see, with broad tree-lined streets, a town square where pioneers built four churches, and the Denison University campus."

He continued, "We have over one hundred buildings on the National Register of Historic Places. Most of the businesses are located in the restored downtown area, where three blocks are dominated by the Avery-Downer House, which houses the Robbins Hunter Museum, furnished with 18th- and 19th-century American and English furniture, paintings, and decorative accessories."

If I had only one word that might describe the Buxton Inn it is "flair." On each of my visits since that now memorable first one, when a very young Amy Orr conducted me on my first tour of the inn and the town, there has been something exciting either accomplished or in the developmental stage. It seems that all of the Orr family, including Audrey, Orville, Amy, and Melanie, have unusual talents that are expressed in the inn.

The Buxton was originally built in 1812, and the Orr family has recreated the atmosphere of an inn of that period, even to the point of having waitresses and hosts and hostesses dressed in carefully researched costumes of the time.

Actually, the inn is a reflection of 175 years of changing styles, with the tastes and fashions of owners and innkeepers of different eras represented in the fabrics and designs. "We tend to collect things from different periods anyway," Audrey told me, "and we've furnished our bedrooms and dining rooms with different themes. Originally, we used period chairs in one of the dining rooms and discovered that they were too small; people were sliding off. So we reluctantly took them out and put in new, larger chairs."

I've always been intrigued by the printed menu at the Buxton Inn, not only because it contains the very interesting history of the inn, but also because it has far more offerings than the average menu, including many varieties of seafood, and such hearty offerings as veal sweetbreads,

baby beef liver à l'orange, Louisiana chicken with artichoke hearts, and others. Be sure to ask about the spareribs with a most marvelous barbecue sauce.

Perhaps it's the atmosphere of a college town that encourages the Orrs to reach out beyond the visible horizon. Many things have been done here over the years I've been visiting. There was the creation of the Wine Cellar and the Tavern downstairs, where the original drivers and settlers would be fed when this was a stagecoach inn after 1812. The gazebo and the fountain, the columns and colonnades in back of the inn, all create a feeling of Roman baths.

The most recent addition is a beautiful dining room, glassed in on three sides and with a glass roof, giving the room a greenhouse feeling. Still more of the nearby homes have been converted into further guest rooms, including the Warner House on the corner.

It is obvious to me that the Orrs are people with dreams and a capacity for inventiveness that has allowed them to continue to turn their dreams into realities—realities that fortunately become wonderful benefits for inn guests at the Buxton.

It's a bit of a distance from Granville, Massachusetts, to Granville, Ohio, but it's always a great pleasure for me.

THE BUXTON INN, 313 E. Broadway, Granville, OH 43023; 614-587-0001. A 16-guestroom inn in a college town in central Ohio near Denison University, the Indian Mounds Museum, and the Heisey Glass Museum. European plan. Lunch and dinner served daily. Closed Christmas Day. Golf, tennis, horseback riding, cultural activities nearby. No pets. Orville and Audrey Orr, Innkeepers.

Directions: Take Granville exit from I-70. Travel north 8 mi. on Rte. 37 into Granville.

THE GOLDEN LAMB
Lebanon, Ohio (1970)

Sandra Reynolds and I were seated in the lobby of the Golden Lamb, waiting for Jack Reynolds to finish a telephone call, and then we were all going to walk up the street to the Warren County Museum.

Just to be in this lobby is to partake of a generous helping of the American past. Among other things, there was a lamp, the base of which was made out of a candle mold, and a curly maple table. An old coal stove that was used 100 years or more ago is still in use today. Always on hand is a big punch bowl, where guests and friends may enjoy a modicum of refreshment. There are quite a few examples of Shaker crafts in the lobby and elsewhere in the inn, including Shaker boxes, dowels, chests, and Shaker-style furniture in the dining room.

"The Shakers came to this section of Ohio during the 19th century and attracted buyers from all over the country with their fine farm stock, medicinal herbs, furniture, and other household essentials," explained Sandra. "Their community, Union Village, was sold by them over a half-century ago, but we have a lot of local interest in their culture, and the Warren County Museum has a considerable area devoted to Shaker memorabilia."

If Ohio could be called the "mother of presidents," the Golden Lamb might be called the "mother of country inns," because it is a significant force in providing inspiration for many innkeepers to preserve the best of the old, and at the same time to back it up with good innkeeping. Throughout the inn are found artifacts, furniture, and furnishings that have been collected from America's past that in a sense give us a real feeling of appreciation for what our forebears thought was beautiful, useful, and promising.

The building dates back to 1815 and was built on the site of an original log cabin erected by Jonas Seaman, who was granted a license in

1803 to operate "a house of public entertainment." Even before roads were built many guests came on foot or horseback to the inn. Here, in the warmth of the tavern's public rooms, they exchanged news of the world and related their own experiences. Many famous people have stopped here, including ten United States presidents as well as Henry Clay, Mark Twain, and Charles Dickens. Overnight guests may stay in rooms that are named for some of the great and near-great, both national and international, who have enjoyed accommodations here in the past.

Since this lovely old inn is a part of the heartland of America, it stands to reason that the main dishes would be representative of American cooking. There is beef in many forms, rainbow trout, and fried Kentucky ham steak. Roast duckling with wild rice dressing, flounder, Warren County turkey, and pork tenderloin are some of the principal entrées. When possible, vegetables from the nearby verdant Ohio countryside are used.

Each guest room is named for a famous guest and is filled with antiques. When the rooms are not occupied, visitors may stroll through the halls and peek at the collection of chests, wardrobes, tables, and beds.

One of the most rewarding times to visit this inn is during the Christmas holiday season, when it is decorated literally "to the nines." Planning starts in July, with decisions on the theme and the menu. It is also the scene for the Cincinnati Art Club annual show.

THE GOLDEN LAMB INN, 27 S. Broadway, Lebanon, OH 45036; 513-932-5065. A historic 20-guestroom (19 private baths) village inn in the heart of Ohio farming country on U.S. Hwys. 63, 42, and 48. European plan. Breakfast served only on Sundays. Lunch and dinner served daily except Christmas. Golf and tennis nearby. No pets. Jackson Reynolds, Innkeeper.

Directions: From I-71, exit Rte. 48N, 3 mi. north to Lebanon. From I-75, exit Rte. 63E, 7 mi. east to Lebanon.

"European Plan" means that rates for rooms and meals are separate. "American Plan" means that meals are included in the cost of the room. "Modified American Plan" means that breakfast and dinner are included in the cost of the room. The rates at some inns include a continental breakfast with the lodging.

THE INN AT HONEY RUN
Millersburg, Ohio (1984)

It was about 6:45 a.m. I was taking a short walk before joining Marjorie Stock for breakfast at the Inn at Honey Run. It was one of those magic times of the day when the moon is still out and the sun is on the rise. In fact, the moon was directly overhead, and the fleecy morning clouds had the wonderful pink, grey, and white tones caught by some of the 18th-century French court painters.

In a sense, I guess that Marjorie is like an artist who had an ideal and set out to accomplish it. The Inn at Honey Run was her ideal, and now on this, my third visit, I told her it has come to full fruition.

"Oh, don't say that," she had said the night before. "I have ideas in my head that haven't even been discovered yet, and here at the inn we are always finding more things to do."

Designed to harmonize completely with the rolling countryside and set amidst a stand of maple, ash, oak, poplar, black walnut, butternut, and hickory trees, the inn is a bird watcher's delight. It is multilevel, with many rooms that give the impression of actually dwelling in the forest.

The guest rooms are a potpourri of styles, including Shaker and Early American. The woods used in the guest rooms reflect the trees of the forest. Everything has been made in Ohio, much of it in Holmes County. Many of the woven and quilted wall-hangings are also done by Ohio craftspeople.

My morning walk had taken me to some of the places where I had joined Marjorie the evening before, with even further views of this rolling countryside, which would have delighted Grant Wood or Thomas Hart Benton. My moon, at the quarter, was still brilliant but I could see it was losing out to the sun. Around me the many trees that have been carefully preserved by Marjorie, as well as the shrubs and bushes, which so beautifully augment the architecture of the inn, would be in their full

autumn glory in a few short days. I couldn't help but reflect on how patient she has been, waiting for all of these things to come together.

This particular area is also to be the locale for "Hobbit Habitats," which will undoubtedly be featured in our next edition.

My morning walk had stirred my breakfast yearnings, so I headed back to the dining room, where meals are made from scratch and include freshly squeezed orange juice in the morning. In the evening there are such things as pan-fried trout from Holmes County waters, vegetables carefully steamed to perfection, and a menu that is impressive for both its offerings and its reasonable prices.

Marjorie's idea of having "Tuesday Tastings," a buffet of about twenty-seven items, has continued to make an impression on the guests, who also provide a continued source of testing to update food.

I walked through the main lobby with its massive chimney fireplace and stepped for a second out on one of the many decks, which seem literally to thrust themselves into the forest. Here, looking toward the eastern sky, I saw that the sun had made its full appearance, and the hues and tones of early fall could now be more easily distinguished.

The Inn at Honey Run is not a quaint, old-fashioned country inn. It is a bold, modern concept that might well be setting the pace for future inns. Instead of reproducing an old inn, Marjorie Stock has built a contemporary inn that makes its own statement, and this statement will be telling something to the inn-goers of 100 years from now about what was contemporary in the 1980s and 1990s.

THE INN AT HONEY RUN, 6920 County Road 203, Millersburg, OH 44654; 216-674-0011. A 25-guestroom country inn located in north-central Ohio's beautiful, wooded countryside. Open all year. Lunch and dinner served Mon. thru Sat. Advance reservations only. Sun. breakfast and lunch served to houseguests only. Breakfast is included in the over-night rate. Ample opportunities for recreation and backroading in Ohio's Amish country. No facilities for small children. No pets. Marjorie Stock, Innkeeper.

Directions: From Millersburg, proceed on E. Jackson St. (Rtes. 39 and 62) past courthouse and gas station on right. At next corner turn left onto Rte. 241. At 1 mi. the road goes downhill. At 1 3/4 mi. it crosses the bridge over Honey Run; turn right immediately around the small hill onto Rte. 203 (not well marked). After about 1 1/2 mi. turn right at inn sign. (Watch out for the Amish horse-drawn buggies.)

WELSHFIELD INN RESTAURANT
Burton, Ohio (1973)

I've been visiting the Welshfield since the late 60s. Skillet-fried chicken, baked ham, fresh fillet of sole, salmon, and apple pie are some of the specialties. Brian Holmes says, "We never use mixes. Our rolls and bread are made from scratch." This is a real country restaurant with real country cooking.

Brian says that the recipe for indian pudding came from Cape Cod. "We took it as a compliment when one of our guests said it tasted exactly like the pudding at the Red Inn in Provincetown."

The restaurant has a very interesting collection of 19th-century antiques and bric-a-brac. The center of interest is an old nickelodeon. The music has a nostalgic flavor and sounds like a combination of mandolin, flute, violin, and piano.

WELSHFIELD INN RESTAURANT, Rte. 422, Burton, OH 44021; 216-834-4164. A country restaurant on Rte. 422, 28 mi. east of Cleveland. No lodgings. Lunch and dinner served weekdays. Dinner only served on Sun. and holidays. Closed the week of July 4 and 3 wks. after Jan. 1. Closed Mon. except Labor Day. Near Sea World and Holden Arboretum. Brian and Polly Holmes, Innkeepers.

Directions: On U.S. 422 at intersection of Ohio 700, midway between Cleveland and Youngstown, Ohio.

Favorite Back Roads

One of our most striking back roads is the delightful, winding, sixteen-foot-wide blacktop roadway that threads its way along the bluff for 21 miles from Harbor Springs to Cross Village. There is a steady succession of tunnels, shaded bowers and bosky dells, as well as historic touches. This is historic Indian country, graced with lingering softwood greens, tinged with hardwood red and purple and gold.

You start at the main intersection in Harbor Springs, head north up the high hill above the town, past Bluff Gardens, and continue on past the well-manicured links of the Harbor Springs Golf Club. This is followed by a solid mile of tree cover that leaps the road overhead; mostly maple, beech, oak, and cedar, with summer homes tucked away, barely in sight.

Continuing through West Traverse, the road passes an old country school and about five miles from Harbor Springs crosses Five-Mile Creek where there is an old mill. Next to it is a tiny "mom and pop" general store, typical of those to be found in Michigan's lumbering communities. Soon, one comes to a unique barnyard golf course where there are no greens fees. Its sporting, rolling, cobby terrain has plenty of hazards and gorse-type rough.

After three miles of winding, woodsy road, you arrive at a scenic turnout high above the rocky beach of Lake Michigan. On the far shore of Little Traverse Bay, the huge greenish globe of the Big Rock Nuclear Plant looks like a marble perched on the beach.

The road continues past the old Indian mission church and on into Good Hart, which has a combination general store–antique shop–post office. About fifteen miles from Harbor Springs, there's a century-old cemetery, nicely kept in its setting of leafy dignity, and then a two-mile stretch of very old, very high, wind-blown sand dunes.

Now the road has taken you to Cross Village, where you can continue along Emmett County Scenic Route 1—twenty miles to Mackinaw City by way of a magnificent array of sand dunes and open beach—or return the way you came, but nearer the lake by taking a couple of optional turns.

Stafford Smith
Stafford's Bay View Inn
Petoskey, Michigan

OLD RITTENHOUSE INN
Bayfield, Wisconsin (1980)

"Jerry was still working on his music degree at the University of Wisconsin, and I had just gotten a teaching job. We came to Bayfield on our honeymoon in 1969, and as soon as we saw this lovely old house we fell in love with it."

At first I thought Mary Phillips was speaking of the present building that houses the Old Rittenhouse Inn, but I soon realized she was really speaking of what was known for many years in Bayfield as "The Mansion."

"In 1973, we came back on a visit and noticed *this* house and wondered how we could have missed it on previous visits. We bought it for a song, and it's been our expanding home ever since." The Old Rittenhouse Inn is a Queen Anne-style mansion with an unusually wide veranda, decorated with hanging flowers and wicker furniture.

The sequel to this interesting episode is that the Phillipses did eventually buy the Mansion and have done it over with the aid of their partner, Greg Carrier. It has been renamed Le Chateau Boutin, and it is now a part of the Old Rittenhouse Inn.

There have been exciting things happening here ever since my first visit in 1979. These two musician-innkeepers have refused from the very start to accept the idea that Bayfield was simply a summertime resort area. They began by staging Christmas and Valentine's Day dinner concerts at the inn, and these developed into many more activities. The success of their programs made it necessary to expand, and so today the original five guest rooms have been augmented with another ten, and Mary finally has a full and proper kitchen.

Antiques being one of Jerry's sidelines, each of the guest rooms has been handsomely outfitted with antique furniture, and a few of them have their own fireplaces.

It may be that Jerry and Mary are best known for their dinners. Jerry, resplendent in a Victorian tailcoat, describes the menu to his dinner guests, and it is also given in detail by the waitress later on. The fixed-price dinners start with several soups and a variety of entrées, including Lake Superior trout cooked in champagne, lamb, seafood crêpes, scallops, or chicken Cordon Bleu. The breads and preserves are all homemade. Their gourmet foods are also on sale at the inn and through a mail-order business that includes jams, jellies, marmalades, candies, fruit cakes, and many other delicious gifts.

The Phillipses have prepared a splendid new brochure entitled "Bayfield–A Place For All Seasons." My copy lists every special event, seminar, festival, workshop, concert, and island adventure that can be enjoyed in Bayfield or on nearby Madeline Island throughout the entire

year. Just to give you a quick idea, there's a quilters' retreat in October, the Christmas Festival in December, ski touring in the winter, a bed-and-breakfast basic conference in February, and winter adventures on Lake Superior. The brochure continues with a "Woman and Money" conference in March, duck decoy wood carving, and such special events as Native American Arts week and, of course, the famous Apple Festival in October. The Phillipses will be glad to send you your copy.

It has certainly been a pleasure for me to visit and revisit the Old Rittenhouse Inn and enjoy good fun, good eating, and wonderful hospitality.

OLD RITTENHOUSE INN, Box 584, 301 Rittenhouse Ave., Bayfield, WI 54818; 715-779-5765. A 15-guestroom Victorian inn in an area of historic and natural beauty, 70 mi. east of Duluth, Minn., on the shore of Lake Superior. European plan. Breakfast, lunch, and dinner served to travelers. Open May 1 to Nov. 1; weekends through the winter. Advance reservations most desirable. Extensive recreational activity of all kinds available throughout the year, including tours, hiking, and cycling on the nearby Apostle and Madeline Islands. Not comfortable for small children. No pets. Jerry and Mary Phillips, Innkeepers.

Directions: From the Duluth Airport, follow Rte. 53-S through the city of Duluth over the bridge to Superior, Wis. Turn east on Rte. 2 near Ashland (1½ hrs.), turn north on 13-N to Bayfield.

SEVEN PINES LODGE
Lewis, Wisconsin (1981)

I parked my car among the tall pine trees and immediately became aware of the sounds of the woods—a combination of water, birds, and wind. The front door of the lodge opened and out scampered a beautiful little golden Labrador retriever, and to the forest sounds were added the delighted and welcoming squeals of what Joan Simpson refers to as "our official greeter."

Joan and David Simpson, along with their son, John-David, and daughter, Tina, are the innkeepers of this rustic hideaway in the Wisconsin forest. It was built in 1903 by Charles Lewis, a grain broker and financier from Minneapolis. Constructed of handhewn logs, the lodge has retained its original appeal and surprising elegance, including an array of interesting antiques that are an integral part of the decor. Ninety percent of the furniture and decorations have been here since Mr. Lewis's time.

Immediately upon my arrival I took a pleasant stroll with Joan, scuffing through the dried leaves to the trout stream, and we passed through a grove of original pine trees, some of which are 115 feet high. Passing over a rustic bridge beside a melodious waterfall, we entered an almost pagodalike, two-story log building with a full screened porch around four sides of the second floor. This is a summer sleeping porch, and I can just imagine the good times enjoyed here by families.

We followed the stream a short distance and came to a sylvan pool with a stone statue of a young Indian boy. As we were drinking in the quiet loveliness of the scene, Joan pointed to a finny denizen and said, "There goes a dinner."

She explained that the brownies, rainbows, and brook trout, all of which are raised on the property, often appear on the menu.

Joan does all the cooking, and David and John-David take care of the tables. Guests frequently sit at the kitchen table while she prepares the Scandinavian bread, desserts, trout dinners, and the hearty meals that are welcomed by guests, who usually have spent most of the day outdoors, whether it be summer or winter. There are miles of cross-country ski trails. "When guests make reservations they are given a choice of one of three main dishes, although most returning guests like the trout."

Accommodations at Seven Pines Lodge are in the main building, where there are five year-round bedrooms, and also in log outbuildings, used only during temperate weather. These have a real "woodsy" feeling.

That evening I joined the other guests around the dinner table, and then we all adjourned to the friendly confines of the living room, where there is a big oval table with an overhead lamp that provides convenient lighting by which to enjoy albums of fascinating photographs of the lodge as it was in earlier times. Some *Portland Oregonian* newspapers

for 1922 provided us all with a good deal of entertainment and laughs.

Joan and a friend had done a wildflower study that catalogued 181 different wildflowers. The fly fishermen oohed and aahed over the brand-new fly display case with beautiful specimens tied by David Crooks. And so the evening passed quite pleasantly in the big rustic living room, where there is no television. There is only one telephone in the lodge itself. There's nothing to disturb the peace and serenity at Seven Pines Lodge.

SEVEN PINES LODGE, Lewis, WI 54851; 715-653-2323. A 10-guest-room rustic resort-inn (most rooms have shared baths) in the Wisconsin woods about 1½ hrs. from Minneapolis. Open year-round. Closed Thanksgiving and Christmas Day. Trout fishing on grounds. St. Croix Falls, Taylors Falls, National Wild River Scenic Waterway nearby. Tennis, swimming, golf, woodswalking, xc, downhill skiing, backroading nearby. Very attractive for children of all ages since the innkeepers also have children. No pets. No credit cards. Joan and David Simpson, Innkeepers.

Directions: From Minneapolis/St. Paul: follow 135W or 135E north to U.S. 8 at Forest Lake, Minn. East on U.S. 8 through Taylors Falls, Minn./St. Croix Falls, Wisc., to Wisc. 35 north to Lewis. Turn right at gas station to T, right 1 mi. to fork in road and turn left ½ mi. to Seven Pines Lodge entrance.

THE WHITE GULL INN
Fish Creek, Wisconsin (1979)

This is actually going to be a tale of not one inn, but two inns. One is the White Gull Inn, where I have been visiting Jan and Andy Coulson and their two daughters, Meredith and Emilie Lindsley, for quite a few years. The other inn is the Whistling Swan, which the Coulsons purchased and have remodeled and redecorated during the last year or more. Both inns are located in the heart of Fish Creek's historic section.

The White Gull is a full-service inn, built as part of a large resort area more than seventy-five years ago, when hundreds of tourists would arrive in Fish Creek from Chicago and Milwaukee aboard steamships. Nowadays, guests drive or fly to Fish Creek because the beautiful waterfront, the main street, and the sparkling atmosphere have remained unchanged.

The main inn is a white clapboard, three-story building with an air of informality. The rooms, which have been increasing in numbers over recent years, are tidy and neat, and have been undergoing a steady redecorating program.

In the Midwest, the White Gull is justifiably famous for its traditional Fish Boils, featuring freshly caught lake fish, boiled potatoes, homemade cole slaw, fresh-baked bread, and cherry pie. Russ Ostrand has been the master boiler for over twenty years. He prepares a roaring fire, and the fish are boiled in two huge iron cauldrons. He also plays the accordion and leads everybody in lots of singing and clapping of hands.

Besides the Fish Boils, the White Gull also has a more familiar evening menu.

Now, to the Whistling Swan, a bed and breakfast inn, with four bedrooms and three suites with antique beds and dressers, comfortable reading chairs and reading lights, carpeting and wallpaper that matches the fabrics. Most of the bathrooms have the original meticulously reglazed tubs, pedestal sinks, and brass fixtures.

A continental breakfast featuring fresh-squeezed orange juice and freshly baked pastry is served in the summer on the huge veranda, and guests take their ease in wicker chairs and rockers. Wintertime guests have a full breakfast at the White Gull. Bookings can be made for the Swan through the White Gull. In fact, dinners are taken at the White Gull by Whistling Swan guests, if desired.

Jan and Andy have also opened the Whistling Swan Shop, which sells unusual gift items plus a distinctive line of women's and children's clothing, elegantly displayed in antique armoires and dressers.

And so Jan and Andy and Joan Holliday and Nancy Vaughn and the remainder of the staff at the White Gull and the Whistling Swan continue to make progress in some respect with each passing year. I'm sure it won't

be long before Meredith, eight years old, and Emilie Lindsley, three and a half, will be taking over some of the innkeeping duties themselves.

Door County is a wonderful place to visit in any season of the year and, thanks to the presence of two fine inns, it's a great place for a holiday.

THE WHITE GULL INN, Fish Creek, WI 54212; 414-868-3517. A 13-guestroom inn with 4 cottages (private and shared baths) and additional guestrooms in the Whistling Swan in a most scenic area in Door County, 23 mi. north of Sturgeon Bay. Open year-round. European plan. Breakfast, lunch, and dinner except Thanksgiving and Christmas. Fish Boils: Wed., Fri., Sat., Sun. nights May thru Oct.; Wed. and Sat. nights Nov. thru April. All meals open to travelers; reservations requested. Considerable outdoor and cultural attractions; golf, tennis, swimming, fishing, biking, sailing, xc skiing, and other summer and winter sports nearby. Excellent for children of all ages. No pets. Andy and Jan Coulson, Joan Holliday, and Nancy Vaughn, Innkeepers.

Directions: From Chicago: take I-94 to Milwaukee. Follow Rte. I-43 from Milwaukee to Manitowoc; Rte. 42 from Manitowoc to Fish Creek. Turn left at stop sign at the bottom of the hill, go 2½ blocks to inn. From Green Bay; take Rte. 57 to Sturgeon Bay; Rte. 42 to Fish Creek.

A number of inns have nearby airports where private airplanes may land. An airplane symbol at the end of the inn directions indicates that there is an airport nearby. Consult inn for further information.

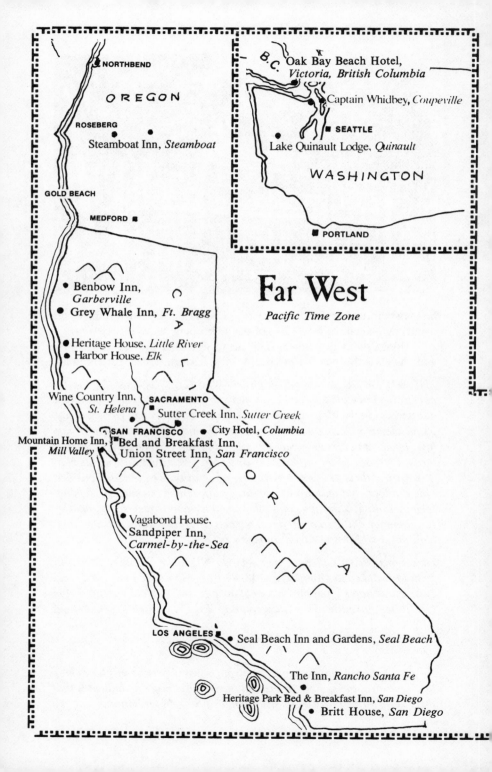

NORTHBEND

OREGON

ROSEBERG

Steamboat Inn, *Steamboat*

GOLD BEACH

MEDFORD

B.C. Oak Bay Beach Hotel, *Victoria, British Columbia*

Captain Whidbey, *Coupeville*

SEATTLE

Lake Quinault Lodge, *Quinault*

WASHINGTON

PORTLAND

Far West

Pacific Time Zone

Benbow Inn, *Garberville*

Grey Whale Inn, *Ft. Bragg*

Heritage House, *Little River*

Harbor House, *Elk*

Wine Country Inn, *St. Helena*

SACRAMENTO

Sutter Creek Inn, *Sutter Creek*

SAN FRANCISCO City Hotel, *Columbia*

Mountain Home Inn, *Mill Valley* Bed and Breakfast Inn,

Union Street Inn, *San Francisco*

Vagabond House,
Sandpiper Inn,
Carmel-by-the-Sea

LOS ANGELES Seal Beach Inn and Gardens, *Seal Beach*

The Inn, *Rancho Santa Fe*

Heritage Park Bed & Breakfast Inn, *San Diego*

Britt House, *San Diego*

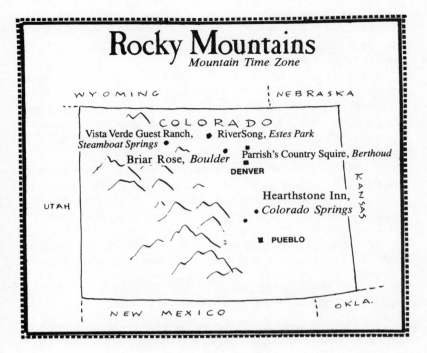

Rocky Mountains
Mountain Time Zone

WYOMING | NEBRASKA

COLORADO

Vista Verde Guest Ranch, • RiverSong, *Estes Park*
Steamboat Springs •

Briar Rose, *Boulder* Parrish's Country Squire, *Berthoud*

DENVER

UTAH

KANSAS

Hearthstone Inn,
• *Colorado Springs*

■ PUEBLO

NEW MEXICO | OKLA.

ARIZONA

Rancho de los Caballeros,
• *Wickenburg*

■ PHOENIX

Lodge on the Desert,
Tanque Verde,
• *Tucson*

THE BED AND BREAKFAST INN
San Francisco, California (1979)

Good, bad, or indifferent, every bed-and-breakfast inn or bed-and-breakfast home on the West Coast owes a debt of gratitude to the Bed and Breakfast Inn in San Francisco. For quite a few years it was the only one of its kind, and now I understand that there are over forty in that city alone. It's a pity they did not all borrow the high standards and admirable objectives, as well as the idea, of the Bed and Breakfast Inn.

It was a wonderful warm morning in mid-September. The sun shone down from a completely cloudless sky, and happy San Franciscans moved briskly up and down the many hills of the city pursuing the day's occupations—the kind of a day in which I knew everything would go right, and it did.

I had walked a few blocks on Union Street, then turned on Charlton Court, and I was standing in front of one of San Francisco's Victorian

houses, painted light green; wooden stairs ascended the front of the building to the very top floor. There were beautiful golden marigolds in boxes and pots placed around the porches and a birdhouse with a very chipper occupant. The sign said, "The Bed and Breakfast Inn."

The reception room apparently was used as one of the breakfast areas. It had a very light and airy feeling, enhanced by white wicker furniture, many flower arrangements, and light touches everywhere. The enticing aroma of fresh coffee filled the room, and some guests were just finishing delicious-looking croissants.

There followed in delightful order my first meeting with Marily Kavanaugh and her husband, Bob; a tour of all the rooms in the inn, and a leisurely chat on the garden deck.

First the lodging rooms: some of them are named after various parts of London. There's Covent Garden, Chelsea, Green Park, and Kensington Garden. Other rooms are called The Library, Autumn Sun, The Willows, Mandalay, and the Celebration. "The Mayfair Flat," has been created in the Kavanaughs' former duplex apartment on the top floor. It has a spiral staircase to a bedroom loft, a double tub, a kitchen, and a view of the Golden Gate Bridge.

Each room provides an entirely different experience. For example, many have completely different sets of sheets, pillowcases, and towels. There are all varieties of beds, including traditional shiny brass bedsteads. There are flowers everywhere, thermos jugs of ice-water, many books, baskets of fruit, electric clocks with an alarm, down pillows, and gorgeous coverlets and spreads. Five of the bedrooms have their own bathrooms, and the others share. Four rooms have the garden view. I saw old-fashioned British ceiling fans in some of the rooms.

The location of the Bed and Breakfast is another virtue. Charlton Court is a little dead-end street off Union, between Buchanan and Laguna. It's within easy walking distance of Fisherman's Wharf. In fact, San Francisco is such a "walking place" that it's convenient to everything. The nicest part of it is that when people get tired of walking, they can always take the cable cars!

THE BED AND BREAKFAST INN, Four Charlton Court, San Francisco, CA 94123; 415-921-9784. A 9-guestroom European-style pension in the Union Street district of San Franciso. Convenient to all of the Bay area recreational, cultural, and gustatory attractions. Continental breakfast is the only meal offered. Open daily year-round. Not comfortable for children. No pets. No credit cards. Robert and Marily Kavanaugh, Innkeepers.

Directions: Take the Van Ness Exit from Rte. 101 and proceed to Union Street. Charlton Court is a small courtyard street halfway between Laguna and Buchanan, off Union.

BENBOW INN
Garberville, California (1974)

I first visited the Benbow Inn in 1973 and was immediately intrigued not only with its location in the glorious redwood country of northern California, but also with its design, which shows definite influences of the Art Deco style of the early 1920s. There are also some touches of an English Tudor manor house found in the half-timbers, carved dark wood paneling, solid oak furniture, bookcases, hardwood floors, handsome oriental rugs, and truly massive fireplace in the main living room.

Some guest rooms are on the terrace and garden levels with private patios. With four-poster beds, antiques, and country fabrics, their decor is most attractive. Three of them have fireplaces. Other guest rooms in the main inn had also been handsomely redecorated, and my own room, Number 313, was on the top floor and looked out over the gardens and a wonderful changing panorama of clouds.

The owners-innkeepers of the Benbow are Patsy and Chuck Watts, whom I have known for many years. The one outstanding quality that each of them has in such marvelous abundance is enthusiasm, and all of the improvements and additions to this truly unusual northern California inn have been undertaken by them with great joy and love.

"Ever since Day One," said Chuck, "we have been very happy and have had a really tremendous time. It's a continuing challenge and we've gotten a great deal accomplished, but I like the idea that the future is big with plans."

"We feel that we are a destination resort-inn, able to accommodate and provide amusement and diversion for all our guests of any age," chimed in Patsy. "We have acquired some fabulous antique pieces, most

particularly a magnificent carved buffet for the dining room. We have added a beautiful carved mantel for the fireplace in the lobby and have installed an antique mantel and a fireplace in the lounge.

"We will be having our wine tasting in November, and this has now become a semi-annual affair, with many of the California boutique wineries represented."

The Benbow is, indeed, a destination resort-inn—in addition to swimming, it offers tennis on two tennis courts nearby, a good golf course within walking distance, hiking, and magnificent backroading. By the way, it's very accessible by public transportation since the Route 101 buses stop almost at the front door.

At Christmastime there's a twelve-foot tree with teddy bears playing drums hanging from every branch. Under the tree there are Patsy's very special antique, oversized toys. An antique sleigh is on the front porch filled with presents and wreaths. Holly and masses of decorations are all over the inn.

On Christmas Day there is a special two-seatings Christmas dinner and everyone has a wonderful time.

Incidentally, in the fall and all through the holidays, English tea and scones are served in the lobby. Chuck's mother, Marie, is the tea lady.

The Benbow also has a film library with over 250 classic films. These are shown every evening. On one of my visits I cheered and wept a little at James Cagney's great portrayal of George M. Cohan in *Yankee Doodle Dandy*.

Patsy, Chuck, and Truffles (their new Afghan hound, the most photographed canine in northern California) are having a wonderful time greeting guests, sharing their enthusiasm, and providing their own bubbling brand of warmth and hospitality. In short, they're model innkeepers. I'm glad they and the Benbow Inn found each other.

BENBOW INN, 445 Lake Benbow Dr., Garberville, CA 95440; 707-923-2124. A 55-guestroom English Tudor inn in the redwood country of northern California. On Rte. 101 near the Benbow State Park. European plan. Breakfast, lunch, and dinner served to travelers daily. Open mid-Apr. to Nov. 28; re-open Dec. 17 for holiday season. Swimming on grounds; golf, tennis adjacent. Hiking and magnificent backroading. Chuck, Patsy, and Muffin Watts, Innkeepers.

Directions: From San Francisco follow Rte. 101 north 200 mi. and exit at Benbow.

BRITT HOUSE
San Diego, California (1981)

Lying abed in the morning in this exquisitely and lovingly furnished bedroom of the Britt House, I couldn't help thinking that Daun Martin, with her attention to important details, has placed her truly valued guests in an atmosphere of at least ninety years ago, with authentic furniture, wallpaper designs, lighting fixtures, and other significant features.

True, to begin with she has a most remarkable Victorian house as you can see from the Jan Lindstrom drawing. A marvelous stained glass window flanking the stairwell is a truly magnificent work. The preservation of the handcarved doorways and moldings and the interior make it an almost living museum.

My mind drifted back to my arrival on the previous afternoon when Daun had shown me to the Camphor Tree Room, a quiet, intimate bedroom done in forest green, teal, and peach, with a carved oak dresser and a matching headboard for the queen-sized bed. True to its name, it has a thrilling view of the eighty-year-old camphor tree surrounded by ferns and flowers, and also has its own balcony where breakfast can be taken. This is typical of other rooms, all of which are done with an abundance of lace curtains, velvet swags, beautiful woods, oversized couches, and marble-top dressers.

The Britt House's answer to "down the hall" bathrooms is to provide their guests with terry cloth bathrobes. It's wonderful to slip into one of these after a shower or a bath.

Daun's affection for animals has created an additional special feature at the Britt House. Not only are there some very nice kitty cats and a couple of amusing dogs on the premises, there is also a collection of stuffed animals of all kinds to be found in every bedroom. Usually they hold a welcoming note, personally addressed to each guest. Some of the animals are even taken out to dinner by guests. I know you won't believe this, but it's true. They sit them at the table, and everybody has lots of fun. (See Inn at Thorn Hill, New Hampshire.)

Because it's the only meal served, Britt House breakfasts are quite special. Freshly squeezed orange juice, hard- or soft-cooked eggs, freshly baked yeast breads, sweet butter and honey, and European coffee, prepared filter-drip style, or tea are provided on the individual trays taken to each room. On Sunday morning, an elegant fresh fruit salad is a special treat.

There are four bathrooms, two on each floor, and one has handsome twin antique bathtubs and bubble bath. The bathroom next to the billiard room offers a luxurious Finnish sauna that is available to all guests.

The Cottage, with its own private bath, just a few steps from the

handsome camphor tree is decorated in cheerful blue and yellow, and has a romantically cozy bed-nook with a canopy, a full-sized bed, a kitchen, and a porch that faces the main house and the beautiful gardens.

These gardens have a remarkably tall hedge that protects the house, and provides excellent privacy. Regardless of what time of year I visit the Britt House, there always seems to be a profusion of flowers in bloom.

BRITT HOUSE, 406 Maple St., San Diego, CA 92103; 714-234-2926. An 11-guestroom bed-and-breakfast inn (private and shared baths) a short distance from Balboa Park with its world-famous zoo, Museum of Art, Man and Natural History, Reuben H. Fleet Space Theater, and the beaches, desert country, and Mexico (13 mi.). Breakfast only meal served (special dinners can be arranged with advance notice). Open all year. Sauna on grounds; jogging, biking, skating, bicycles nearby. No pets. Not particularly suitable for young children. Daun Martin and Robert Hostick, Innkeepers.

Directions: Take Airport-Sassafrass turnoff coming south on Hwy. 5. Proceed on Kettner. Turn left on Laurel; left on Third; right on Nutmeg; right on Fourth St., and come down one block to the corner of Fourth and Maple.

CITY HOTEL
Columbia, California (1987)

I felt almost as if I were a participant in a shoot-out on the main street of Columbia. All of the late-19th-century props were certainly in place: the board sidewalks protected by the overhead balconies, the express office, two saloons where you can still step up and put your money on the bar, and several other stores of western mining-village vintage. We needed only a Matt Dillon or John Wayne to complete the picture.

Columbia was a gold rush community that flourishes today, much as it did in the late 19th century. A visit there recreates the lusty history, the people, and the lifestyle of the gold rush. It is not a ghost town and is much more than a museum—it's a living tribute to the excitement of the gold mining days.

The City Hotel flourished too during those exciting times, and today continues to provide real hospitality to travelers from all over the world. One steps inside to the reception desk and then up the stairs leading from the main dining room to a second-floor parlor, where houseguests may gather and get acquainted and also enjoy a rather fulsome continental breakfast. The Victorian motif is authentically maintained throughout the hotel to the extent that guest rooms have half-baths, with two showers "down the hall."

The object of my search, the innkeeper at the City Hotel, Tom Bender, came around the corner, and I was relieved to see that he was not wearing a six-gun. He proved to be very genial and well informed about the area, and an enthusiastic hotelier.

Among many other things, I learned that nearby there is still another old-time hotel in the historic district of Columbia—the newly restored Fallon. Right next door is the Fallon House Theatre, also newly renovated, with year-round productions. At the time of my visit they were playing *The Sound of Music*. The Fallon Hotel has wonderfully restored oak with that marvelous blond finish almost throughout, and the City Hotel is more on the darker, mahogany side; otherwise, the hospitality is the same in both places.

I talked with Tom about the menu at the City Hotel. "Oddly enough," he said, "the menu is classic French. This is because so many of the people involved here during the gold rush days came from many different countries, and the French played a very important role. Our menu includes fresh oysters, excellent produce, poultry, and such regional game as duck and quail. We are proud of our poached lobster in a whiskey cream sauce; our Caesar salad is done at the table; we have oysters baked with a mushroom-duxelle and glazed in a champagne cream sauce, and an excellent lemon and chocolate soufflé for dessert. Our dining room waiters are dressed in tuxedo shirts, but we don't request our guests to be in formal attire; they can be casual since they are on vacation. However, many guests do dress up a bit."

There's much more to the Columbia Historic State Park–City Hotel story, and I must say that the entire experience was most rewarding. The restorations and activities are in extremely good taste, and the emphasis is just the opposite from the honky-tonk atmosphere that I found in other places in the gold rush country. I visited in March, which is a great month to go, as it can be quite crowded during the summer and through October.

We're delighted to welcome the City Hotel to the pages of *Country Inns and Back Roads* for the very first time in this issue.

CITY HOTEL, Main St., P.O. Box 1870, Columbia, CA 95310; 209-532-1479. A 9-guestroom (private ½ baths) restored gold rush hotel in Columbia Historic State Park, 2½ hrs. east of San Francisco. Reservations can also be made for the 13-guestroom Fallon Hotel. Lunch and dinner served to the public every day except on Christmas Day and on Mon. from Nov. 1 to Apr. 1. Open year-round. Conveniently located to enjoy the truly unusual gold country historic and natural attractions. Tom Bender, Innkeeper.

Directions: The historic section of Columbia is restricted and cars are not allowed. Coming from Sonora to Columbia on Rte. 49, look for a sign to the City Hotel on the right and turn there to park.

THE GREY WHALE INN
Fort Bragg, California (1980)

Ever since the first edition of this book in 1966, I have visited inns that were formerly gristmills, poorhouses, majestic mansions, carriage houses, stagecoach taverns, farmhouses, and log cabins. However, the Grey Whale is the first inn that began life as a hospital!

"The inn was built in 1915," explained John Bailey, who with his wife, Colette, acquired it in 1978. "It was the Redwood Coast Hospital before it was transformed into an inn in 1974."

John, Colette, and I were browsing through the fourteen guest rooms, twelve of which have private baths. Its early life as a hospital creates a distinct advantage for present-day inn guests, because the rooms are quite large, with many generous windows.

The Grey Whale features an unusual variety of textures and colors, ranging from the rich brown stain of the exterior boards to the brilliant colors of the interior carpeting and the wide selection of original contemporary paintings. The guest rooms have comforters with matching pillow covers, bright decorator sheets, and one has a working fireplace.

Each room contains a folder describing all of the sights and attractions of Fort Bragg and the Mendocino Coast, including the redwood forest, art galleries, the Botanical Gardens, the beautiful Pacific Ocean beaches, the Skunk Railroad, and a brief summary of some of the restaurants. (The Grey Whale offers bed and breakfast.)

When we passed through the second-floor dining room, Colette explained that she bakes all the breads and coffee cakes that are served on the continental breakfast. "These can be enjoyed right here, or the tray may be taken to the bedroom. Many guests like to eat breakfast in bed," she said.

Colette received two blue ribbons at the Mendocino County Fair and Apple Show—her apricot-prune coffee cake and the lemon-yogurt bread were winners, and St. Timothy's coffee cake won a third prize. John said, "Competition was keen, but no match for the specialties that we serve our guests at the Grey Whale Inn." These are now available in the Grey Whale Cookbook.

Motorists passing through Fort Bragg on Highway 1 just can't miss the Grey Whale, because it stands at the north end of town surrounded by a large grass and turf area with some very colorful plantings of marguerite, California poppies, amaryllis, African daisies, and geraniums.

"Whale watching is one of our great pastimes," said John. "The whale watch starts in mid-December and from then on through March there are programs planned at various points along the coast."

Along with the whale-watching programs, there is a whale festival that includes a whale art exhibit. Many nationally known marine artists

will be coming to Fort Bragg again this year for the concurrent whale art exhibits at the Grey Whale Inn and the Wildlife Gallery in nearby Mendocino.

It was from John that I learned of the many activities and attractions in this section of northern California. "We have theater, crafts shows, scuba diving, fishing, hiking, and many museums," he reported. "We appeal to the art buff, the whale-watcher, the beachcomber, and anyone who wants to have some unhurried hours away from pressures."

Whether the traveler is headed north or south along the Mendocino coast, or bent on staying a few days, the Grey Whale provides a unique country inn experience.

THE GREY WHALE INN, 615 No. Main St., Fort Bragg, CA 95437; 707-964-0640. (California toll-free reservations: 800-382-7244.) A 14-guestroom inn located on Hwy. 1 at the north end of Fort Bragg. Continental breakfast included in room rates. (Only meal served.) Open every day in the year. Advance reservations important. Many natural, historic, and recreational attractions within a short distance. Beachcombing, scuba diving, fishing, and hiking nearby. Available by Greyhound Bus and Skunk Train. John and Colette Bailey, Innkeepers.

Directions: From the south, follow Hwy. 101 to Cloverdale, take Rte. 128 west to Hwy 1, and follow north to Fort Bragg. Alternate route: Exit Hwy. 101 at Willits, then west on Rte. 20 to Fort Bragg. Driving time from San Francisco, 4 hrs. Another alternative: Hwy. 1 along the coast. Driving time from San Francisco: 6 hrs.

HARBOR HOUSE
Elk, California (1975)

Here I was on the opposite side of the continent from New England, far away from my home in the Berkshires, but enjoying still another of my "second homes"—this time on the cliffs of the blue Pacific at Harbor House.

This is another good place to greet spring, because spring comes lustily and vigorously in this part of the world, and the sea in its many moods washes ashore gently or raucously, but the rhythm never ceases. I awaken in the morning to look through the trees to the great rock formations that seem to have been thrown almost helter-skelter from the end of the headlands. Helen and Dean Turner, the innkeepers, had thoughtfully provided a very comfortable chair in the window, with a perfect view of the sea stacks and tunnels, which, along with the arches, caves, and small islands, provide an unusual view from the inn.

This particular group of rock formations was at one time a staging area for the loading and the unloading of lumber schooners. Fortunately, the story of this community has been graphically presented in the unusual brochure of the inn, with dramatic photographs showing just the scenes that I have described.

The subtitle for Harbor House on the rustic sign on Route 1 is "By the Sea." Fewer words are more apt than these. Although the main entrance is on the highway, the immediate focus of all the attention is in the rear of the inn, which looks out over the Pacific, and almost every guest room has this view.

The main building of the inn was built in 1916 as an executive residence. The construction is entirely of virgin redwood from the nearby

Albion Forest. In fact, it is an enlarged version of the "Home of Redwood" exhibit building of the 1915 Panama–Pacific International Exposition in San Francisco.

Guest rooms in the main building and adjacent cottages are individually heated and have private baths. Fireplaces and parlor stoves are stocked with wood, and some of the accommodations have sun decks.

I reflected that were it not for the dominance of the sea, the view from the *other* side of the house across the meadows and into the low coastal hills could be thought of as very beautiful.

Because Helen and Dean Turner have always had a great deal of involvement and interest in the arts, from time to time Harbor House presents programs by soloists and chamber music players. The living room with its wood paneling provides an ideal atmosphere. One such recent guest artist was Carolyn Verse Steinbuck, a resident of Elk with a master's degree in music. She has performed frequently in the San Francisco Bay area. As Helen says, "So many artists live on the coast and an intimate concert in the living room is a wonderful way to hear them."

One reader wrote me, "Our dinner was the nice, slow, mellow kind I love and get so rarely. It was such pleasant, unhurried service. We were free to be alone together or speak to others if we wished, a wonderful blend of solitude and society.

"We got wonderful pictures of all the colorful flowers and scenery. . . . Beautiful as the pictures are, they do not capture what it was like to be there, or explain why I felt homesick when I had to leave."

HARBOR HOUSE, 5600 S. Hwy. #1, Box 369, Elk, CA 95432; 707-877-3203. A seaside inn with 5 guestrooms in the inn and 4 cottages, 16 mi. south of Mendocino, overlooking the Pacific. Modified American plan omits lunch. Breakfast and dinner served daily to houseguests. Open year-round. Ocean wading, abalone and shell hunting, fishing, and hiking on grounds. Golf, biking, boating, ocean white-water tours, deep-sea fishing, and canoeing nearby. Unsuitable for children or pets. No credit cards. Dean and Helen Turner, Innkeepers.

Directions: Elk is approx. 3 hrs. from Golden Gate Bridge. Take Hwy. 101 to Cloverdale, then Hwy. 128 west to Hwy. 1. Continue on Hwy. 1 south 6 mi. to Harbor House.

The date in parenthesis in the heading represents the first year the inn appeared in the pages of Country Inns and Back Roads.

HERITAGE HOUSE
Little River, California (1971)

"You simply cannot get a full appreciation of this wonderful coastline and the outstanding sculptures created by the sea and wind by driving your automobile on Coastal Route 1." That is a quotation from innkeeper Don Dennen, who has lived here at Heritage House for almost all of his life. "It is necessary to seek out the paths and the beaches and do some walking to get away from the sound of the automobiles and really feel nature right down to your shoetops."

I like to make contrasts and comparisons, but I have to admit that I'm at a loss as to what to compare with this section of the northern California coast. The closest thing might be the Cabot Trail on Cape Breton in Nova Scotia, but it doesn't have the twisting, turning, convoluted roads. The Skyline Drive in Virginia has many wonderful vistas, but it doesn't have the sea.

I can't believe that it is all of eight years since scenes from *Same Time Next Year* were filmed here at Heritage House. There is an area at the inn devoted to various bits of memorabilia, including some very good early articles by travel writers, and it is interesting to see just how long Heritage House has been recognized for what it really is—an outstanding country inn. Some of the articles go back a great many years. Many gifts presented to the inn are also displayed, including old photographs and books; one book is in Chinese. The walls are adorned with some remarkable paintings and scenes of the headlands on which the inn is located.

One of the more spectacular views is from the Apple Room, located in the rear of the original main building. It has sweeping views of the waves breaking on the many partially submerged rocks.

I arrived as the sun was definitely on its journey into the Pacific Ocean, but still relatively high in the sky, shining brilliantly on the water and providing dramatic lighting for the gorgeous, huge eucalyptus trees that are everywhere.

Heritage House is different. It has a pleasant, intimate atmosphere without room telephones or television. There are no planned activities; however, there are beautiful drives and walks along the ocean and in the forests and mountains and valleys nearby.

Guests are provided with ample information about circle tours along the coast and into the great woods. There are no amusements or special entertainment for children. Quite a few of the guest accommodations are in cleverly designed little cottages that nestle up against the side of the hill and enjoy a view of the ocean and headlands.

In California, where bed and breakfast is almost a cult expression, Heritage House not only serves dinner but makes the modified American plan obligatory. Credit cards are not accepted and gentlemen are encouraged to wear jackets and ties at dinner.

I walked from the Apple Room down the sloping lawn past guest houses with such names as "Firehouse," "Schoolhouse," "Chartroom," "Ice Cream Parlor," "Barber Pole," and "Stable." Most of these are furnished in antiques and have their own fireplaces.

Anyone planning a visit for a weekend should reserve months in advance. It might be a little easier in the middle of the week, but even then early reservations should be made.

From San Francisco, 140 miles distant, I believe the fastest way to Little River is via Route 101 to Cloverdale and then Route 128 west to the sea. Coastal Highway 1, through Bodega Bay, Jenner, and Point Arena, sometimes seems to hang by its fingernails to the cliffs over the ocean.

HERITAGE HOUSE, Little River, CA 95456; 707-937-5885. A 67-guest-room elegant oceanside inn on Coast Highway 1, 144 mi. north of San Francisco, 6 mi. south of Mendocino. Modified American plan omits lunch. Breakfast and dinner served to travelers daily by reservation. Open from Feb. thru Nov. No amusements or special facilities for children. No pets. No credit cards. Don Dennen, Innkeeper.

Directions: From San Francisco (a 3-hr. drive) follow Rte. 101 to Cloverdale then Rte. 128 to Coast Highway 1. Inn is 5 mi. north of this junction on Hwy. 1.

HERITAGE PARK BED & BREAKFAST INN
San Diego, California (1987)

"Yes, we call ourselves a bed and breakfast inn, but since we offer dinner to our guests, I guess that makes us a full-service inn." Lori Chandler and I were enjoying a candlelight dinner in the unusually commodious Queen Anne dining room, with a waitress costumed in late Victorian fashion. This remarkably restored mansion is located in the seven-acre Victorian preserve of Old Town, San Diego. "Yes, it has won us a 'People in Preservation' Award," Lori proudly told me.

"It stood vacant here in the Park for two-and-a-half years collecting mold, dry-rot, and severe floor and roof damage," she said. "Then my mother, my two sisters, their husbands, and I saw the possibilities and we spent hundreds of hours in research. Fortunately, we found the original floor plan, which enabled us to restore the house very authentically."

Heritage Park is set in a very quiet enclave of painstakingly restored Victorian homes, surrounded with flowers and shrubs. The pleasant cobblestone street is for pedestrians, and cars are parked in the back.

"The mansion was built in 1889," Lori pointed out, "and has the typical Queen Anne characteristics, including a variety of chimneys, shingles, a two-story corner tower, and an encircling veranda. Featured in the *Golden Era* magazine in 1890, it was called an 'outstanding, beautiful home of southern California.'"

There are nine distinctive guest rooms, each furnished and decorated in a popular style of the late 19th century. Incidentally, the antiques and collectibles are offered for sale, and as Lori says, "You can keep your special occasion with you forever."

Our catered dinner, at which we were joined by Lori's mother, Mary, consisted of five courses, and I could have chosen from baked chicken marinated in herbs, lemon, and butter or roast leg of lamb; however, I opted for large shrimp served with feta cheese. There is also a simpler Victorian country supper.

The full breakfast includes omelets, quiches, soufflés, a fruit cup with fresh fruit, and Lori's very special award-winning Strawberry Jam Loaf.

"I hope you will share with your readers the joy that we feel about Old Town, San Diego," she said, as we walked out to the front veranda to enjoy dessert and coffee. "It was a mission at first, established in 1769. Old Town, San Diego, was officially classified as a State Historic Park and incorporated in 1968; there are tours available to visit the original buildings.

"I've done a lot of other things up to this time in my life," she said, sighing contentedly. "However, I think that my background in antique collecting, interior designing, entertaining, public relations, and teaching

has finally come to one focal point, and I'm content to be an innkeeper indefinitely."

I found a little poem on the antique dresser of my guest room:

MY GUEST
Sweet be thy sleep, my guest,
Peace come to thee and rest
Throughout all the quiet night.
And with the morning light,
Awake thee and rise refreshed.

HERITAGE PARK BED & BREAKFAST INN, 2470 Heritage Park Row, San Diego, CA 92110; 619-295-7088. A 9-guestroom (private and shared baths) restored Victorian mansion in the heart of Old Town, San Diego. A choice of catered dinners is offered. Breakfast included in tariff, as well as evening refreshments, and nightly showing of vintage films. Open year-round. Special festivities at Christmas. Balboa Park, the famous San Diego Zoo, and other cultural activities and entertainment in the San Diego area. No accommodations for children under 14. No pets. No smoking. Lori Chandler, Innkeeper.

Directions: From Los Angeles follow I-5 south to Old Town Ave. off ramp; turn left on San Diego Ave., and right on Harney.

THE INN
Rancho Santa Fe, California (1974)

I was seated on the patio of my little bungalow at the Inn at Rancho Santa Fe, catching one more hour of the fantastic March sunshine, hoping to return to New England that evening with a faint blush of sunburn or even suntan. It was wonderful and quiet except for the twittering of a few birds inhabiting the lush green shrubbery and eucalyptus trees found everywhere in this beautiful southern California community.

I had just completed a two-week tour of California from Mendocino to San Diego and had found a very quiet haven. The mood here is untrendy. Perhaps it is set by the Royce family, including owners Danny and his sister, Dorothy, who are very much in evidence, along with their assorted now grown-up offspring, also on the inn staff.

For example, Danny, who is a proud alumnus of Hamilton College in Clinton, New York, as was his father, Steve, was dressed in a tweed coat with a button-down shirt and tan chino trousers. I think that guests, whether from the East or West Coast feel very comfortable in this conservative and not-at-all-stuffy atmosphere. Somehow or other, gentlemen just naturally seem to feel more comfortable wearing coats and ties for dinner, and the smart shops and boutiques, a few paces away in the village, cater to the tastes and preferences of the female guests at the inn.

I have visited here in many different seasons, and find that the guests, some of whom stay for a week or two at a time, cut across the categories of age and preference. They are quite apt to be into tennis, golf, swimming, and the beach. They enjoy some of the excellent attractions in the area, including Balboa Park and the San Diego Zoo. It's an inn where one would spend many days without leaving the area. Guests can rest and read by the swimming pool or even join in a game of croquet on the front lawn.

The town of Rancho Santa Fe is one of the most attractively designed that I have ever visited. It has been well described as a "civilized planned community." The homes and estates have been created in perfect harmony with nature's generous endowment of climate and scenery. One of the dominating factors is the presence of the gigantic eucalyptus trees.

The "family" feeling is extended even further when guests learn that the stunning framed needlepoints, very much in evidence through the main lobby and living rooms of the Inn, have been done by Danny's mother. For example, there is one very large, extremely handsome piece showing a large eucalyptus tree. It has become the symbol of the Inn and is found on all the stationery. My favorite is a needlepoint clock on one wall of the cathedral-ceilinged living room.

Cottages are scattered among the towering trees, and there's recreation for everyone here, including the younger set. The Inn has membership in nearby private 18-hole golf courses, and there are three tennis courts and a croquet green on the grounds. The swimming pool has an outdoor terrace where luncheon and refreshments are available. Also, the Inn has a beach cottage at nearby Del Mar for use during the summer months.

One of the most useful and gratifying amenities at the Inn is a map showing many short motor trips to points fifty miles away, including Lake Elsinore to the north and Tijuana, Mexico, to the south. I am personally acquainted with the rolling ranch and orchard country to the east as far away as Julian. All of these trips make a stay at the Inn worth several extra days.

Readers who use this book as a travel guide will recognize that I have not confined myself to any one particular *genre* of inn. What I look for is some important common denominators, including a friendly warmth from the innkeepers and staff, as well as an ambience that makes every guest feel wanted and taken care of.

I've been reporting about guests being taken care of at Rancho Santa Fe since 1974.

THE INN, P.O. Box 869, Rancho Santa Fe, CA 92067; 619-756-1131. A 75-guestroom resort-inn, 27 mi. north of San Diego Freeway #5 and 5 mi. inland from Solana Beach, Del Mar. European plan. Breakfast, lunch, and dinner served to travelers daily. Open year-round. Pool, tennis, and 6-wicket croquet course on grounds. Golf and ocean nearby. Daniel Royce, Innkeeper.

Directions: From I-5, take Exit S8 and drive inland about 6 mi.

MOUNTAIN HOME INN
Mill Valley, California (1987)

"Mount Tamalpais has been an international meeting place for many years. Transplanted Europeans, missing their tradition of hiking the Alps, came here, and there were Swiss, German, Austrian, English, Norwegian, Italian, Yugoslavian, and French tourists and hikers who mingled with the Bay Area residents, enjoying the wonderful mountain wilderness and trails."

Susan Cunningham and I were seated on the deck of the Mountain Home Inn, overlooking the truly gorgeous panoramic scenery that stretched out to include a view of the northern San Francisco Bay. "Actually, the inn was once accessible only by taking a train up the mountain to a small railroad stop and hiking the rest of the way up. Thank heavens, today our guests can drive all the way up to our front door. A wagon road wasn't built until 1884, and then the railway came a couple of years later. It was known as 'the crookedest railroad in the world,' with 22 trestles and 281 curves. It cost $1.00 from Mill Valley and only $1.40 from San Francisco for the round trip."

Susan left me for a moment to greet some new guests, and I thought of other places that I had visited with such tremendous views—Chateau Chevre d'Or overlooking the Mediterranean in southern France and the Snowbird Mountain Lodge in North Carolina. Views of the Bay, the Tiburon Peninsula, the East Bay Hills, and Mount Diablo can be enjoyed from each of the guest rooms, most of which have their own private balconies. Every one of the ten handsome guest rooms has an original design; some have jacuzzis, and there are also some with fireplaces. Built in three tiers, with hardwood floors, skylights, and a lobby dominated by four giant indoor redwood trees, the inn is decorated in the basic colors of beige and tan, which certainly blend well with the natural, rugged setting.

Susan returned with her eyes sparkling. "It took Ed and me four years to bring this building to the point where we felt we were ready to reopen it. Actually, it's the first luxury inn and restaurant on the mountain for many, many years. There used to be several of them, when people came up from San Francisco to enjoy the view and the hiking. At one time, I'm told, there was a Bavarian beer garden, where Germanic hikers, artists, and poets gathered to have a good time."

There are seemingly endless possibilities for hikes and drives through the mountain woods. Bird and sea-life sanctuaries are within easy driving distance, as are Stinson Beach and Point Reyes National Seashore. Horseback riding and tennis are also nearby.

Although the outdoorsy atmosphere is somewhat rustic, the menu at Mountain Home is quite sophisticated and extensive. The fish courses include mesquite grilled fillet of ono fish, served with slivers of ginger root, and poached fresh fillet of salmon with sorrel sauce. The meat and poultry selections include roast fillet of pork, with calvados and apple brandy sauce, and medallions of milk-fed veal served in a cream sauce. A dining room and outside dining deck are reserved especially for overnight guests, and they may choose to have their complimentary continental breakfast outside on warm, sunny days. Lunch and dinner are served to other visitors in an upper-level dining room and deck.

Only a twenty-five-minute drive from San Francisco's financial district, there may be no other inn in the world that is so conveniently close to a major city and yet is so splendidly isolated from the everyday world.

We are happy to welcome Mountain Home Inn to *Country Inns and Back Roads* for the first time this year.

MOUNTAIN HOME INN, 810 Panoramic Hwy., Mill Valley, CA 94941; 415-381-9000. A 10-guestroom (private baths) mountainside inn just 15 min. north of the Golden Gate Bridge. Breakfast and lunch served daily; dinner every night except Mon. Open year-round. Endless hiking possibilities with over 250 mi. of trails in Mt. Tamalpais State Park and adjacent lands. Near Muir Woods National Monument, Stinson Beach, Point Reyes National Seashore, horseback riding, and tennis. No pets. Susan and Ed Cunningham, Innkeepers.

Directions: From the Golden Gate Bridge, exit right on Hwy. 1 at Mill Valley following all Mt. Tamalpais signs. After 3 mi. turn right on Panoramic Hwy. and go 3.25 mi. to the inn on the right side of the road.

THE SANDPIPER INN
Carmel-by-the-Sea, California (1981)

It was a very stimulating morning at the Sandpiper because it had rained during the night in Carmel, and all of the flowers and bushes in the gardens in front of the inn were glistening with water, and birds were twittering merrily, going about from branch to branch. Inside, in the impressive cathedral living room, a good fire was burning and at the far end there were guests enjoying breakfast and reading the morning papers. In the reception area there was the pleasant hustle and bustle of departing guests promising to meet again next year.

Graeme and Irene Mackenzie, looking as bright and fresh as the morning, were moving from guest to guest making arrangements, expressing concern and hospitality in their clipped British accents. I happened to hear Graeme explaining what I took to be the inherent nature of Carmel to one of the guests.

"We who live here think that Carmel is a city of serendipity," he said. "We have houses and cottages with sunny balconies and courtyards, and I'm sure you've experienced the collection of small streets." I might add that Carmel's white beaches, narrow cypresses and magnificent seascapes are further rewards for the visitor.

"We're a kind of sleepy village," he continued. "There are no street lights, no sidewalks in residential districts, no street numbers, and, I guess most important, no neon signs."

I drifted over to another group where Irene was carrying on a lively conversation in French. She is quite at home with many other languages as well.

Each time I visit I'm impressed with the resemblance of this inn to an English country house hotel. Irene and Graeme fit beautifully into this ambience because they are both Scottish, so one might say that they blend right into the English and French antiques, oil paintings, flowered quilted bedspreads, wallpapered bathrooms, and freshly picked nosegays. Some of the bedrooms have wood-burning fireplaces, but there are no TVs or telephones in the rooms, ensuring peace and quiet. A recent innovation has been the addition of a third top sheet to each bed under the bedspread.

The inn itself is about seventy yards from the beach with sweeping views across Carmel Bay to Pebble Beach. The wide beach has white sand and is a marvelous place for sunning and picnicking. Both Irene and Graeme are very much interested in outdoor sports, including golf, tennis, and racquet ball, and are happy to introduce their houseguests to some of the clubs on the peninsula in which they have membership. There are also excellent back roads, as well as a tour of wineries in the area. The new Aquarium on Cannery Row is well worth a three-hour visit.

Later, after things had calmed down a bit and guests had gone off to play golf, walk the beach, or just sit in a quiet corner reading a book, I asked Graeme how an inn happened to be in this section of Carmel, where I had noted there were only private homes.

"The original guest house was built in 1930," he explained. "It came into existence before the very stringent zoning laws went into effect; hence our guests have the advantage of being in a very quiet section of the village and still only a few steps from the beach.

"We recently celebrated our tenth anniversary at Sandpiper, and both Irene and I find the greatest satisfaction in the number of returning guests each year."

THE SANDPIPER INN at-the-Beach, 2408 Bayview Ave. at Martin St., Carmel-by-the-Sea, CA 93923; 408-624-6433. A 15-guestroom bed-and-breakfast inn and cottages near the Pacific Ocean. Breakfast only meal offered. Open all year. Carmel and Stuarts Cove beaches, Old Carmel Mission, Point Lobos State Park, 17-Mile Drive, and Big Sur State Park nearby. Ten-speed bicycles available; jogging and walking on beach. Arrangements can be made to play at nearby private golf and tennis clubs with pools and hot tubs. Children over 12 welcome. Please, no pets. Graeme and Irene Mackenzie, Innkeepers.

Directions: From Hwy. 1 turn right at Ocean Ave., through Carmel Village, and turn left on Scenic Dr. (next to Ocean). Proceed to end of beach to Martin St. and turn left.

I do not include lodging rates in the descriptions, for the very nature of an inn means that there are lodgings of various sizes, with and without baths, in and out of season, and with plain and fancy decoration. Travelers should call ahead and inquire about the availability and rates of the many different types of rooms.

THE SEAL BEACH INN AND GARDENS
Seal Beach, California (1981)

Like many other people, I am a natural born fan; such charismatic people as Frank Gifford, Casey Stengel, Leslie Howard, Marilyn Horne, Martha Graham, and Marjorie Bettenhausen will find me in the front row, cheering with everything I've got.

I became a Marjorie Bettenhausen fan when I first visited the Seal Beach Inn, which at that time was little more than a motel from the 1920s. It had one very important thing going for it, however, and that was Marjorie's vision, talent, and enthusiasm.

Here are some observations from Marjorie herself about the inn: "It is a fairyland of brick courtyards, old ornate street lights, blue canopies, objets d'art, fountains, shuttered windows, window boxes, and vines. We are a family-run inn, a place of character, a thoughtfully designed place where guests are pampered and our service is friendly and caring.

"From the very start we saw the opportunity to create an inn that would have the ambience of inns that we have visited in southern France. We've been very fortunate since 1980, when you first visited, Norman, in having been discovered by many feature writers and also in having been on TV many times."

The French Mediterranean appearance is enhanced by the truly extraordinary gardens. All of the lodging rooms are named after flowers, including fuchsia, gardenia, and camellia. The full-time gardener keeps the flowers blooming even in winter with considerable aid from the mild year-round weather in this part of California. There are rare vines, climbing vines, flowering bushes, sweet-smelling bushes, deciduous trees, evergreen pear trees, and a wonderful variety of a cascading willowy tree that look like a weeping willow, but really isn't. It stays green all year.

Lush plantings and antique newel posts are beside each guest room door, and in the rooms, lovely burgundy, rust, and peach comforters and dust ruffles set off the wrought-iron headboards. The bridal chamber, with its very own veranda beside the pool, is much in demand.

In addition, there are the Royal Villas, six of the most romantic, lavish suites imaginable. Marjorie says, "In all of California there are none that are more exquisite!"

The entrance to the inn from the street is through a three-sided square, around which the guest rooms are situated, and this is indeed a flower-filled courtyard, lit by street lamps that were rescued from the scrap pile at nearby Long Beach. There is a red English telephone booth in one corner, and a kiosk (that would be quite at home in Nice) has notices of all the nearby attractions. The library is an elegant guest salon with an impressive fireplace, books, and games. Breakfast is served in a small, cozy French-style tea room, presided over by a cheerful hostess.

Kay Trepp is responsible for the ambrosial breakfasts. Among her many accomplishments, she recently won first place for two entries in an important contest among other southern California innkeepers. When you visit the inn, ask about her "Chocolate Love Package."

Marjorie maintains that it takes many years to establish an inn par excellence and declares that "we finally are reaching the end of inn adolescence and moving into golden maturity. We want to be the best inn in the state, not just in beauty but in the warmth and love in which we serve."

So now it can easily be seen why I am a Marjorie Bettenhausen fan.

THE SEAL BEACH INN AND GARDENS, 212 5th St., Seal Beach, CA 90740; 213-493-2416 or 213-430-3915. A 22-guestroom village inn located in a quiet residential area of an attractive town, 300 yds. from beach. Breakfast only meal served. Open all year. Near Disneyland, Knott's Berry Farm, Lion Country Safari, Catalina Island (20 mi. offshore), and California mountains and lakes 2 hrs. away. Long Beach Playhouse, Long Beach Music Center nearby. Swimming pool on grounds. Tennis, beach, biking, skating, golf nearby. No pets. Marjorie and Jack Bettenhausen, Innkeepers.

Directions: From Los Angeles Airport take Hwy. 405 Freeway south to Seal Beach Blvd. exit. Turn left toward the beach, right on the Pacific Coast Hwy., left on 5th St. in Seal Beach, which is the first stoplight after main street. Inn is on the left, 2 blocks toward the beach on 5th St.

SUTTER CREEK INN
Sutter Creek, California (1969)

It was 1967 when I first flew to the West Coast in search of country inns. I had been persuaded by Jane Way at the Sutter Creek Inn to visit the gold fields of California. She was sure that I would love it. Well, Jane was right, and I have been visiting California and writing about the Sutter Creek Inn ever since.

It is, in fact, an inn with its New Hampshire heritage much in evidence in the porches and high, pointed roof. There are grape vines, tomato plants, gardenias, trumpet vines, Virginia creepers, hollyhocks, chrysanthemums, gooseberries, zinnias, and roses in abundance.

On that first visit and every time since, at the end of the day, I have joined the other guests on the porch to watch the huge, old white owls that live in the barn circle over the backyard and fly off to the redwood trees to spend the rest of the night.

The only meal served at this inn is breakfast, but it is really an experience. When the bell rings at 9 a.m., everyone sits at long, family-style tables. "Our breakfasts are big and hearty," says Jane. "It's a good basis for a full day of exploring the mother lode country."

Ten of the several bedrooms of the inn have fireplaces and four have swinging beds that hang from the ceiling on chains. These, by the way, can be stabilized. Jane fell in love with the idea while traveling in the tropics. They are the most popular rooms at the inn. "Very romantic, indeed," says Jane.

I should caution our readers that reservations in advance are almost always necessary in order to avoid disappointments. There is a two-day minimum stay on weekends, either Friday and Saturday or Saturday and

Sunday. "Sometimes," said Jane, "we do have last-minute cancella-tions." With this in mind, a telephone call to Jane on a Thursday might provide a very pleasant surprise.

"You might also point out to your readers," Jane added, "that we are rather small, so children are not encouraged as guests. In addition, pets and cigar smoking are a 'no-no.'"

At the Sutter Creek Inn, deep in the mother lode country, fireplaces blaze in cold weather and there are warm lazy summer days to be spent in hammocks, or out exploring the gold rush country. Sutter Creek, Volcano, Murphy's, Angel's Camp and Sonora are all part of the great living legend of gold in California and they are all on or near Route 49, which runs along the foothills of the Sierras.

It's great fun on Halloween day. All the staff don hilarious costumes. Even the shopkeepers and townspeople are dressed in funny clothes. Jane says, "It's like becoming a child again. . .all giggly and silly."

For many of her guests, Jane Way and the Sutter Creek Inn are the "first" country inn experience. "People frequently ask me," she said, "about the essential qualities for successful country innkeeping.

"I reply that the most important is unlimited love for people."

SUTTER CREEK INN, 75 Main St., Box 385, Sutter Creek, CA 95685; 209-267-5606. A 19-guestroom New England village inn on the main street of a historic mother lode town, 35 mi. from Sacramento. Lodgings include breakfast. No meals served to travelers. Open all year. Water skiing, riding, fishing, and boating nearby. No children under 10. No pets. Mrs. Jane Way, Innkeeper.

Directions: From Sacramento, travel on the Freeway (50) toward Placer-ville and exit at Power Inn Rd. Turn right and drive one block; note signs for Rte. 16 and Jackson. Turn left on Fulsom Rd., approx. 1/4 mi.; follow Rte. 16 signs to right for Jackson. Rte. 16 joins Rte. 49. Turn right to Sutter Creek. From San Francisco, follow Freeway (80) to Sacramento and take previous directions or drive via Stockton to Rte. 49.

I do not include lodging rates in the descriptions, for the very nature of an inn means that there are lodgings of various sizes, with and without baths, in and out of season, and with plain and fancy decoration. Travelers should call ahead and inquire about the availability and rates of the many different types of rooms.

UNION STREET INN
San Francisco, California (1981)

"We are Edwardian, not Victorian."

Helen Stewart and I were having breakfast, seated in the sunny garden at the rear of the Union Street Inn. The fragrance of lilacs, camellias, and violets filled the air, and an occasional hummingbird darted from blossom to blossom. Some guests were enjoying breakfast on the spacious deck overlooking the garden, and there was the unmistakable aroma of fresh coffee and croissants. In this quiet retreat it was difficult to realize that we were in the heart of one of San Francisco's most attractive shopping and entertainment areas.

"I say Edwardian," Helen continued, "because we're rather proud of the fact that in a city that has so much Victoriana, we are a bit different. The Edwardians, already into the 20th century, were less ostentatious than their elders. Their ornamentation was tempered by a new conservatism, and we like to feel that many of our decorations and furnishings are understatements."

Helen is a former San Francisco schoolteacher, who found herself involved in a mid-life career change. She restored and remodeled this handsome turn-of-the-century building, using tones and textures that are not only in the period, but also increase the feeling of hospitality.

The five bedrooms have such intriguing names as Wildrose, Holly, Golden Gate, and English Garden. Two have private bathrooms, and the others have running water in the rooms and share two bathrooms.

Two of the bedrooms have queen-sized beds with canopies, two have gleaming brass beds; all have really impressive, carefully chosen antiques. The brochure of the inn explains the different color schemes for each room. "If reservations are made sufficiently in advance, and the guests can anticipate a mood, these can all be coordinated." Helen made this comment with the faint suggestion of a twinkle.

My room had one of the queen-sized beds with very pleasant dark green wallpaper and matching draperies, which were most helpful in keeping the sun from intruding too early. The walls were adorned with two of the well-known Degas prints of ballet dancers. I thought they were quite appropriate, remembering King Edward's fondness for pretty women.

One end of the room had been turned into an alcove containing a rather elegantly decorated wash basin with mirrors and generous, fluffy towels. A very handsome antique mahogany dressing table had a three-way oval mirror. This is typical of the appointments of the other bedrooms, and I found many welcome living plants in all of the bedrooms.

Helen has converted the old carriage house at the bottom of the garden into a very fetching accommodation, with a large bay window

overlooking the garden, and its own jacuzzi. The garden has been remodeled, and a Victorian-looking curved fence with a lovely old-fashioned gate has been added. It truly does resemble an English garden.

A glance at the comments from the guest book told me the story: "Happiness is staying here!" "What a refreshing change from typical hotel stays." "Like returning to visit an old 'friend.' " "We'll be back for a second honeymoon."

"How far are you from Fisherman's Wharf?" I asked, helping myself to another tasty croissant. "Oh, we're just minutes away," she said. "Our guests walk to Ghirardelli Square, the Cannery, and Pier 39. It's possible to take streetcars and cable cars to almost every point of interest in San Francisco."

UNION STREET HOTEL, 2229 Union St., San Francisco, CA 94123; 415-346-0424. A 5-guestroom (3 rooms share 2 baths) bed-and-breakfast inn. Convenient to all of the San Francisco attractions, including the cable car line. Breakfast only meal served. Open every day except Christmas and New Year's. Unable to accommodate children under 12. No pets. Helen Stewart, Innkeeper.

Directions: Take the Van Ness exit from Rte. 101 to Union St.; turn left. The inn is between Fillmore and Steiner on the left side of the street.

VAGABOND HOUSE
Carmel-by-the-Sea, California (1976)

I had joined a group of other Vagabond House guests in the parlor, where we were all enjoying a continental breakfast. The conversation turned to the squirrels who were knocking on the windows and disporting themselves in the trees and the gardens. Manager Bruce Indorato explained that they consume about thirty pounds of peanuts a week, and so saying, he opened up the window just enough to put some more peanuts on the outer ledge. "Every once in a while one gets inside," he said, "and then it's hilarious. Of course, they are very tame and they really do know how to find their way out again, but it's fun while it lasts."

I'll have to explain next that the breakfast we were enjoying was a *true* continental breakfast, with fresh pastries, cheese, hard-boiled eggs, and lots of coffee and tea. One of the guests remarked that it was like the continental breakfasts he had come to enjoy while traveling in Europe.

The Vagabond House is a delightful experience that begins when guests walk up the stone steps and enter an atmosphere that seems almost magical. There is a three-sided courtyard enhanced by many trees, including mock orange, magnolia, and live oaks. The plantings include camellias, primroses, tulips, and daffodils in great profusion, along with impatiens, rhododendrons, fuchsias, and many other varieties of flowers.

Accommodations are in eleven completely different cottage rooms or suites, many of which have their own woodburning fireplaces. The rooms are large and pleasingly furnished with Early American maple furniture, quilted bedspreads, and antique clocks; some have kitchens. Most rooms are supplied with coffeepots and fresh ground coffee for brewing.

Actually, reservations for three different inns may be arranged through the Vagabond House, and each provides a different kind of atmosphere. The Vagabond House itself is the best known and most popular of the three.

The other two are equally interesting in their own way. The San Antonio House, somewhat European in nature, is a smaller building in a very quiet residential section. Each large room has its own fireplace.

On the other hand, Lincoln Green, in another residential section of Carmel, is particularly adaptable for children, with much more space for running about. The four little dwellings, called Maid Marian, Robin Hood, Little John, and Friar Tuck, offer a total of four suites, each with a living room and bedroom able to accommodate four people comfortably. In each living room is a stone fireplace and a sofa that turns into a bed.

Carmel is justly famous for its shopping and galleries, and a walk along Ocean Avenue will afford the chance to browse on the way down to the spectacular beachscape.

Another point of interest in the area is Point Lobos, just south of Carmel. Its six-mile-long, unbroken coastline encompasses many spectacular views, as does the 17-Mile Drive. Incidentally, the main road south through Big Sur is now open, after being closed by mudslides.

Golf is one of the main reasons to come to this part of the world, and during the annual Bing Crosby tournament, many of the touring pros have reserved for years in advance at the Vagabond House.

VAGABOND HOUSE, Fourth & Dolores Streets, P.O.Box 2747, Carmel-by-the-Sea, CA 93921; 408-624-7738 or 408-624-7403. An 11-guestroom village inn serving a European continental breakfast to houseguests only. No other meals served. Open every day of the year. Bike renting, golf, natural beauty, enchanting shops nearby. Not ideal for children. Attended, leashed pets allowed. Dennis and Karen Levett, Owners; Honey Jones, Innkeeper.

Directions: Turn off Hwy. 1 onto Ocean Ave.; turn right from Ocean Ave. onto Dolores, continue 2½ blocks. Parking provided for guests.

I do not include lodging rates in the descriptions, for the very nature of an inn means that there are lodgings of various sizes, with and without baths, in and out of season, and with plain and fancy decoration. Travelers should call ahead and inquire about the availability and rates of the many different types of rooms.

THE WINE COUNTRY INN
St. Helena, California (1978)

Three or four of us who were attending a meeting of the CIBR innkeepers were seated around the pool at the Wine Country Inn, enjoying the warm, welcome sunshine. "It looks a lot different than it did yesterday," said Jim Smith, who is the innkeeper of the inn. "We've had heavy rains and quite a little high water the last couple of days, but things have really calmed down now."

One of the innkeepers complimented Jim on what was then a new pool and Jacuzzi. "Thank you very much," he responded. "I've never received as many compliments about the inn as I have this year and a lot of that has to do with the pool. It's become a popular area for socializing and swapping stories as to which winery tours to go on and which restaurants to enjoy."

It was a wonderful day in March. There were new leaves on the trees, the spring flowers were in profusion, wild geese were flying, and the small vineyards in the little valley just below the inn were starting to perk up. The natural wild mustard, lupines, poppies, and live oak trees blended with plantings of oleanders, petunias, and Chinese pistachios. This inn, which I saw almost the first day it was opened, has now taken on the patina that comes as buildings put on additional years.

The guest rooms are furnished almost entirely in antiques; some have intimate balconies and some have patios leading to the lawn. Many of the rooms have fireplaces, canopied beds, tufted bedspreads, and handmade quilts, along with a generous supply of magazines and books, and big, comfortable, fluffy pillows.

Visitors to the Napa Valley enjoy visits to the many wineries, as well as to mineral baths, geysers, a petrified forest, and several Robert Louis

Stevenson memorial sites. There are also a number of antique shops in the area. Dotted with century-old stone bridges, pump houses, barns, and stone buildings, all of which are a delight to both painter and photographer, the manicured agricultural beauty of the valley contrasts with the rugged, tree-covered hills surrounding it.

In the many years since the Wine Country Inn was the first bed and breakfast inn in the Napa Valley there have been other inns created. However, I am convinced that it is still for me the most enjoyable experience in the valley. Patience and constant attention to details and maintenance have allowed the building, the trees, shrubs, and flowers to take on a real character of their own. It's hard to realize that it was actually built in 1975 as an inn. The architecture is batten board with a center section of stone and a mansard roof that is quite in keeping with the other winery architecture of this part of California.

On a more personal note I have to say that becoming acquainted with people like Ned and Marge Smith and their sons, Jim and Jeff, and watching the progress of such families over the years has always been a great source of satisfaction for me. I think other innkeepers in California are fortunate to have such a model inn after which to fashion themselves. The care and consideration that have gone into the designing, and the result, prove that a country inn doesn't have to be old to be legendary.

It's the spirit that matters.

THE WINE COUNTRY INN, 1152 Lodi Lane, St. Helena, CA 94574; 707-963-7077. A 25-room country inn in the Napa wine valley of California, about 70 mi. from San Francisco. Continental breakfast served to houseguests, no other meals served. Open daily except Dec. 22–27. This inn is within driving distance of a great many wineries and also the Robert Louis Stevenson Museum. Swimming pool and spa on grounds. Golf and tennis nearby. No children. No pets. Jim Smith, Innkeeper.

Directions: From San Francisco take the Oakland Bay Bridge to Hwy. 80. Travel north to the Napa cutoff. Stay on Hwy. 29 through the town of St. Helena, for 1¾ mi. north to Lodi Lane, then turn east ¼ mi. to inn.

"European plan" means that rates for rooms and meals are separate. "American plan" means that meals are included in the cost of the room. "Modified American plan" means that breakfast and dinner are included in the cost of the room. The rates at some inns include a continental breakfast with the lodging.

STEAMBOAT INN
Steamboat, Oregon (1984)

I was on the Umpqua Highway (Route 138) on my way for a visit with Jim and Sharon Van Loan at the Steamboat Inn, a country inn that is a steelhead fisherman's dream.

This is the heartland of Oregon, and after a pleasant trip from Crescent City and Eureka, California, up Routes 101 and 199, I thrilled to the scenery on I-5 from Grants Pass to Roseburg.

Now, having left the Interstate and turning east, I was getting the feeling of what inland Oregon is really like. There were many cattle farms and fruit orchards gradually giving way to the beautiful upland country, and soon the road was running parallel to the North Umpqua River.

The road was getting steeper and the river more rambunctious. I remembered that Jim and Sharon had suggested in their inn folder that even though it's a challenge, they discouraged guests from trying canoe or boat trips on this river.

This idyllic trip along the river ended as I arrived at the Steamboat Inn and was immediately taken in tow again by both Jim and Sharon, who are two very friendly people, quite suited to innkeeping.

I was shown to one of the eight original rustic cabins, all of which are joined by a deck that extends out over the river, and soon I was enveloped in the euphoria created by the melodious, ever-present sounds of the water rushing by on its way to the Pacific Ocean.

I joined the other guests on the new back porch of the lodge in time to be well introduced by Jim and Sharon and to admire the original paintings that line the walls. After hors d'oeuvres we were all invited to sit down around the great harvest table in the dining area and enjoy the main course. Sharon explained that a typical dinner includes several vegetables, homemade bread or pasta, and a selected entrée of the evening. Our main dish that evening, appropriately enough, was game hens with a fruited wild rice stuffing, which won the $5,000 grand prize in a Best-of-Country Inns recipe contest in a recent national competition.

Guests for longer stays at Steamboat will not have the same main course at dinner twice. By the way, dinner is generally served a half hour after dark each night during the summer months and around seven during the winter.

Following dinner, I had a chance to talk with Jim and Sharon about how they came to be located here. "Originally, we came because of Jim's enthusiasm for fly-fishing," Sharon responded. "Then it occurred almost simultaneously to all of us that this would be a wonderful place to raise a family, and it seemed like a viable way of involving everyone and still being able to make financial progress. It's worked out wonderfully and all of our children are involved."

Jim continued, "Although fishing is a big activity here about three months of the year, the rest of the time there are many non-fishing guests who arrive with the intention of remaining for one night and who extend their stay for two or three. It's an excellent place for families, because the cabins can accommodate up to four people quite comfortably, and we have another new building that can accommodate even more."

"Our guests enjoy the wonderful presence of the river," Sharon commented. "They can explore the waterfalls, swim in the creek, and

return at night to put their feet up on the porch railing and read a good book. We also have frequent cooking classes that many of our guests enjoy. Information about classes is included in our brochure."

So we see the Steamboat Inn is a combination of a great many things, but the real, compelling attraction is the river—its sound, color, and ever-changing textures.

STEAMBOAT INN, Steamboat, OR 97447; 503-496-3495 or 503-498-2411. An 8-guestroom rustic riverside inn in one of Oregon's most spectacular nature areas. Open all year. Breakfast, lunch, and dinner served daily; breakfast is not included in the room rate. Dinner ½ hr. after sundown in summer, 7 p.m. in winter. Fishing, backpacking, and hiking in abundance. Sharon and Jim Van Loan, Innkeepers.

Directions: From Roseburg drive 38 mi. east on Rte. 138.

THE CAPTAIN WHIDBEY INN
Coupeville, Washington (1973)

I'm going to share with you the contents of my yearly letter from John Stone, the innkeeper of the Captain Whidbey Inn. I think it shows that country inns are continually adjusting and changing to meet the preferences and needs of their guests.

First, a word about the Captain Whidbey. It's an old-fashioned New England inn, way up in the northwest corner of the state of Washington. The New England part of it comes quite naturally because the original owners were Steve and Shirley Stone. Steve is a native of Nantucket Island, off the coast of Massachusetts in the East, and a good example of the old saying, "You can take the boy out of Nantucket, but you can't take Nantucket out of the boy"; the tweedy look, the unmistakable accent, and the corncob pipe are all there. John refers to his father as the "Innkeeper Emeritus."

The exterior of the inn, built in 1907, is of the distinctly regional peeled madrona logs, a shiny, red-hued wood, a large relative of the manzanita. The inn remains just about the same as it has always been, with highly polished log walls decorated with antiques and bric-a-brac.

The natural center of the inn is the living room, with a very big fireplace made of round stones. Here, everybody—houseguests and dinner guests alike—sits around talking and leafing through the dozens of magazines.

Some of the guest rooms are upstairs in the main house and an additional number of rustic lodges, called Lagoon Rooms, were built in the woods across the road from the main house a few years ago, and they overlook their own private lake. The guest rooms are tastefully furnished with antiques, and those in the main house have down comforters and feather beds. A nice area for general relaxing has been set aside for houseguests on the second floor with floor-to-ceiling bookshelves jam-packed with books.

Now, to John's letter: "This year we have added a gazebo by the lagoon and a dining deck overlooking the Cove. The gazebo enhances the inn as a great spot to have a wedding. The dining deck is ideal for lunch alfresco; guests can enjoy the warm sun, gentle breezes, and spectacular vistas with sailboats on the Cove and snowcapped mountains in the distance.

"Our mussel festival was a great hit. It was won by a young lady from Belgium who said it was only natural that she won, because mussels are the 'national food of Belgium.' We also had a mussel recipe contest and an all-mussel dinner. We will be repeating that every year.

"I have my Coast Guard license to carry passengers for hire on both power and sail vessels, and I've been taking guests on short cruises of

Penn Cove on Saturdays and Sundays, similar to the sail you and I had on the *Wind Song*. Both the guests and I enjoy getting out on the water for a refreshing sail, and it gives me an hour or so to get to know at least six of our guests.

"My wife, Mendy, is in her second year teaching at the Oak Harbor Co-op Preschool. She also takes care of the fresh flowers inside and outside the inn. Our 7-year-old son, Andrew, continues the tradition of the Stones as a 'reading family.' Ian is $4\frac{1}{2}$, and says he wants to be an innkeeper and sailor like his Dad."

The Captain Whidbey, located on the shore of Penn Cove, with the Cascades to the east, dominated by Mount Baker at more than 10,000 feet and Mount Olympus on the west at almost 8,000 feet, provides a most unusual and scenic country-inn adventure.

THE CAPTAIN WHIDBEY INN, Rte. 1, Box 32, Coupeville, WA 98239; 206-678-4097. A 25-guestroom (4 cottages) (private and shared baths) country inn, on protected Penn Cove off Puget Sound, 50 mi. north of Seattle, 3 mi. north of Coupeville. European plan. Breakfast, lunch, and dinner served daily to travelers. Open year-round. Boating and fishing on grounds. Golf nearby. Pets allowed in cottages only. The Stone Family, Innkeepers.

Directions: Whidbey Island is reached year-round from the south by the Columbia Beach–Mukilteo Ferry, and during the summer and on weekends by the Port Townsend–Keystone Ferry. From the north (Vancouver, B.C., and Bellingham), take the Deception Pass Bridge to Whidbey Island.

LAKE QUINAULT LODGE
Quinault, Washington (1976)

It was ten o'clock on a summer evening and the big living room of the Lake Quinault Lodge was filled with a number of guests reading, talking, doing puzzles, and playing bridge. In one corner some people were singing softly to the accompaniment of a guitar. The moon had risen over the lake and a light breeze was stirring the leaves of the great trees on the mountains.

One of the guests who had been there about a week, dropped a couple of aromatic birch bark logs on the fire. Although it was a mild night, a small fire was quite welcome.

"Well," he asked me, "what did you do all afternoon?"

I replied that I spent most of the time just walking in the woods getting the feel of the great trees. "Yes," he replied, "I think that's what almost every newcomer does. It takes time to get used to these two- and three-hundred-foot giants that surround us."

This is indeed big tree country with cedars, redwoods, spruces, Douglas firs, hemlocks, and pines in profusion. My afternoon walk in the woods was an inspiring experience.

"It's interesting to watch people come into this relaxing atmosphere for the first time," my new friend continued. "They arrive tired and tight from city living and I can see them unwind. Finally, they're sitting around like all of us without a worry in the world. I think that the saunas, jacuzzi, and indoor swimming pool help out a great deal, too," he added.

In 1890, two brothers of the pioneer Olson family built a crude log hotel, which served as the only haven for travelers coming to Quinault. Another temporary structure was built to provide additional shelter for travelers in 1923, and finally, in 1926, the site for Quinault Lodge was selected in a natural clearing, and the lodge was constructed with great care and the finest materials.

The present innkeepers, Marge and Larry Lesley, have worked very hard to preserve the best of the old and, of course, to incorporate some of the improvements of today's conveniences. The result is a growing lodge in which many of the rooms look out over the lake and command an excellent view of the mountains.

The Lesleys are also the owners of Kalaloch Lodge, overlooking the beautiful Pacific Ocean, a few miles north on Route 101.

The Lake Quinault Lodge is a year-round resort-inn about three hours from Seattle and Tacoma. Frankly, I feel totally inadequate to describe the tremendous scope of the trees and the entire forest, mountain, and lake experience.

Everything about the lodge is homelike and comfortable, and is clearly a source of pleasure to the many families staying there. The irrepressible younger set spends many an enjoyable evening in the dandy recreation room with its variety of games.

With so much time spent out of doors, it is easy to see why the dining room is an important part of the inn experience. I found homemade baked bread, Yankee pot roast of beef, and many other typical country inn items interspersed with things that are found only in the Northwest, like alder-smoked Quinault salmon.

As the evening moved on, I strolled over to the corner where the people were singing to a guitar and joined the widening circle. About

thirty minutes later, the great old grandfather's clock in the corner tolled eleven. With this, the group started to break up and say good night, all of them headed for another deep sleep here in the woods.

LAKE QUINAULT LODGE, Southshore Rd., Quinault, WA 98575; 206-288-2571. A 55-guestroom resort-inn in the Olympic National Forest of the State of Washington, about 40 mi. from Aberdeen. European plan. Breakfast, lunch, and dinner served daily to travelers. Open every day of the year. Indoor swimming pool, chipping green on grounds. Hiking, mountain climbing, fishing, nature walks nearby. Fee for pets; must be attended. Marge and Larry Lesley, Innkeepers.

Directions: Use Quinault exit from Rte. 101. Proceed 2 mi. on south shore of Lake Quinault to inn.

A number of inns have nearby airports where private airplanes may land. An airplane symbol at the end of the inn directions indicates that there is an airport nearby. Consult inn for further information.

OAK BAY BEACH HOTEL
Victoria, British Columbia (1979)

"Really, one of the most spectacular sights in this part of the world is the view of Victoria from the water at Christmas time!"

There were three of us enjoying the superb seaside view from the Tudor Dining Room at the Oak Bay Beach Hotel. There was Bruce Walker, the owner, whom I met at least twelve years ago on my first visit to this spectacularly beautiful part of the world, and his son, Kevin, who is the general manager of the hotel. Kevin's wife, Shawna Dee, had just excused herself to do a little shopping in the hotel gift shop.

"Actually, Christmas starts about the eighth of December for us," explained Kevin. "We start having buffet luncheons with special holiday season specialty items. The daily afternoon high tea also has some special holiday touches. These are in effect for the entire month.

"We have carolling in the lobby each night, featuring the Victoria Operatic Society, starting on the twentieth. That's when we serve roasted chestnuts and Christmas beverages."

"Our Christmas Eve gala buffet is really an extravaganza," Bruce offered. "Christmas dinner starts at 4:30 in the afternoon and there are two seatings.

"Everything continues up to and including the thirty-first, when we come to a smashing climax with our New Year's Eve dinner."

I understand that very few of you will actually be able to be at the Oak Bay Beach Hotel during the Christmas season; however, I'm sharing it with you to illustrate the real *esprit* which is present much of the time at Victoria's only seaside hotel.

For me, Victoria is the most English of all Canadian cities, and the Oak Bay Beach Hotel is like a visit to England's North Devon coast or Cornwall. Like the Mermaid in Rye, it also has the handsome Tudor-style half-timbers.

The English theme is carried out in the guest rooms, and in fact the third floor has the same white plaster and Tudor half-timber finish as the exterior of the building. The rooms and suites, all furnished with handsome antiques, have such names as Samuel Pepys, Prince Albert, and Queen Anne. The rooms in the back of the house overlook the Straits of Haro, with a view of Discovery Island and the San Juan Islands. Mount Baker rises ten thousand magnificent feet in the distance.

There are pleasant walks in the hotel's gardens and along the pathway down to the sea, as well as through the surrounding residential streets, with their attractive houses and the shops of Oak Bay Village. The Oak Bay golf course is a ten-minute walk away, and the hotel will arrange charter-boat fishing. Killer whales, seals, and salmon are often spotted offshore.

"How does one see Victoria's Christmas lights from the water?" I asked. "That's very easy," Kevin replied. "We hold Christmas lights cruises on board our yacht, the *Mesouda*. It's a two-hour cruise, departing the inner harbor daily about 4:30. Not only that, but we're happy to provide hors d'oeuvres befitting the occasion. Our yacht has proven to be one of our most popular diversions during the summer. We have sunset dinner cruises in which guests are taken on a three-hour excursion around the beautiful Oak Bay waters and Victoria's inner harbor."

Now we could see Mount Baker in the distance dramatically lit by the sun's rays, and high tea was beginning to be served in the Tudor Dining Room. I started doing some mental figuring on how to be able to take a cruise on board the *Mesouda* myself.

OAK BAY BEACH HOTEL, 1175 Beach Dr., Victoria, B.C. Canada V8S 2N2; 604-598-4556. A 48-guestroom seaside inn located in one of the quiet suburbs of Victoria. European plan. Breakfast, lunch, and dinner served to travelers. Open every day in the year. A short distance from the spectacular scenery and recreational resources of British Columbia. Swimming on grounds. Daily yacht cruises. Golf, tennis, fishing, sailing, and Butchart Gardens nearby. No pets. Bruce R. Walker, Innkeeper.

Directions: Take Johnson St. or Fort St. from downtown Victoria, east to Oak Bay Ave., which leads into Newport Ave. Turn left into Windsor Ave. to Beach Dr. Turn right and continue to 1175 Beach Dr. If arriving by air at Victoria Airport, I suggest you take public transportation to the center of the city and then take a taxi to the hotel.

THE LODGE ON THE DESERT
Tucson, Arizona (1976)

The slanting rays of the western sun, providing spectacular back-lighting for the great banks of clouds that seemed to skim the jagged peaks of the Santa Catalina Mountains, streamed through the casement window and lit up the interior of my spacious studio bedroom at the Lodge on the Desert.

Even though the afternoon temperature in September reached 85 degrees, I knew that later that evening I would want a fire in my fireplace to ease the chill of the cool desert night.

My bedroom was really most impressive, with three windows on two sides and a patio facing north. The two double beds had rich bedspreads that complemented the orange curtains, and an armful of freshly picked flowers lent an air of gaiety to the dark tones of the carved

wooden tables and chests. The full-sized closet reminded me that many people come here to spend weeks at a time, enjoying the benefits of a friendly climate in both summer and winter, plus the many opportunities for outdoor recreation, as well as the pursuit of the arts.

Tucson is one of the most sophisticated cities in the Southwest, with many fine homes and attractive shops in the downtown area. The University of Arizona is an active cultural center with a continuing program of music, drama, and arts and crafts exhibitions.

"We are now into our second fifty years of family ownership. My father built the Lodge on the Desert outside Tucson in 1936," commented Schuyler Lininger, the *patron grande* of this resort-inn. "Now the city has grown up around us; fortunately, we have no tall buildings to disrupt our guests' view of the mountains, and yet we are set apart by the hedges around the property. However, many of our guests find nearness to the center of things in the city most desirable."

Here in the Southwest desert, during the outdoor weather, everybody gathers around the swimming pool, and here is where many conversations and lasting friendships start.

For cooler days, the Lodge has a very spacious and inviting living room with lots of books, which guests are free to take to their rooms, a chess game, a jigsaw puzzle, and many opportunities just to sit and relax.

The guest rooms of the inn have been designed after the manner of Pueblo Indian farmhouses, the beige adobe color frequently relieved by very colorful Mexican tiles.

Although the dining room features many dishes of the Southwest, I found there were also such favorites as Chateaubriand for two, roast rack of lamb, and several veal dishes. Schuyler explained that he and Helen have gone to great lengths to bring milk-fed Wisconsin veal to the table in different versions. Incidentally, one of the most popular features of the inn is breakfast served on the patios of the guest rooms in the beautiful early-morning sunshine.

I believe another guest succinctly summed up my feelings about the Lodge on the Desert while we were at the pool, taking advantage of that bright September sun to get a few more degrees of tan.

"What I like about it here," she said, "is the really endless variety of things that are going on in Tucson—the Art Center, the many different theaters, the new museum, the exhibition of Indian arts, the opera company, the ballet, the Tucson Symphony, the golf courses, the racetrack, and all kinds of sports events—it's so *civilized!*"

THE LODGE ON THE DESERT, 306 N. Alvernon Way, Tucson, AZ 85733; 602-325-3366. A 40-guestroom luxury inn within the city limits. American and European plans available in winter; European plan in summer. Continental breakfast included in European plan. Breakfast, lunch, and dinner served to travelers every day of the year. Near several historic, cultural, and recreational attractions. Swimming pool and lawn games on grounds. Tennis and golf 1 mi. Attended, leashed pets allowed. Schuyler and Helen Lininger, Innkeepers.

Directions: Take Speedway exit from I-10. Travel about 5 mi. east to Alvernon Way, turn right (south) onto Alvernon (3/4 mi.). Lodge is on left side between 5th St. and Broadway.

RANCHO DE LOS CABALLEROS
Wickenburg, Arizona (1971)

"The idea of a winter vacation on a guest ranch in Arizona never occurred to us," said the letter from Michigan. "Wickenburg seemed like such a long way and we weren't quite sure what kind of people would be there. We certainly weren't horseback riders and we thought we might feel out of place. However, we were reading your book about how much you enjoyed the noon buffet around the pool at Rancho de los Caballeros and getting some horseback riding tips from Dick Frederickson, and we began to think that maybe we would enjoy it too.

"The trip from Detroit to Phoenix was quite short and the ranch car met us at the airport. When I talked with Ann Giles on the telephone she assured me that we'd feel right at home and that we should bring our tennis rackets. She mentioned that golf clubs could be rented if we didn't

want to carry them. We literally dragged our two early-teenage sons with us, and did their faces light up, when almost as soon as we arrived they noticed other young people. I don't believe we saw them for the rest of the two weeks.

"You were right about Dick, and by about the third day I began to feel as if I had almost been born on a horse. We decided to spend Christmas there next year."

Rancho de los Caballeros. . . "The ranch of the gentlemen on horseback." The name alone has an unusually romantic, melodic sound, and its location in the high country is equally romantic. As my correspondent from Michigan said later on in her letter, "The mountains and the desert literally grow on you."

I love to sit on the terrace at sunset and watch the changing colors and dimensions of the Bradshaw Mountains far across the valley.

Rancho de los Caballeros is a rather elegant ranch-inn. A continuous program of watering and irrigation makes it a green jewel in the desert. This is especially true of the 18-hole championship golf course. Many of the guest rooms and suites are built around a carefully planned cactus garden and oversized putting green, and are decorated in Arizona desert colors with harmonizing hues of tan, yellow, and brown. Each accommodation or "casita," as they are called in this part of the world, has a private patio, and many of them have fireplaces.

A program of planned activities for younger people is one of the reasons this ranch experience is so popular with families. "We feel that it is a good balance," says innkeeper Rusty Gant, "because children of all ages have several activities every morning, and in the afternoon they can join their parents for more trail riding or tennis or a swim in the pool. At dinner the children's counselor gathers them all together, and they even have their own dining room. They are kept occupied until bedtime. This has proven to be an excellent idea for both children and their parents."

I've visited Rancho de los Caballeros many times since my initial visit in 1971, and have always had a marvelous time, so I am not at all surprised at the experience of my friends from Michigan.

RANCHO DE LOS CABALLEROS, Wickenburg, AZ 85358; 602-684-5484. A 73-guestroom luxury ranch-resort, 60 mi. from Phoenix in the sunny, dry desert. American plan. Breakfast, lunch, dinner served to travelers daily. Open from mid-Oct. to early May. Swimming pool, horseback riding, hiking, skeet shooting, putting green, tennis, and 18-hole championship golf course on grounds. Special children's program. No pets. No credit cards. Dallas C. Gant, Jr., Innkeeper.

Directions: Rtes. 60, 89, and 93 lead to Wickenburg. Ranch is 2 mi. west of town on Rte. 60 and 2 mi. south on Vulture Mine Road.

A number of inns have nearby airports where private airplanes may land. An airplane symbol at the end of the inn directions indicates that there is an airport nearby. Consult inn for further information.

I do not include lodging rates in the descriptions, for the very nature of an inn means that there are lodgings of various sizes, with and without baths, in and out of season, and with plain and fancy decoration. Travelers should call ahead and inquire about the availability and rates of the many different types of rooms.

TANQUE VERDE
Tucson, Arizona (1970)

The postmark on the letter was "Caldwell, New Jersey." It said in part: "We've been reading about your last visit to Tanque Verde Ranch, just outside of Tucson. It sounds very intriguing. My wife and I are enthusiastic about the prospect of a new vacation experience in the desert country. The idea of staying at a ranch that may have even survived Indian raids, and your description of steak over mesquite fires and bird watching, are most inviting. However, it is a long way for us to go, and neither of us has ever been astride a horse. We're both about fifty years old and we'd like a little more advice as to whether we should venture forth on this trip."

Until my first visit to Tanque Verde in 1969, horseback riding for me consisted of a couple short hauls on a Tennessee walking horse and one or two rides on the gentlest nag in my local livery stable. When I went out to Tanque Verde, I talked this over with the head wrangler, and he picked out a horse that he thought was the right size for my weight and had enough experience to guide me.

On that ride (the first of many during subsequent visits), I met a husband and wife from the Boston area, who were at a Western ranch for the first time and out on their first morning trail ride. We left the corral in single file and rode out into the desert. The entire experience was so exhilarating that by the time we got back to the ranch my Massachusetts neighbors were inquiring as to whether they could have more active horses and go for a longer ride the next day.

By the end of the week, these people had purchased some blue jeans, western shirts, cowboy hats, and boots, and knew all the horses by their first names.

Tanque Verde is a completely different type of country inn. There are many diversions, including both indoor and outdoor pools and an active tennis program. I spent one New Year's Eve there and had a great time with all the parents and children who had been there since Christmas.

In Tanque Verde's 100-year-old history as one of Arizona's pioneer guest cattle ranches, there are even stories of Indian raids. The ranch is set back in a semicircle of mountains, about a thirty-minute drive from downtown Tucson and the airport. The accommodations are in almost luxurious individual *casitas,* all of which have their own Spanish-style corner fireplaces. Everyone eats at long tables in the vaulted dining room, and there's nothing like the desert air to encourage big appetites.

One further point: Tanque Verde is open throughout the entire year, and during the summer there are many guests from Europe and Asia enjoying the full holiday in the desert. As innkeeper Bob Cote says, "We have so many guests speaking different languages, we could almost advertise that it's a good place for children to get some language tutoring."

This guest ranch was the first such accommodation to be included in *CIBR.* In subsequent years I have added a few others, both east and west. Tanque Verde, with geniune cordiality extended to all guests and its infectious informality, has served as a model for me.

TANQUE VERDE, Box 66, Rte. 8, Tucson, AZ 85710; 602-296-6275. A 65-guestroom ranch-inn, 10 mi. from Tucson. American plan. Breakfast, lunch, and dinner served to travelers by reservation. Open year-round. Riding, indoor and outdoor pool, tennis, sauna, exercise room, and whirlpool bath on grounds. Robert Cote, Innkeeper.

Directions: From U.S. 10, exit at Speedway Blvd. and travel east to dead end.

I do not include lodging rates in the descriptions, for the very nature of an inn means that there are lodgings of various sizes, with and without baths, in and out of season, and with plain and fancy decoration. Travelers should call ahead and inquire about the availability and rates of the many different types of rooms.

BRIAR ROSE BED & BREAKFAST
Boulder, Colorado (1983)

I'm going to share a part of a sparkling letter I received from Emily Hunter, the innkeeper at the Briar Rose:

"Briar Rose is filled with people who have come to see the CU–Ohio football game. There is a bouquet of autumn leaves in the Briar Rose window seat, screening the bird feeder from the activity at the dining room table. A flock of grosbeaks has taken up residence in the lilac bushes and lost all hesitations, sitting for hours, sharing pounds of sunflower seeds with Rusty the squirrel.

"We built the first fire of the season yesterday. The big poplar out front is turning that great marigold yellow that I look forward to every year. The fire alarms are all checked, the firewood ordered and to be split next week, and the down puffs go back on the beds tonight. It feels like all the appropriate gestures have been made to stave off the cold and dark and snow for a few more months."

The ground floor exterior of the inn is a beautiful rose-colored brick, with Queen Anne shingles on the second story. I noticed several other small houses in Boulder that featured some of the same basic design.

The Briar Rose has also undergone some extensive redecorating in the public rooms, dining rooms, and some of the bedrooms in a small building immediately adjacent. Almost all of the furnishings are Regency Victorian, and there are splendid additional touches, such as roses in the guest rooms, baskets of fruit on the nightstands, and the aforementioned down puffs on the beds.

More as an accommodation to the guest than anything else, the Briar Rose offers a modest dinner consisting of a single entrée of different types of casseroles with puff-pastry tops. There's usually a choice of beef with onion, wine, and mushrooms or turkey with cream, onions, and carrots. This is augmented by a simple dessert that goes along with dinner.

As Emily says, "Boulder is a great restaurant town, and there are good restaurants within walking distance, but we want to be able to offer dinner to those guests who are arriving really tired from a long trip and who don't want to take the trouble to go out for dinner. This is particularly true of businessmen, and if they want to have dinner in front of the fire or at the table—or even on the back porch in the summertime—they can take their tray and enjoy it wherever they like."

During the past few years Emily has gained a considerable reputation for conducting conferences and seminars whose basic subject is "how to open a bed-and-breakfast inn." These are held several times a year and I'd suggest contacting her to find out all of the details.

Emily's letter went on: "We have an ideal climate here in Boulder with four distinct and wonderful seasons. There are over 300 sunny days a year and many things for visitors to enjoy, both recreational and artistic. Of course, the mountains offer everything, including climbing, hiking, cross-country skiing. Some people say that the powder snow offers the best downhill skiing in the world. Biking is also very popular here in this part of Colorado and there are bicyclists everywhere, as well as joggers and runners."

Emily's letter continues: "At this moment my dining room here at home is filled with six-foot-long cardboard boxes, in turn filled with dried whole roses that I dried in my attic. A friend, who is a floral

designer, has begun just this week to market 'Briar Rose Potpourri.' A friend gave me a plastic pink flamingo that now resides hidden in the water lilies of the fish pond. Only the most observant guest is treated to the sight of our own 'Loch Ness Flamingo.' "

BRIAR ROSE BED & BREAKFAST, 2151 Arapahoe Ave., Boulder, CO 80302; 303-442-3007. A 12-guestroom (some shared baths) inn located in a quiet section of a pleasant, conservative Colorado city, approx. 1 hr. from Denver. Open all year. Breakfast included in lodging rate. Evening meal available upon request. Afternoon tea served. Convenient for all of the many recreational, cultural, and historic attractions nearby. Limousine service available to and from Denver airport. Emily Hunter, Innkeeper.

Directions: From Denver, follow I-25 north and Rte. 36 to Boulder. Turn left on Arapahoe Ave. Briar Rose is on the right on the corner of 22nd St.

THE HEARTHSTONE INN
Colorado Springs, Colorado (1979)

It was a most agreeable early August morning at the Hearthstone Inn. This time I was paying a visit in midsummer, when I could see the inn's beautiful lawn and flowers at their very best, and also sit on the front porch in one of the new handsome Tennessee country rockers.

I watched with amusement while a father, mother, and their four-year-old boy romped on the lawn, and then one of the staff came out and set up the croquet set. I had arrived just a few moments earlier, driving down from Denver and Boulder, and was immediately offered my choice of coffee or iced tea. "The coffee is on from early in the morning," explained Dot Williams, who with Ruth Williams (no relation), is the innkeeper at the Hearthstone.

Now I watched the few cars go by on Cascade Avenue, one of the most impressive streets in Colorado Springs, and reflected on the many changes I have seen in the considerable number of years since the first night I landed in Denver. I had been picked up by Dot and Ruth and driven out to the "Springs." These two women had opened up the first inn in Colorado Springs, overcoming many difficulties. At that time there was only one house; now there are two houses, cheek-by-jowl.

The most recent development is the completion of Sheltering Pines, a totally different type of accommodation in nearby Green Mountain Falls. I had visited it when it was just a bit more than a gleam in the innkeepers' eyes.

"It is slowly developing its own following," Dot said. "The cool of the mountain evenings and the clear air of our mountain days make this part of Colorado a real boon for those who suffer from heat or allergies.

Family reunions or groups are enjoying the patio, barbecue grill, and the many trees. It's quite a bit higher than Colorado Springs."

Sheltering Pines is actually a duplex with two completely separate living areas. Each has a completely equipped kitchen with everything provided, including all of the bedding and towels. In the summer it is rented only by the week, but the rest of the year it's available for shorter stays with a two-night minimum.

The Hearthstone itself is well known from coast to coast as being one of the truly impressive Victorian restorations. Every room has been furnished entirely with Victorian furniture and decorations, and the outside of this wonderful combination of two rambling houses has been finished in carefully researched Victorian colors. Visitors will be surprised, as was I, to see how gracefully they reflect the Mauve Decades.

I always look forward to breakfast at the Hearthstone, and there is a wide variety of hearty breakfast offerings, not just the usual. "We never serve the same guest the same breakfast twice," Ruth declared.

Dot and Ruth joined me on the front porch, and we watched the squirrels, Minnie the Moocher and Pearl the Squirrel, and their friend, Jaws, eat themselves silly on sunflower seeds.

"I've always hoped that you would come out during Christmas some year," Ruth said. "Our guests all gather around for eggnog and the tradition of decorating the tree. Many guests bring a homemade ornament, and we tag each one with their name and the year, and it becomes a permanent part of each tree's decorations. Why don't you plan to come next year?"

I certainly would enjoy that experience very much!

THE HEARTHSTONE INN, 506 N. Cascade Ave., Colorado Springs, CO 80903; 303-473-4413. A 26-guestroom bed-and-breakfast inn within sight of Pike's Peak, in the residential section of Colorado Springs. Complimentary full breakfast is the only meal served. Open every day all year. (Housekeeping units also available in Green Mountain Falls.) Convenient to spectacular Colorado mountain scenery as well as Air Force Academy, Garden of the Gods, Cave of the Winds, the McAllister House Museum, Fine Arts Center, and Broadmoor Resort. Golf, tennis, swimming, hiking, backroading, and Pikes Peak ski area nearby. Check innkeepers for pet policy. Dorothy Williams and Ruth Williams, Innkeepers.

Directions: From I-25 (the major north/south hwy.) use Exit 143 (Uintah St.); travel east (opposite direction from mountains) to third stop light (Cascade Ave.). Turn right for 7 blocks. The inn will be on the right at the corner of St. Vrain and Cascade—a big Victorian house, tan with lilac trim.

PARRISH'S COUNTRY SQUIRE
Berthoud, Colorado (1987)

A terrific clap of thunder rolled over the mountains, followed by an even greater clap. The patch of blue sky to the south would soon be covered by ominous blue-gray clouds that were already moving over the ranch.

Donna and Jess Parrish and I had just finished dinner, and were sitting on the front deck of Parrish's Country Squire, which is nestled down in a little valley north of Boulder, Colorado. I've experienced thunderstorms all over the world, and as far as such things are concerned, we New Englanders bow to no one, but I have yet to see a prelude that would be the equal of what we were now experiencing. It was thrilling.

Earlier, we all had sat out on this deck overlooking the Little Thompson River and the cottonwood trees. Only a few advance clouds warned of the coming storm, and Donna's soft accents mixing with Jess's twang made me a part of this Colorado family, as I shared their dinner and began to understand some of their hopes and dreams and the reasons that they lived here in the foothills of the great Rockies.

Parrish's is a working ranch. It is where Jess and Donna and their family, including their small grandson, live and work. When you walk through the front door you are in their home, sitting in their cathedral-ceilinged log living–dining room. It's a wonderful opportunity to be with a real Western family on a small ranch. There is a television set and stereo, and on the mantelpieces of the great stone fireplaces are photographs of the family, taken at various times. There are pictures of their kids, of weddings, and even of previous guests.

They have set aside two bedrooms, especially for guests, and there is another room on the top floor that is very good for kids of all ages.

Donna told me dinner "might be steak over the charcoal grill, which we are having tonight, baked potato, and salad. We serve meat casseroles and fresh-baked things. We're not real sweet eaters, so we don't make a big thing out of desserts. We suggest fruit and cheese. We use our own steers for beef."

I asked her about the wild animals. "We have lots of them, and we can often see them from right here on the deck. There are rabbits, prairie dogs, coyotes, raccoons, and, of course, dozens of varieties of birds. Last Sunday was a beautiful evening, and we watched deer appearing from all directions. We were really surprised to see a fawn come out of the plum bushes. Sometimes they come right up to the lawn."

Her voiced trailed off as if in reverie, and Jess picked up the tune with a more practical view: "We raise cattle and hay, but we're getting into more recreational ranching now. We are still a working cattle ranch, but we rent horses to guests for trail rides."

Earlier, they had taken Emily Hunter, the innkeeper at the Briar Rose in nearby Boulder, and me up a long, curving road that can be seen from the front deck. From a higher point it is possible to see considerably more of the countryside with the wonderful high foothills. This is one of the places that the ranch guests go for their horseback rides. We were accompanied on this short journey by their border collie, Lacey.

In many respects, Parrish's reflects the early hospitality of Colorado, before the great resorts and big hotels took over. It's a wonderful, natural experience offered by people who have opened their home to a few guests at a time.

As you can see, I was entranced.

PARRISH'S COUNTRY SQUIRE, 2515 Parrish Rd., Berthoud, CO 80513; 303-772-7678 or 678-8834. A 3-guestroom (private and shared baths) working cattle ranch in the foothills of Rocky Mountain National Park in northern Colorado. Complimentary ranch breakfast; evening meal is available at an additional charge. Open year-round except Dec. Telephone in advance. Swimming, hiking, horseback riding, trail rides with guides, on grounds. Carter Lake nearby has sailing, boating, and fishing. Suitable for younger children. No pets. No credit cards. Jess and Donna Parrish, Proprietors.

Directions: From Denver, take I-25 north to the Lyons and Estes Park turnoff and go west on Hwy. 66. Turn north on Rte. 287 to County Rd. 4, also marked 41600W. Turn west for 5 mi. and look for the ranch sign on left as the road enters the foothills.

RIVERSONG
Estes Park, Colorado (1987)

As I meandered through the grounds in front of RiverSong, I noticed that the grass had been allowed to seek its own level, along with the wildflowers and various flowering bushes. I noted, too, a couple of ponds and pools and a gazebo with a fireplace for cooking out. Through the trees I could see to the top of the great Continental Divide, which in August was still snowcapped. This view is even better from several of the guest rooms in RiverSong. It is reminiscent of an Albert Bierstadt painting.

Now I crossed a narrow little stone bridge into a lovely tiny glade of evergreens, with two benches, and wandered to the edge of still another pool. There is a series of connecting pools where all the wonderful music of splashing water can always be heard. It reminded me of the same wonderful tinkling sounds I've heard in the fountains of Spanish *paradores*.

The first time I walked through the front door, I knew that this was a small, intimate inn whose owners understood what it means to provide a place for guests to come together and exchange ideas and conversation. In the middle of the living room was a large, crescent-shaped couch, which faced the fireplace at one end and a spectacular view of the great peaks of the Rockies at the other end. It was a room with many, many books of all kinds—books indicating an active literary and intellectual curiosity on the part of Sue and Gary Mansfield. As Gary says, "Although we are an inn that basically appeals to outdoor-minded people—they want to hike on the trails or ski or just go outside and smell the fresh air after a rain—we know that when the day is through there are times when a good book is exactly what is needed."

Every one of the guest rooms has been furnished most uniquely. I'll just describe the honeymoon suite, which has a queen-sized bed, a working fireplace with a raised hearth, a semi-cathedral ceiling with a skylight, and a little unicorn. In fact, there are unicorns in all of the guest rooms. This suite has its own patio, looking up through the ponderosa pines. The bathroom has a sunken tub and a double redwood shower with a skylight. A few steps away is a carriage house with some very attractive additional rooms.

Sue told me that almost all of the antiques in the inn have been handed down through her family; the carved bed and dresser in one room belonged to her father's parents, and the quilts were made by her maternal grandmother. The antique silver and dishes have come from both sides of the family. As she says, "It's nice to be able to share these things with other people who really appreciate them."

The talk turned to breakfast. Apple pan dowdy, blueberry and rhubarb cobblers, baked cinnamon apples, along with such favorites as cinnamon rolls, bran muffins, and homemade raspberry jam or Emily Hunter's lemon curd are some of the offerings. Dinner is served on advance request, and the rather simple one-dish meals have proven to be very satisfactory for those guests who do not want to drive "downtown" to Estes Park for the evening meal.

"Oh, I wish you could come here at Christmas!" Sue exclaimed. "It is truly a magical time, with the deer and the elk returning and the serenity and beauty of our little inn on the banks of the Big Thompson River. I do wish you could join us." I've never had a better invitation.

We are happy to welcome RiverSong to *Country Inns and Back Roads* for the first time.

RIVERSONG, P.O. Box 1910, Estes Park, CO 80517; 303-586-4666. A 7-guestroom (private and shared baths) mountain inn at the foot of the great Continental Divide, 70 mi. from Denver. Breakfast included in room rate; simple dinners offered on advance request. Open all year. Downhill and xc skiing, hiking, walking, golf, tennis, antiquing, and exploring, all most convenient. Boarding kennel nearby for pets. No smoking. Gary and Sue Mansfield, Innkeepers.

Directions: From Denver: Estes Park is only 70 mi. from central Denver with no mountain passes to cross. Any choice of roads is wonderfully scenic. Ask the inn for directions from the center of Estes Park.

VISTA VERDE GUEST RANCH
Steamboat Springs, Colorado (1987)

There seemed to be a ruckus in the side yard next to the main lodge at the Vista Verde Guest Ranch, where some children were practicing with the lariat. There was a great deal of shouting and laughing because they had lassoed one of the wranglers, and he was now on the ground. They were all standing around him like the Lilliputians stood around Gulliver. The other adult guests in the dining room and I crowded to the window to see what was going on. One of the mothers seated at my table noted somewhat wryly that this was the first night her young daughter hadn't worn bluejeans, and it was obvious that her little flowered frock was going to be grass-stained.

Afterward we all drifted back to the tables and most of the talk was about the day's rafting trip down the Colorado, and the guests who had been here previously said that it was always a different adventure.

Vista Verde is an activity-oriented guest ranch, with the major focus centered on horseback riding. However, as Frank Brophy pointed out, "We have lots of things like gold panning and guided hiking expeditions for people who may not care for riding."

It was my first real Colorado guest ranch experience, and I must say that I was tremendously impressed. It is situated at an elevation of 7,800 feet, surrounded by a national forest and a wilderness area. Guests share the environment with elk, deer, bears, foxes, coyotes, beavers, porcupines, and golden and bald eagles.

Lodgings are in individual hand-hewn cabins with hooked rugs, calico curtains, and Early American furnishings. All of them are car-

peted, with spacious living rooms, cozy fireplaces, kitchens and baths, and from one to three cheerful bedrooms.

Guests are on the American plan rates, which include three meals a day, and what meals they are! Everybody is summoned by a ranch dinner bell, and, as you might imagine, home cooking is the rule. There are homemade breads, pies, and pastries, and fresh eggs from the henhouse. Meals are served family-style in the main lodge or on picnic tables near the outdoor fireplace. Breakfast cookouts, steak barbecues, and fish fries all add to the fun. There's evening entertainment almost every night, with such diversions as a rodeo, square dancing, sing-alongs, story-telling, and even some guest talent as well.

There is an extensive children's program with a children's counselor. As Frank says, "In short order, we can have a five-year-old riding better than an eighteen-year-old."

For both the summer and winter guests, there is a spa and exercise center with a whirlpool, sauna, and exercise facilities to help them relax after a day out of doors, either in the saddle, on hiking trails or on skis.

In winter, there is cross-country skiing, horse-drawn sleigh rides, snowshoeing, and ice fishing right on the ranch, or just relaxing in front of the fire.

This account of Vista Verde's virtues must of necessity be somewhat limited, and I hope that it will pique your interest enough to write for a brochure, which contains far more extensive suggestions. I can assure you that it is right on the mark.

We are happy to welcome Vista Verde to *Country Inns and Back Roads* for the first time.

VISTA VERDE GUEST RANCH, Box 465, Steamboat Springs, CO 80477; 303-879-3858. A 40-guest-capacity working ranch, high in the Colorado Rockies. Full American plan includes breakfast, lunch, and dinner. Open year-round. Inquire about minimum stays. Horseback riding and instruction; xc skiing on grounds and nearby in winter. Colorado River float trips, hunting, fishing, hot-air ballooning, tennis, swimming, golfing, and other summer sports nearby. No pets. Special cancellation policy. Mr. and Mrs. Frank Brophy, Innkeepers.

Directions: American Airlines and PSA will have nonstop jet service to Steamboat Springs during the winter with access from fifty major U.S. cities. In summer, the best plan is to fly to Denver and transfer to Continental Express Airways or drive to Steamboat Springs. Once there, telephone the ranch for further instructions.

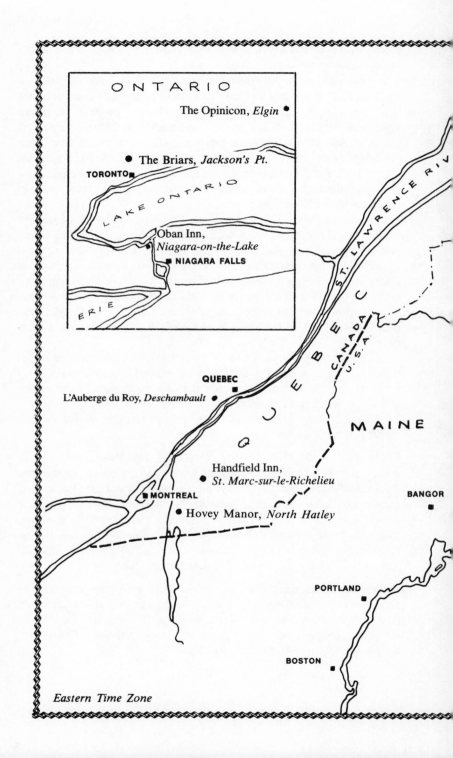

ONTARIO

The Opinicon, *Elgin*

The Briars, *Jackson's Pt.*

TORONTO

LAKE ONTARIO

Oban Inn,
Niagara-on-the-Lake

NIAGARA FALLS

ERIE

ST. LAWRENCE RIV

QUEBEC

CANADA
U.S.A.

MAINE

L'Auberge du Roy, *Deschambault*

Handfield Inn,
St. Marc-sur-le-Richelieu

MONTREAL

Hovey Manor, *North Hatley*

BANGOR

PORTLAND

BOSTON

Eastern Time Zone

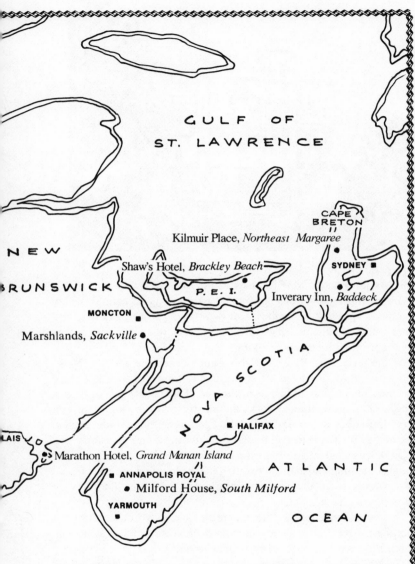

GULF OF ST. LAWRENCE

CAPE BRETON

Kilmuir Place, *Northeast Margaree*

Shaw's Hotel, *Brackley Beach*

SYDNEY

NEW BRUNSWICK

P. E. I.

Inverary Inn, *Baddeck*

MONCTON

Marshlands, *Sackville*

NOVA SCOTIA

HALIFAX

Marathon Hotel, *Grand Manan Island*

ATLANTIC

ANNAPOLIS ROYAL

Milford House, *South Milford*

YARMOUTH

OCEAN

Eastern and Maritime Canada

Atlantic Time Zone

MARATHON INN
Grand Manan Island, New Brunswick (1976)

Grand Manan is a quiet, unspoiled island of great natural beauty fifteen miles long and four miles wide—a paradise for naturalists, bird watchers, photographers, artists, divers, and rock hounds. The best way to experience the island is by walking.

As the ferry from Black's Harbour approached the wharf at North Head on Grand Manan Island, I could readily see that this was a place where men made their living from the sea. There were fishing boats, seining weirs, and weathered docks on tall stilts; a necessity because of the very high tides in the Bay of Fundy. I could see the Marathon Inn at the top of the hill—a gleaming, three-story building with a mansard roof.

On this particular trip Jim Leslie had suggested in a very mysterious way that something unusual and exciting had been going on at the inn on at least two occasions during the year, and said that he would fill me in when we had a chance to chat.

The owner-innkeepers of the inn are Jim and Judy Leslie, and Jim's mother, Fern. The Leslies are all Canadians. Fern is from Saskatchewan, and both Judy and Jim were brought up in Toronto.

The first thing I did on arrival was to take a plunge in the heated swimming pool and arrange for a game of tennis. Jim joined me about an hour before dinner on the front porch overlooking the harbor.

"Our guests often like to take advantage of the chance to go deep sea fishing for herring, pollock, and haddock with the island fishermen. There are also boating trips to Gannet Rock, Machias Seal Island, and Tent Island. Children seem to have a wonderful time here, and that is very gratifying.

"We have some excellent spring programs that are available to our guests at a slight additional charge," Jim said. "There are three four-day birdwatching tours in May and June conducted by Mary Majka. Also in June we have a special photographic workshop conducted by Freeman Patterson and a watercolor seminar by John Austen. We also have a super dark room.

"During the fall months we have a program called 'Ocean Search' that enables our guests to learn more about the great whales off the island and also to go out on the sea in boats. Our naturalist shows slides several evenings during the week with special emphasis on those great mammals during that time."

Finally, I could contain myself no longer. "What is this mystery you're talking about?" Jim smiled broadly and replied, "That's exactly what it is: an old-fashioned 'whodunit' mystery, in which our guests can hunt down clues and suspects. We supply them with a complete kit of clues when they arrive on Fridays. Before the weekend is out we've had a 'crime' with suspects and detectives, and finally we solve the mystery by figuring out who the culprit was.

"We did two of these last year and they were a huge success. We're already booked for some additional weekends this year, as well. You don't have to be a fan of Miss Marple or Sherlock Holmes, but it helps to get into the swing of things. Everybody has a terrific time. Tell your readers that they will have to telephone in advance to make a reservation."

So, I have now solved part of the mystery; however, I made a reservation on the spot for one of the 'whodunit' weekends at the Marathon Inn. Doesn't the idea sound intriguing?

MARATHON INN, North Head at Grand Manan, New Brunswick, Canada EOG 2MO; 506-662-8144. A 38-guestroom resort-inn on Grand Manan Island in the Bay of Fundy, 40 mi. from St. John in New Brunswick. Modified American and European plans. Closed in winter months. Breakfast and dinner served to travelers daily. Heated swimming pool, tennis courts on grounds. Beachcombing, bird watching, swimming, fishing, hiking, diving, bicycles, golf nearby. Whale watching in season. Pets allowed on ground floor annex. Jim, Judy, and Fern Leslie, Innkeepers.

Directions: Grand Manan Island is reached by ferry from Black's Harbour, just off Rte. 1, midway between Calais, Maine, and St. John, New Brunswick. Check inn for schedule.

MARSHLANDS INN
Sackville, New Brunswick (1975)

Every year I hear from a great many readers who have driven across Maine into New Brunswick to reach Nova Scotia and Prince Edward Island by the land route.

Almost all of these letters make some reference to the Marshlands Inn, just a few miles from the Nova Scotia border and the Prince Edward Island ferry. I'd like to reach back into the past to 1975 and share a portion of a letter from a honeymooning couple.

"Our itinerary from Calais, Maine, took us to the Marathon Inn off the coast of New Brunswick and then to the Marshlands Inn for a late lunch. The setting, decor, and food exceeded our expectations. We never expected to find such a sophisticated inn so far north.

"While paying our bill we found a copy of *Country Inns and Back Roads*, perused the table of contents, and noted your entry regarding the Marshlands. We found that we were in complete agreement with your comments and enjoyed your personal observations."

What was true in 1975 is for the most part still true these many years later. There has been one change recently at the Marshlands Inn. My dear friends Herb and Alice Read have leased the inn to Mary and John Blakely. Mary worked for four years at Marshlands as a hostess. She and John both come from England, where Mary's family had an English-style country inn in the Derbyshire hills. Their eldest son has returned to Marshlands, and is now involved in the family inn business. However, Herb and Alice are still very much on the scene in Sackville, and they are extremely pleased with the way the Blakelys are doing things.

In a conversation that I had with Mary, she filled me in on some of the new offerings being prepared by their French chef.

"Our chef calls the appetizer the entrée and the main dish, dinner," Mary told me. "He does traditional French cuisine as well as a little bit of nouvelle. One of his specialties is sauces.

"We have many new things on the menu, including cultivated mussels from Prince Edward Island or Nova Scotia. We serve them in wine or in stock, depending on the preference of the guest. We also have an excellent Caesar salad. We have specials three or four days a week, with appetizers and entrées. Incidentally, our chef does a halibut mousse with a pink peppercorn sauce and also a smoked cod mousse made with red peppers. We also have a Middle Eastern dish called cous-cous. This is a lamb dish with semolina.

"Of course, we still have the same dishes for which the Marshlands has gained such a fine reputation, including Atlantic and Miramichi salmon. Many of our guests ask for fiddlehead greens almost as soon as they check in."

The first thing that a newly arrived guest sees when entering Marshlands is the graceful, curving staircase, a carved settee, and many ancestral portraits. There are two high-ceilinged parlors for houseguests and diners waiting to be shown to their tables.

The guest rooms are almost all furnished in antiques and Persian rugs, and runners muffle footsteps in all the halls. Each guest room has a four-poster bed and is decorated in a different color scheme and period wallpaper. My favorite room is on the third floor under the eaves, where there is a bow-shaped window with a sitting alcove, a leather-topped writing desk, a marble reading lamp, and a high dresser with a pedestal mirror.

One of the enduring traditions at Marshlands is the delicious hot chocolate, served every evening around ten o'clock. It's a time when guests who may have been otherwise occupied find themselves congregating and talking over the day's experiences.

Let me reassure my honeymooning couple from 1975 that the Marshlands Inn is all that it was during their visit and perhaps a great deal more.

MARSHLANDS INN, Box 1440, Sackville, N.B., Canada EOA 3CO; 506-536-0170. A 10-guestroom (mostly private baths) village inn near Tantramar Marshes and Fundy Tides. European plan. Breakfast, lunch, and dinner served to travelers daily. Open from Feb. thru late Nov. Golf, xc skiing, curling, hiking, and swimming nearby. John and Mary Blakely, Innkeepers.

Directions: Follow Trans-Canada Highway to Sackville, then Rte. 6 for 1 mi. to center of town.

INVERARY INN
Baddeck, Cape Breton, Nova Scotia (1972)

We were all gathered in the living room at Inverary for our annual meeting of all the *CIBR* inns in the Canadian Maritimes. There was a very cheerful fire burning against the chill created by a late October rainstorm. Surrounding us were the trappings that I had seen so often in Scottish inns, such as Tartan drapes, family portraits, and books and magazines of interest to people of Scottish heritage. There were not one, but two, grandfather clocks and very comfortable chairs and settees, where the innkeepers were gathered to exchange ideas and tell stories. It was wonderful to see them here again.

In between the rain showers we had taken walks down along the shore of Lake Bras d'Or, past the heated outdoor swimming pool, the new lakeside tennis courts, and the new house of Scott MacAulay and his wife, Terri. They, by the way, became the parents of Matthew Scott MacAulay on last All Saints Day. His grandfather and grandmother are Danny and Isobel MacAulay, the innkeepers of the Inverary Inn.

Our tour also took us past the waterside seafood restaurant set among the pine trees, where lobster, fresh fish chowder, and other Nova Scotia seafood are offered. The restaurant has a most attractive view of a boatyard, and some of the fishing boats and sailboats can easily be seen while enjoying one of the those delicious Nova Scotia lobsters. A pontoon boat, moored next to the Fish House, takes inn guests out in the evening, and Dan MacAulay is the skipper.

Our walk also included a visit to the wee chapel on the grounds of the inn. "It was the gift of one of our guests," Isobel said. "For everyone it has become a haven of quiet and peaceful serenity. I'm sure to visit here almost every day myself."

But she had other news for us. "I think our biggest news is that the Inverary Inn is now open year-round," she exclaimed. "We feel that this is going to be a wonderful place particularly for people in the Maritimes to come for a 'getaway weekend.' This is especially true because of the addition of our new indoor swimming pool." All of the innkeepers present cheered and congratulated her for such an interesting innovation. Unless I am poorly informed, this is one of the few inns in Nova Scotia to be open twelve months of the year.

The Inverary Inn has several types of accommodations; some are in the main house and others are in adjoining outbuildings and cottages. The newer lodging rooms are principally used to accommodate bus tours. With this in mind, *CIBR* travelers should indicate that they are from *CIBR* when they call to make reservations, and at that time specify the kind of accommodation they prefer. The main house and the Old Barn have the more traditional kinds of rooms.

A letter I received from a couple from Gaithersburg, Maryland, read, in part: "Recently my wife and I enjoyed a portion of our honeymoon at the Inverary Inn. The thing that captured our admiration was the stunning ambience and the warmth and friendliness we experienced from every staff member. We carried away from the Inverary Inn two hearts full of fond memories."

INVERARY INN, Box 190, Baddeck, Cape Breton, N.S., Canada BOE 1BO; 902-295-2674. A 50-guestroom resort-inn on the Cabot Trail, 52 mi. from Sydney, N.S., on the shore of Lake Bras d'Or. European plan. Breakfast and dinner served to travelers daily. Lunch available from June thru Oct. Open year-round. Heated outdoor pool, indoor pool, tennis courts, bicycles, and children's playground on grounds. Boating and small golf course nearby. Isobel MacAulay, Innkeeper.

Directions: Follow Trans-Canada Hwy. to Canso Causeway to Baddeck.

I do not include lodging rates in the descriptions, for the very nature of an inn means that there are lodgings of various sizes, with and without baths, in and out of season, and with plain and fancy decoration. Travelers should call ahead and inquire about the availability and rates of the many different types of rooms.

KILMUIR PLACE
Northeast Margaree, Cape Breton, Nova Scotia (1972)

"I've never used a mix in my life, and never will." Isabel Taylor stood with her hands on her hips and tossed her head back, her eyes flashing. "After all, my mother and father started this place over fifty-five years ago and our guests love the old-fashioned ways. I can tell the difference when something is made from a mix and I'm sure that everybody else can, too."

"Indeed, they do, and I'm a guest who's been coming for forty straight years."

This time the speaker was a lady from Philadelphia, who walked into the Kilmuir Place kitchen as if on cue.

"In those days it took some persistence and motivation to come out to the Margaree," she said, settling down into one of the comfortable upholstered chairs in one corner of the kitchen. "Now you can get here from Sydney in about an hour and a half and from Halifax in about three and a half hours. In the old days the roads weren't paved and sometimes it was necessary to get a team to pull us out of the mud."

Built by a merchant, deep in the unspoiled Nova Scotia countryside in 1885, Kilmuir Place was named for a parish house on the Isle of Skye, off the northwest coast of Scotland. The inn can accommodate six people comfortably, and operates on the modified American plan, serving breakfast and dinner to houseguests only. It's necessary to have firm reservations. The home is filled with treasures and other dear things collected over the years. In the dining room, the beautiful mahogany set and the silver are outstanding. It is an old-fashioned country inn offering a unique, almost rustic, and peaceful lifestyle. Homegrown vegetables accent meals of old-fashioned Nova Scotia fare, including, of course, the famous salmon served in the family dining room along with hot coffee and good conversation.

The inn is on the Cabot Trail that winds between the Gulf of St. Lawrence and the Atlantic Ocean, claiming some of the world's most breathtaking scenery.

Kilmuir Place is a delightful home base for salmon and trout fishing, bicycling, hiking or picnicking. Community suppers and dances in the area are plentiful, and summertime's many Canadian holidays provide stimulating cultural activities, including Canada Day, July 1, featuring the traditional Gathering of the Clans and the Fisherman's Regatta. The end of July brings Margaree Days, and in August the Gaelic Mod presents bagpipe music, Gaelic singing, and Scottish cultural programs.

There are guides available for fishing on the world-famous Margaree River for Atlantic salmon and trout, and the beaches are twelve to fifteen miles away on the warm waters of the Gulf Coast on the Northumberland

Strait. Incidentally, there's excellent bird watching, with many bald eagles.

In recent years Isabel Taylor has given over the innkeeping chores to her daughter and son-in-law, Nancy and Guy Parry; however, she still is in residence and eager to talk on any subject in the world to her many returning guests.

Nancy asked the Philadelphia guest whether she would like to have another piece of the famous Kilmuir chocolate cake; however, the lady demurred, saying that she couldn't possibly eat another bite. I'm also

happy to report that the blueberry crop was sensational during the past year, so there were lots of blueberry muffins and marvelous blueberry cake to add to the repertoire, as well as a great blueberry meringue for dessert.

When you come to Kilmuir, be prepared to wish fervently on the day you leave that you could stay several days longer.

KILMUIR PLACE, Northeast Margaree, Cape Breton, N.S., Canada BOE 2HO; 902-248-2877. (U.S.A. reservations: 800-341-6096; Maine: 800-492-0643). A 5-guestroom country inn on Rte. 19, 28 mi. from Baddeck. Some rooms with shared baths. Modified American plan. Breakfast and dinner served to houseguests only. Open from June to mid-Oct. Salmon fishing in the Margaree River, touring the Cabot Trail, and both fresh-water and salt-water swimming nearby. Not suitable for children under 12. Mrs. Ross Taylor, Guy and Nancy Parry, Innkeepers.

Directions: After crossing Canso Causeway to Cape Breton, follow either Rte. 19 (coast road to Inverness) and turn right on Cabot Trail at Margaree Forks, or Rte. 105 and turn left on Cabot Trail at Nyanza.

MILFORD HOUSE
South Milford, Nova Scotia (1974)

The time was 7:30 a.m. I awakened to the sound of the lake water lapping against the shore, and looked out of the window of my cabin to see an errant canoeist drifting by in the middle of the lake. I bounded out of bed, in and out of the shower, and dressed rapidly so as not to miss a single moment of my time at this "almost-wilderness" resort-inn in southern Nova Scotia.

My accommodations, like all the others, were in a tidy, rustic cabin where there were two bedrooms and a large combination sitting and dining room with windows overlooking still another view of the lake. There are over two dozen of these cottages situated well apart along the wooded shores of two lakes, within walking distance of the main lodge. Each cottage has its own lakeside dock, two to five bedrooms, a living room with a fireplace, electricity, and a bathroom with a tub or a shower. Some of them are insulated and contain housekeeping facilities ideal for a cross-country skiing holiday or just a secluded winter vacation. There were fresh flowers in my cabin and although the furnishings were plain, everything was absolutely spic and span. All the cottages are provided with maid service, ice, wood, and kindling, delivered daily.

I walked down to the end of the lane and up the woods road toward the main lodge for breakfast, happening to meet another guest bound in the same direction. "Oh, I think it's a wonderful place here," she said. "We left the windows open and just loved listening to the loons. My husband and I are going to stay and take a canoe trip."

We continued on up to the main lodge with its comfortable living room, large dining room, library and games room. Milford House guests take their breakfasts and dinners at the main lodge, where there are vegetables from the garden, roasts, fresh fish, native blueberries, raspberries, and ample home-baked breads and pastries. Breakfast consisted of bacon, eggs, pancakes, homemade muffins, and coffee—and, especially, lots of conversation with other guests.

For a number of years, even before my first visit in 1973, the Milford House has been expertly managed by Margaret and Bud Miller. It was their daughter Wendy who gave me my first tour, and about whom I have written continuously over the years. For the benefit of Wendy's many friends, she has joined the Canadian Armed Forces and has finished her officers' training course at the Air Force in British Columbia. I do miss seeing that twelve-year-old young lady who showed me around not so very many years ago.

The Millers' other daughter Linda visits in August, too, with her three children, who are becoming well known at the inn. Linda designed and hooked a wall hanging of the Milford Inn with symbolic figures

around the outside of the oval picture. It has truly been a conversation piece. Margaret told me that she was planning to have some Christmas cards made of it.

What has made the Milford House attractive to many repeating guests is the fact that the area is virtually unspoiled; however, it is easily traversable by canoe.

When I left, the remaining guests stood on the porch waving. And when I passed the big tree at the corner, true to the Milford House tradition, I didn't look back. A lovely, old-fashioned custom.

MILFORD HOUSE, South Milford, R.R. 4, Annapolis Royal, N.S., Canada BOS 1AO; 902-532-2617. A rustic resort-inn with 27 cabins on 600 acres of woodlands and lakes, 90 mi. from Yarmouth, N.S., near Kejimkujik National Park. Modified American plan. Breakfast and dinner served daily with picnic lunches available. Open from June 15 to Sept. 15; fall and winter by special reservation. Tennis, fishing, croquet, canoeing, birdwatching, and swimming on grounds. Deep-sea fishing and golf nearby. Warren and Margaret Miller, Innkeepers.

Directions: From Yarmouth follow Rte. 1 to traffic lights in Annapolis Royal. Turn right and continue on Rte. 8, 15 mi. to inn. The Blue Nose Ferry from Bar Harbor to Yarmouth N.S., arrives in time for guests to make dinner at the Milford House.

"European plan" means that rates for rooms and meals are separate. "American plan" means that meals are included in the cost of the room. "Modified American plan" means that breakfast and dinner are included in the cost of the room. The rates at some inns include a continental breakfast with the lodging.

THE BRIARS
Jackson's Point, Ontario (1981)

When prospective guests contact the Briars for information, in addition to some very informative literature, they also have the benefit of an unusually large full-color map of the Briars and Lake Simcoe, prepared by innkeeper John Sibbald.

I'll go into details about this map in just a moment, but first let me tell you about the Briars, a lush 200-acre estate on the south shore of Lake Simcoe, about forty-five miles north of Toronto. Guests are accommodated in cottages clustered by the lake or in handsome guest rooms in the Manor and its new wings. The inn is set in expanses of deep green lawns surrounded by sculpted hedges and giant pines. A peaceful river meanders through the golf course, and little streams wander under wooden bridges in the scenic woods and fields. I would term the Briars a distinctive Canadian resort that blends its rich past with modern facilities to offer an attractive holiday for guests with family or friends.

In the more than twenty years that I've been traveling in North America, I've come to the conclusion that while Canadians and Americans have lived side by side for many years and both speak the same language, there are still some subtle differences. For one thing, Canadians are basically more conservative than Americans. In this respect they are more like the English. I found that they prefer some of the more quiet things of life, such as good walking, quiet fireside reading, and a little less flamboyant approach to life in general.

And now to the map. In one corner it details a most interesting history since 1819, and traces ownership through more than 170 years to the present Sibbald family.

Actually, the Briars takes in so much territory and so many activities that it really requires this map to give a good overview. It shows the relationship of the Briars to the Red Barn and Peacock House, the

gardens, the tennis courts, the wilderness, and of course the 18-hole golf course, the lake, and the village of Jackson's Point.

It shows the location of all of the many lakeside cottages and the golf clubhouse, as well as Saint George's Church, which I visited for the first time with John Sibbald a number of years ago, and the route of a great circle tour around Lake Simcoe with many points of interest.

With this map in hand it's easy for the guest to locate the many recreational possibilities at the Briars. In winter the property becomes a snowy paradise for walking and cross-country skiing, skating, tobogganing, and snowshoeing. When the temperature falls there is a beautiful indoor pool, sauna, and whirlpool.

In summer, there are two outdoor pools, all of the lake's recreational advantages, the golf course, lighted tennis courts, lawn sports, and wooded walking trails. There's fishing every day of the year on Lake Simcoe.

Early on, one of the things that intrigued me greatly about the Briars was the fact that the Canadian novelist Mazo de la Roche lived in this area, which undoubtedly supplied her with the atmosphere later portrayed in her famous *Whiteoaks of Jalna* books. She was a guest in one of the cottages at the Briars during the last five summers of her life.

I pored over this map for at least an hour, discovering things that I had never known before about the Briars and Lake Simcoe.

On the wall in the reception area there is a quote from Stephen Leacock, who had a longtime association with the Briars. "There is a wild grandeur in those highlands of Scotland, and the majestic solitude where the midnight sun flashes upon the ice peaks of Alaska. But to my thinking, none of these will stand comparison to the smiling beauty of the waters, shores, and bays of Lake Simcoe and its sister lake, Couchiching."

THE BRIARS, Jackson's Point, Ontario, LOE 1LO Canada; 416-722-3271. A resort-inn on the shores of Lake Simcoe, approx. 45 mi. north of Toronto. Open every day. Breakfast, lunch, and dinner served to non-residents. Summer activities include 18-hole golf course, two outdoor swimming pools, indoor swimming pool, whirlpool, sauna, lakeshore swimming, 5 all-weather tennis courts, and many lawn sports. Winter sports include xc skiing, skating, tobogganing, snowmobiling, ice-fishing, and curling. There is a children's program during the summer and Christmas holidays. Excellent for families in all seasons. John and Barbara Sibbald, Innkeepers.

Directions: Jackson's Point is located near Sutton, Ontario. From Hwy.401, via Hwy. 404/Woodbine. Continue to Sutton and then Jackson's Point, ½ mi. east on Hedge Rd.

THE OBAN INN
Niagara-on-the-Lake, Ontario (1977)

"January, February, and March are wonderful times to be here in Niagara-on-the-Lake."

We were passing through the reception area, and innkeeper Gary Burroughs deftly drew an Oban Inn brochure from the rack and pointed out that there were two photographs of the inn, one in summer, showing the flowers and lawns, and the other in winter, with ample snow and a beautifully decorated Christmas tree.

"The village and shops are still here, but this is before our famous Shaw Festival brings crowds, and summer folks come in, and the feeling here at the inn is slower and more relaxed and such great fun. As you know, we do not salt our roads; instead they are rolled after each snowstorm, so once again there's a lovely sort of country-village feeling

during the wintertime. Also I want to point out that the really exceptional Niagara Historical Society and Museum is open and it provides both Canadians and Americans with an extensive and interesting background of the area. We have a wonderful collection of beautiful old homes, along with English-style shops, that make our village one of the most pleasant places to walk on a brisk winter's day."

Well, it was far from winter during my last visit, and Gary and I were touring the golf course that almost surrounds the inn on two sides. When we got to a point where there is a little lighthouse, he pointed out that we could see the lights of Toronto in the distance, across the corner of the lake, and on the other side, almost close enough to throw a dollar across the river, is Fort Niagara on the American side. "It was originally a French fort and it was right here that there were some skirmishes between the Canadians and the Americans during the War of 1812. That's the mouth of the Niagara River out there," he pointed out.

I can well understand why I get letters from guests who enjoyed their stay, not only in Niagara-on-the-Lake, but also at the Oban itself. There is a wonderful, distinctively Canadian feeling to this inn, and while literally thousands of Americans visit the town and the inn each year, that wonderful Canadian feeling continues undisturbed.

For example, in the inn there is a pub with a magnificent oil painting of George Bernard Shaw, along with photographs of stars of theater and cinema who have appeared at the Shaw Festival during past years. The luncheon fare is typical of what I've enjoyed at pubs in England many times. Real English porridge is served at breakfast.

The dining room overlooking the lake is considerably enhanced by the care and attention given to the flowers by Gary's mother, and here is still another Canadian quality reflected in the inn—the love of flowers.

The dinner menu also reveals the Oban's mix of the old world and the new. For example, among the appetizers is a homemade paté, a tradition in England and on the Continent. The main menu items have the ring of the English countryside: roast prime ribs of beef with Yorkshire pudding and calves' sweetbreads with bacon served on toast. The patrons of the inn include businessmen from the town, as well as a few Canadian-American visitors. In the evening, there are informal, jolly sing-alongs around the piano in the corner, as well as quiet entertainment.

Our swing around the golf course was coming to an end, but we were being treated to a really sensational sunset. Here, in mid-July, nightfall takes its time about coming, and even well after nine o'clock there were sailboats returning from the lake or the river. Gary even found a golf ball. It was obvious that this generous and sensitive man really loves the town and loves the inn, and it was such a pleasure to be with him. "I think it's dinnertime now and I know Sarah will be waiting. Are you ready?"

You bet I was.

THE OBAN INN, 160 Front St., Box 94, Niagara-on-the-Lake, Ontario, Canada LOS IJO; 416-468-2165. A 23-guestroom village inn on a quiet street in one of Canada's historic villages, approx. 12 mi. from Niagara Falls, N.Y., on the shores of Lake Ontario. All plans available. Breakfast, lunch, dinner served daily to travelers. Open every day of the year. Near Ft. George and Ft. Niagara, and the Shaw Festival. Golf, xc skiing, sailing, fishing, tennis nearby. Owner-controlled pets welcome. Gary Burroughs, Innkeeper.

Directions: Exit Hwy. 55 at St. Catharines from the Queen Elizabeth Hwy. Follow signs to Niagara-on-the-Lake.

THE OPINICON
Chaffey's Locks, Elgin, Ontario (1981)

Ever since I was a boy I've been hearing about those wonderful, almost inaccessible, fishing and hunting resorts in Canada that are always situated on sylvan lakes and surrounded by primeval forests. Friends of my father would disappear a couple of times each year and return with tales of fish that practically leapt into the boat and game in Paul Bunyan dimensions. There were stories about highly voluble guides and idyllic days spent in the forest and on the water, followed by trenchermen's meals, very often including the day's catch.

In the summer of 1980 I found such a Canadian retreat with all of the virtues listed above, plus many more that make it a wonderful place for a rusticated vacation.

The Opinicon resort-inn is situated on a lovely wooded hill overlooking Opinicon Lake, and surrounded by seventeen acres of well-groomed lawns, giant oaks, a large flower garden, and quiet spots in the woods or on the lake from which to observe nature. Accommodations are in the main building, an old-fashioned, two-storied, yellow clapboard residence with completely modernized rooms, many opening onto a porch or balcony. In the woods, set back from the lakeshore, are a series of cottages accommodating from two to eight persons each.

The cheerful dining room offers three sumptuous meals a day under the American plan, and I understand they've had the same chef for many years. Guests' freshly caught fish can be cooked and served at any meal, and the dining room is conducted like many old resort inns that have now disappeared. I sat at the same table and had the same waitress for all my meals. She and the other waitresses were friendly young ladies from the area.

Innkeeper Al Cross, whose Bay State accent I recognized immediately, is from Newton, Massachusetts. His wife Janice's family has been running this resort-inn for many generations. Al is a somewhat rumpled type of man who is always on the go, greeting guests, taking care of their needs, and keeping the staff members on their toes.

With over 200 lakes in the area, the Opinicon is known for its great fishing. It appeared to me that about fifty percent of the guests in residence during my visit were interested in this sport, for which boats and experienced local guides can be arranged. The inn provides basket lunches, if desired.

On the other hand, many people enjoy the great variety of recreational activities available, including boating, lake and pool swimming, tennis, croquet, shuffleboard, horseshoes, ping-pong, volleyball, and for the occasional inclement days, a good lending library. There's also an honest-to-gosh country store.

One of the most interesting things to do is to take the short walk to Chaffey's Locks, which are a part of the Rideau Canal System. This system was opened in 1832 to connect Kingston with Ottawa, thus avoiding the rapids of the St. Lawrence. It is still a navigable waterway, and the locks, models of stone engineering construction, are operated by hand by two gatekeepers.

The Opinicon is a great place to take the entire family for a real Canadian woods holiday. Rates have been structured in such a way that it is within the financial means of the average North American family, especially when you think of hungry kids eating three meals a day.

THE OPINICON, Chaffey's Locks, RR 1, Elgin, Ontario, Canada KOG 1CO; 613-359-5233. An 18-guestroom resort-inn on Opinicon Lake, part of the Rideau Canal System of eastern Ontario; accommodations also available in rustic cottages. Full American and modified American plan. Open early April to late November. Fishing, boating, tennis, heated swimming pool, shuffleboard, bicycles on grounds, golf course nearby. Excellent for children of all ages. No credit cards. Personal checks accepted. Albert and Janice Cross, Innkeepers.

Directions: From south: Interstate 81 to 1000 Island Bridge to Ontario Rte. 401 west. Turn off Exit No. 645 at Rte. 32 (right), go north to Rte. 15, turning right (north). Follow to 2 miles beyond Elgin (bypassed). Turn left on Chaffey's Locks Rd. From east: Rte. 401 west to Exit No. 696 (Brockville), turn north (right) on Rte. 42, follow Rte. 42 to Crosby, turn south (left) on Rte. 15 for 2 miles and turn right on Chaffey's Locks Rd.

SHAW'S HOTEL
Brackley Beach, Prince Edward Island (1975)

I'm certain a great many of our readers enjoyed the Public Television presentation of *Anne of Green Gables,* an adaptation of Lucy Montgomery's splendid novel about a girl growing into young womanhood on Prince Edward Island. If you missed it, be sure to catch the reruns. Anne may never have actually existed, but her spirit is there, as well as an attractive, typical gabled house that she *might* have lived in.

Prince Edward Island is one of the great surprises of North America. For one thing, ocean water temperatures along the wide P.E.I. beaches average sixty-eight to seventy degrees in summer and the sun is excellent for tanning. It has one of Canada's finest national parks, stretching twenty-five miles along the Gulf of St. Lawrence. There are wild seascapes, breathtaking views, and an atmosphere of hospitality, because this has been a resort area for more than a century.

During the summer months there is an excellent theatre at the Confederation Centre of the Arts of Charlottetown, offering a choice of musicals that play to capacity houses almost every night.

Prince Edward Island is very popular in July and August, so reserve well in advance and be sure to obtain ferry information.

I first visited P.E.I. and Shaw's Hotel in 1974 and never thought that I could be this far north and find ocean water so wonderfully warm and enjoyable.

I had taken the ferry from Caribou, Nova Scotia, that morning. There is another ferry from Cape Tormentine, New Brunswick. It is possible to stay at the Marshlands Inn in Sackville and take the ferry over the next morning. I had driven down from the Inverary Inn on Cape Breton in northern Nova Scotia, so the Caribou crossing was more convenient.

I found that Shaw's was part of an original pioneer farm started in 1793; had become a hotel in 1860; and today, still has many of the characteristics of an operating farm.

Some of the accommodations are single and double rooms in the main building, a Victorian house with a brilliant red mansard third story. There are also individual cottages, accommodating from two to eight people. This is most convenient for families who return every summer. The cottages are spaced far enough apart to insure privacy. Five of them have their own fireplaces.

Shaw's Hotel is surrounded by many trees and broad meadows. The view from the dining room might include a sailboat bobbing along on the bay. There is a good mix of both Canadian and American guests, and Robbie Shaw says that there are always a few people from California, Washington, New York, and Alberta.

One of the most attractive features about Shaw's Hotel is the fact that it is only a short distance through the woods to the beach. All of this summertime outdoor activity, including swimming, sailing on the bay, deep sea tuna fishing, golf, tennis, bicycling, walking, and horseback riding, contribute to very big appetites, so the main dishes include fresh salmon, lobster, mackerel, cod, and halibut. Dinners are fun because everyone is eager for a hearty meal, and enthusiasm is high after a day of recreation.

Children are particularly happy in this atmosphere. Robbie Shaw said he has had as many as twenty to thirty children at one time at the height of the season. "There is always plenty of elbow room," he said. "We don't have any trouble keeping the parents of the children amused either. Besides the beach, there are riding horses nearby, and it is fun to ride along the beach and on the bridle paths. I have been doing it all my life. My father, who passed away in 1985, always loved the children."

SHAW'S HOTEL, Brackley Beach, Prince Edward Island, Canada COA 2HO; 902-672-2022. A 24-guestroom and 10 guest cottages (some shared baths) country hotel within walking distance of Brackley Beach, 15 mi. from Charlottetown. American plan. Breakfast and dinner served to travelers daily. Open from June to Sept. Tennis, golf, bicycles, riding, sailing, beach and summer theater nearby. Pets allowed in cottages only. **Robbie Shaw, Innkeeper.**

Directions: Prince Edward Island is reached by ferry from either Cape Tormentine, New Brunswick (near Moncton), or Caribou, Nova Scotia. In both cases, after arriving on P.E.I., follow Rte.1 to Charlottetown, then Rte. 15 to Brackley Beach. P.E.I. is also reached by Eastern Provincial Airway, VIA Rail Canada, and Air Canada.

HANDFIELD INN (Auberge Handfield)
St. Marc-sur-le-Richelieu, Quebec (1983)

The Richelieu River, part of the waterway that carries boats to the Saint Lawrence and down to the tip of Florida, was blue and sparkling in the summer sun. I was relaxing on the grassy banks directly in front of the newest group of traditional Quebec houses, which had been redecorated and furnished by Conrad and Huguette Handfield and named Maison LaFlamme. The marina in front of Auberge Handfield ("auberge" is really the French word for inn) had several visiting boats, and there were people sitting around the swimming pool enjoying animated conversations in both French and English.

In thinking about the new accommodations, I realized that the inn would become, with the tennis courts to be added very shortly, a resort-inn, since there were a great many things to do on the grounds or nearby.

Guest rooms in the main inn are furnished in the old Quebec style but with touches of modern comfort, including tile bathrooms and controlled heating. Many of them have rough wooden walls and casement windows overlooking broad fields. Huguette told me that most of these guest rooms are decorated either with antiques or furniture made by local craftsmen. Maison LaFlamme's guest rooms have a water view.

A summer visit here is really not complete without attendance at the summer theater presentation in a very cleverly converted ferry boat. The plays are all French comedies and have been commissioned by Huguette especially for performances at Auberge Handfield.

However, let's get back to the "country inn" aspects of Auberge Handfield. Certainly one of them would be the cuisine. As Conrad said, "There are two menus—one is traditional French cuisine and the other is nouvelle cuisine. So you see our guests can really have a choice for whatever may be their preference." I won't take the time here to list the main dishes except to say that I like French cuisine in any form, particularly the wonderful pastries on display for dessert.

The main dining room is very cozy and warm, and tables are on the sunny, converted, glassed-in porch. The natural wood contributes to a feeling of comfort and warmth. An interesting point is that the dining room is open all afternoon, so that guests can always get something to eat. It's open from breakfast until ten o'clock each night.

Auberge Handfield is essentially French and it is not necessary to travel very far from any place in the United States or Canada to enjoy as French an experience as you would have in any village in France. The language is French, the villagers greet you in French, and the stores are French. They will help you out if you are in any difficulty. Essentially, it's a wonderful French experience.

I should also mention that "sugaring-off" parties are held from March until the end of April and are very popular with inn guests. They are held in a rustic sugar shack in a maple grove just a few miles from the inn. I have enjoyed them myself very much.

The Handfield Inn is a great many things: it is a venerable mansion that has seen a century and a half of history; an enjoyable French restaurant; a four-season resort; and perhaps best of all, it is an opportunity to visit a French–Canadian village that has remained relatively free from the invasion of developers. Its ancient stone houses and nearby shops remain untouched, and its farms still raise good vegetables and poultry.

HANDFIELD INN (Auberge Handfield), St. Marc-sur-le-Richelieu, Quebec, JOL 2EO, Canada; 514-584-2226. A 45-guestroom (some shared baths) French–Canadian country inn about 25 mi. from Montreal. Different plans available. Please consult with inn in advance. Open year-round. Breakfast, lunch, and dinner served daily to travelers. Ladies are expected to wear a skirt or dress and gentlemen a coat at dinner. All summer and winter active sports easily available. Many handcrafts, antique, and historical tours in the area. No pets. M. and Mme. Conrad Handfield, Innkeepers.

Directions: From Champlain, Victoria, or the Jacques Cartier bridges, take Hwy. 3 to Sorel, turn right at Hwy. 20. From the east end of Montreal, go through the Hyppolite LaFontaine Tunnel. Rte. 20 passes through St. Julie, St. Bruno, and Beloeil. Leave Hwy. 20 at Exit 112, turning left on Rte. 223 north. Handfield is 7 mi. distant.

HOVEY MANOR
North Hatley, Quebec (1983)

The entire six pages of an article on Hovey Manor which appeared in the June issue of *Sel & Poivre*, Quebec's leading food magazine, were in French, and even if my French is a bit sketchy I could see that there were many, many compliments for some of the wonderful dishes prepared by Belgian chef Marc de Canck.

A letter from Steve and Kathy Stafford at Hovey Manor indicated that they were both very pleased that the magazine was in agreement with them regarding Marc's talent. "Marc loves Hovey Manor and he will be here for many years to come. By the way, we have received new dinnerware from Europe with our own logo."

Hovey Manor is a traditional inn with all the resort facilities for a complete vacation experience. In the summer there are canoes, paddle boats, fishing, and tennis on the grounds.

Windsurfing has proved to be very popular with the guests, and lessons are available for everyone from kids to grandmothers. It's a fine, exhilarating exercise and offers a good escape without taking too much time. Sailboats and water skiing are also available at reasonable rates. By the way, there are ten golf courses within a half-hour's ride, and there is summer stock at the Piggery Theatre and concerts at the Mount Orford Arts Center nearby.

There seems to be something special going on at all times during the summer—beach barbecues, a lake cruise to Ripplecove Inn at Ayer's Cliff where you can have lunch if you like, chamber music concerts, poetry readings with wine and cheese, and various other events.

Festival Lac Massawippi runs from mid-July to mid-August, and the Abenaki Room at Hovey Manor will be the site of one of Festival Lac Massawippi's art exhibits, featuring the works of Eastern Township artists.

Nine new bedrooms and an expansion of the dining room have been completed. As Steve describes them, "the bedrooms are quite deluxe, many with fireplaces, private balconies, four-poster beds, and whirlpool baths, which are particularly attractive to cross-country and alpine skiers." Steve hastened to add that Hovey's atmosphere will not change.

The new guest rooms are furnished with a combination of antiques, antique reproductions, and works of local cabinetmakers, as well as artwork by Eastern Township artists.

I mentioned skiing, and actually, Hovey has 150 kilometers of groomed cross-country ski trails right from their door, and also a ski package offering inn-to-inn skiing, where the inn transfers the cars and the baggage. Ski instruction is also available. Downhill skiers enjoy an interchangeable ticket, valid at four big mountains in the area, all with extensive snowmaking equipment. There's a great apres-ski atmosphere in Hovey's historic Tap Room, where, on selected evenings, the chefs broil steaks and fresh salmon over the live charcoal hearth.

The two-language menu is quite European, and chef Marc de Canck emphasizes contemporary cuisine featuring beautiful presentation and lighter sauces. Desserts are sinfully good— or bad— depending on your viewpoint.

HOVEY MANOR, North Hatley, Quebec, Canada JOB 2CO; 819-842-2421. A 36-guestroom resort inn (12 with woodburning fireplaces) on Lake Massawippi, ½ hr. from U.S./Canada border. Modified American and European plans. Breakfast, lunch, dinner served every day. Open all year. Lighted tennis court, two beaches, sailing, canoeing, paddleboats, water skiing, windsurfing, fishing, xc skiing on grounds. Downhill skiing, horseback riding, racquet sports, and golf (10 courses) nearby; also many scenic and cultural attractions nearby. Sorry, no pets. Stephen and Kathryn Stafford, Innkeepers.

Directions: Take Vermont I-91 to Vermont/Quebec border and follow Rte. 55 to No. Hatley Exit 29. Follow Rte. 108E for 5 mi. to T junction at Lake Massawippi in North Hatley. Turn right for ¾ mi. to Hovey Manor sign and private drive on left.

L'AUBERGE DU ROY
Deschambault, Quebec (1987)

Let's assume that you are planning a trip to Quebec—a delightful experience. In addition to stopping outside of Montreal at Auberge Handfield, described in the previous pages, let me suggest another French country experience near Quebec City.

If I thought Auberge Handfield was a French adventure, then L'Auberge du Roy turned out to be even more so. It is owned and kept by two very vivacious and obliging French–Canadians, Isabelle and Jean-Claude Lisita. Jean-Claude is the chef and is most voluble in one language only: French. Isabelle is the hostess and fortunately is conversant in English.

Upon my arrival, Isabelle showed me to my room on the second floor and at the same time gave me a tour of all the other guest rooms as well. Everything—the floors, the windowsills, the beds, the closets, just every possible surface—was immaculately clean.

L'Auberge du Roy is totally French–Canadian. Among the decorations in the dining room, for example, are hanging plants, painted plates decorating the wall, and a bottle of wine on the table which is both a suggestion and a decoration. There were many, many little figurines on tables and mantelpieces. The rugs, paintings, and prints were unmistakably French.

Also, there was an aroma from the kitchen that spelled nothing else but French cuisine. I had an opportunity to talk with Isabelle and Jean-Claude about this, and learned that he had been a French chef for many years in nearby Quebec City. It was their dream to own an auberge in the countryside.

After discussing the menu, I decided on a special duckling dish, cooked with black olives. I must admit that I was tempted by the salmon with lemon and also the medallions of beef. I'm very fond of sauces, and I guess I had come to the right place. The dessert menu featured a chocolate mousse made with brandy, as well as a sugar tart named after Isabelle—I think I can understand why.

The Lisitas acquired this property a few years ago at a time when it was very run-down, and they have put much into making it an engaging country inn.

Within a few steps of the inn is a stream with a wonderfully melodious waterfall, which can be heard from the guest rooms and the front porch. The lawn extends to the grassy bank, where the brook ripples across the dam and drops down into a little pool below, continuing a short distance to the Saint Lawrence River. It is delightfully quiet and cool.

I had a very good time and a happy stay at L'Auberge du Roy. I think Isabelle and Jean-Claude viewed my halting French with good humor,

and I made the acquaintance of a bilingual neighbor, Maurice Angers, who explained some of the things that I needed for this book in greater detail.

In closing, may I say that I haven't yet found an inn to my taste that also serves dinner in Quebec City, but L'Auberge du Roy is close enough so that the traveler will have all the advantages of visiting that historic city, and at the same time, an opportunity to return to the countryside for peace and quiet.

We are happy to welcome L'Auberge du Roy to *Country Inns and Back Roads* for the first time.

L'AUBERGE DU ROY, 106 Rue St.-Laurent, Deschambault, Quebec GOA 1SO; 418-286-6958. A 6-guestroom (private and shared baths) French-Canadian countryside inn, just a few miles from Quebec City. Breakfast, lunch, and dinner served every day. From Oct. 1 to May 1 the inn is closed on Mon.; the remainder of the year the inn is open 7 days a week. Tennis court and swimming pool on grounds. Many historic and scenic attractions nearby. No amusements for children under 12. Isabelle and Jean-Claude Lisita, Innkeepers.

Directions: From the north, take Hwy. 40 up the north side of the St. Lawrence River to Quebec City. Exit at Deschambault. From the south, use Exit 156 (Villeroy), off Rte. 20. Then follow Rte. 265 to Deschaillons, and Rte. 132 to the Deschambault-Lotbinière ferry.

Upper South

Eastern Time Zone

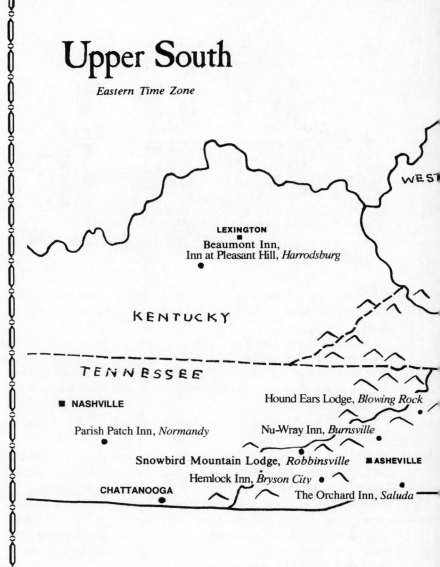

WEST

LEXINGTON
Beaumont Inn,
Inn at Pleasant Hill, *Harrodsburg*

KENTUCKY

TENNESSEE

NASHVILLE

Hound Ears Lodge, *Blowing Rock*

Parish Patch Inn, *Normandy*

Nu-Wray Inn, *Burnsville*

Snowbird Mountain Lodge, *Robbinsville*   ASHEVILLE

Hemlock Inn, *Bryson City*

CHATTANOOGA

The Orchard Inn, *Saluda*

THE DAVID FINNEY INN
New Castle, Delaware (1986)

In April 1985, I was literally the first guest ever to sign the David Finney Inn guestbook! On my second trip, innkeeper Judy Piser pointed out that fact to me: "You were our very first overnight guest!"

First, a word about the town, whose historical and architectural treasures are a well-kept secret. The earliest settlement began around 1638, shortly after the Swedish government established a new-world foothold in nearby Wilmington. The early colonists were not only Swedish but also Finnish and Dutch adventurers in search of readily available farmland. Ships' ballast and building bricks from Holland have been found in excavations. Such colorful personalities as Peter Stuyvesant also figured prominently in the early history. He purchased about thirty miles of land along the west bank of the Delaware River and established Fort Casimir, which also became the name of the town. When the English arrived, they renamed it New Castle.

Aside from this fascinating continuing history, the real charm of New Castle lies in the fact that in the historic part of the town the architecture and building design remains almost totally pre-1800. As trite as it may sound, a walk across the village green is indeed an experience akin to stepping back in time. This green is dominated by the Immanuel Church and its grounds, where there are graves of men who in earlier days helped to build the United States of America. There are many other beautifully harmonizing residences and buildings of varying architectural styles that blend in extremely well.

The inn property is part of a 1650s Dutch land grant. The building dates back to 1685, with major additions in every century since. It has been a large, luxurious home, hosting some of America's most important people. At least three signers of the Declaration of Independence knew it well.

Furnished with antiques, it is an exceptionally fine restoration/renovation, featuring four two-room suites and thirteen double rooms, all with private baths. Breakfast, lunch, and dinner are served in the restaurant, and there is courtyard dining in season. Entertainment is offered in the tavern, where the nautical theme is heightened with museum-quality model ships.

The evening menu, which changes daily, includes charcoal-grilled swordfish steak with teriyaki butter, and grilled breast of duck with water chestnuts, snow peas, and ginger sauce. It's a little hard to pin the cuisine down because it reflects not only the area, but a Continental theme as well. A continental breakfast is complimentary and tea is served to houseguests in the afternoon.

Five museums in the town display life as it was lived in the Dutch

and English Colonial periods with guides to explain every detail. It is a delightful experience to walk along the Strand and other streets lined with antique homes, or to visit the marketplace and the village green.

Among the seasonal events and festivals in historic New Castle are "A Day in Old New Castle" on the third Saturday in May, which includes a tour of private homes, gardens, and public buildings; "May Market," the first weekend in May; "Separation Day," the first Saturday in June, celebrating the separation of Delaware from England. There are also numerous other art and antique shows and a Christmas candlelight tour.

There is history aplenty in New Castle, and fortunately for the enthusiastic country-inn-goer, the town and area are splendidly served by the David Finney Inn. What a pleasure for me to be the first guest!

THE DAVID FINNEY INN, P.O. Box 207, 216 Delaware St., New Castle, DE 19720; 302-322-6367. A 21-guestroom (private baths) meticulously restored 18th-century inn in a historic riverfront village, 35 mi. south of Phila. Continental breakfast included in tariff. Breakfast, lunch, and dinner served every day of the year. Many historic, recreational, and cultural attractions in New Castle or nearby. Convenient off-street parking available. No entertainment facilities for children under 10. No pets. Tom and Louise Hagy, Proprietors; Judy Piser, Innkeeper.

Directions: Coming south on the New Jersey Tpke., take the first exit after crossing the Delaware River Bridge and turn south on Rte. 9, which goes directly into New Castle. The inn is located in the historic section of Old New Castle.

BEAUMONT INN
Harrodsburg, Kentucky (1979)

"Oh, I wish you could have known Miss Pauline, she was here for so many years, and everybody loved her."

Mary Elizabeth Dedman and I had taken a few moments to talk about the history of the Beaumont Inn, and I found that not only was she a gold mine of wonderful, interesting anecdotes, but she had actually written a history of the inn and some of its furnishings, which is available to the guests.

The Beaumont, with its stately Grecian columns set against a dark red brick background, was built as a school for young ladies in 1845 and later became known as Daughter's College. Later on it was Beaumont College. In 1916, it was purchased by Mr. and Mrs. Glave Goddard and converted into the Beaumont Inn. The ownership and management passed from Mrs. Goddard to her daughter, Mrs. Dedman, and then to Mrs. Dedman's two sons. Today, Bud Dedman is the owner-manager, and his son, Chuck, following tradition, becomes the fourth generation to be trained here in the innkeeper's art. Moreover, Chuck has two children, one of whom is already showing great promise as an innkeeper of the future!

Each time I visit I find something I have not seen on my many previous visits. This time I discovered that Mary Elizabeth has a collection of saltcellars—handsome small dishes that were used everywhere before the saltshaker came into being. She must have at least one hundred or more in a glass case, and handsome they are indeed—many of glowing cut glass in various shapes and shades. It's just an example of the kind of memorabilia that is found throughout all of the public rooms, hallways, and guest rooms of the inn.

The decorations and furniture in all the parlors and guest rooms reflect American history. The hallways on the main floor have several cabinets with beautiful old china and silverware. The sitting rooms have elegant fireplaces and wallpaper decorated with roses.

The inn also has a very extensive gift shop, and some of the items that have the Beaumont Inn label are cornmeal batter-mix, brown sugar syrup, green tomato relish, sweet pickle relish, chicken-cheese casserole, creamed chicken, frozen fruit salad, soda biscuits with chopped country ham, and many different sauces. These are also served in the Beaumont Inn dining room, and besides that there is the famous Beaumont Inn cookbook with special recipes (also compiled by Mary Elizabeth), which was done many years ago and has been enlarged and revised, and is now in its second printing.

It's well worth noting that the traditions at the Beaumont also include a high interest in Kentucky horses, and it's just a short distance

to Keeneland, the Red Mile Harness Racing Track, and, of course, Churchill Downs, home of the Kentucky Derby.

A guest at the Beaumont is visiting the Dedman family, and there's always somebody named Dedman within earshot or at least just around the corner, and this includes Chuck and Helen's young son, Dixon, who is very much in evidence riding the tractors or in the kitchen or helping with the redecorating. In Kentuckey, where families and relatives play such an important role in everyone's life, I'm sure it must be a source of great pride to Bud Dedman to see his grandson, Dixon, already shaking hands and greeting people like a good innkeeper should.

BEAUMONT INN, Harrodsburg, KY 40330; 606-734-3381. A 29-guest-room country inn in the heart of Kentucky's historic bluegrass country. European plan. Lunch and dinner served to travelers; all three meals to houseguests. Lunch not available Mon. Open every day from mid-March to mid-Dec. Tennis, swimming pool, shuffleboard on grounds. Golf courses and a wide range of recreational and historic attractions nearby. No pets. The Dedman Family, Innkeepers.

Directions: From Louisville: Exit 48 from east I-64. Go south on Ky. 151, to U.S. 127 south to Harrodsburg. From Lexington: U.S. 60 west, then west on Bluegrass Parkway to U.S. 127. From Nashville: Exit I-65 to Bluegrass Parkway near Elizabethtown, Ky., then east to U.S. 127.

THE INN AT PLEASANT HILL
Shakertown, Kentucky (1971)

Betty Morris and I were driving down the twisty road that leads to the Shaker Landing on the Kentucky River, just a few moments from the Inn at Pleasant Hill. Soon, a handsome paddlewheel river boat, the "Dixie Belle," came into view, and already there were people waiting to board her for the morning cruise.

This cruise, very popular with the inn guests, follows the seventy-five mile course of the river, bordered by impressive 315-foot limestone cliffs. Betty, who is manager of the Inn at Pleasant Hill, told me that a running history of the Kentucky River, including its importance to the economy of 100 years ago and the contributions made by the Shakers, is part of this cruise.

By an interesting coincidence, just as she pointed out the great railroad trestle that traverses the river, a freight train went by, right on cue.

The Inn at Pleasant Hill is located in a restored Shaker community in one of the most beautiful sections of central Kentucky. The Shakers were members of a religious sect, the United Society of Believers in Christ's Second Appearing. They were actually an offshoot of the Quakers. The founder was Mother Ann Lee, who brought her ideas to America late in the 18th century.

The Shakers held some advanced social ideas. They were hospitable to visitors and took in orphans and unwanted children. Their fundamental beliefs were in hard work and austere discipline that sought perfection. This sense of perfection was extended into the design of their furniture, and many people learn about Shakers for the first time as a result of being attracted by the beauty and simplicity of the functional Shaker designs.

The Shakers lived in communal dedication to their religious beliefs of celibacy, renunciation of worldliness, common ownership of property, and public confession of sins, which culminated in the frenetic dances that gave them the name of Shakers.

There were five "families" at Pleasant Hill, established in 1805. By 1820 it was a prosperous colony of five hundred persons. "Family" had a particular meaning, since the Shakers did not believe in marriage. Men and women, they maintained, could live more happily as brothers and sisters helping one another, but living personally apart.

The Civil War, plus 19th-century industrialism and worldliness, seeped into Pleasant Hill, and the celibacy rules prevented the natural increase in their numbers. In 1910 they were dissolved.

The reception area of the inn is located in the Trustees' House, one of twenty-five or more restored buildings clustered along the single country road. To construct buildings of enduring strength, some with walls three or four feet thick, the Shakers quarried limestone from the

river bluffs and hauled granite slabs a mile uphill from the river. Most of the buildings are a deep red brick or limestone.

The restaurant is on the first floor of the Trustees' House, and the guest rooms on the second and third floors are reached by two marvelous twin-spiraled staircases of matchless craftsmanship. There are many additional bedrooms on the second floor of restored Shaker buildings.

The experience of sleeping in a Shaker room is most refreshing. In my room were two single beds, each with its own trundle bed underneath. The Shaker rockers were classic, and the extra chairs were hung by pegs on the walls.

For the third time in fifteen years, the three-day international meeting of the Independent Innkeepers Association was held at Pleasant Hill last fall. It was a resounding success.

THE INN AT PLEASANT HILL, Shakertown, KY. P.O. address: Rte. 4, Harrodsburg, KY 40330; 606-734-5411. A 63-guestroom country inn in a restored Shaker village on Rte. 68, 7 mi. northeast of Harrodsburg, 25 mi. southwest of Lexington. European plan. Breakfast, lunch, dinner served daily to travelers. No tipping. Open year-round. Suggest contacting inn about winter schedule. Closed Christmas Eve and Christmas Day. Ann Voris, Innkeeper.

Directions: From Lexington take Rte. 68 south toward Harrodsburg. From Louisville, take I-64 to Lawrenceburg and Graeffenburg exit (not numbered). Follow Rte. 127 south to Harrodsburg and Rte. 68 northeast to Shakertown.

THE INN AT BUCKEYSTOWN
Buckeystown, Maryland (1987)

This elegant Victorian inn immediately appealed to me because one of its themes is "clowns." I've always been very attached to clowns and have, in fact, played two of Shakespeare's most famous clowns on stage, Feste in *Twelfth Night* and Touchstone in *As You Like It*.

There are enough clowns and pictures of clowns and clown dolls and clown posters to satisfy the most avid of clown enthusiasts. Some are reproductions of famous paintings, including the famous Rouault clown, and there are clowns laughing, crying, playing instruments, clown dolls on each of the beds, books on clowns, and a wonderful collection of china clown dolls in a case on the second floor, where there is also a little shop with clown dolls for sale, along with candies, jams, and other craft items, some of which are directly connected with the Inn at Buckeystown. Because innkeepers Dan Pelz and Marty Martinez are true collectors, there are many other collectibles, having to do with American Indians, glassware, early California art, postcards, and Victorian posters.

However, I think the main theme at this inn is hospitality, and this is best personified by the evening meal. A different set menu is offered each night of the week. Wednesday, the night I was there, happened to be "Ethnic Night," and since this was the third Wednesday of the month we had Basque chicken. Other dishes in the ethnic category for Wednesdays include Mexican, German, Country French, and Curry. Dinner is served family style around a big table at seven o'clock each night, with no smoking in the dining room. Everyone sits down together, and thanks to Dan and Marty, all of the guests soon become well acquainted. As Dan says, "It is in the tradition of the late 18th and early 19th century in this part of Maryland." He added, "Our guests prefer to dress a little for dinner and men wear coats and ties."

Another extremely hospitable feature is a perfectly wonderful wraparound front porch with rocking chairs and other comfortable furniture. Stepping off the porch, you'll find yourself on broad grassy acres, which are part of the parklike surroundings, with many varieties of trees and bushes.

The guest rooms are all authentically furnished in beautiful Victorian style, with such modern comforts as electric blankets and air conditioners.

Buckeystown is within an hour of Washington, D.C., Baltimore, and Gettysburg, and within a half-hour of New Market (the antiques capital of Maryland), Harper's Ferry, and Leesburg. Dan points out that the area is a paradise for architecture buffs, historians, antiquers, and outdoors people. Nearby Frederick is a beautifully restored historic town with many sites of interest, beautiful shops, and all city conveniences.

I would be remiss if I failed to mention that the other innkeepers besides Dan and Marty are Amos, a big shaggy dog, a Maine coon cat named Joshua, and assistant innkeeper Becki, who is at the heart of the inn.

We welcome the Inn at Buckeystown to the pages of *Country Inns and Back Roads* for the first time in this edition.

THE INN AT BUCKEYSTOWN, Buckeystown, MD 21717; 301-874-5755. An 8-guestroom (shared baths) inn in a historic village. Rates include dinner and breakfast. Open year-round except for the last 2 wks. of Jan. and July. Minimum stay of 2 days required on all holidays and on weekends from Oct. 1 to Jan. 1, and from Apr. 1 to July 1. Conveniently located to enjoy all of the historic and cultural attractions of the region. No facilities for children under 16. No pets. Dan Pelz, Marty Martinez, Innkeepers.

Directions: Buckeystown lies 4 mi. to the south of the Buckeystown exit off I-270 in Frederick, and 5 mi. to the south of the Buckeystown exit off I-70 in Frederick. Inn is located on Maryland Rte. 85.

I do not include lodging rates in the descriptions, for the very nature of an inn means that there are lodgings of various sizes, with and without baths, in and out of season, and with plain and fancy decoration. Travelers should call ahead and inquire about the availability and rates of the many different types of rooms.

MARYLAND INN
Annapolis, Maryland (1970)

This time I was approaching Annapolis from the south and east, coming along U.S. 50 over the thrilling expanse of the Bay Bridge, with its two suspended roadways over the Chesapeake. There were a number of freighters in the shadowy mist making their way up through the bay, and several sailboats were running before the wind.

I turned off at the sign for the Naval Academy and followed Maryland Route 450, continuing on between the Naval Academy and St. John's College. Then, using the steeple of St. Ann's Church as a heaven-pointing guide, I made a right turn and came into Church Circle and the Maryland Inn. The discreet sign at the front door indicated that Charlie Byrd was appearing in the King of France Tavern. Some folk singers were scheduled for later on.

I couldn't help but think that Thomas Hyde, who built the original inn and advertised it as "an elegant brick house in the dry and healthy part of the city . . . one of the finest houses in the State for a House of Entertainment," would be quite pleased with the many different aspects of the Maryland Inn today.

I'm certain that the guest rooms far exceed any of Mr. Hyde's wildest dreams. I have been visiting the Maryland Inn since the late 1960s, and I've seen all of the rooms undergo an impressive restoration of both furnishings and decor.

The modern equivalent of innkeeper Hyde is Paul Pearson, who has recently added four other historic inns to this first love, the Maryland Inn.

All are 18th-century buildings, tastefully restored and furnished. They include one of the most remarkable of all the restoration projects in Annapolis—the 1747 Reynolds Tavern. When asked if Washington slept at any of his inns, Paul declares that there is no truth to any such rumor. Indeed, it seems clear that Washington's greater contributions to his country were made during his waking hours, many of which were spent in and about the family of inns that surround the famous Maryland State Capitol, where Washington resigned his commission in the Continental Army and where the first meeting of patriots leading to the drafting of the United State Constitution took place exactly 200 years ago. To walk among these lovely buildings is to savor the same atmosphere experienced by George Washington and other men and women who were forming the destinies of our country. Reservations for these inns can be made through the Maryland Inn.

Over a cup of tea in the Treaty of Paris dining room, I asked innkeeper Peg Bednarsky, a dear friend of many years, about the menus of the restaurants in the inn. "Well, as you know we're located right on Chesapeake Bay, so we have eight to ten fish offerings every day, including red snapper, grouper, trout, swordfish, mako shark, cohoe salmon, pompano, monkfish, flounder, and rockfish. We musn't forget the famous crab bisque, the popovers, and cornsticks." I agreed with that, as I took another delicious bite of a cornstick.

Mr. Hyde, there's lots of toe-tapping excitement at your Maryland Inn these days.

MARYLAND INN (HISTORIC INNS OF ANNAPOLIS), Church Circle, Annapolis, MD 21401; 301-263-2641. (U.S. reservations: 800-847-8882; within Md.: 800-638-8902.) A 44-guestroom village inn in a history-laden town, 20 mi. from Baltimore and Washington. Near the U.S. Naval Academy and Chesapeake Bay. Breakfast, lunch, and dinner served to travelers daily. Open year-round. Music nightly in the King of France Tavern. Tours can be arranged to historic and scenic points of interest. Paul Pearson, Proprietor; Peg Bednarsky, Innkeeper.

Directions: From Baltimore, take Rte. 2 south to first directional turnoff "Washington/Annapolis." From Washington, take Rte. 50 east to "Annapolis Naval Academy/Rowe Blvd." exit.

The date in parenthesis in the heading represents the first year the inn appeared in the pages of Country Inns and Back Roads.

ROBERT MORRIS INN
Oxford, Maryland

The Robert Morris is on the eastern shore of Maryland beside the Tred Avon River. One of the ways to reach it is via the famous Cape May-Lewes ferry, which I've been riding ever since my first visit. Oxford is, surprisingly enough, still one of the most unspoiled villages in North America. It has several pre-Revolutionary and Federalist houses that are remarkably well preserved. Incidentally, you can get a copy of "This and That About Olde Oxford, Maryland" by Howard B. Gerhardt at the front desk of the inn. It's an extremely well-written informal history of Oxford.

The news from the inn is that the Sandaway Lodge has been completely done over in a country-romantic theme with handmade pine, pencil-post king-sized beds, love seats, and country furnishings. One bathroom has an antique chandelier over the bathtub. Two of these rooms are for nonsmokers, which now gives the inn a total of six rooms set aside for nonsmokers.

The decorations in the main house have always attracted attention and the murals in the dining room depict some scenes from other places in North America, including Natural Bridge, Virginia, and Boston Harbor. The guest rooms in the main house are decorated in a casual motif with country rugs and coverlets and a variety of interesting knickknacks on the walls, among which are the tops of china serving dishes of many different designs.

The inn's location in the Chesapeake Bay area means that there is considerable emphasis on seafood at lunch and dinner—crabcakes, baked seafood au gratin, lobster pie, seafood pot pie, and fresh fish with a Robert Morris special sauce. There are, of course, other poultry and meat offerings as well.

The inn starts taking reservations on the tenth of January for the current year, and accommodations should be reserved as early as possible, even for midweek stays.

A letter from Wendy told me that she and Ken recently sent some Robert Morris crabcakes to author James Michener in Sitka, Alaska, where he is working on his next book. "We heard that he was homesick for the Eastern Shore and our crabcakes. They made it via Federal Express in under forty-eight hours."

The Gibsons are extremely "family oriented" people. During a part of 1987, Ken, Wendy, and their two sons, Kent, 15, and Ben, 13, will be traveling to *CIBR* inns in North America and Britain.

ROBERT MORRIS INN, Oxford, MD 21654; 301-226-5111. A 33-guest-room waterside inn and lodge (mostly private baths) in a secluded Colonial community on the Tred Avon, 10 mi. from Easton, Md. (Some rooms with private porches and some non-smoking rooms; two cottages only available for children.) European plan. Breakfast, lunch, and dinner served to travelers and guests daily. Open year-round except Christmas Day and Feb. 1 till mid-Mar. Tennis, golf, seasonal river swimming, sailing, fishing, and bicycles nearby. Recommended for children over 10. No pets. Wendy and Ken Gibson, Owners; Jay Gibson, Innkeeper.

Directions: From Delaware Memorial Bridge, follow Rte. 13 south to Rte. 301 and proceed south to Rte. 50, then east on Rte. 50 to Easton. From Chesapeake Bay Bridge, follow Rte. 50-301 to Rte. 50 and procced east to Easton. From Chesapeake Bay Bridge Tunnel, follow Rte. 13 north to Rte. 50 and proceed west to Easton. From Easton, follow Rte. 322 to Rte. 333 to Oxford and inn.

A number of inns have nearby airports where private airplanes may land. An airplane symbol at the end of the inn directions indicates that there is an airport nearby. Consult inn for further information.

"European plan" means that rates for rooms and meals are separate. "American plan" means that meals are included in the cost of the room. "Modified American plan" means that breakfast and dinner are included in the cost of the room. The rates at some inns include a continental breakfast with the lodging.

HEMLOCK INN
Bryson City, North Carolina (1973)

"What's it really like at the Hemlock Inn?" I've been joyously answering that question for a great many years as a result of some really inspiring visits with Ella Jo and John Shell. This time, however, I'm going to share with you a letter I received from Mr. and Mrs. J. Brooks Brown, which apparently was mostly written by Helen Brown. I think it puts us right into the picture at the Hemlock Inn.

"We have stayed fifteen times at the Hemlock Inn and would like to share with you some observations about it. My husband, Brooks, and I, who are in our mid-sixties, travel by car from our home in Jacksonville, Florida, in just one day's time for that delicious 6:00 p.m. casual, family-style dinner. . . .

"How great it is to sit around the large Lazy Susan tables with guests who seem to be in concert with our same needs—not all seeming to need the entertainment of radio, TV, golfing, swimming, guided hiking or walking tours, but, instead, much-needed rest and freedom from pressing responsibilities. There is the freedom to converse without competitive conversation, to spend one's day in quietness together in those beautiful surroundings—most particularly for us in long walks or hikes down at the historic Deep Creek region. This can be a short or long hike.

"At each Hemlock stay we find renewal in having had our day started by John's loving prayer of grace in the lodge; new expressions of love for each other in tranquil, quiet, beautiful wild-flowered surroundings; discussing and working out a few problems of our own or those of friends;

making plans for grandchildren, family, or friends, or in stopping by the wonderful melodious stream to picnic or just to enjoy.

"You might say that we have the freedom here to catch up on the 'loose ends of life' at our own pace and to celebrate life during this getaway week at a slower tempo. . . .

"Another uniqueness about Hemlock is the freedom of choice of accommodations. There are all kinds of guest rooms, including some in cottages with even room for our grandchildren. Of course, all of them have private baths.

"We have played the shuffleboard that you have described and noticed that many guests enjoy a good game of ping-pong, the outdoor porch rockers, quiet reading or game playing in the cheerful book-filled mountain-view room or in front of the large stone fireplace. Many couples, singles, or families hop in their cars and manage to take untold trips to interesting 'nobs' or 'overlooks,' or hike on the scenic trails. Ella Jo says that there are over 700 miles of maintained trails in the Great Smokies.

"So, I might end by saying, if you have survived this long letter so far, Brooks and I leave Hemlock with renewed vigor, memories for our memory bank, healed spirits to continue to meet a busy life, and, as John Shell says, 'a grateful reverence for those God-given things we certainly have in abundance.' "

Thank you, Brooks and Helen Brown. I've taken a few editing liberties with your splendid letter, and I am delighted to share your feelings for the Hemlock Inn. Perhaps we'll meet there sometime in the near future.

HEMLOCK INN, Bryson City, NC 28713; 704-488-2885. A 25-guest-room Smoky Mountain inn, 4 mi. from Bryson City and 60 mi. from Asheville. Modified American plan omits lunch. Breakfast and dinner served to travelers by reservation only. Sunday dinner served at noon-time. Open late April to early Nov. Near Fontana Dam, Cherokee, and Pisgah National Forest. Shuffleboard, skittles, ping-pong, hiking trails on grounds. Tubing, rafting, and tennis nearby. No pets. No credit cards. Ella Jo and John Shell, Innkeepers.

Directions: From 19-A (19 Bypass) take the Hyatt Creek Rd.–Ela exit. Bear right until you reach old Rte. 19. Turn left on Rte. 19 for approx. 2 mi., and turn right at inn sign. Take paved road to top of mountain.

HOUND EARS LODGE
Blowing Rock, North Carolina (1971)

There are very few sights more inspiring to the golfer in me than to look over the golf course on a pleasant June morning from the balcony of Hound Ears Lodge. In the foreground is a lake fed by a small mountain stream that winds its way through the valley. This lake also serves as a hazard for the final hole and a very good 9-iron shot to the green is necessary to stay out of trouble.

The fairways that stretch out in the distance toward Grandfather Mountain are being watered by great fountains sent forth by the automatic watering system. When this is completed and the mist burns off, there is revealed a ring of mountains around the entire area. However, in the meantime, the greenskeepers are busy sweeping off the moisture that has accumulated overnight and the head greenskeeper can be seen tootling about in his golf cart, making sure that everything is ready for another day's play.

I had arrived at Hound Ears early in June, just at the time when the special golf packages, in effect since April, were being replaced by the regular social season. It was a good opportunity for me to have a pleasant visit with David Blust, the assistant manager at Hound Ears, who actually started as a bellboy a number of years ago. It's hard to imagine a more enthusiastic devotee of not only Hound Ears, but of golf and of North Carolina. We enjoyed a few moments of listening to Gene Fleri, who plays piano in the pleasant lounge before dinner and in the dining room during dinner. It is said that he can play any song that anyone can name.

Hound Ears is a golf- and ski-oriented country inn, but is somewhat different in atmosphere than the other *CIBR* inns in North Carolina. It is a luxurious, modified American plan resort-inn and the rates reflect the additional services and elegance. In the many, many years that I have been revisiting Hound Ears I've always found a very gratifying number of *CIBR* guests.

Among the many amenities offered are turn-down service each evening, the *Charlotte Observer* at the door every morning, fresh towels supplied to the rooms while guests enjoy dinner, and a careful monitoring of guests at the main gate by courteous custodians. Advance reservations are to be preferred; however, occasionally there are some guest rooms available.

The property surrounding Hound Ears has been purchased by home-owners who have built attractive, luxurious vacation homes, and who are very much involved in the future and welfare of the entire resort complex.

A great many of the guests are from Florida, and during the warm weather they escape to this very high mountain area to enjoy all of the relative coolness, as well as the golf.

During the winter, in addition to being near several downhill ski areas aided by snowmaking, Hound Ears also has its own beginners' and intermediate slopes, providing enjoyment for those of us who are looking for a less vigorous downhill experience.

The staff at Hound Ears is made up for the most part of students from nearby Appalachia College in Boone. These are very pleasant, alert young people who have grown up in the area, for whom Hound Ears is a source of pride.

The furnishings, appointments, interiors, and exteriors are carefully harmonized. For example, my room was done in complementary shades of brown and yellow. All of the buildings are set among the rhododen-drons and evergreens, and in many places huge handsome boulders were allowed to remain where they rested. The road was built around them, curving and twisting and climbing.

Nearby Grandfather Mountain is a place where the Scottish clan gathering is held during the second week in July. Scotsmen gather from all over the globe to take part in athletic competitions, dances, and piping. There are also a great deal of other cultural and recreational events held at the same time.

HOUND EARS LODGE AND CLUB, P.O. Box 188, Blowing Rock, NC 28605; 704-963-4321. A luxurious 25-guestroom resort-inn on Rte. 105, 6 mi. from Boone. Near natural attractions. American plan. Meals served to houseguests only. Open year-round. Tennis, 18-hole golf course, swimming, and skiing on grounds. David Blust, Innkeeper.

Directions: From Winston-Salem, follow Rte. 421 west to Boone, then travel south on Rte. 105 to inn. From Asheville, follow Rtes. I-40 east to Marion then Rte. 221 north to Linville and Rte. 105 north to inn. From Bristol, Va., and I-81, follow Rte. 58 east to Damascus, Va., then Rte. 91 to Mountain City, Tenn., and Rte. 421 to Boone, and Rte. 104 south to inn (5 mi.)

THE NU-WRAY INN
Burnsville, North Carolina (1973)

The drive from Hound Ears Lodge in Blowing Rock to the Nu-Wray Inn in Burnsville, North Carolina, on a sunny morning in June is most enjoyable. It provides an overview of the various intriguing altitudes in this part of North Carolina, which has the highest mountains east of the Rockies. Traveling next to Grandfathers Mountain, we start out literally in the high clouds and drop through various layers of mists to reach a more fertile farming country.

The Nu-Wray Inn provides an interesting contrast to the Hound Ears, a sophisticated, somewhat elegant country club resort. The Nu-Wray is a North Carolina inn that has been in existence since the 19th century and has remained much the same, thanks to the members of the Wray family who have carefully preserved some of the best of the past.

On the village square in Burnsville, the Nu-Wray now enjoys a well-deserved recognition for its venerability and individuality, especially in light of the proliferation of inns in North Carolina. My first visit goes back quite a few years when I met the late innkeeper emeritus,

Rush Wray, and spent the better part of the evening listening to his fascinating accounts of history and literature in North Carolina. It was also my introduction to the distinctive regional cooking at the Nu-Wray, characterized by the fried chicken and wonderful country hams.

At a bountiful breakfast on one of my later trips, after introducing everybody seated at the long harvest tables, Rush went into particulars about dinner:

"On Monday, Wednesday, and Friday we have fried chicken; Tuesday, Thursday, and Saturday we have baked country ham. The vegetables and desserts vary each day according to what's fresh from the various farms in the area. We have corn on the cob, fresh tomatoes, beans, carrots, and similar vegetables. One of the things we've been serving is homemade scalloped potatoes. We have found that a great many of our guests have sort of forgotten about scalloped potatoes and many have asked for our recipe."

The inn is really a very old building and the hallway walls are made of tongue-in-groove paneling, which in some cases is painted. Different sections of the building obviously have been put together at various times during the past 100 or more years, so that there are some interesting variations in interior design. It has been on the National Register of Historic Places for many years.

There is an assortment of bedrooms at the Nu-Wray. Those on the top floor are a bit smaller and in a lower price range. The inn also has an assortment of parlors and sitting rooms including one on the second floor with an old A.B. Gate & Co. piano of beautiful wood and several handsome antique tables and a chest of drawers.

Almost all the letters I get about the Nu-Wray say that it's different. Almost everyone mentions the rousing bells rung at 8:00 and 8:30 a.m. to announce breakfast. It's good to get an early start here in this part of North Carolina, because the flora and the fauna and the back roads provide a most rewarding vacation experience.

A word about my dear friend, Rush Wray, who passed away in July of 1985. Rush was really a one-of-a-kind individual, giving freely of himself to friends and strangers alike. I'll miss the long talks and good-natured joshing that we both enjoyed. He was a true innkeeper.

However, I'm sure that Howard and Betty Wray Souders, who have been the working innkeepers in recent years, will carry on his tradition of warm hospitality and friendliness.

THE NU-WRAY INN, Burnsville, NC 28714; 704-682-2329. A 35-guest-room village inn on town square on Rte. 19E, 38 mi. north of Asheville. Breakfast and dinner served every weekday to travelers. Noon dinner served on Sun. only. Open daily May to Dec. 1. Golf, swimming, hiking, and skiing nearby. A few miles from Mt. Mitchell. Howard and Betty Souders, Innkeepers.

Directions: From Asheville, go north on Rte. 19-23 for 18 mi., then continue on 19. Five miles from Burnsville, Rte. 19 becomes 19E. From the north via Bristol or Johnson City, Tenn., take Rte. 19-23 to Unicoi. Turn left on 107 to N.C. State Line. Take Rte. 226 and turn right on Rte. 197 at Red Hill to Burnsville.

THE ORCHARD INN
Saluda, North Carolina (1985)

On my first visit to this mountaintop inn in Saluda a few years ago, innkeeper Ken Hough and I picked our way over all the building paraphernalia that was scattered around both the interior and exterior of the inn. At that time he and Ann, his wife, were busy restoring this building, which has had a most interesting history as a vacation retreat for Southern Railway employees. Now the work has been done, the workmen are finished, and the results are worthy of their toil.

This restoration (by the way, I think this is the Houghs' seventeenth) combines country farmhouse warmth with many touches of southern plantation elegance. The inn reflects not only Ken and Ann's love of restoration, but also their passion for collecting. It has oriental rugs, original artwork, baskets, quilts, and Flow Blue china, which Ann has been collecting for some time. To that list I must add a great emphasis on flowers, painting, music, and intellectual curiosity.

With an extensive background in interior design, Ann has exercised a splendid restraint in decorating the ten guest rooms with antiques, including some with iron and brass beds and hand-woven rag rugs.

This inn has one of the most interesting second-floor hallways I have ever seen. Several bookshelves are loaded with books and magazines, including very old but readable ones. There are all kinds of unusual curios, dolls, childrens' toys, a dollhouse, and contemporary drawings, watercolors, and prints from the French Impressionists.

Outside, there's a path that leads down through the woods, past a couple of beehives and many, many flowers, both wild and cultivated.

The inn takes its name from the many orchards nearby, and much of their fresh fruit comes from those orchards.

Ken, who is the chef, has a background as a headmaster at a college preparatory school in Charleston and also as an operatic tenor. He has created such things as chilled peach soup, creamed seafood over rice, and chicken Madras. Broiled fresh mountain trout is a specialty. The desserts include apple crumble, blackberry cobbler, and pecan pie from a special New Orleans recipe.

The May 1986 *Gourmet* contained a partial description of Ken's culinary arts, and both Ann and Ken were very pleased at this recognition. "Ken's cooking school has been very successful and is offered every winter," Ann told me. "Last winter, mostly men came—their wives came along to sit by the fire and knit. We all had fun as well as good cooking!"

The dining room is in the wonderful, long, glassed-in porch overlooking the splendid, rolling mountains of the Warrior Mountain Range. It was really quite magical after dusk had fallen—every table was candlelit and the strains of Schumann, Mozart, and Scarlatti wafted out into the gathering night.

I would be greatly remiss if I did not call your attention to the really spectacular views, which are as much a part of the Orchard Inn as the interior design and Ken's cuisine. I have watched the changing tones and colors as they are affected by the mist off the mountains at various times of day.

THE ORCHARD INN, Box 725, Saluda, NC 28773; 704-749-5471. A 10-guestroom mountaintop (2500 feet) inn a short distance from Tryon in western North Carolina. Open year-round. Breakfast included with room rate. Lunch and dinner available. Antiquing, hiking, wild flower collecting, birdwatching, and superb country roads abound. Pets in cottages only. No credit cards. Ann and Ken Hough, Innkeepers.

Directions: From Atlanta, come north on I-85 to Hwy. 5. Inn is 2 mi. off I-26. From Asheville, take I-26 south.

I do not include lodging rates in the descriptions, for the very nature of an inn means that there are lodgings of various sizes, with and without baths, in and out of season, and with plain and fancy decoration. Travelers should call ahead and inquire about the availability and rates of the many different types of rooms.

SNOWBIRD MOUNTAIN LODGE
Robbinsville, North Carolina (1973)

Bob and Connie Rhudy and I were seated where everyone sits at Snowbird Mountain Lodge—on the terrace that almost hangs over Lake Santeetlah, at least 1,000 feet below. Gazing over the railing we could see a tiny automobile on the thin, winding sliver of road climbing the adjacent mountain. Directly in front of us, almost close enough to touch, were at least fifteen majestic peaks with heights, from 4,000 to 5,000 feet.

Since my first visit to Snowbird quite a few years ago, I have always associated it with the increasing number of birds that make this area their habitat. I understand that some guests can identify as many as 110 different species. In the last couple of years wildflower walks have become extremely popular.

Connie and Bob were especially enthusiastic about the nature hikes led by several knowledgable guides in the past two years. "They have become enormously popular," Connie said. "There are wildflower, bird, and plant hikes, and our guides are acknowledged authorities in their fields. They are each here at different times during the spring and summer, and we have many reservations for next spring's adventures already."

Rustic Snowbird Mountain Lodge, built of chestnut logs and native stone, harmonizes beautifully with its mountain setting. Two huge stone fireplaces add beauty and warmth. (There is also steam heat for the cooler months.)

The main lounge is paneled in butternut, the dining room in cherry, and guest rooms are paneled in a variety of native woods with custom-made furniture to match. The comfortable beds have bright bedspreads.

The Rhudys have two excellent assistant innkeepers in their daughter, Becky, who is now enrolled at the University of North Carolina, and their son, Bobby, who will complete his junior year at Furman University in June. All of the Rhudys have combined to make this mountaintop lodge a veritable haven for guests who enjoy the many outdoor activities in the area.

Boxed lunches are provided in lieu of lunch at the lodge, if guests prefer. Snowbird is on the full American plan.

"Last year we did something for the first time that we're going to continue," explained Bob. "We decided to add one final weekend to our season and call it 'Fall Finale at Snowbird.' Fresh hot coffee starts the Friday afternoon and then after the evening meal, which will have fresh mountain trout and homemade coconut cream pie, we'll gather in front of a roaring fire to enjoy music from some of our local musicians. After breakfast on Saturday morning, a packed lunch will be available for

anyone wishing to explore the Joyce Kilmer–Slickrock Wilderness Area. Following a dinner of Rock Cornish game hens we'll retire to our sitting room for another evening of reading, games, and swapping stories of the day's activities. The weekend closes on Sunday morning with a delicious breakfast of country sausage and blueberry pancakes."

Sounds like a wonderful way to wind up the autumn.

SNOWBIRD MOUNTAIN LODGE, Joyce Kilmer Forest Rd., Robbinsville, NC 28771; 704-479-3433. A 22-guestroom inn on top of the Great Smokies, 12 mi. from Robbinsville. American plan (room and 3 meals). Open from end of April to early Nov. Lunch and dinner served to travelers by reservation only. Shuffleboard, table tennis, archery, croquet, horseshoes, badminton on grounds. Swimming, fishing, hiking, backroading nearby. Guided walks for nature lovers by reservation. Not suitable for children under 12. No pets. The Rhudy Family, Innkeepers.

Directions: The inn is located at the western tip of No. Carolina, 10 mi. west of Robbinsville. Approaching from the northeast or south take U.S. 19 and 129; from the northwest take U.S. 129, then follow signs to Joyce Kilmer Memorial Forest.

A number of inns have nearby airports where private airplanes may land. An airplane symbol at the end of the inn directions indicates that there is an airport nearby. Consult inn for further information.

PARISH PATCH INN
Normandy, Tennessee (1986)

"Cortner Mill stayed with the same family from 1848 until the late 1950s. It was a working mill for that entire time. We've kept some of the original equipment right here, including the scale and some of the wonderful grain chutes."

Marty Ligon, the innkeeper at Parish Patch Inn, and I were seated on the porch at Cortner Mill in Normandy, Tennessee. Here above the dam, the waters of the Duck River seem so placid until they drop over the dam and gather momentum from their fall. Upstream on both banks the branches of the trees hang out over the water, and one branch has a rope swing, where one could swing out over the river, let go, and splash right into the water just like a lad in a Norman Rockwell painting. The sound of the water has a wonderful soporific effect. It's the kind of place to sit and read a book, maybe take a nap in one of the beautiful ladder-back rockers, or possibly even *write* a book.

The Mill, which also has its own accommodations, is actually part and parcel of Parish Patch Inn, the main house being just a few moments away. The combination of the two places provides a most interesting contrast in a country inn experience. The Mill has a pleasant rustic elegance, with four different guest rooms, including one bunk room with seven twin beds. I think the most impressive feature, of course, is the presence of the river and the dam.

The main house of the Parish Patch presents an entirely different aspect. This is a lovely board-and-batten structure with comfortable rooms, private baths, fireplaces, patios, rose gardens, and a swimming pool with an attractive poolhouse. Fresh-cut flowers and homemade pumpkin bread are some of the extra touches that make it enjoyable. The guest rooms are not at all rustic, unless you count the beautifully varnished overhead beams. All have splendid views of the rolling Tennessee countryside, and the outdoors is immediately available, in some cases, through a sliding door onto a balcony. There's a mixture of natural woods, with some excellent antique pieces and well-designed lamps and other necessities. All of the guest rooms have two double beds and a television.

Dinner is served in a very pleasant dining room, for houseguests only, by reservation. I asked Marty what kind of a menu is offered. "Well, we serve only one main dish," she replied, "and that could be meat loaf, fried chicken, chicken cordon bleu, roast beef, or stuffed pork chops. All of the breads, muffins, rolls, and coffee cakes are homemade right here. Mildred Kimbro is the cook, along with her daughter, Kay, and she is happy to take suggestions."

Provisions are made for people traveling with children, with some outdoor swings, slides, bars, and other equipment. The house itself overlooks great cornfields on two sides, and the whole immediate area is surrounded by an old-fashioned Tennessee split-rail fence.

I'd like to suggest that readers making reservations at the Parish Patch Inn talk over their preferences with Marty or Phyllis Crosslin, the innkeeper, because there are a number of options.

Everything at both locations is beautifully maintained and cared for, and yet within just a few moments' walk you're in the beautiful Tennessee countryside.

PARISH PATCH INN, Normandy, TN 37360; 615- 857-3441. A 10-guest-room elegant inn in the verdant Tennessee countryside. European plan. Evening meals are served to houseguests only with advance reservation. Open all year. Closed Christmas Day. Swimming pool on grounds. Fishing, boating, canoeing, picnicking, bicycling, bird watching and backroading nearby. Personal checks accepted. Marty Ligon, Innkeeper; Phyllis Crosslin, Manager.

Directions: From Shelbyville continue south on 41-A for 7.2 mi. and look for a left turn at the sign for Normandy. Turn left onto Dement Rd. and follow signs to inn. From I-24, take Exit 97 (Beechgrove-Shelbyville-Hwy. 64 Exit). Take Hwy. 64 west to Wartrace. In Wartrace do not cross RR tracks. Take Hwy. 269 east. Pass shops and turn left at yellow light, up hill. Inn is 4 mi. from Wartrace.

GRAVES' MOUNTAIN LODGE
Syria, Virginia (1972)

Of all of the thousands of inn and hotel brochures that I have seen, none is more handsome, better designed, or more informative than "Mountain Hospitality," the booklet that describes literally five generations of innkeeping at Graves' Mountain Lodge.

For over 130 years, five generations of the Graves family have been innkeepers in the shadow of the Blue Ridge Mountains near Syria, Virginia. In the early 1850s, Paschal Graves opened an "ordinary," or inn, along the Blue Ridge Turnpike on land now part of the Shenandoah National Park. The ordinary was a natural stopping point for travelers making the seventy-mile journey between Gordonsville and New Market. Here horses were changed to make the climb over the mountains, and farmers on foot herded their livestock to market along the turnpike or hauled wagonloads of bark and carts of apples, corn, and chestnuts.

Around 1857 the Graves family moved to their present location and for 100 years "took in" travelers and vacationers in their rambling farmhouse. Today's innkeeper is Jim Graves, and he can recall as a boy growing up the fun and work of having visitors arrive. Their cook fried chicken, baked hams and fresh fruit pies and cakes. Dinner was served family-style and people came from all around to have chicken. As he said, "When we had a lot of guests in the summer, our family moved out of the bedrooms and slept on the porch. We didn't mind because vacationers usually brought children for us to play with. We became friends with many of them and later some came back to work on the farm."

A lot of very exciting things have happened since Jim was a young boy. He met and married Rachel Lynn Norman, who shared his enthusiasm. Even during their courting days they drew sketches and developed ideas about a rustic but modern mountain resort. They discovered that they had the same pedigree; they are both descendants of Captain Thomas Graves, who sailed to Jamestown in 1608. Rachel's family stems from Thomas Graves' oldest son, born in England, and Jim's family is descended from a younger son, born in Virginia. Twelve generations later their marriage united two branches of a 375-year family tree. By the way, this tree is pictured in "Mountain Hospitality."

One of the most colorful figures connected with Graves' Mountain Lodge was Jim's father, "Mr. Jack," who was still on the scene during my first visit many years ago. It was a common sight to see him come to dinner fresh from his farm chores, but in clean overalls, to be on hand to meet all of the guests.

As I leafed through the pages of the booklet, I realized that very little has changed since the original concept of Graves' Mountain Lodge four generations ago. The new lodge is a unique collection of old and new buildings, each with a history all of its own. Over the years I have described the outbuildings that also serve as guest quarters. In recent years two additional buildings with tastefully furnished motel-type bedrooms enjoy a fantastic view of the great valley filled with cattle, sheep, farmland, and acres and acres of peach and apple trees.

What about the food at Graves' Mountain Lodge? Well, here is Suzanne Haney telling me, during a visit I made last November, about Sunday night supper at Graves' Mountain Lodge. "Sunday night dinner will be country ham, cold fried chicken, country-fried potatoes and onions, green beans, baked tomatoes, corn pudding, coleslaw, maybe one or two other vegetables, and probably spiced peaches or apples. Usually on Sunday night we have hot fudge cake for dessert.

"Tonight, we will have between 250 and 300 people. Last Sunday, we had about 700 people."

The original Graves family, including Mr. Jack, I'm sure, would be glad to know that everybody is served family-style inside the lodge and on the porch.

Although the lodge is operated on the American plan—three meals a day with lodging—those who want to stop by for a meal can call for a reservation and are always welcome.

GRAVES' MOUNTAIN LODGE, Syria, VA 22743; 703-923-4231. A 41-guestroom secluded, rustic resort-inn, including cottages and 2 motel units, on Rte. 670, off Rte. 321, 10 mi. north of Madison, Va., 38 mi. N.W. of Charlottesville, Va. American plan. Breakfast, lunch, dinner served to travelers by reservation only. Closed Dec. 1 to late Mar. Swimming, tennis, horseback riding, hunting, fishing, a special nature walk, rock hunting, and hiking on grounds. Golf nearby. Jim and Rachel Graves, Innkeepers.

Directions: Coming south from Wash. D.C., take I-66 to Gainsville. Follow Rte. 29 south to Madison, turn right onto Rte. 231 west, go 7 mi. to Banco, turn left onto Rte. 670 and follow 670 for 4½ mi. to lodge.

THE INN AT GRISTMILL SQUARE
Warm Springs, Virginia (1977)

Bruce McWilliams was explaining the workings of the waterwheel at Gristmill Square:

"The waterwheel is known as an 'overshot wheel,'" he said. "It is driven by the weight of the water flowing into the buckets at the top of the wheel. It was manufactured in 1900 by the Fitz Waterwheel Company in Hanover, Pennsylvania, and operates from this little brook. There's been a mill on this site continuously since 1771, although the present mill building was erected in 1900."

Gristmill Square is built around a three-sided square, formed by an old mill, a blacksmith's shop, and a hardware store. Guest rooms were created in the old hardware store and there are three country stores in the former blacksmith's shop. Most of the guest rooms are furnished with antiques and old prints, although some are done in a more contemporary style.

There are other bedrooms available in period buildings adjacent to the inn or across the village street from Gristmill Square. Both the Virginian Room and the Miss Jenny Payne Room, two rooms in the Steel House, have four-poster beds and fireplaces.

The Waterwheel Restaurant has been artfully fashioned from the grain mill, which was operated by the waterwheel. The heavenly aroma of the grain, the beige patina of the walls, and the geometric patterns created by the beams and posts make a most unusual setting for a candlelight dinner.

The menu features roast duckling with apricots, pan-fried trout with black walnuts, veal à l'orange, and broiled mountain trout.

The McWilliams family has also provided additional amenities for guests who enjoy longer stays. The Bath and Tennis Club has a swimming pool and tennis courts that are playable for most of the year, and there is a sauna in the Steel House. In one of the golfing capitals of the world, the famous Cascades and Lower Cascades golf courses are a short drive away. The Warm Springs Pools are within walking distance.

There is horseback and carriage riding nearby as well as exceptional trout fishing, downhill and cross-country skiing, and some of the most beautiful backroading and hill-walking to be found west of Scotland.

Adding to the cultural attractions of the area are the Garth Newel chamber music concerts, performed on summer weekends.

Bath County is located in the west–central portion of Virginia. The 540-square-mile area is within one day's drive of half the population of the northeastern United States. The elevations range from 4,477 above sea level to 1,140 feet, where the Cowpasture River flows into Allegheny County. Visitors began coming to the springs of Bath County as early as 1750 and it's been increasing in popularity every year since.

THE INN AT GRISTMILL SQUARE, P.O. Box 359, Warm Springs, VA 24484; 703-839-2231. A 14-guestroom unusual restoration with a restaurant and many resort attractions in a small country town in the Allegheny Mtns., 19 mi. no. of Covington. European plan. Restaurant open for dinner daily Tues. – Sun., and Sun. lunch. Lunch served May 1 to Nov. 1, Tues. – Sun. Restaurant closed Mon. Suggest calling for details. Tennis courts, swimming pool, and sauna on grounds. Golf at nearby Cascades or Lower Cascades. Skiing at Snowshoe, West Va., about an hr. away. Skating, riding, hiking, fishing, hunting, antiquing, and backroading nearby. Children welcome. The McWilliams Family, Innkeepers.

Directions: From Staunton, Va. follow Rte. 254 to Buffalo Gap; Rte. 42 to Millboro Spring; Rte. 39 to Warm Springs. From Lexington, take Rte. 39 to Warm Springs. From Roanoke, take Rte. 220 to Warm Springs. From Lewisburg, W. Va., take I-64 to Covington; Rte. 220 north to Warm Springs. From northern W. Va. travel south to Rte. 39 east to Warm Springs. The inn is on Rte. 645. From Rte. 220 going north, turn left on Rte. 645 in Warm Springs. From Rte. 39W turn left on Rte. 692 and left again on Rte. 645 at Warm Springs.

JORDAN HOLLOW FARM INN
Stanley, Virginia (1985)

I'm not sure of the protocol, but I think I'm godfather to a colt. It all happened on a visit to Jordan Hollow Farm, when a foal was born and Marley Beers named him "Norman"—I have his most recent photo, and he's a beauty.

"He'll have to earn his keep," she said, "because we are a working horse farm. We raise German Holsteiner and thoroughbreds, as well as keeping pleasure horses for our guests. However, it's not necessary to be a horse rider to enjoy yourself here. Many of our guests who have never ridden in their lives and have come for the wonderful Shenandoah Valley mountain experience begin to feel at home with these beautiful animals,

and we have persuaded them to try one of our beginners' rides. We never take out more than five or six people at a time and we have both English and Western saddles. There are some very quiet trail horses that are trustworthy for beginners and we have advanced horses for experienced riders.

"In most other places there is a walking trail ride and everyone goes in a long line. You see the scenery but you don't really have too much of an equestrian experience. We do things differently because we want everybody to enjoy as many experiences as possible."

Marley and her Dutch husband, Jetze (pronounced Yet-sah), purchased this former Colonial horse farm several years ago and began creating an inn for the enjoyment of their guests. Jetze speaks several different languages, and both of them have traveled widely and are sophisticated hosts. They met in Africa.

This African influence is mirrored in one of the three dining rooms with decorations from Africa. In many ways, they seemed quite in place with the rest of this wonderful atmosphere that is so removed from the hubbub of the city.

One of the engaging features of the inn is the pub, called the "Watering Trough." Jetze has built an adjoining fountain and gardens with umbrella tables and chairs. On the night of my visit I sat up rather late with the innkeepers and another couple from Washington. I asked the gentleman what he enjoyed most about being here, and he said, "Just the peace and quiet and opportunity to read, take walks, and enjoy good food and good company."

This convivial atmosphere continues at dinner. Marley is the cook and describes the food as "country French" style, with plenty of fresh fruits and vegetables, and homemade breads and desserts. She particularly recommends their roast quail and rib eye steaks.

In regard to the guest room furnishings, *Country Decorating Ideas* saw fit to photograph the interior of one of the bedrooms for a splendid feature in their magazine. The guest rooms are all furnished with comfortable, cozy country-inn furniture, with different types of beds and other pieces in each room, as well as dried flower arrangements, calico comforters, and wonderful, thick, fluffy towels.

On a guest's birthday, along with a birthday cake, Marley and Jetze have revived the old Virginia custom of buttering that person's nose, thus "helping him to slide through the next year without difficulty." I guess I'll have to return to Jordan Hollow on Norman's birthday and butter his nose!

JORDAN HOLLOW FARM INN, Rte. 2, Box 375, Stanley, VA 22851; 703-778-2285 or 2209. A 20-guestroom restored Colonial horse farm 6 mi. south of Luray in the northern Shenandoah Valley of Virginia. Open year-round. Breakfast, lunch, and dinner served daily to houseguests. Restaurant open to public Wed. thru Sun. The horse center is on the property with a wide variety of horses and lessons from beginner thru advanced. Scenic trail rides are planned for various levels of skill. Swimming, volleyball, ping-pong, board games, walking, and xc skiing on the premises. Hiking, canoeing, fishing, skiing, golf, tennis, auctions, museums, antiques, crafts shops nearby. Sorry, no pets; boarding kennel nearby. Marley and Jetze Beers, Innkeepers.

Directions: The inn is located 6 mi. south of Luray, Va.; 12 mi. from the Skyline Drive; and 19 mi. from I-81 at New Market. Go south from Luray 6 mi. on Rte. 340; turn left on Rte. 624; left on Rte. 689; and right on Rte. 626.

MAPLE HALL
Lexington, Virginia (1987)

It is always somewhat in the nature of a homecoming for me to return to Lexington, Virginia. I lived in nearby Lynchburg for five years and made many trips through the beautiful Blue Ridge Mountains to follow the fortunes of the Virginia Military Institute and Washington and Lee sports teams. There are many lovely old buildings on both of those college campuses, and even the downtown business buildings have a weathered and attractive appearance. Lexington has a gentle quality of the past, and indeed is a most historic place, at the same time keeping pace with the present and the future. There is an informal walking tour of downtown Lexington, which will reveal many unexpected architectural delights.

Susan and Peter Meredith and the many members of their family have been developing Historic Inns of Lexington for the past few years. It began with the Alexander-Withrow House, which I first visited many years ago, and continued with the McCampbell Inn. Both of these offer bed and breakfast, and are conveniently located in the business district. These two have now been joined by a most imposing old plantation called Maple Hall, a few miles north of Lexington.

This lovely old red brick mansion with its handsome white columns has always been admired by all who pass it by. The small red brick house next door may have been the original plantation house. This is now the guest house, offering three guest rooms, a living room, and kitchen.

The guest rooms in the main house are generously sized and appropriately furnished. There are fireplaces and modern conveniences.

Don Fredenburg, who is the manager of all three of the Historic Inns of Lexington, told me that Maple Hall was built on 257 acres around 1850. "It is of the typical mansion-plantation architecture that characterized the South during the pre-Civil War days," he said.

At the time of my visit, the dining room was open for dinners on Wednesday through Saturday and for a very impressive Sunday brunch. "Our guests from the Alexander-Withrow and the McCampbell also enjoy dinner here.

"Peter has built a pier on the pond at Maple Hall and stocked it with fish. There are also several miles of hiking trails cut through the fifty-six acres of woods and pastures so that guests can take a leisurely stroll or perhaps even do some running."

Dinner is served in the quiet, impressive dining room. I had chosen fresh salmon fillets from a menu that included four or more other main items.

"Lexington is certainly a growing place," Don remarked. "For one thing, the Virginia Horse Center is now being built, and we had the governor here for the ground-breaking ceremonies. A number of dignitaries from Texas and Virginia were also in Lexington in September to commemorate Sam Houston's birthplace across the road from Maple Hall."

Readers who want to stop at Maple Hall may check in directly at Maple Hall, while guests at the Alexander-Withrow and the McCampbell Inn should check in at the main reception desk at the McCampbell Inn in the center of Lexington.

The Merediths have always been great builders and designers and restorers, and I'm happy to say that Maple Hall is a credit to their craft and enthusiasm. Located as it is in such a beautiful area of the Blue Ridge Mountains, I'm sure that it is going to provide a real Southern country-inn flavor for inn devotees and business travelers.

MAPLE HALL (Historic Inns of Lexington), 11 No. Main St., Lexington, VA 24450; 703-463-2044. A 16-guestroom (private baths) mansion-inn, just 7 mi. north of Lexington. Hearty continental breakfast included with room rate. Dinner served Wed. thru Sat.; Sun. brunch. Open all year. Ideal for back-road wanderers or business travelers on I-81 and I-84. Lexington has many activities both summer and winter besides those at Virginia Military Institute and Washington and Lee University. The Blue Ridge Parkway is just a few miles away. Golf, hiking, Appalachian Trail, and canoeing also available. No pets. Mr. and Mrs. Peter Meredith and sons, Owners; Don Fredenburg, Innkeeper.

Directions: Maple Hall is 7 mi. north of Lexington on Rte. 11. From I-81 take Exit 53.

MEADOW LANE LODGE
Warm Springs, Virginia (1982)

I was wandering about in the great barn at Meadow Lane Lodge, located in Bath County, Virginia, a few minutes from the famous Cascades Golf Course in Warm Springs. Here, sheep and goats graze and gambol. Chickens, ducks, guinea fowl, geese, and turkeys inhabit the old horse stalls in the large stable and freely wander in the areas around them. Cats and kittens mingle, as do the farm dogs. No one hurts anyone and there is respect everywhere.

A few moments earlier I had reluctantly gotten up from a wonderful breakfast featuring a special recipe for scrambled eggs blended with some aromatic herbs, prepared by innkeeper Philip Hirsh. Although Phip, as he is called, is a retired executive, he still takes great pride in occasionally doing the Meadow Lane breakfast.

In the beautiful Allegheny Mountains, Meadow Lane Lodge is an integral part of the Hirsh estate, comprised of 1,600 acres of woods, fields, and streams. In such an atmosphere, tranquility and relaxation are almost guaranteed.

Two suites and three double bedrooms are available in the main house, while Craig's Cottage, named for a Hirsh grandson, will accommodate two to four people. The cottage boasts a big stone fireplace in a lovely high-ceilinged bedroom with a large picture window looking over the meadows and mountains.

Cathy Hirsh led me off to one corner, saying, "Yesterday, Phip and I took a couple of hours off, and with two of the dogs went up into the woods to walk around the horse exercise track, which was hewn out of the forest by Phip's father. We saw lady-slippers in bloom and lots of

trillium and dwarf iris. Then we drove along the Jackson River to the trout ponds and the spring where the wild azalea and dogwood are flowering, and the watercress is a great patch of vivid green. Our river is one of Virginia's designated scenic rivers and two miles of it flow right through the farm.

"On cool spring and fall mornings and evenings, the two fireplaces in the living rooms of the lodge are always in use. I'm sure you noticed that the upstairs rooms have screened-in porches with delightful views and breezes. Later on, our large front porch with its wicker furniture will be a scene for lots of relaxing and chatting with other inn guests."

Additional accommodations are offered in the center of the village of Warm Springs in the Francisco Cottage, which has been restored and furnished in the manner of the log house originally erected on the site, circa 1820. This cottage offers a very pleasantly furnished living room, porch, bedroom, kitchen, and bath, and an impressive view of the hillsides.

Cathy and Philip are excited about the newest addition to Meadow Lane. "It has been designed like an old Pennsylvania barn with an overhang and beautiful stonework at one end," Cathy told me. "There are two guest rooms with baths, plus a vaulted-ceiling living room with a big picture window. The building looks old and fits in beautifully with the rest of the farm."

MEADOW LANE LODGE, Star Route A, Box 110, Warm Springs, VA 24484; 703-839-5959. A 10-guestroom lodge-inn on a portion of a large estate about 10 min. from the center of Warm Springs and near the famous Cascades Golf Course. Guestrooms are in the main house and a cottage on the grounds and also in Francisco Cottage in Warm Springs. A full breakfast is the only meal served. Open Apr. 1 thru Jan. 31. Minimum stay in the lodge is 2 nights; in Francisco Cottage, 3 nights. Dinners are available at nearby restaurants. Tennis court, swimming, horseback riding, and excellent fishing on grounds. Also, miles of hiking and walking trails. Golf, skeet, and trap shooting nearby. Children over 6 welcome. Small dogs accepted with prior approval. Philip and Cathy Hirsh, Innkeepers.

Directions: From Staunton, Va., follow Rte. 254 west to Buffalo Gap; Rte. 42 south to Millboro Spring; Rte. 39 west to Warm Springs. From Lexington, take Rte. 39 west. From Roanoke, take Rte. 220 north to Warm Springs and Rte. 39 west to Meadow Lane Lodge.

MORRISON HOUSE
Alexandria, Virginia (1987)

Although this book is about "country inns," over the years I have received requests for my recommendations of places in cities. About twelve years ago, I included the Algonquin Hotel in New York City as a discreet "country inn in the city," and since then, I have recommended a few others.

Similarly, Morrison House in Old Town, Alexandria, about twenty minutes from downtown D.C., is not a country inn on a back road, but it is the answer to having quiet, elegant lodgings in an atmosphere that is quite reminiscent of Knightsbridge, London. Further, if you have business or pleasure in the nearby nation's capital it is a most rewarding experience to return to Old Town, with its rows of 18th- and 19th-century houses, diverting shops, and safe walking at night.

The new four-story, Federal-style building is red brick with black shutters, with a main entrance reached by twin curved staircases encircling a fountain and rising to a portico supported by Greek columns.

Seated in the small courtyard in front of the hotel, I was enjoying the freshness of the early morning air and thinking back over the events of my first visit on the previous evening. When I pulled up in front of the entrance, my automobile door was opened by a properly attired butler— not a bellboy, but a butler. I learned that this gentleman is a very important part of the service offered at Morrison House. He was relaxed, efficient, not pompous, extremely accommodating, and a veritable fountain of information about where to go in the D.C. area and how to get there. In the meantime, my car had been whisked away to the hotel's underground parking garage.

Off the first-floor reception area was a pleasantly elegant guest lounge with camelback sofas, Chippendale chairs, and loveseats upholstered in satin brocade. Gracefully draped floor-to-ceiling windows looked out over a quiet street.

If all of this talk of butlers and European elegance seems a little stiff, let me assure you that it is quite relaxed, and designed to provide a very pleasant stay.

This is also true of the guest rooms, which have mahogany fourposter and canopied beds, made up in the European style with triple sheets. The bathrooms are done in Italian marble, and there are terrycloth robes and little reminders to the effect that should a traveler have forgotten such things as a toothbrush, comb, shaving cream, and so forth, the same can be obtained by calling the reception area.

All of the additional thoughtfulness and amenities reflected in this hotel are the result of the extremely broad travel experiences of owners Mr. and Mrs. Robert Morrison. I had a very enjoyable chat with them about various European and British hotels that we both have enjoyed, and, not surprisingly, one mutual favorite was La Residence du Bois in Paris, included in the European edition of this book.

As might be expected, part of the Morrison adventure is the restaurant with the intriguing name of Le Chardon d'Or (the Golden Thistle). There are two menus for both lunch and dinner: à la carte and fixed-price. The à la carte prices are more expensive than those of many country inns, but very much in line with other restaurants in the D.C. area. French contemporary cuisine is the order of the day, served by formally clad waiters.

We are happy to welcome Morrison House to *Country Inns and Back Roads* for the first time.

MORRISON HOUSE, 116 S. Alfred St., Alexandria, VA 22314; 800-367-0800 or 703-838-8000. A 47-guestroom elegant, luxury hotel in a historic section of Alexandria, 20 min. from D.C. Restaurant open for breakfast, lunch, and dinner; Sunday brunch. Open year-round. Conveniently located to visit all of the D.C. area historic, recreational, and cultural attractions. Attractive weekend rates. Mr. and Mrs. Robert Morrison, Owners; Thor Halvorsen, General Manager.

Directions: From National Airport, drive south on Geo. Washington Pkwy. to King St. Turn right and continue for 2 blks. and turn left on S. Alfred St. The hotel is on the left at midblock. From the Beltway/U.S. 495, take Exit U.S. 1 north to Prince St. Turn right and continue for 1 blk. to S. Alfred St. Hotel is on right side.

PROSPECT HILL
Trevilians, Virginia (1979)

"Welcome to our home, Prospect Hill." Bill Sheehan, resplendent in a blue blazer, with his red mustache carefully groomed, stood in the middle of the dining room at Prospect Hill surrounded by his friends—innkeepers from *Country Inns and Back Roads*—all seated at the candlelit dinner tables, anticipating another highly enjoyable meal and good times. His wife, Mireille, her face beaming with pleasure, was seated at a circular table in the corner.

My thoughts turned to a similar meeting here about six years earlier of CIBR innkeepers from Virginia, West Virginia, Maryland, and even some from Pennsylvania and New Jersey. Various regional meetings are held periodically on a rotating basis among the inns.

Bill, as he does at every dinner, explained exactly what was on the menu for the evening and then returned to the kitchen to supervise the meal and join us later on.

On the previous occasion the tranquility of the inn—the antiquity of the house and the little buildings; its setting in a parkland of trees, flowers, and many birds—impressed all of us. The rooms in the main house have a wonderful feeling of quiet and dignity, and there is a lovely veranda on the back and an open gallery on the second floor.

Between the main course and dessert, Bill told us that this plantation dates back to 1732 but that the real history began in 1840. "During the War Between the States, the son of the owner returned to find everything in a completely rundown condition and of course the slaves were gone. One way of surviving was to 'take in' guests from the city, and in 1880 additional bedrooms were added to the manor house, and the slave quarters were enlarged to accommodate guests."

The innkeepers' tour of the guest rooms had included three of the outbuildings—Uncle Guy's House, with rooms both upstairs and down, the Overseer's Cottage, with a suite, and the Boys' Cabin. "The first half of the Boys' Cabin is early 18th century," Bill told us, "having been built in the early 1730s as a cabin for the boys in the family. As you see, it's only twelve feet square, with the original fireplace, log walls, and pine flooring. We added a new addition to the rear wall and called it '20th-century Californian,' because it has a very modern bath, complete with a whirlpool soaking tub and a deck for morning coffee."

Our bill of fare that night was a leek and potato soup, salad vinaigrette garnished with egg, veal sautéed in butter with a mushroom and wine sauce, and fresh asparagus and wild rice. When it came to the dessert course, Bill said, "If you eat all of your vegetables, you get a strawberry cream tart." Ordinarily, there is one seating at 8:00 and Bill rings the bell to summon the guests to the dining room.

Guests enjoy an intimate and personal experience at Prospect Hill and there is ample opportunity to meet and make friends with other guests.

Our meeting at Prospect Hill was once again a resounding success. As one innkeeper put it, "I can hardly wait until it's time to come here again!"

PROSPECT HILL, Route 613, Trevilians, VA 23170; 703-967-0844. A 7-guestroom country inn on a historic plantation 15 mi. east of Charlottesville, Va.; 90 mi. southwest of Washington, D.C. Bed and breakfast-in-bed Sun. thru Tues. Modified American plan with full breakfast-in-bed and full dinner Wed. thru Sat. Dinner served Wed. thru Sat. by reservation. Dining room closed Sun., Mon., and Tues. Breakfast always served to houseguests. Swimming pool. Near Monticello, Ashlawn (Pres. Monroe's home), Univ. of Virginia, Castle Hill, and Skyline Drive. Children welcome. No pets. Bill and Mireille Sheehan, Innkeepers.

Directions: From Washington, D.C.: Beltway to I-66 west to Warrenton. Follow Rte. 29 south to Culpeper, then Rte. 15 south thru Orange and Gordonsville to Zion Crossroads. Turn left on Rt. 250 east 1 mi. to Rte. 613. Turn left 3 mi. to inn on left. From Charlottesville or Richmond: take I-64 to Exit 27; Rte. 15 south ½ mi. to Zion Crossroads; turn left on Rte. 250 east 1 mi. to Rte. 613. Turn left 3 mi. to inn on left.

A number of inns have nearby airports where private airplanes may land. An airplane symbol at the end of the inn directions indicates that there is an airport nearby. Consult inn for further information.

THE RED FOX INN AND TAVERN
Middleburg, Virginia (1979)

While I strolled with the chef through the immaculate kitchen at the Red Fox, he proudly announced, "We make all our own ice creams, all our own breads and desserts. We also make all our own sauces and soups, and bone our own meats. We are very adaptable in our cuisine, with some nouveau, some Italian, and some classic French things. We make all our own pasta and our own ravioli, and we use only sweet butter. You won't find preservatives or coloring in any of our food."

There are not many country inns in North America that have remained in the same building for more than 200 years; however, the Red Fox in Middleburg, Virginia, which started as a simple way station when the road to the west was known as "Ashby's Gap Turnpike," has passed the midway point of its third century and is an integral part of American history.

Joseph Chinn was the first proprietor and the inn became known as Chinn's Ordinary. His first cousin was George Washington, who was engaged by Lord Fairfax to survey the area around the tavern, which in turn became known as Chinn's Crossroads.

It's probably true that soldiers from both the American and British lines stopped at this local tavern during the war for American independence. During the War Between the States, Confederate General Jeb Stuart needed lodging for the night and chose the large rooms above the tavern. It was in these rooms that Colonel John Mosby and his Raiders had a celebrated meeting with Stuart, and it was downstairs in the tavern where many of the wounded received care. Among modern-day celebrities who have visited the Red Fox is President John F. Kennedy, who held a rare press conference in the pine-paneled Jeb Stuart Room.

The main entrance leads directly into one of the two low-ceilinged dining rooms where the thirty-inch-thick walls are appropriately decorated with fox-hunting regalia and sporting paintings. There are seven dining rooms in all. Cheery fires are always lit during the chilly months. A secluded terrace at the rear of the inn underneath the trees has an intimate outdoor feeling and is very popular during the clement weather.

Guest rooms in the Red Fox Inn and Tavern are carefully furnished in the 18th-century manner with period antiques and four-postered beds, most with canopies. Some of the rooms have original fireplaces, and all have private baths, direct-dial telephones, and central air conditioning. Fresh flowers, current issues of local country magazines, thick, cotton bathrobes, besides sweets and a *Washington Post* each morning, are some of the extras that make an overnight stay enjoyable.

In keeping with the tradition of naming rooms for famous local personalities, one is called the "Duffy Room" in memory of a colorful fox-hunting and steeplechasing personality, Louis Duffy.

Just a stone's throw from the Red Fox is the Stray Fox Inn, built as a private dwelling long before the Civil War. Guest rooms are carefully furnished with fabrics, furniture, wallcoverings and accessories in the 18th-century style. Stenciled floors and walls, hooked rugs and original wooden mantelpieces preserve the traditional character of the building. The McConnell House, the very latest addition, provides five more guest rooms.

An interesting gallery specializing in 19th-century animal and sporting art has been opened in the old stables of the Stray Fox, and various oil paintings and watercolors, oriental rugs, and bronzes of that period are also featured.

THE RED FOX INN AND TAVERN, Middleburg, VA 22117; 703-687-6301. A 20-guestroom historic village inn (13 of the rooms in the Stray Fox) near the Blue Ridge Mountains, approx. 40 mi. from Washington, D.C. European plan. Breakfast, lunch, and dinner served to travelers. Open every day of the year. Near Manassas Battlefield, Oatlands, and Oak Hill (President Monroe's White House), Upperville Horse Show, Foxcroft School, and Nat'l Beagle Trials. Spectator sports such as polo and steeplechasing available nearby. No activities for small children. Sorry, no pets. The Reuter Family, Innkeepers.

Directions: From Washington D.C., exit the Beltway (495) at Rte. 66 west, to Rte. 50 west. Follow Rte. 50 west for 22 mi. to Middleburg. From Winchester and the Shenandoah valley, take Rte. 81 and exit at Winchester onto Rte. 50 east for 30 mi. to Middleburg.

SILVER THATCH INN
Charlottesville, Virginia (1986)

The visiting innkeepers from *CIBR* had finished a tour of the guest rooms at the Silver Thatch, and we were seated under a beautiful Siberian elm tree in a little courtyard formed by a new building with four additional bedrooms. Cathy Hirsh from Meadow Lane Lodge clapped her hands and said, "Come on everybody, lunch is ready and it is really scrumptious." So we filed over the red brick wall, remarking on how happy the birds sounded and what a beautiful day in May it was.

It was Bill Sheehan, the innkeeper at Prospect Hill in nearby Trevilians, Virginia, who first suggested that I visit the Silver Thatch.

"It is really exceptional," he declared, "and Tim and Shelley Dwight are doing wonderful things at dinner as well."

Phil Hirsh from Meadow Lane Lodge also backed up Bill Sheehan's praise, so when I arrived to meet the Dwights and see the inn I was already prepared for something special. I certainly wasn't disappointed. The inn is a Colonial structure of much charm, dating back to 1780. I learned, with some amusement, that the original construction was performed by Hessian soldiers who were taken prisoner during the battle at Saratoga, New York, and marched south to Charlottesville. The original two-story log cabin section of the building is now called the Hessian Room. Of course, there have been several additions through the years, including a recent one by the Dwights themselves.

The addition of the new guest wing, which was constructed in the same Colonial architectural style, now brings the total of guest rooms to eight, all with their own private baths and decorated with Colonial antiques and folk art and antique beds and country quilts, dressers, and armoires.

Tim, as maitre d', greets guests, and Shelley enjoys her cooking duties. The three dining rooms are elegantly appointed with white tablecloths, sparkling glassware, and soft candlelight. The menu, featuring Continental cuisine with emphasis on Southern specialties, changes every month. For instance, in October, there was Autumn Chicken, chicken breasts with apple brandy and fresh pears in a light cream sauce; Tangier Island duckling with peaches and cinnamon; redfish Provençal, sautéed with mushrooms, tomatoes, and olives in a white wine sauce; filet mignon with a bleu cheese demi-glacé sauce; and veal Virginia, veal medallions in a brandied cream sauce with crabmeat and capers.

Tim and Shelley have found that being fifteen minutes from the Blue Ridge Mountains means that spring and fall are particularly busy times.

The nearby attractions are exceptional. The inn is located just eight miles from downtown Charlottesville and minutes away from the University of Virginia, the Skyline Drive, and the Blue Ridge Parkway. Thomas

Jefferson's Monticello and James Monroe's Ash Lawn provide an interesting experience, as does a visit to Michie Tavern. The area also has fox hunting and steeplechase events.

Tim tells me that their swimming pool and tennis courts get quite a workout during the summer, while in the winter, after a day skiing or browsing in the many antique shops, everyone's favorite spot is in front of the fireplace in the cozy lounge.

Although we were having a special light lunch that day, Wendy Gibson from the Robert Morris Inn in Oxford, Maryland, was exclaiming over the dinner menu for that evening. "Just look at this," she said, "they

are having Raspberry Chicken or roast duckling served with peach brandy sauce and black walnut pasta—that's pasta cooked with sautéed chicken strips, walnuts, and apples in a teriyaki ginger sauce. I think we ought to stay for dinner, too."

SILVER THATCH INN, Off Rte. 29 at 3001 Hollymead Rd., Charlottesville, VA 22901; 804-978-4686. An 8-guestroom country inn on the outskirts of Charlottesville, 15 min. from the Blue Ridge Mtns. Lodgings include breakfast served to guests only. Dinner is served Tues. thru Sat. evenings. Open year-round. Closed last 2 wks. of June and Christmas. Swimming and tennis on premises. Golf, horseback riding, hiking, skiing, biking, jogging, and wonderful back roads are all available nearby. Convenient to visit Monticello, Ash Lawn, and the University of Virginia. Not readily adaptable to children under 10. Tim and Shelley Dwight, Innkeepers.

Directions: The inn is 2 hrs. south of Washington, just off Va. Rte. 29. Turn east 1 mi. south of the airport road intersection onto Rte. 1520 and proceed ½ mi. to inn.

TRILLIUM HOUSE
Wintergreen, Nellysford, Virginia (1985)

First, I'd better explain Wintergreen. This is a ten-thousand-acre residential community-cum-four-season resort on the slopes of the Blue Ridge Mountains, three hours southwest of Washington, D.C., and an hour from Charlottesville. Tucked away in the mountains is an 18-hole golf course, an extensive tennis compound, a sixteen-acre lake, landscaped swimming pools, an equestrian center, and ten ski slopes.

The Wintergreen gate is just one mile from the Reeds Gap exit of the Blue Ridge Parkway.

Now, Trillium House. A rambling cedar building with dormers and pitched roofs, this country inn at Wintergreen is named after one of the many species of wildflowers that grow in abundance in these mountains.

Rustic, but quite modern, the Trillium House makes an excellent first impression. After stopping at the gate, Trillium guests receive from

the courteous gatekeepers a pass and directions upward through various clusters of condominiums to Trillium, on one of the highest points at Wintergreen. It happens to be directly across the road from the Wintergarden, a brand-new recreation complex with both indoor and outdoor swimming pools, exercise rooms, and a very attractive restaurant looking out on a splendid view of the Blue Ridge Mountains. It is just a short walk to one of the many ski lifts. Strange as it may seem to some northerners, this part of Virginia has first-rate cross-country and downhill skiing.

I stepped through the double entrance doors at ground level into the "great room" with a 22-foot cathedral ceiling and Jefferson sunburst window. A massive chimney with a woodburning stove dominates the room. Across the back of this room and up a short flight of steps stretches a balcony with a most impressive library, and on the other side of the fireplace is a big-screen TV-watching room and gathering place.

Hallways stretch out from both sides of this room, along which are guest rooms and suites, many of them containing heirlooms that Ed and Betty Dinwiddie have brought from their former homes.

The dining-room windows put the guest on almost intimate terms with the 17th fairway and green, and watching the chipmunks and squirrels and birds around the feeders provides entertainment at breakfast.

I would describe Trillium House as being basically informal. It is, after all, an area where one would come to enjoy all of the great outdoors, from walking and hiking to golf, tennis, and swimming. Gentlemen are comfortable with or without jackets at dinner, and Ed and Betty have a way of immediately making everyone feel at home.

Speaking of dinner, it is available on Friday and Saturday nights with advance reservations. Talk it over with either Ed or Betty when you make your reservations. Betty says that she cooks the same kind of meals she has cooked for the twenty-five years she has been married, dishes that either family or friends have liked. "I do different things with shrimp and chicken and, of course, roasts. We always have a salad. It's a single entrée meal. I make almost all the desserts—lemon pie and chess pie, and dishes that most of our returning guests enjoy."

If by some chance you are arriving unannounced, it's necessary to have the gatekeeper phone ahead to Trillium House so that you can be introduced.

The Trillium House country inn experience is much greater than I can describe in one edition. The entire area—the beauty of the mountains, the vistas, and the splendid facilities are almost beyond my descriptive powers.

TRILLIUM HOUSE, Wintergreen, P.O. Box 280, Nellysford, VA 22958; 804-325-9126. A 12-guestroom country inn within the resort complex of Wintergreen. Breakfast included in room rate. Dinner served Fri. and Sat. on request. Open year-round. Please call for reservations at times other than the dinner hour. Extensive four-season recreation available, including golf, tennis, swimming (indoor and outdoor pool), and downhill skiing, hiking, bird watching, and horseback riding. Ed and Betty Dinwiddie, Innkeepers.

Directions: From points north and east take the Crozet/Rte. 250 exit from I-64. Go west on Rte. 250 to Rte. 6 and turn left. Follow Rte. 151 south to Rte. 664; turn right on 664 to Wintergreen entrance. From Blue Ridge Parkway, exit at Reeds Gap, going east on Rte. 664.

WAYSIDE INN
Middletown, Virginia (1971)

The flickering candlelight in the Slave Kitchen cast our shadows on the smoke-blackened beams overhead and was reflected in the pewter plates, pitchers, and old windows. The fireplace radiated a warm glow and two cast iron pots on the crane gurgled and boiled.

"This room was hidden," Leo Bernstein, the owner of the Wayside Inn, told me. "It was discovered by accident, and restoring it was a great deal of fun. Those are the original brick walls, and I see you've already noticed the adz marks on the beams. All of the tools are from the Colonial period."

The Wayside Inn dates from at least 1797. It is correctly referred to as a historic restoration. It was carefully restored to its present form after 1960, when Leo, a lawyer and banker from nearby Washington, happened to drive through the main street in Middletown and recognized the inn's tremendous possibilities. The inn is an antique lover's paradise. Its rooms are packed with a mind-boggling collection of tables, chests, paintings, and *objets d'art*.

In earlier days the Wayside Inn served as a way station, where fresh teams of horses waited to harness up to arriving stagecoaches traveling the Shenandoah Valley Turnpike. Soldiers from both the North and South frequented the inn, then known as Wilkinson's Tavern, seeking refuge, comfort, and friendship during the War Between the States.

Americana abounds in each of the seven dining areas, uniquely decorated according to their names: the President's Room, Portrait Room, Senseny Room, Main Dining Room, Captain's Den, Lord Fairfax Room, and of course the Slave Kitchen. A new addition is Wilkinson's Tavern, which has a very rustic flavor.

Hearty meals with entrées like roast leg of lamb or crab Imperial are served for dinner. Lunch, served from 11:30 to 3:00, features Brunswick stew, chicken pot pie, salads, and sandwiches.

Guest rooms at the Wayside Inn are decorated in many different styles because of Leo's passion for collecting. He has an eye out for antiques of any kind; hence, each lodging room is quite apt to be a potpourri of anything from Byzantine to Victorian pieces.

Patrons at the inn have always had a wealth of diversions at their disposal, including the Wayside Theater, which has extended its season through December. Dinner is served starting at five o'clock on show nights to provide guests enough time to walk the one-and-a-half blocks to the theater.

Guests are also invited to visit Wayside Wonderland, a 250-acre recreational park with natural woodlands, offering swimming at Half Moon Beach, hiking, fishing, boating, and a tour of Crystal Caverns.

Late in the summer of 1985, the Wayside inn suffered a devastating fire that nearly destroyed the entire building. Complete restoration and repair of the inn was immediately started. The inn has since reopened with full service, while a much larger kitchen is planned for the summer of 1987.

Today, the Wayside Inn is many different things. It has history, regional offerings on the menu, an opportunity for guests to spend an extended vacation enjoying all of the attractions in the Shenandoah Valley, and it is a haven for collectors of all kinds.

WAYSIDE INN, Middletown, VA 22645; 703-869-1797. A 24-guestroom country inn in the Shenandoah Valley, about 1½ hrs. from Washington, D.C. European plan. Breakfast, lunch, and dinner served Mon. through Sat. Breakfast and dinner served on Sun. Open every day of the year. Professional Equity Theater, Belle Grove, Cedar Creek Battlefield, Blue Ridge Parkway, Wayside Wonderland, Hotel Strasburg, Washington's Headquarters, Wayside's Gallery One, and Strasburg Antique Emporium nearby. Convenient to Apple Blossom Festival. Carolyn Hammack, Innkeeper.

Directions: Take Exit 77 from I-81 to Rte. 11. Follow signs to inn.

I do not include lodging rates in the descriptions, for the very nature of an inn means that there are lodgings of various sizes, with and without baths, in and out of season, and with plain and fancy decoration. Travelers should call ahead and inquire about the availability and rates of the many different types of rooms.

THE COUNTRY INN
Berkeley Springs, West Virginia (1975)

"Let me tell you about our West Virginia spring-house water, which is from right here in Berkeley Springs and is shipped as far away as Miami, Florida!"

Once again I was having lunch in the Garden Room at the Country Inn with Jack and Adele Barker, whom I have been visiting for more than half of the twenty-two years that I've been writing this book.

Although it was a very warm midsummer's day, the atmosphere in the Garden Room was really springtime. It has a translucent ceiling, and its many, many growing plants, red and white tablecloths, strings of tiny white lights, and flags from all countries create a very festive air.

Jack continued, "There is a TV station in Miami that did a test on bottled water, and our water came out number one. It's just plain good spring water, and we're happy that it satisfies the folks in Miami."

I had landed earlier that morning at the Washington airport and made the relatively short trip through the countryside to this eastern panhandle of West Virginia well in time for lunch.

The first thing we did was to tour Country Inn West, the new building I wrote about in the previous edition. Each floor has a different decorative color scheme, and there is an elevator and rooms for the handicapped. Guest rooms in the new building are larger, with more sumptuous bathrooms, and provide an interesting contrast to the rooms in the older building, with their brass beds and individual furnishings.

The hallways throughout both of the buildings of the Country Inn are hung with prints, reflecting Jack's interest in paintings and art. In fact, one entire living room has been set aside to display these well-chosen works of art for sale to the guests. There are reproductions of Italian, Flemish, French, and English masters, as well as American primitives. In particular, there are excellent and reasonably priced reproductions of turn-of-the-century French theatrical posters.

Jack was particularly enthusiastic about the completed spa, where it is now possible "to take the mineral waters," for which this section of West Virginia is famous, right at the inn.

The talk at lunch turned to the theme of dinner menus and events that have been developed over the past few years. There is a Hawaiian night, a Mexican fiesta night, a French night, and a Greek night, with appropriate ethnic specialties. "The Hawaiian night is the most popular," Adele said. "We have a professional Hawaiian band, entertainment, with dancers in grass skirts, and every guest receives a Hawaiian lei, and they wear their bright shirts. It's very festive and very popular during the winter months."

The regular menu at the inn has such country items as ham, smothered chicken, duckling with orange sauce, and homemade hot breads. Desserts on the luncheon menu include chocolate mousse cake, black cherry cake, whiskey cake, pecan pie, coconut cream pie, and cheesecake.

Almost since the very start I've seen continuing changes and improvements at the Country Inn, and since 1972 there has always been something "in the works." "The completion of our spa will provide the use of relaxing Swedish techniques and deep muscle massage," Jack commented. "And we expect that our facial massage and make-up analysis will be equally attractive to our guests."

This section of West Virginia, identified as the Potomac Highlands, offers boating and fishing as well as many, many antique shops and excellent backroading in every season. Guests come in the winter to enjoy the quiet peacefulness, and now, with the opening of Country Inn West and the new spa and massage facilities, more and more people will be able to enjoy this truly country-inn hospitality.

THE COUNTRY INN, Berkeley Springs, WV 25411; 304-258-2210. A 72-guestroom (some shared baths) resort inn on Rte. 522, 34 mi. from Winchester, Va., and 100 mi. from Washington, D.C., or Baltimore, Md. European plan. Breakfast, lunch, and dinner served to travelers. Open every day of the year. Berkeley Springs Spa adjoins the inn. Hunting, fishing, hiking, canoeing, antiquing, championship golf nearby. Jack and Adele Barker, Innkeepers; Bill North, General Manager.

Directions: Take I-70 to Hancock, Md. Inn is 6 mi. south on Rte. 522.

The date in parenthesis in the heading represents the first year the inn appeared in the pages of Country Inns and Back Roads.

GENERAL LEWIS INN
Lewisburg, West Virginia (1973)

I had just returned from a walking tour of Lewisburg with its 19th-century residences and generous sprinkling of historic markers. I paused for just a moment at the bottom of the crescent-shaped drive that leads to the inn to read a marker that said, "Confederate troops under General Henry Heth on May 23, 1862, were repulsed by Colonel George Crook's Brigade."

As I settled into one of the rocking chairs on the long, shaded veranda, Mary Hock Morgan came out and joined me. "Well, what do you think of our little town?" she asked. I readily admitted that, as always, I was still completely captivated by Lewisburg.

"It was established in 1782 and is the third oldest town in the state," she said proudly. "It was named for General Andrew Lewis, who defeated the Indians at the first battle in the American Revolution in 1774.

"The old part of the inn, where the dining room is located, was built in 1798 as a private dwelling. My mother and father purchased the house in 1928 and hired a well-known architect, Walter Martens, who designed the West Virginia Governor's Mansion, to add on the section that embraces the lobby and the matching west wing. Care was taken to capture the feel of the early period, including the use of hand-hewn beams from the slave quarters in the dining room and lobby areas. Work was completed in 1929. It took my parents many years to collect all of these antiques, including the four-poster canopy bed you are going to sleep in tonight."

We were joined by innkeeper Rodney Fisher. "I usually seat the dinner guests in the evening," he told me, "and I try to learn a little about them. It's also a good time to tell them a little about the General Lewis and its history, and about the town of Lewisburg and other country inns that might be on their route."

The General Lewis Inn is like a permanent flashback to old West Virginia. It is furnished almost entirely in antiques. There is a sizable collection of old kitchen utensils, spinning wheels, churns, and other tools used many years ago, as well as an unusual collection of chinaware and old prints. The parlor has a friendly fireplace flanked by some of the many different types of rocking chairs that are scattered throughout the inn. The atmosphere is made even more cozy by the low-beamed ceilings.

The inn is surrounded by broad lawns, and in the rear there are fragrant flower gardens, tall swaying trees, and even a small rock garden.

The menu has many things that I associate with country cooking—pork chops with fried apples, pan-fried chicken, apple butter, country ham, and home-baked rolls and biscuits, to name a few. The entrée selection includes new specialties such as chicken Randolph, Coquille

St. Jacques, and a lean, smoky pork barbecue. The dessert menu includes many new mouthwatering items.

Rodney told me they have added four tables with umbrellas to their garden area. "This has given us a delightful and very popular outdoor dining area. Weather permitting, we serve lunch there every day. It is really a hit with the local ladies."

Dusk had fallen while we were talking, and the gaslights that illuminate the tree-lined streets began to dot the late twilight. Our talk turned to some of the famous golf courses here in the Greenbrier area, and we discussed some circle tours of the mountains that would include the fabulous scenery and a generous glimpse of rural West Virginia.

I have a letter from a recent guest who writes, "We returned to the General Lewis for our first anniversary, and our second stay was every bit as romantic and wonderful as the first. . ."

Small wonder that some call it "almost heaven."

GENERAL LEWIS INN, Lewisburg, WV 24901; 304-645-2600. A 30-guestroom (private baths) antique-laden village inn on Rte. 60, 90 mi. from Roanoke, Va. European plan. Breakfast, lunch, and dinner served daily. Dinner reservations necessary. Dining room closed Christmas Day. Famous golf courses nearby. Mary Hock Morgan, Proprietor; Rodney Fisher, Innkeeper.

Directions: Take Lewisburg exit from I-64. Follow Rte. 219 south to first traffic light. Turn left on Rte. 60, two blocks to inn.

RIVERSIDE INN
Pence Springs, West Virginia (1977)

I happen to be very fond of roast duckling. I've had this succulent dish, I'm sure, in more than half of the country inns in this book. On this particular occasion I was having fruit-stuffed duckling prepared for two at the Riverside Inn. Ashby Berkley, complete with a long leather vest over a dashing white shirt with billowing sleeves, set the plate in front of me and twirled his mustache. "I know how you feel about duckling," he said. "So, I'm anxious to see what you say about this."

The menu at the Riverside Inn might include Colonial meat pies, mountain rainbow trout, fresh seafood pie in a cheese pastry, baked glazed chicken, lamb chops, and steak. The famous scalded English slaw, a hot cabbage salad with bacon-vinegar dressing, is now traditional. The English mulled cider served before each meal is made from fresh cider pressed especially at the nearby Morgan Orchard.

As odd as it may seem, Ashby Berkley has created at the Riverside Inn the ambience of 17th-century Jamestown, Virginia, and I dare say that the impressive log building is probably a great deal more substantial than the accommodations the Jamestown settlers enjoyed.

The Riverside Inn has the intimacy of a Colonial roadside tavern where travel-weary guests once refreshed themselves with the tablefare of their hosts. It is located on the bank of the Greenbrier River, whose placid waters ran amock last year and unfortunately completely wiped out the inn's foundation, floors, kitchen, porches, cottages, grounds, and in fact almost everything. "We were closed eight months, but did reopen on July 4, and everything is normal once again," Ashby told me.

I asked him whether or not he had been tempted to move away from this valley where he had grown up. "Oh, I wouldn't think of leaving this beautiful place," he said. "I know I am prejudiced, but it is the perfect

place for anyone who appreciates being close to nature. We are the fourth most rural state in the nation and are eighty percent forested. It is almost like an undiscovered island set down in the middle of the busy East Coast, and all you have to do to commune with nature is to open the doors and windows and let it come in.

"It's difficult to concentrate with the sun streaming through the brilliant fall foliage hanging over the green of the valley, alive with birds and all the river life. Each season here is so uniquely different. Spring is like living in a wildflower garden. The lush, green, quiet summer can shut out the world. Fall is a parade of color and splendor that I have never seen matched anywhere, and the majesty of our untamed mountains—stripped of their blanket of leaves during winter—is not unlike the mystery and strength of the ocean, a force bigger than man. I think you can see why I stay here."

The two of us sat for awhile staring at the rugged massive fireplace, and the light from the fire flickered on the tops of the massive oak tables, which were set off by the pewter underplates and the pistol-handled knives.

In response to a question, Ashby explained that at the moment there are only token lodgings available; however, there will be some very interesting additions and changes shortly.

I must confess that all the time that Ashby and I were talking I was enjoying one of the most delicious roast ducklings that it has ever been my pleasure to eat. Augmented as it was by orange, baked and glazed carrots, bourbon sweet potatoes, and stuffed acorn squash, I couldn't help but think a little guiltily that the settlers of early Jamestown could not have fared one-tenth as well.

RIVERSIDE INN, Rte. 3, Pence Springs, WV 24962; 304-445-7469. A country restaurant on the Greenbrier River on Rte. 3 in the beautiful West Va. mountains, between Hinton and Alderson; 12 mi. from Lake Bluestone. Limited lodgings. Dinner served 5 to 9 p.m. Mon. thru Sat. from May 31 to Labor Day; open Wed. thru Sat., April 15 to May 31 and Labor Day to Oct. 31; open Fri. and Sat., Nov., Dec. Closed Christmas and Jan. to April 15. Lunch served by special reservation only. Skiing, boating, hiking, swimming, spelunking, white-water canoeing nearby. O. Ashby and Kelley Berkley, Innkeepers.

Directions: From the east, take Alta exit off I-64, follow Rte. 12S to Alderson, then 8 mi. on Rte. 3W to Pence Springs. From the west, from W. Va. Tpke. follow Rte. 3 from Beckley through Hinton to Pence Springs. The inn is located in Pence Springs on Rte. 3 between Hinton and Alderson.

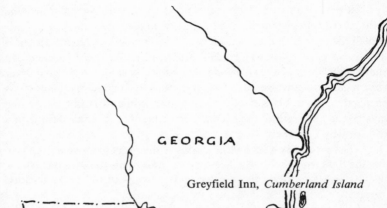

SOUTH CAROLINA

GEORGIA

Greyfield Inn, *Cumberland Island*

FLORIDA

■ JACKSONVILLE

■ ORLANDO

Chalet Suzanne,
Lake Wales •

MIAMI

Hotel Place St. Michel, *Coral Gables* •

Lower South

Eastern Time Zone

CUMBERLAND ISLAND

Cumberland Island is the southernmost and largest of a chain of barrier islands that starts at Cape Hatteras and extends to the Florida-Georgia border. It is eighteen miles long and three miles wide at its widest point. There are 26 varieties of wild animals and 323 species of birds identified. The island has one road, Grand Avenue, a dirt and shell affair, which traverses the length of the island through the live oak.

In recent years the National Park Service acquired a great portion of the island and has taken the necessary action to forever maintain it as a nature preserve.

Marshland fringes much of Cumberland's shores protecting them from the current and the tide. Its principal inhabitants are the ubiquitous fiddler crabs and long-legged wading birds. The live oak avenues create an atmosphere akin to a cathedral.

The eighteen-mile beach is the most striking feature of the island and one can walk for hours in delicious solitude except for the sanderlings that scurry out of the clutching fingers of the waves, and the pelicans skimming the water. Shells abound and it's impossible to come back empty-handed.

The dunes, which are carefully protected, provide still another intriguing atmosphere. At the edge of the forest there is a group of lakes, which have their own particular wildlife. Egrets and herons fish these waters as well as ducks who stop off as they travel north and south.

Besides the wildlife there is a rich history of the island that covers pre-Columbian times as well as occupation by the Spaniards, the British, and later on some enterprising men from the new American republic. In the early 1800s there were a few plantations on the island, but after the War Between the States the island was dominated by the presence of the Carnegie family who raised an impressive mansion of brick and stone at Dungeness with formal gardens, swimming pool and stables. Unfortunately, it burned in 1959.

GREYFIELD INN
Cumberland Island, Georgia (1982)

This is the story of Grandma Ferguson, who was once married to Thomas Carnegie (brother of Andrew), and the Ferguson family—including her great-grandsons, Andy and Mitty—and of the flora and fauna of one of the last remaining impressive nature preserves on the East Coast. It is only a part of the story of Greyfield Inn, located on Cumberland Island, off the southern coast of Georgia.

I paid my first visit to this gorgeous, haunting part of the world in 1975. I had the pleasure then of spending part of a day with Lucy Ferguson, known to everyone as "Grandma." It was Grandma who first introduced me to Cumberland Island, with its seventeen-mile stretch of beach, fascinating dunes, and secret ponds. She also showed me the ruins of Dungeness, built by her great-grandparents, which unfortunately burned in 1959.

Once again, as on my first visit, I was on the ferry boat, *R.W. Ferguson,* and Captain Mitty Ferguson was updating me on Greyfield Inn. We left Fernandina Beach at 3:00 p.m. and were making the hour-and-a-quarter run up the passage between the island and mainland to the Greyfield dock.

"Of course, everything is much the same as it was when you were here the first time," he said, keeping a guiding hand on the wheel. "The Fergusons, including Grandmother, are still very much in the picture, so that we are a family team dividing the chores. We also have some excellent staff, which makes everything much more of a pleasure."

By this time the ferry was within sight of the Greyfield dock, and I could see once again the gleaming, three-story mansion through the mysterious grove of live oaks. Andy waved to us, and soon, with the other guests, I was bundled into the jeep and driven to the impressive front entrance of the inn with its majestic steps and broad veranda. As soon as I stepped inside, it all returned to me: the paintings, the oriental rugs, the mahogany furniture, the silver on the sideboard, the great fireplaces, and the great collection of books. Andy showed me to my corner room and then joined me in front of the fire for a cup of late afternoon tea as we renewed our acquaintance.

I joined the other guests at dinner in the candlelit dining room and the conversation dealt with the wonders of the unspoiled beach, where the magnificent loggerhead sea turtles lay their eggs, and where guests sometimes can see the young hatching. The shore birds and the marine life are there, as are deer, wild horses, wild turkeys, and the dense live oak forest.

The newest acquisition is a gazebo that stands in the meadow between the primary and secondary dunes—a great spot in which to get out of the sun at midday, to watch the sun rise and set, or just to lie about reading and watching the shore birds.

There were several guests who had been at Greyfield for many days who were saying, "It takes a day just to find out what is here, and at least two days more to explore it."

Several of the guests had seen a recent issue of *Audubon Magazine* with the article by John Mitchell on Cumberland Island and Greyfield Inn.

It was wonderful to be back at Greyfield once again.

Do not plan on visiting the Greyfield Inn if you have only one night, and be certain to check with the inn about the ferry schedules. Incidentally, the 1735 House in Fernandina Beach is an excellent overnight stop before taking the afternoon boat to the island. The Greyfield Inn is the only public overnight accommodation on Cumberland Island.

GREYFIELD INN, Cumberland Island, GA (mailing address: Fernandina Beach, FL 32034); 904-261-6408. An 8-guestroom mansion on an island off the coast of southern Georgia. Accessible from Fernandina Beach, Fla., or on a Natl. Park Service ferry from St. Mary's, Ga. Check with inn on ferry times. Rates include full breakfast and dinner, as well as either box lunch or informal noon meal. Open every day in the year by reservation only. Beachcombing, swimming, fishing, clam digging, photography, birdwatching, bicycles, walking and driving tours, natural history tour. No pets. The Ferguson Family, Innkeepers.

Directions: The R. W. Ferguson leaves from the public dock at Fernandina Beach, Fla., at either 3 or 5 p.m., depending upon the day of the week (check with inn). Also check with inn on National Park Service ferry schedule from St. Mary's, Ga. Autos are left on the mainland. Island also accessible by small plane or helicopter.

CHALET SUZANNE
Lake Wales, Florida (1973)

After my first visit to Chalet Suzanne a number of years ago, I wondered if it really did happen or was it like the musical *Brigadoon*, in which the fictional Scottish village returns for one day every 100 years. This is a reaction I frequently get from guests who visit this unusual country inn in central Florida. Sometimes they can hardly believe it.

However, there is no doubt that Chalet Suzanne is a real place. The bridges, steeples, cupolas, minarets, peaked roofs, flat roofs, castle towers, domes, treasures, antiques, and pagodas are all there. It's a world of pastels in Bavarian, Swiss, Oriental, French, English, Turkish, Chinese, and every other style you can think of, and the nice part of it is that the guest rooms are all comfortably furnished in this wonderful Arabian Nights atmosphere.

It was all started in the early 1930s by Bertha Hinshaw, and now her son, Carl, and his wife, Vita, are continuing with their own touches—the newest of which is a spectacular new covered walkway to the dining area, graced by a beautifully carved window with Tiffany angel roundels from All Angels Episcopal Church in New York City.

To the people who live in Florida, Chalet Suzanne is best known for its exceptional food. In fact, it was recently awarded the "Golden Spoon" for the eighteenth consecutive year of being listed among the top twelve restaurants in Florida. *Mobil Guide* has given it four stars and it has the *Travel-Holiday Magazine* award for fine dining.

Dinner is served in the wonderful around-the-world ambience of the dining room, with Persian tile tables, Venetian glass lamps, clocks, statuary, stained glass windows, an old piano, and an eclectic collection of goblets and stemware—no two tables are set alike. By the way, there is a very intriguing little table for two set in the front window, which is reserved for honeymooners, if possible.

Most of the guests visiting Chalet Suzanne for the first time order the well-known chicken Suzanne, beautifully browned and glazed. It is prepared by Carl, who, in addition to being the "chief pilot" of the airfield (oh, I forgot to mention the airfield), is also the "principal stirrer" in the soup factory, and in addition to everything else is the chef at the inn.

Dinner also can include the original baked grapefruit centered with a sautéed chicken liver, the famed Chalet Suzanne romaine soup, hearts of artichoke salad, petite peas in cream and butter, a grilled tomato slice, deliciously hot homemade rolls, a mint ice, and tiny crêpes Suzanne.

The remark "It's almost like a Disney movie" is frequently heard at Chalet Suzanne, and I guess it's more than a coincidence that Disney World and many other famous attractions, including the beautiful Cypress Gardens waterskiing shows, are just a short distance away.

Oh yes, there is a 2,450-foot airstrip at Chalet Suzanne and it comes out of Carl Hinshaw's lifelong love of flying. The flying tradition continues because Carl and Tina's son, Eric, is also a pilot.

Some of the best news of all is that Eric Kindle Farewell was born in 1986 to Bob and Tina, who is Carl and Vita's beautiful daughter.

CHALET SUZANNE, P.O. Drawer AC, Lake Wales, FL 33859; 813-676-6011. A 30-guestroom phantasmagoric country inn and gourmet restaurant, 4 mi. north of Lake Wales, between Cypress Gardens and the Bok Singing Tower near Disney World. European plan. Dining room open from 8 a.m. to 9:30 p.m. Closed Mon. from June to Nov. Pool on grounds. Golf, tennis nearby. Lots of opportunity for good jogging. Not inexpensive. The Hinshaw Family, Innkeepers.

Directions: From Interstate 4 turn south on U.S. 27 toward Lake Wales. From Sunshine State Pkwy., exit at Yeehaw Junction and head west on Rte. 60 to U.S. 27 (60 mi.). Proceed north on U.S. 27 at Lake Wales. Inn is 4 mi. north of Lake Wales on 17A.

I do not include lodging rates in the descriptions, for the very nature of an inn means that there are lodgings of various sizes, with and without baths, in and out of season, and with plain and fancy decoration. Travelers should call ahead and inquire about the availability and rates of the many different types of rooms.

HOTEL PLACE ST. MICHEL
Coral Gables, Florida (1985)

As soon as I walked through the canopied entrance between the potted trees and into the long, narrow lobby of the Hotel Place St. Michel I felt that I had been there before.

Its very stylish three-story facade, with many vines and awnings, is as European as one could possibly imagine, maybe even more Parisian than Paris itself.

As I continued strolling through the hotel, seeing the gleaming hand-tiled floors, soaring arches, and vaulted ceilings, I thought here was a place that should have an "in-house" poet or at least an artist-in-residence. This gave me a clue to my sense of *déjà vu*, and I leafed through the pages of *Country Inns and Back Roads, Continental Europe* to find the Hotel de France in Luxeuil-les-Bains, France. The Hotel Place St. Michel, like its French counterpart, has all the elements of a stage setting.

The original inspiration for this Coral Gables hostelry was the Art Deco world of Paris in the 1920s. Fortunately, Stuart Bornstein and Alan Potamkin, the present owners, decided to return it to its former style and elegance, and this small hotel has undergone a refurbishing that does it proud.

The concierge's desk is on the lobby level, where there is a parquet floor and a European brass and glass chandelier.

The Restaurant St. Michel, off the lobby, has banks of greenery, Art Nouveau lighting fixtures, and framed prints reflecting an old-world elegance and a discerning attention to detail.

My notes about some of the bedrooms include Number 302, which has parquet floors, built-in bookcases, and two double beds with very handsomely carved headboards. The decorations are a combination of Art Nouveau and Art Deco with some sensible contemporary furniture. This particular room had dried flowers and some attractive stenciling on the walls. Guests' shoes left outside the door at night are polished and returned early the next morning, along with a morning newspaper. The air conditioning in the guest rooms is supplemented by overhead fans— very Paris!

A continental breakfast of freshly baked croissants with an assortment of marmalades and jams, fruit juice, and hot coffee is included in the room rate, and may be taken in the guest room, if preferred.

The dinner menu includes such intriguing main dishes as breast of chicken sautéed with wild mushrooms, several scrumptious crêpes, as well as filet mignon served in a green mustard sauce. The dessert tray had a Charlotte Russe, a chocolate mocha torte, and many kinds of little cookies, cakes, and fruits.

Luncheon is served with a selection of crêpes, quiches, omelets, salads, and patés. The newly built Stuart's Lounge offers guests an opportunity to enjoy a lighter meal as well as some sophisticated jazz.

Stuart Bornstein pointed out that a strict building and zoning code has kept Coral Gables, an integral part of Miami, visually attractive and appealing. White-pillared plantation-type homes on broad green lawns, Spanish haciendas with barrel tiled roofs, and large coral rock homes dominate the architectural scene. Residential streets are shaded by decades-old gigantic oak and banyan trees.

HOTEL PLACE ST. MICHEL, 162 Alcazar, Coral Gables, FL 33134; 305-444-1666. A 30-guestroom charming, restored, 1926 European-style hotel in the heart of Coral Gables, 7 min. from Miami Int. Airport and 10 min. from downtown Miami. All rooms with private baths and air conditioning. Open year-round. Continental breakfast included in room tariff. Dining room open daily for breakfast, luncheon, and dinner. Sunday brunch. Within 3 blocks of shopping mecca of Miracle Mile, and easy walking distance to theaters, galleries, and boutiques. Children welcome. No pets. Stuart Bornstein and Alan Potamkin, Owners.

Directions: Follow I-95 south into U.S. 1 (Dixie Hwy.). Continue south to Ponce de Leon Blvd. Turn right onto Ponce, continuing to 2135 Ponce. Turn right onto Alcazar.

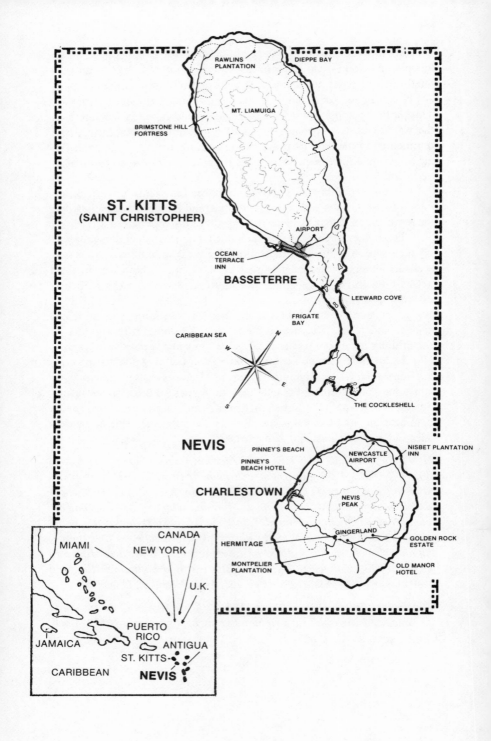

RAWLINS PLANTATION

DIEPPE BAY

MT. LIAMUIGA

BRIMSTONE HILL FORTRESS

ST. KITTS
(SAINT CHRISTOPHER)

AIRPORT

OCEAN TERRACE INN

BASSETERRE

LEEWARD COVE

FRIGATE BAY

CARIBBEAN SEA

THE COCKLESHELL

NEVIS

PINNEY'S BEACH

NEWCASTLE AIRPORT

NISBET PLANTATION INN

PINNEY'S BEACH HOTEL

CHARLESTOWN

NEVIS PEAK

GINGERLAND

HERMITAGE

GOLDEN ROCK ESTATE

MONTPELIER PLANTATION

OLD MANOR HOTEL

MIAMI

CANADA

NEW YORK

U.K.

PUERTO RICO

JAMAICA

ANTIGUA

ST. KITTS

NEVIS

CARIBBEAN

NEVIS AND SAINT KITTS

Nevis and Saint Kitts are two islands that lie in the northern part of the Leeward Islands in the eastern Caribbean. After quite a few years of association with Britain, they attained a full independence in 1983, and the Federation of Saint Kitts and Nevis is now a country of its own, with a population of 44,000, of which 35,000 live on Saint Kitts and 9,000 on Nevis.

A travel-writer colleague of mine, Jennifer Cecil, suggested Nevis to me when I said that I thought I was ready for my first Caribbean vacation in at least twelve years. This idea was further strengthened for me when I learned that two longtime friends of mine from the Berkshires, Dr. Frank Paddock and his wife, Sis, had been coming to Nevis for many, many years. A great deal of what I am sharing with you in this section has been greatly enhanced by their having generously shared with me their enthusiasm for both of these lovely islands.

Although the land is beautiful, the sea and the surroundings are gorgeous, I think it is the Nevisians and the Saint Kittitians who make this a really fulfilling experience.

There are some interesting differences and similarities between the two islands. Saint Kitts is much larger, has a greater population, and is really much more sophisticated than Nevis. This is partly attributable to the fact that the cruise ships can come in to Basseterre and their passengers may walk around the downtown shops. Also, it's possible to fly from New York or Miami directly to Saint Kitts on the jumbo jets. The longer runways and larger airport on Saint Kitts make the country directly available from almost anywhere in the world.

On the other hand, I learned that the Nevisians are quite happy with the state of affairs that makes it necessary to reach Nevis either by ferry from Saint Kitts or by smaller airlines from Antigua. Taxis are available at both airports and also at the ferry landings.

The two islands lie in the tropics. Air temperature ranges from a minimum of 74° F. to a maximum of 84° F., with an average of 79° F. The average water temperature is 80° F., average annual rainfall is 55 inches, and the average duration of sunshine per day is more than 8 hours. These islands are warm, and the climate is very pleasant and healthy, with extremes tempered by the breezes from the northeastern trade winds. Usually dry and mild weather is experienced during the period from November to April; the period from May through October is warmer with higher rainfall.

A passport is required except for holders of proofs of identity issued to nationals of Canada and the United States visiting for a period of less than six months.

The currency used is the East Caribbean dollar (EC $). Currency may be exchanged at any bank, and at the time this went to press the rate of exchange for the U.S. dollar was approximately EC$ 2.68 to U.S. $1. I did not find that credit cards were widely accepted. Inns accept personal checks.

Various car-rental firms offer different makes and types of cars. A refundable deposit is frequently necessary. I personally rented a Mini-Moke from Mr. Johnson while I was on Nevis and would recommend it to anybody. It is a sort of overgrown golf cart with a canvas top and no sides. They're really fun.

Before driving any vehicle, including motorcycles, a local temporary driver's license must be obtained from the traffic department either in Basseterre or Charlestown in Nevis. Driving on both islands is on the left side of the road. The British ways are given up very slowly.

As far as entertainment and sports are concerned there is an 18-hole international championship golf course on Saint Kitts, available to all visitors.

Most inns on both islands have their own tennis courts, or arrangements can be made to use nearby courts. These are generally hard surfaced.

Swimming may be enjoyed at several white sand and black volcanic sand beaches on both the Caribbean and Atlantic sides of the islands. Of course, there are wonderful facilities for scuba diving, snorkeling, deep-sea fishing, sailing, cruising, and surfing. Arrangements can be made through each inn.

Horseback riding and hiking tours are also available, and tours by a horse-drawn carriage are a lot of fun.

There are several restaurants on both islands.

There are duty-free shopping facilities, and available goods range from perfumes to textiles and high-fashion clothing to porcelain, crystal, and jewelry.

Locally produced batik and tie-dyed clothing, fabrics, and hangings are among the local handicrafts, which also include a wide range of articles made of coconut shell or fiber, as well as straw goods, basketware, and ceramics.

The main vacation or holiday season runs from mid-December to mid-April. This is when there are more visitors. However, there is no rainy season and the islands are at their best during the summer, when the inns offer accommodations at reduced tariffs.

Light summer clothing, preferably in cotton or cotton mixtures rather than nylon, is recommended. Dress is informal at most inns.

Electricity is basically 230 volts AC; however, transformers may be supplied by inns and some have direct 110 voltage.

The water is safe, even the tap water.

I'm further indebted to Sis Paddock for presenting me with a copy of an excellent book by Joyce Gordon: Nevis: Queen of Caribees, *which should be read by all visitors to Nevis before, during, or after their trip. It's available from stores on both islands.*

Because the economy of the islands was supported in early times by the sugar plantations, a great many so-called Great Houses were built, most of which have been abandoned by what came to be impoverished owners. Some of these houses, along with their sugar factories, still remain, and it is possible to walk through them and get a very strong impression of what life was like in those halcyon days. Many of the inns I visited had at one time been a part of these sugar plantations.

There are two disparate figures in history forever connected with Nevis. One is Alexander Hamilton, who was born on the island in 1757. A very impressive museum has been built on the foundations of his birthplace and is maintained by the Nevis Historical and Conservation Society.

The other figure is Horatio Nelson, whose first encounter with Nevis would make a very good movie. I'll leave that for the reader to discover in Joyce Gordon's book. However, the woman to whom he proposed and who subsequently became his wife lived here. This was long before he became such a heroic figure in British Naval history.

I visited an excellent small museum devoted to Nelson memorabilia, and it contains every possible category of artifact from china, pottery, paintings, and tinted prints to all kinds of published books—novels, fiction and non-fiction—dealing with this man, who later became the hero of Trafalgar and subsequently the subject of much controversy.

This museum, called Morning Star, is the private collection of Mr. Abrahams and is open to visitors most mornings. March, 1987, marked the 200th wedding anniversary of Lord Horatio Nelson to Francis "Fanny" Nisbet, and the wedding was re-created for all to see and participate in. Some of the events included a sail-in of large ships from various islands around Nevis, authentic costumes, historical drama, and an actual wedding ceremony, held at Montpelier Plantation, the original site of the wedding. It was followed by a gala ball.

A full information kit may be obtained from the Saint Kitts-Nevis Tourist Board, 414 East 75th St., New York, NY 10021, 212-535-1234.

NISBET PLANTATION INN
Nevis, West Indies (1987)

I left Frank and Sis Paddock playing tennis with some of their island friends, and wandered down the truly impressive aisle of palms, which leads from the lovely old stone main building of Nisbet Plantation to the shore of the Atlantic. I could see a number of beach chairs already in place. Inn guests were adding to their generous tans or, perhaps for first-timers like me, getting a faint tinge of red.

Each side of this spacious aisle had very pleasant little bungalows or cottages, usually designed with two suites in each. They are all very neat and tidy, with screened-in porches and very attractive plantings and exterior design. Guests stay in these buildings and congregate and take their meals at the main house.

The private beach has a bar and restaurant, serving breakfast and lunch daily, and an off-shore reef protects the swimming area and provides good snorkeling. Equipment is available.

I wandered back up to the tennis game, which was just ending, and was introduced to several more guests, of whom there seemed to be an equal number of Britons and Americans. Of course, we chatted about Nevis and how relatively undiscovered it really is and how much they were enjoying their holiday.

The main building, which includes the dining room, is a very handsome structure with a screened-in veranda, which wraps around three sides. The chintz-covered furniture, along with the many plants, photographs of Nevis, and a bookshelf that also has many classical recordings, lends an air of hominess to the entire scene.

The adjoining beach and the many waterside activities make Nisbet Plantation Inn a popular vacation getaway.

NISBET PLANTATION INN, Nevis, West Indies. U.S. reservations: 218-722-5059. A 33-guestroom (private baths) oceanside resort inn. Modified American plan includes breakfast and dinner. Open year-round, but sometimes closed for 1 month midsummer. Swimming, snorkeling, tennis, croquet, fishing, boating, water-skiing, horseback riding, guided mountain climbing on premises or nearby. Not recommended for children under 12. George G. Barnum, Jr., Managing Director; Michael Mudd, Resident Manager.

Directions: See general travel information on Nevis. Nisbet Plantation is a short taxi ride from the New Castle Airport.

CRONEY'S OLD MANOR ESTATE
Nevis, West Indies (1987)

Each of the inns of Nevis and Saint Kitts has some memorable feature. Here at Croney's (as it is known locally), I learned that the special feature was the cuisine.

I had been assured and reassured many times by my dinner companion (arranged through the courtesy of owner Vicki Knorr), a college professor from the Northeast, that the food here was little short of superb. "I have been coming here for many years and I have never had anything but the most fabulous meals," he declared.

Later, Vicki came out of the kitchen, where she does all the cooking, and we had a chance to talk about some of her favorite dishes.

"One of our appetizers, which our guests love, is sautéed shrimp, dipped in coconut. We have a set meal every night, and frequently we serve a baked half lobster, filled with a conch dressing and basted in butter. Everyone likes this."

She warmed to her subject. "Curried chicken we do with many condiments. We import our lamb from the States rather than New Zealand, but it is the seasonings that make it unusual. We use a lot of rosemary. We also stuff a leg of lamb with a very good spicy dressing."

Croney's is a restored sugar plantation dating back to a 1690 land grant, on the slopes of Mount Nevis, 800 feet above sea level on the tradewind side of the island. The garden, which utilizes the stone hearth kitchens of the plantation, is a lovely outdoor facility for lunches and is the scene on each Friday evening of the steak and lobster buffet with dancing to a steel band.

The *National Geographic* magazine mentioned it as being the best and longest-lived inn of all the Nevis plantations. One of the really intriguing features is the fact that a lot of the machinery connected with the original plantation has been left in place. This is the mid-19th-century mechanized machinery, and it has the look of modern mechanical sculpture.

There are ten guest rooms, all with verandas and colorful quilts, and some with sitting rooms.

There is a fresh-water swimming pool surrounded by tropical foliage. The Cooperage Dining Room, a room where the coopers once made barrels for the sugar mill, provides another attractive ambience.

As I was leaving, Vicki pointed out that the temperature, year-round, ranges between 69 and 82 degrees Fahrenheit, which calls for a light blanket at night and definitely suggests a sweater for bare shoulders after dark.

CRONEY'S OLD MANOR ESTATE, P.O. Box 70, Charlestown, Nevis, West Indies, Leeward Islands; 809-469-5445. U.S. reservations: 800-223-9815. A 10-guestroom former Nevisian sugar estate. American plan. Open year-round, but check if planning to come in midsummer. Swimming pool on grounds. Free beach and town transportation. Horseback riding, sailing, snorkeling and more sports available. Not suitable for children under 12. No credit cards. Vicki and Gregg Knorr, Owner-Managers.

Directions: See general directions to Nevis and St. Kitts. Take taxi from airstrip and make arrangements to rent a car for a longer stay.

HERMITAGE
Nevis, West Indies (1987)

On this typical February morning in Nevis, which reminded me very much of June temperatures in the Berkshires, I was on the road that circles the island on my way toward a daytime visit to the Hermitage. I had enjoyed dinner there the previous evening with owners Maureen and Richard Lupinacci, along with Frank and Sis Paddock and Pam Barry. It had been one of those idyllic Nevisian evenings, with great food and lots of laughter.

Now I turned off onto a narrow road that was nothing more than two concrete tracks, with grass growing up between and brushing the bottom of the car. I was going ever upward toward Mount Nevis.

The night before I had learned that the main house of the Hermitage is one of the oldest on Nevis, and is featured in a book of Caribbean architecture. The photographs of the Hermitage in the book have some details that are quite impressive. This has been Maureen and Richard's home for some years, and relatively recently they turned it into an inn. They have roots in Quakertown, Pennsylvania, and Richard is with the bank in nearby Charlestown.

Alexander Hamilton Museum

There are three guest rooms in the main house and other guest rooms in outbuildings connected with the original plantation. Each guest room in the cottages has a gallery overlooking the swimming pool and a working kitchen, so it's possible to stay at the Hermitage on the European plan.

The wood walls of the dining room are adorned with some beautiful English china, patterned in light blue flower patterns, and paintings of native Nevisians. The living room has a very high peaked ceiling, and is decorated with a combination of antiques, prints of British soldiers in uniform, and maps.

There is a set meal every night—a three-course dinner with an emphasis on such Caribbean fish as red snapper, grouper, and parrot fish. I enjoyed their baked chicken with rice and papaya. Fish baked in banana leaves is another popular dish.

Incidentally, both Maureen and Richard are very much involved in restoration and preservation projects on Nevis, and are an excellent resource in helping the guests experience the Nevis of the past and present.

HERMITAGE, Nevis, West Indies; 809-469-5477. An 11-guestroom former plantation, now a comfortable Nevisian country inn. Modified American, or European plan on a weekly basis. Open year-round. Swimming pool on grounds. All of the activities of Nevis are nearby. Transportation to the beach can be arranged. Children over 6 can be accommodated in apartments en famille. *No credit cards. Richard and Maureen Lupinacci, Owners.*

Directions: See the main directions to both St. Kitts and Nevis. Consult with the inn about transport from the airstrip.

GOLDEN ROCK ESTATE
Nevis, West Indies (1987)

There were quite a few of us going home that morning: Ernie and Jane, Bill and Brucie, Shirley and Henry, and me. Tessa would stay on for another four or five days, and John and Nancy would leave the next day. However, we all made arrangements with Pam Barry, the innkeeper at Golden Rock, to return again in February of next year.

I believe, as is the case with other guests, we were all drawn together by the courtyard at Golden Rock, one side of which is formed by the mellowed old stone walls of a sugar plantation and the other by a bordering garden. The third side is open to the sea and faces east to the Atlantic.

It was here in the courtyard that we gathered for breakfast and lingered on for long chats, lots of laughter, and frequently arranged outings on Nevis. The courtyard also was the setting for lunch each day, although we did have the option of a picnic lunch that could be anything from hamburgers to broiled lobster at the inn's hut on a nearby beach, which was reached conveniently by car or by the Golden Rock bus. On one night a week the scene changed completely, when a Caribbean string band held forth, led by a clever flutist, and we were wafted away on the wings of the music.

My accommodations were similar to the others—a large bedroom, ample enough for two people to share without any difficulty at all. Like the others, it had its own terrace overlooking the Atlantic. From mine, I could watch the morning and afternoon games of tennis, while others shared the view of the swimming pool. There are also two- and three-bedroom villas for families or friends traveling together.

Like most of the other inns I visited on Nevis and Saint Kitts, Golden Rock is a former sugar plantation, and the gray stone main building has a lounge and reception area as well as a dining room. It is situated above the ocean in the foothill area of Mount Nevis.

There is an eleven-acre stretch of sandy beach owned by Golden Rock on the wild and surfy windward side of the island. There you can put on your mask and fins and experience some of the best inshore snorkeling that Nevis has to offer.

Now, as we gathered for one final breakfast and talked about returning, I learned that for some it would be the third or fourth trip. I can imagine that along about the first of December I'll start to figure out ways to return to Golden Rock again.

GOLDEN ROCK ESTATE, Nevis, West Indies; 809-469-5346. U.S. reservations: 800-223-5186 (Northeast), 800-223-5581 (nationwide). A 12-guestroom (private baths) inn with additional larger accommodations for families or couples traveling together. Modified American plan in-

cludes breakfast and dinner. Open year-round. Swimming, tennis, beach, sports available on premises. Numerous opportunities for visiting historic sites such as the Alexander Hamilton birthplace, Fig Tree Church, and others nearby. Arrangements can be made to rent Mini-Moke automobiles. Pam Barry, Innkeeper.

Directions: To reach Nevis consult earlier section.

MONTPELIER PLANTATION INN
Nevis, West Indies (1987)

While the guests at Golden Rock Plantation were predominantly American and the mix at Nisbet Plantation Inn was about equally divided between Britons and Americans, the percentages at Montpelier slightly favored the British guests.

Perhaps this can be partially attributed to the fact that proprietors James and Celia Milnes Gaskell are themselves quite British, and the ambience of this resort inn, with its beautiful English furniture and oil portraits of ancestors, is decidedly Albionesque.

When you phone or write for information and reservations, be sure to ask for a copy of the mimeographed general information on Montpelier; a more informative précis of what to expect I have seldom read. As well as mentioning the hillside location overlooking the sea, the "fast-playing hard (tennis) court in lovely surroundings," and the many other amenities, it includes what it does *not* have, such as no telephones in the guest rooms, no dress code, no tennis pro. A very handsome four-color brochure has some lovely views of the stone buildings and gorgeous gardens, as well as the swimming pool and the private beach nearby.

Some of the guest rooms, in individual cottages, have an ocean view and the others have an inviting view of Mount Nevis. Since the general outlook is to the west, guests can sit on their private patios and watch the sun go down. It's fun to wander around Montpelier, with its stone terraces and gardens.

In its description of the cuisine at Montpelier, the general information mentions fresh lobster and conch, "imaginative use of local produce," and that Montpelier keeps its own pigs and sheep. "The outside dining terrace gives views past floodlit palm trees to the ocean two miles away and to the lights of Saint Kitts, twelve miles distant."

James Gaskell summed up Montpelier for me: "It is known to a few perceptive travel writers and agents, and to a number of guests who hope that it will retain its personal nature, its consistently good food, and its happiness. They need not worry."

MONTPELIER PLANTATION INN, Nevis, West Indies; 809-469-5462. U.S. reservations: 203-438-3793. A 16-guestroom resort-inn on a hill-

side overlooking the sea, with mountain views. All rooms have two double beds and showers. Modified American plan includes breakfast and dinner. Lunch, if desired, additional. Private beach house on Pinney's Beach with transportation provided. Tennis, swimming pool, water sports, hiking, ocean beach available on premises or nearby. Not recommended for children under 12, especially in winter season. No credit cards. James and Celia Milnes Gaskell, Owners.

Directions: See general directions for transportation to the island of Nevis. Take a taxi from the airstrip to Montpelier, although arrangements can be made to rent a car in Charlestown en route. It is necessary to stop at the police station to get a Nevis driving license.

RAWLINS PLANTATION
Saint Kitts, West Indies (1987)

Philip Walwyn and I were strolling about the grounds and gardens of the Rawlins Plantation, which is family owned and managed and has the atmosphere of an English country house.

"The first Walwyn came to Nevis in 1677," he told me. "Later, the family moved to Saint Kitts, and in 1790 became owners of the plantation. The original house burned down some years ago, and the new buildings designed by us in 1970 have been carefully blended into the ruins of the old plantation works.

"This boiling house that you see here is a hundred years old and was used to manufacture fancy molasses, but is now a cool courtyard, where we dine every day.

"We are about 350 feet above sea level and Mount Misery, behind us, rises to nearly 4,000 feet. That island you see off the coast is Statia."

Earlier, I had picked up my rented car at Basseterre, the principal town on Saint Kitts, where the big jets land. I had driven out to the far end of the island and turned into the sugar cane fields, where the waving stalks were half again as high as my automobile. I parked my car on the grass, and a gentleman with faded blue shorts and a blue shirt appeared almost instantly and introduced himself as Philip Walwyn, the proprietor.

As we continued our pleasant walk, he pointed out the eight cottage accommodations, including a windmill, originally built in the 17th century to provide power to grind sugar cane. It has been converted into a suite, complete with a bathroom and sitting room. There are also guest rooms in the plantation house. These are all light and airy and attractively furnished.

"I would say that we offer peace, unpolluted air, beautiful surroundings, relaxation, and excellent food, most of which is homegrown. We have a set meal every evening at 8:00 p.m., and we have provisions for

special diets. Our cuisine is not really French, and the local meats and vegetables are prepared in more of a western style.

"I'd say that Saint Kitts, and particularly Rawlins, is not for the person who is looking for the 'bright lights.' There's plenty to do; the rain forest and the craters are accessible to those who enjoy vigorous walking, and we have a pool fed from our own spring in the mountain. There are two golf courses near Basseterre, and we have our own 75-foot catamaran. By the way, the five-minute drive to the beach is provided without charge."

As we walked back to my car, I heard Philip use that wonderful expression that seems to be so typical of English hoteliers and innkeepers, "Do tell your readers about Rawlins Plantation here on Saint Kitts; we're a small inn so we can look after people very well."

RAWLINS PLANTATION, Box 340, St. Kitts, West Indies; 809-465-6221. U.S. reservations: 617-367-8959. Modified American plan includes breakfast and dinner, afternoon tea, and laundry service. In season minimum stay 4 days. Open year-round. Swimming pool, grass tennis courts, and lawn sports on grounds. Golf, tennis, walking and hiking, beach and water sports nearby. Open year-round. No credit cards. Philip and Frances Walwyn, Owners.

Directions: See the general directions for reaching St. Kitts by air. Arrangements can be made with Rawlins Plantation for either a taxi or a car rental.

INDEX